CONSTRUCTING CORPORATE AMERICA

Constructing Corporate America

History, Politics, Culture

edited by
KENNETH LIPARTITO AND DAVID B. SICILIA

OXFORD
UNIVERSITY PRESS

OXFORD

UNIVERSITY PRESS

Great Clarendon Street, Oxford OX2 6DP

Oxford University Press is a department of the University of Oxford.
It furthers the University's objective of excellence in research, scholarship,
and education by publishing worldwide in

Oxford New York

Auckland Bangkok Buenos Aires Cape Town Chennai
Dar es Salaam Delhi Hong Kong Istanbul Karachi Kolkata
Kuala Lumpur Madrid Melbourne Mexico City Mumbai Nairobi
São Paulo Shanghai Taipei Tokyo Toronto

Oxford is a registered trade mark of Oxford University Press
in the UK and in certain other countries

Published in the United States
by Oxford University Press Inc., New York

British Library Cataloguing in Publication Data
Data available

Library of Congress Cataloging in Publication Data
Data available

ISBN 0-19-925189-4 (hbk.)
ISBN 0-19-925190-8 (pbk.)

1 3 5 7 9 10 8 6 4 2

Typeset by Newgen Imaging Systems (P) Ltd., Chennai, India
Printed in Great Britain
on acid-free paper by
Biddles Ltd., King's Lynn, Norfolk

For Thomas Cochran and Alfred D. Chandler, Jr.

CONTENTS

ACKNOWLEDGMENTS

We are grateful for the privilege of working with the contributing authors to this volume and with other scholars over the past three years in exploring social, cultural, political, and economic dimensions of the evolution of the American corporation. Thanks to the generous support of several individuals and institutions, we have been able to come together to share our work, our criticisms, and our insights. Our first formal gathering was a conference on "The Corporation as a Social and Political Institution," hosted by the Hagley Museum and Library in Wilmington, Delaware, and funded by the Alfred P. Sloan Foundation. Our special thanks to Hagley's former Director, Dr. Glenn Porter, and to Sloan's Dr. Gail Pesyna, who took an early interest in our modest efforts to explore, through a historical lens, the place of the corporation in society, a question at the center of the Sloan Foundation's funding mission.

As the present volume took shape, the Sloan Foundation stepped in again by co-sponsoring a second conference, this time at Harvard University's Kennedy School of Government. Additional funding was provided by two units within the Kennedy School: the Center for Business and Government (thanks to the special efforts of Ira Jackson, its former director, and David Hart) and the Hauser Center for Nonprofit Organizations (thanks to Professor Peter Dobkin Hall).

Our home institutions – Florida International University and the University of Maryland, College Park – also have supported this enterprise. Catalina Toala at UM deserves a special note of gratitude.

David Musson at Oxford University Press saw merit in this project at an early stage and, with the help of his able staff, ushered it forward to publication with efficiency and grace.

As always, our families have been a wellspring of love, humor, and – perhaps above all when it comes to this sort of thing – patience.

ABOUT THE CONTRIBUTORS

Gerald Berk is Associate Professor of Political Science at the University of Oregon. He is author of *Alternative Tracks: The Constitution of Industrial Order, 1865–1916*, which received the American Political Science Association's J. David Greenstone Prize for the Best Book in History and Politics in 1995. He is currently completing a book with the working title *Accounting for Power: Antitrust, Associations and Accounting in the United States from the Turn of the Century to the New Deal*. This project has been supported by fellowships from the American Council of Learned Societies, the American Philosophical Society, the Hagley Museum and Library, and the National Endowment for the Humanities. His email address is gberk@oregon.uoregon.edu.

Charles Dellheim is Professor and Chair of History at Boston University. He earned his doctorate in History at Yale University. His writings include *The Face of the Past: The Preservation of the Medieval Inheritance in Victorian England* (1982), *The Disenchanted Isle: Mrs. Thatcher's Capitalist Revolution* (1995), and "The Creation of a Company Culture: Cadbury's," *American Historical Review* (1987). Dellheim has held fellowships from the National Endowment for the Humanities, Harvard University, and the University of Pennsylvania's Center for Advanced Judaic Studies. He is currently working on a history of the rise and fall of Jewish art dealers in modern Europe. His email address is dellheim@bu.edu.

Colleen A. Dunlavy is Professor of History at the University of Wisconsin – Madison, where she teaches the history of capitalism, business history, and the history of technology with an emphasis on the United States. She is the author of *Politics and Industrialization: Early Railroads in the United States and Prussia* (1994), which was co-winner of the Thomas Newcomen Prize for the best book in business history published in 1992–94; and of *Shareholder Democracy: The Forgotten History* (forthcoming). She has held fellowships or grants from the American Council of Learned Societies, the German Academic Exchange Service (DAAD), the German Marshall Fund of the United States, the Russell Sage Foundation, and the Alfred P. Sloan Foundation. Her email address is cdunlavy@facstaff.wisc.edu.

Melissa Fisher received her Ph.D. in Anthropology from Columbia University. She teaches in the Department of Anthropology at Columbia University and the Metropolitan Studies Program at New York University. Her research and teaching focus on the ways gender and class relations are changing within global cities. She is editing a volume with Gregory Downey, entitled *Frontiers of Capital: Ethnographic Reflections on the New Economy*. Her email address is msf2@columbia.edu.

Louis Galambos is Professor of History and Editor, The Papers of Dwight David Eisenhower, at Johns Hopkins University. He is also a codirector of the Institute for Applied Economics and the Study of Business Enterprise at Hopkins. Among his publications are *The Rise of the Corporate Commonwealth: US Business and Public Policy in the Twentieth Century* (1988), with Joseph Pratt, and the award-winning *Networks of Innovation: Vaccine Development at Merk, Sharp and Dohme, and Mulford, 1895–1995*, with Jane Eliot Sewell. He can be reached at galambos@jhunix.hcf.jhu.edu.

Eric Guthey is Associate Professor of American Studies in the Department of Intercultural Communication and Management in the Copenhagen Business School in Denmark, where he coordinates and teaches in the department's interdisciplinary Masters Program in Intercultural Management. His research has appeared in various journals and anthologies, and he is currently completing *Ted Turner/Media Legend/Market Realities: The Cultural Politics of Business Celebrity*. His email address is eg.ikl@cbs.dk.

David M. Hart is Associate Professor of Public Policy at the John F. Kennedy School of Government, Harvard University, and author of *Forged Consensus: Science, Technology, and Economic Policy in the U.S., 1921–1953* (1998). He is currently writing a book about the role of the high-technology industry in American politics since 1970, and his edited volume, *The Emergence of Entrepreneurship Policy: Governance, Start-Ups, and Growth in the Knowledge Economy*, was recently published by Cambridge University Press. He holds a Ph.D. in political science from MIT and can be contacted at david_hart@harvard.edu.

Naomi R. Lamoreaux is Professor of Economics and History at the University of California, Los Angeles, and a Research Associate at the National Bureau of Economic Research. She received her Ph.D. from Johns Hopkins University. She has written *The Great Merger Movement in American Business, 1895–1904* (1985) and *Insider Lending: Banks, Personal Connections and Economic Development in Industrial New England* (1994), and edited *Coordination and Information: Historical Perspectives on the Organization of Enterprise* (1995) with Daniel M. G. Raff, and *Learning by Doing in Firms, Markets, and Nations* (1999) with Raff and Peter Temin. Her email address is lamoreaux@econ.ucla.edu.

Kenneth Lipartito is Professor and Chair of the Department of History at Florida International University. He is the author of *The Bell System and Regional Business: The Telephone in the South* (1986), *Baker and Botts in the Making of Modern Houston* (1989) with Joseph Pratt, and, most recently, *Investing for Middle America: John Elliott Tappan and the Origins of American*

Express Financial Advisors (2001). Lipartito is Editor of *Enterprise & Society, The International Journal of Business History*. He works on the intersection of organization, technology, and culture. He can be reached at lipark@fiu.edu.

David B. Sicilia is Associate Professor of History at the University of Maryland, College Park. He received his Ph.D. from Brandeis University. His research and teaching focus on ways that entrepreneurs and institutions marshal technology and attempt to shape public opinion for strategic advantage. His books include *The Entrepreneurs* (1986) with Robert Sobel, *Labors of a Modern Hercules: The Evolution of a Chemical Company* (1990) with Davis Dyer, *The Engine That Could: Seventy-Five Years of Values-Driven Change at Cummins Engine Company* (1997), and *The Greenspan Effect* (2001), both with Jeffrey L. Cruikshank. Sicilia is Associate Editor for Reviews of *Enterprise & Society, The International Journal of Business History*. His email address is dsicilia@umd.edu.

Juliet E. K. Walker is Professor of History at the University of Texas at Austin and Walter Prescott Webb Chair Fellow. She is author of *Free Frank: A Black Pioneer on the Antebellum Frontier* (1983), *The History of Black Business in America: Capitalism, Race, Entrepreneurship* (1998), editor of the *Encyclopedia of African-American Business History* (1999), and founder/director of the Center for Black Business History, Entrepreneurship, and Technology at UT – Austin. Her current research project is "*Oprah Winfrey: An American Entrepreneur.*" She can be reached at jekwalker@mail.utexas.edu.

Introduction: Crossing Corporate Boundaries

Kenneth Lipartito and David B. Sicilia

The corporation invokes strong associations – profit, efficiency, technology. It also conjures up a number of anxieties – about bureaucracy, economic power, insularity. For more than a century, the corporation has been the preeminent economic institution in the world's capitalist economies.[1] It is the instrument used by most entrepreneurs and managers to marshal the resources needed to do business: the capital, the technology, the workers. Through the corporation, businesspeople market products, forge contracts with suppliers, and enter into strategic alliances with other firms. When successful, corporations are the wellspring of economic growth. Along with the market itself, the modern corporation has become the quintessential institution of capitalism.

Although business can take and has taken many forms, the corporation remains the most common way business is organized. This is especially so in the United States, which pioneered the modern managerial corporation. More economic activity in the United States is conducted under the corporate form than under alternatives such as sole proprietorships and partnerships.[2] Although popular opinion has long been critical of traditional large firms and recently has celebrated small enterprise, the fact remains that large corporations continue to employ the majority of workers and earn the majority of profits in most sectors. Indeed, one of the most striking facts about the American economy is how important and powerful large-scale corporations remain. Through downsizing, rightsizing, outsourcing, acquisitions, re-engineering, and refocusing, big businesses were expected to become leaner, meaner, and more profitable. Many analysts predicted that bureaucratically organized business would be eclipsed by networks, alliances, entrepreneurial firms, and individual initiatives.

There is little doubt that corporations have changed substantially. But they have not disappeared. Indeed, many have thrived and expanded their global reach. In 1998, U.S. corporations garnered 73 percent of total business income – a modest 6 percent decrease on what they earned in 1980. The largest of the breed (those with $250 million or more in assets) control some 87 percent of all assets in mining, manufacturing, wholesale and retail trade, services, and finance. Companies with more than 1000 workers provide fewer jobs than they once did, but their overall contribution to the labor force has dropped by a minuscule 1.6 percent since 1980. Real pre-tax corporation profits have grown slightly faster than U.S. GNP since 1975.[3]

Since the nineteenth century, the corporation has offered some compelling legal advantages – most notably limited liability – and for many enterprises it offers tax advantages. In some cases, it has provided distinct economic benefits as well. As we discuss in greater detail below, Oliver Williamson and other leading economists who write about the corporation have argued that the chief advantage of the corporate form – its *raison d'être* – is its ability to lower the transaction costs associated with its multifarious activities. If firms had to contract with other firms to research, finance, manufacture, and market their products, this argument goes, the costs of forming, maintaining, and enforcing those relationships would far exceed the advantages of independent ownership.[4] Other leading students of the corporation, most notably business historian Alfred D. Chandler, Jr., counter that the large corporation offers not merely transactional advantages, but also *strategic* ones. According to Chandler, the corporation's managers can coordinate many of the functions needed to run a large and complex business enterprise better than markets.[5]

While all of this is true, it is far from complete. To view the corporation solely in transactional and coordinative terms is to miss a great deal of its salience. In many historical contexts – the contributors to this volume will argue – the corporation's economic functions play secondary roles to its political or social or cultural missions. In this sense, the American corporation (and corporations in other capitalist societies, a topic touched upon but not examined rigorously in this volume) has at various times been as much a cultural, political, or social institution as an economic one.

The distinction between the traditional economic analysis of the corporation and our approach can be summarized by Fig. I.1. Traditional theory has tended to focus on the left hand side of the diagram, and also to assume that all three boxes are tightly linked. We move the analysis to the right-hand side and argue that the three are not tightly linked. It is not necessarily true, for example, that large firms must operate with concentrated ownership and formal managerial principals to the exclusion of informal arrangements. More generally, we argue that it is possible to do political or cultural analysis of large, formal business organizations, as has been carried out for small business or public bureaucracy.

To be sure, the American corporation always has attracted scrutiny for its extra-economic roles in society. This scrutiny began with the republican heritage of the revolutionary and antebellum periods, when corporations were viewed as dangerous concentrations of power for a free society. It continued with the "robber baron" tradition of muckraking journalism in the Gilded Age and Progressive Era, which in turn fed a New Deal anti-monopolist sentiment.

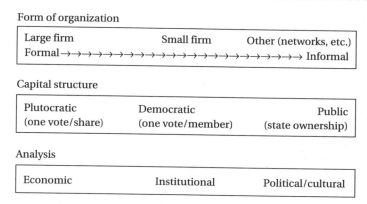

Fig. I.1. **Spectrums of corporate definition**

In these eras corporations aroused suspicions for their power and tendency to concentrate wealth and monopolize key resources. Post-Second World War anxieties about organizational depersonalization and corporate–state collusion extended this critique into new social and cultural realms. Recent debates about "corporate social responsibility" have occasionally lauded the American corporation, but more often have indicted it as detrimental to the public good, particularly in such areas as health, safety, and the environment.

Our purpose in this volume is not to correct any imbalance in the corporation's cultural or political balance sheet, but rather to question this very way of thinking about the corporation as a social actor. Rather than seeing the corporation as neatly bounded by its legal status or its economic functions, we see its borders as permeable, at times even indistinguishable from the broader society and culture. The boundaries of the corporation, we argue, look different when viewed through a cultural or political lens than through an economic one. But even when approached in economic terms, there is more than one fruitful vantage point for surveying the corporation. A small army of economists has mulled over this issue – why some corporate functions are internalized, others outsourced, and so on – but nearly all have been soldiers trained at the neo-classical academy. When one considers, however, the culturally constructed mental maps that shape corporate decision-making, the neoclassical model begins to lose its explanatory power.

In the parlance of post–structural analysis, the corporation has been reified as an economic actor. And it has not been given sufficient attention as a social, cultural, and political one. Many traits attributed to the American corporation need to be scrutinized, perhaps even dismantled. Economists have tended to assume that these traits appear almost automatically, or else are acquired in a simple, rational manner. Among the aspects of the corporation we question are the rationality of managerial decision-making; the exclusive focus on efficiency and profits; the supposedly impersonal, merit-based procedures governing employee conduct; the purported distance between the corporate world and the nitty-gritty of politics; and the assumed disinterest of corporate managers in such "nonpractical" matters as ideology, values, and cultural conflict. As the chapters in this volume argue, each of these assumptions about the corporation should be rejected, or at least seriously qualified.

The authors of these chapters arguably are predisposed, by both training and inclination, to question long-standing definitions and categories regarding the American corporation. They bring diverse backgrounds to this collective effort: two are political scientists, one is an anthropologist, one is trained in American Studies, another in public policy, and one is a professor of both history and economics. The rest of us reside in history departments. What unites our efforts is our devotion to the evolution of institutions and cultures, especially economic ones, with the corporation a "usual suspect." But whatever the formal training and current institutional affiliations of the contributors to this volume, all were invited to participate because they possess (among other analytical strengths) a historian's sensibility about complexity, contingency, and causality. Each, in other words, has something interesting and important to say about how the American corporation has been constructed and reconstructed over time and in varying contexts.

Along with the fallacy of the reified corporation as economic actor, most writing about the American corporation has given us a remarkably static institution. Collectively and individually, the authors of this volume see something different: a construct every bit as changeable – and indeed changing – through historical processes as other key constructs in our national past, whether "liberalism," "family," "law," "the military," "the Left," or "race." In the Afterword of this volume, we reflect on some new ways of characterizing and periodizing the American corporation in light of the work presented in *Constructing Corporate America*.

But first we need to situate this book more precisely within the onrushing currents of scholarship about the corporation. It is a rich and stimulating literature. Just as we hope to cross definitional borders, so we aspire to speak across several disciplinary boundaries, and in that way move closer to a common discourse about this crucial institution.

WHAT IS THE CORPORATION? THEORETICAL BEGINNINGS

A proper starting-point seems to be the question: What is a corporation? Here, we can provide no single, *a priori* definition. As we have suggested, that is hardly fitting for a volume that looks at the corporation in evolution over time, as it changed shape, form, and function. The very definition of the term, moreover, is caught up with theoretical debates that this volume engages.

We can note, however, some of key attributes of corporate enterprise. Formally, classically, corporations are legal entities with certain characteristics: limited liability, wide public distribution of shares, and managerial hierarchies characterized by the separation of ownership and control. Few of us would be satisfied with a formal, legal definition, however. More importantly, the legal definition of the corporation has evolved, reflecting the different roles, functions, and uses to which this form of enterprise has been put.

Corporations have also been linked closely with issues of size, market power, and economic concentration. Certainly for critics, these characteristics have been the most salient and troubling. To them, corporations are opposed to free markets, or to more equitable distributions of wealth and power. They look for the end of bureaucratic business and the flowering of small-scale, competitive firms providing innovative, enriching job environments. These oppositions miss much of the story. A great deal of the competition in modern capitalism happens between and among the large firms that dominate many industries. Corporate enterprise remains different from the classic, small-scale, atomistic firm of textbook economics, if such firms ever truly existed. As noted previously, moreover, the corporation's role in the American economy has diminished less than one might expect, given all the emphasis on alternative structures.

The word "corporation" travels closely with its companion term, "big business." It is hard to define one without leaning hard on the other. Big business generally refers to firms that grow large relative to the market, certainly larger than most forms of business enterprise in history. But big business has a second, even more important meaning: managerial enterprise, or firms that operate through a complex, functional division of labor, with a hierarchy ranging from production workers to middle managers to executives. This managerial structure carries out the routine, everyday tasks of business, but also takes strategic action for the firm as a whole. It engages in planning that affects the macroeconomy. Usually this form of big business – perhaps better termed "managerial capitalism" – is seen as deriving from certain technical features of industries and certain market conditions that emerged by the late nineteenth century.

The work of Alfred D. Chandler, Jr. and his many students has been the starting-point for investigations of managerial capitalism. Looking at technological changes that permitted large-scale production and at concomitant improvements in infrastructures of communications and transportation, Chandler described the rise of managerial capitalism as a functional outgrowth of these technical and market developments. Big corporations were a necessary response to the realities of the changed economic environment.

Chandler's explanation had the advantage of delimiting the space of the corporation, while also shifting attention from legal form to managerial structure. Corporations arose – not because of quirks of the legal or political environment – according to Chandler, but because this legal entity provided a useful way of structuring managerial enterprise.[6] Conversely, small firms and alterative enterprises survived because not every sector of the economy had the same technical and market characteristics. Seen from the perspective of top managers who take their surroundings as given, Chandler's model seemed to offer the flexibility to explain the why, where, and how of the corporation's appearance and spread. As rational actors, managers adopted organizational structures that fit environmental constraints.

BUSINESS HISTORY AND ECONOMICS: A FLEETING FUNCTIONALIST CONSENSUS

New moves in economics reinforced this view of the corporation. In the 1970s, organizational and institutional economists took a second look at the corporation, and found that it might be a useful institution after all. Traditionally, economists had condemned large firms and managerial bureaucracy as drags on market efficiency.[7] In the work of economist Oliver Williamson, however, much of the Chandlerian model of the corporation was confirmed, though with a twist.

Williamson attempted to place in theoretical language what Chandler had discovered from his close investigations of historical case studies. In doing so, Williamson shifted emphasis from production and production technologies to transactions (or exchange). Starting from the work of Ronald Coase, who in a brilliant article had asked, "Why do firms exist?", Williamson and his followers answered by pointing to the cost of market transactions, and to the ways in which firms could reduce those costs.[8] The firm now had a reason to exist. It could save money and increase economic efficiency. By extension, corporations, with their large, complex managerial structures, no longer appeared as lumbering bureaucracies stubbornly clinging to life in the face of simpler, more efficient market mechanisms. They were, in Williamson's view, vast transactions cost-reducing machines, complex perhaps, and subject to periodic breakdown, but like any technology, useful tools.[9]

For a time, business historians joined forces with transactions cost economists. Both turned to older work by sociologists associated with Carnegie Mellon University in the 1950s and 1960s. There, Herbert Simon, James March, and others had applied the tools of social psychology to corporations and other large bureaucratic organizations. They inquired more about behavior than structure, however. Simon, for example, argued that members of large organizations intended to act rationally, but could not always do so. Organizations were shaped by imperfect information and the cognitive limits of human actors. Additionally, managers could only command so many subordinates. They could only investigate so many new lines of business before becoming overwhelmed by information and by day-to-day operational realities. In response, the Carnegie School emphasized, organizations broke down tasks into smaller units and separated everyday operations from planning and strategy. Corporations rationalized behavior as best they could by employing routines and standard operating procedures.[10] Williamson and economists of the transaction school adopted some of these insights too, arguing that organizations were partly a response to bounded rationality, information limitations, and the opportunism that subordinates could exercise in the face of imperfect supervision and control.

For a time, it seemed that a new paradigm of the corporation might emerge, a historically grounded theory that explained change in economic institutions and behavior over time. Drawing on insights from economics, sociology, and psychology, this new model seemed to offer the best understanding of the corporation yet. That did not happen, however. In fact, over the past decade, what had seemed a strong consensus on the corporation, and on economic institutions generally, has become severely frayed.

This is where our volume enters. Although the insights of Chandler and Williamson and the transactions cost, institutional, and organizational schools have been valuable, they clearly are not enough. Some of their fundamental assumptions and explanatory vehicles – including methodological individualism, functionalism, and rational choice – are now under question.

The fragmentation of momentary consensus began with a crucial but suppressed difference between business historians and organizational economists. Despite fruitful borrowings, historians looked at change, development, and specific cases and scenarios that could never quite be brought under the abstract, generalized models of organization proposed by economic theory. On the other hand, Williamson (following Coase) had taken the firm as an unnatural entity that needed to be explained. Such a starting-point, while perhaps analytically useful, was in tension with the historian's concern with context, with placing institutions in their own time and place. Viewed over the long term of history – where institutions, politics, law, and even what is taken to be "human nature" may change – firms are no less problematic than markets themselves; both need to be explained. In short, the highly functionalist nature of transactions costs and related microeconomic theory proved to be too limited for writing real history.

In truth, much of the Chandlerian model was equally functionalist. In Williamson's view, corporations existed only because they made markets function better. To Chandler, corporations existed because they provided a high level of throughput in production processes that, for technological reasons, had to run at a large scale. Yet, the historical perspective never closed off other, nonfunctional investigations and explanations. Some historians continued to emphasize corporate power, questioning assumptions about efficiency. Others followed the broader social and cultural implications of the revolution in organizations touched off by the rise of big business at the end of the nineteenth century.[11] Before we turn to these important departures, however, it is useful to review the crucial, if seemingly intramural, differences between how economists and business historians conceptualize corporations.

Williamson and his colleagues had looked largely at the formal structure of enterprise, and left people pretty much out of play. But Michael Jensen and other economists investigating "principal-agent" conflict looked more carefully at the practice of management and the people who occupied those offices.

Run by agents who sought to maximize their own wealth and prestige (or "satisfice" in the words of Simon and the older Carnegie School), corporations were no match for individuals (principals) operating in the market when it came to investing capital and seeking profitable opportunities.[12] Believing that the interests of managers could never perfectly match the interest of owners, Jensen posited that public corporations were in eclipse, although he offered no explanation as to why they had arisen and lasted so long.

Principal-agent and related economic theories of institutions focused attention on another fundamental difference between the economic and historical view of the corporation. They treated the corporation as a collection of self-interested individuals bound by a "nexus of contracts." Seen in this way, corporations, and indeed all economic institutions, were nothing more than the sum of their parts. The value of firms was assumed to be fully reflected in the current market price for their stock.

One can debate the philosophical legitimacy of this point of view. Individuals may be ontologically prior to institutions and organizations. But this does not mean that organizations are simply the sum of their parts. On this point historians began to split with their one-time allies in economics. Chandler and his followers reaffirmed the primacy of the firm in their work, over and above the individuals who make it up. In place of the nexus of contracts, institutional historians, with some new allies from business schools, offered a view of the firm as a collection of specific assets, a repository of skills and knowledge, and a site of technological inventiveness. Corporations were seen as structures of economic resourcefulness that could not be replicated by individuals acting freely in the marketplace.

Work along these lines reemphasized the difference between corporations and other economic units. Big firms were unique value-creating entities. Their managers discovered vital investments, created new organizational forms, and took strategic actions that realized potentials only latent in technology and markets. Such coordination of activity did not happen automatically. Managers learned from experience – often unique, non-replicable experience – that generated important tacit knowledge of how to perform successfully. "Managerial enterprise, meaning industrial concerns in which operating and investment decisions are made by a hierarchy of salaried managers," Chandler concluded, "have been engines of growth and social transformation for the past 100 years."[13] These managers "drove economic growth and played a critical role in the rapid reshaping of commercial, agrarian, and rural economies into modern, urban, industrial ones."[14] Without their creative work, the economy would not have progressed as it had. William Lazonick expanded these insights into a more general, comparative theory of capitalist development that contrasted the favorable experiences of nations such as the United States, Germany, and later Japan in creating value through managerial coordination, with the unfavorable experiences of faltering nations such as Great Britain.[15]

This renewed emphasis on learning, experience, and the context of decisions connected business history with a bold new departure coming out of economics itself. Some of the most fruitful work moving away from the conventional assumptions of microeconomic theory has come from a new group of "evolutionary" economists. Although not central to our volume, evolutionary theory, broadly conceived, helps point the way to a new historical paradigm for understanding the corporation. For that reason, it is worth exploring here in greater depth.

EVOLUTIONARY PERSPECTIVES

In place of the functionalism that has long dominated economic discussions of institutions, evolutionary economics offers a model of organizational change based on variation and selection. Subsuming both the economist's concern with transactions costs and the sociologist's focus on bounded rationality and information flows, evolutionary economics posits two ways that organizational change can take place. Firms may grow through a "Darwinian" process, whereby the successful survive and thrive and the maladapted fall by the wayside. This approach takes firm operations and behavior as relatively fixed, due to bounded rationality and other criteria. Organizational change happens at the population level, as inefficient firms leave and better adapted ones emerge and grow.[16]

To business historians focused on the firm, and on large corporations in particular, the second variant of evolutionary theory has been of more interest. Organizational change happens as incumbent organizations learn and adapt. Although there is no denying that new actors often enter the picture, organizational learning helps to explain the endurance of corporations, both at the individual level and as an institution of capitalism that has weathered more than a century of change in markets and technology. This sort of evolutionary economics has helped historians refocus on the firm as a whole, while relating firms to their environment.

The importance of learning, innovation, and adaptation accords with the original Chandlerian focus on the firm and production, as opposed to transactions and contracts. At the same time, evolutionary theory opens research to the full range of possible things firms can learn and do. Beside working on plants of efficient size and scale, or pondering the tradeoffs of vertical integration, firms also groom their labor forces, burnish their public images, and forge connections with institutions of scientific research, higher education, and government funding. The corporation need not be restricted to one structural type formed at one particular moment in time. Networks, cooperative and strategic alliances, and organizational change to flatter hierarchies; all can be seen as options for managers deeply engaged in trying to understand the constraints and opportunities of their environment.

Much recent work on the history of the corporation has followed this approach, to excellent effect. Using a "dynamic capabilities" framework, David Teece, Richard Langlois, and others have combined the insights of institutional and evolutionary economics with a historical perspective on business development. Emphasizing the "radically uncertain" nature of economic activity, they see firms as creative actors in a market defined, in part, by what firms do. Over time, and by watching other firms, strategically placed managers learn how best to compete, and put their firms through the difficult but necessary process of changing fixed routines. A key capability becomes the ability to learn and make organizational changes. Firms that are adept at such processes thrive, and economies that encourage such adaptation tend to do better than economies that do not.[17] The range of possible choices, however, is broad, with firms moving to or away from market-like structures depending on circumstances.

Here, the corporation becomes just one possible way to coordinate and organize economic activity, albeit an important and creative one that cannot be explained away as a reaction to market imperfections. As repositories of skills, knowledge, and learning capabilities, firms are a necessary part of the market system. Economic activity is not a division between markets and hierarchies, but a combination of both. Especially crucial are the interactions between firms, and the choices among different structural options.[18]

As a model of change, variation, and selection, evolutionary economics has much to recommend it. Unlike functionalist models, it does not depend on *post hoc* theorizing, or on writing "just so" stories that make economic institutions the best possible adaptation to how the world "should" work. Nor does it privilege one form of organization, a tendency in the Chandlerian paradigm, which takes the large corporation as it emerged in the United States in the late nineteenth century as an icon of capitalist success. Evolutionary models permit unexpected, unforeseen, or unintended outcomes in technology, markets, and organization. They allow for "path dependency," or the movement of institutions through history, not because they are driven by some optimal solution to a market or social problem, but rather because of chance or unforeseen consequences. Feedback loops of technology, skill, learning, or standards may lock in a path of change and shape its future direction toward non-functional, less than efficient outcomes. In other words, history matters to economic institutions.

THE MUTUAL CONSTITUTION OF CORPORATION AND SOCIAL ORDER

Variation and selection, however, is still only one way that history moves. Thus far, writing in this mode has had a highly technical flavor, with learning a matter of rational, if constrained, adaptation to changing environmental circumstances. Although cutting-edge work in this field has begun to emphasize the contextual nature of behavior, and has noted the way in which culture, the state, and the larger situational environment help define or construct what counts as rational, evolutionary theory does not offer sufficient scope for understanding the multiple ways in which corporations intersect with society. Sometimes, for example, economic outcomes occur because they are intended by actors, or because certain actors have the power to make them happen. Other institutional patterns are not rational, intended, or even chance adaptations to circumstances, but rather part of a more general pattern of social order.[19]

Our purpose in this volume is to move the debate another step away from the strict individualism and rationalism of traditional microeconomics and other approaches influenced by this theory. In the Chandlerian world, for example, managers are creative actors, but we still know little about the forces that affect managerial initiative and creativity. We know far less about managers as people than about the fixed "roles" they play. Evolutionary and managerial models also assume that firms react rather narrowly to the environment, seeking solutions to a set of economic problems largely rooted in production. It is equally possible, though, that managers are more broadly situated social actors who respond to many influences. Problems, rather than being presented clearly by the environment, may be obscure. Efforts to gain clarity and reduce uncertainty may force on all actors certain simplifying assumptions and unquestioned routines which construct the problem to be solved. Neil Fligstein, for example, has noted how conceptions of management have changed over time, in response to broad social and economic changes, defining different appropriate strategies for the firm. These strategies are not defined simply by optimizing or profit-maximizing criteria, but by a broader cultural milieu, or by the power relations within organizations that determine who gets to say what matters. In this case, the scope of rational action is situational rather than universal.[20]

In the chapters that follow, we examine more closely the "environment" in which corporations operate, what in evolutionary models is called the selection environment, and what in traditional economics is left largely unexamined, or examined only from a narrow perspective of individual self-interest. We inquire also about the identity and agency of those who manage and work in corporations. In doing so, we draw on new approaches to economic institutions that take society, culture, and politics into greater account.

In business history, the triumph of the Chandlerian paradigm was a victory over alternatives that had given greater weight to social context. This narrowing of the field began at Harvard Business School in the 1940s, where N. S. B. Gras defined business history as the study of business policy and administration. The internal workings of the firm received primary attention, at the expense of politics and culture. Despite attempts by Chandler's contemporary, Thomas Cochran, to reintroduce culture back into the study of business, the internal focus prevailed.[21]

Prompted by moves in social and cultural history over the past decade, business historians have begun to re-travel some of the field's less traveled roads. Here, they have been aided by advances in the study of culture and society that offered a more subtle view of the relationship between institutions and their environment.

Increasingly, business historians have recognized that the relationship between firms and their environment is likewise complex. As historians have turned to such matters as the interaction of firms and consumers, the political and legal structures that affect corporate strategy and structures, and the cultural milieu of business, they have portrayed firms as much more fully rounded social institutions. They have shown how, throughout history, corporations have had the ability to promote, or hold back, changes in work, family life, gender relations, and equal opportunity. The new scholarship has also cut against the grain of the large manufacturing firms, once taken as emblematic of modern capitalism. Indeed, the very term "business" is up for grabs. In the case of minorities and women, for example, much economic activity has taken place in the home, the neighborhood, and other settings outside the firm.[22] To understand why corporations exist, how they behave, and what role they have to play in our history, we have no choice but to unpack the business environment and to recognize that no strict and simple line can be drawn to divide the corporation from the rest of the social order.

NEW INSTITUTIONAL SOCIOLOGY

New theoretical work can aid in this endeavor. In particular, a literature grounded more in sociology than economics but focused on economic institutions holds great promise for advancing a more rounded conception of the firm as a social institution. This work, termed the new institutional sociology or economic sociology, has followed a course similar to that of the new economic institutionalism, but with a different starting-point.

Sociologists have long recognized that institutions are something more than collections of individuals. The very word "institution," if it has any added value, implies a structure that becomes permanent and fixed enough to influence and constrain, and also enable, individuals. That structure may well arise from individual actions, from rational, means–ends seeking behavior; but at some point it takes on a life of its own. There is a crucial difference here from the neoclassical economic definition of institution. For economists, institutions are largely compensations for market failure. Such a limited view implies that they are nothing more than a set of rules for purely instrumental behavior. If institutions have an existence beyond this, it is because of their market power or due to path dependencies and other technical limits to market processes. The sociological approach, by contrast, recognizes that as *social* institutions organizations may be more than rational, functional entities. They are sense-making, value-laden structures of "practical" or unreflective reason as much as of fully discursive reason. Rather than being constituted by individual actions, institutions are notable for the lack of "action" or conscious, thought-out behavior by their members. Individuals operating within institutional structures are given to following rule-like patterns or scripts.[23]

Originally, the sociological focus remained confined largely to what went on within corporations. Parallel to the emphasis on efficiency by institutional economists, sociologists sought to explain how organizations responded to environmental constraints to survive and reduce uncertainty.[24] They also noted the limitations of strategic action in corporate bureaucracies, consistent with Carnegie School's focus on cognition and rational action. Organizations attempted to reduce uncertainty and optimize, given their resource constraints. Other sociological work took a somewhat wider view, looking at the "informal" structures and organizational cultures within firms that subverted or operated along side formal, rational bureaucracy.[25] But this human relations school conceived of the informal structures as a problem, one that interfered with the full optimization of organizational behavior. As with much economics, the focus on internal organizational behavior left the environment largely unexamined.

Since the 1970s, there have been important breaks with this tradition. Work in organizational sociology began to pay attention to the various ways in which organizations interacted with their environment. Beside seeking to optimize resources, for example, organizations also seek "legitimacy," or status as accepted, valuable parts of society. Legitimacy may also confer power, by presenting the norms of the organization as true, just, right, efficient, and inevitable. There is no reason that organizations must behave as admonished in textbooks of bureaucratic rationality.

Some theorists tried to reconnect this expanded view of organizational behavior to optimization and market efficiency. In seeking legitimacy, for example, corporations may be conforming to certain societal expectations and following certain rules or scripts in order to make their actions clear and predictable in an obscure and uncertain environment. "Organizational ecologists" argued that the environment may be able to select out or differentiate between those organizations that actually perform well and those that only give the appearance of performance. Those that actually perform well grow and thrive; those that merely follow the rules are winnowed out. Those that hope to survive must learn and adapt. Once again, the corporation proposes, but the market disposes.[26]

Such plausible rationalizations for bureaucratic behavior, however, face some strong theoretical objections. Organizational behavior may, for example, become institutionalized, so that what begins as a functional response to environmental constraints turns into an unwritten rule of conduct that takes on a life of its own.[27] Institutional forms can be subject to path dependencies, whereby what is created at one moment in time cannot be changed easily or without cost. Limits of human creativity and cognition create "competency traps" that ensnare even creative managers. What works reasonably well overshadows untried, but potentially superior alternatives. Norms and standards of behavior that make the chaotic world clear and readable act as blinkers against creative thought, locking organizations into existing patterns.[28]

As with evolutionary economics, moreover, we have to know how the selection environment works before we can say that it moves institutions to some optimal structure. If the environment is a field of similar organizations, and if all organizations seek legitimacy and follow certain rules or scripts of legitimate behavior, it is unclear that the market can separate the efficient from the non-efficient. If a belief in the efficacy of a certain organizational form is widespread, all firms may have no choice but to conform to this belief. State structures, regulatory policies, and professional norms absorbed by managers may also limit organizational variation. Creative action from outside the field of existing organizations can break this logjam, of course, but such radical creativity is also unusual and sometimes long delayed. New entrepreneurs generally do not enter markets as organizational virgins, with no preconceived ideas of how they should behave. Their behavior, too, is influenced by prevailing industry norms. Large, powerful entities, including incumbent firms, as well as the state, often limit the degree of radical change by structuring the selection environment in a manner favorable to themselves.

Empirical evidence also stands in the way of efficiency driven explanations of organizational evolution. Many organizations end up conforming to a narrow set of behaviors, despite rather different circumstances or points of origin. They become more alike over time, or isomorphic. At the same time, organizations tend to differ substantially across nations or other significant cultural boundaries. If efficiency were at work, one would expect, on one hand, greater convergence across national boundaries and, on the other hand, greater diversity among competing organizations.

Such problems have changed the focus of institutional studies in two ways. First, rather than taking an institution as a "given," attention has focused on the institutionalization process. Anything might become an institution – family structure, the law, voting, cuisine, the corporation – but what actually is institutionalized depends on specific circumstances of history and culture. Different things will be institutionalized at different times and places. By this way of thinking, the corporation is not inherently an institution, but it has *become* one in America and other capitalist nations. The chapters here help to unpack the institutionalizing process by explaining how the corporation became a normal way of doing business, to the point that, while contested, it gained a powerful sense of legitimacy as the way business should be done.

EMBEDDING THE CORPORATION IN ITS ORGANIZATIONAL FIELD

New sociological work also has shifted attention from specific organizations or practices as the site of institutionalization to the larger environment. What gets institutionalized is the environment, not the individual organization. Once again, this approach blurs the line between environment and organization. Such work has emphasized the "organizational field" in which organizations sit – the competitors, suppliers, and other organizations that interact with each other. For corporations, the field varies by industry, but generally the assumption is that firms watch each other and adopt practices that are considered normal and appropriate. Just and you or I might figure out how to mow the lawn by watching our neighbors, rather than reading a book on landscape architecture or reinventing lawn maintenance, so managers watch their peers in the field. The field also may be influenced by the state, in the form of laws and regulations, or by investment banks and professionals such as lawyers and engineers who work with the firm. These actors have their own norms of behavior, which they bring to the corporation, influencing structure and action.[29]

For the study of business, this new sociological institutionalism offers two possible moves. First, one may emphasize the "embedded" nature of economic activity. Corporations sit in a field of social relations, which influences how they behave, what they can do, and what they see as legitimate strategic action. This approach tends to slight formal organization by focusing directly on social relationships within the firm and between actors in different organizational fields or settings. Thus, as studies of technology and innovation indicate, successful corporations plug themselves into networks of scientists, engineers, and university faculties in order to gain critical knowledge. This network of relations also constrains strategic action: To be successful, firms must conform to the national innovation system in which they operate.[30] Other work, along similar lines, emphasizes the importance of trust and cooperation, cemented by social and cultural bonds that are outside – but vital to – organizations. The degree of trust and the values of society influence how firms will organize. In places where trust and social bonds are high, firms may rely on less bureaucratic, less formal methods of operation.[31]

This contextual approach has shown how, even in advanced capitalist societies composed of large corporations, social relations remain important. Once we reject the textbook model of perfect competition, once we admit that rational action is bounded, information limited, and competition defined by interaction among firms, it becomes apparent that economic behavior cannot be stripped of its social content and reduced to narrow, universal rational action. Real markets consist of real actors, who bring to the marketplace their values, identities, and feelings. Trust, recurrent relationships, prejudice, assumptions, and values matter to market (or organizational) behavior. In textbook economic exchange, problems like the Prisoner's Dilemma and opportunism may arise; with real actors who share complex social relations, they may not. Markets and organizations work not despite the messy, multifaceted humanness of actors, but because of it.[32]

From the point of view of embeddedness, the corporation is a product of the particular social relations of society. The formal, rational organization we commonly observe is thus "modified and overlaid" by culture and society.[33] The second sociological alternative, however, returns to the formal structure once more, but with a critical cultural eye. It is possible that a structure like the corporation, while forming in a particular social environment may, nonetheless, become institutionalized in ways that render those social relations less obvious, and that reinforce formal structures.

Robert Freeland has shown, for example, that Alfred Sloan, the executive par excellence in Alfred Chandler's business history, had to violate the formal rules of decentralization in order to gain the consent of lower-level line managers at General Motors. The embedded social relations of General Motors, not the formal order, made the firm efficient. Yet the formal order of management, which in this case proved to be "irrational," could not be eliminated. Eventually, it overwhelmed Sloan's carefully crafted system of informal relations.[34]

In explaining the rise of the corporation, it is necessary to account for the institutionalization of formal order. To do so requires an engagement with issues of power and politics. Some forms of organization may be adopted because powerful actors have an interest in them. For corporations, the network of lawyers, investment bankers, and regulators is most relevant in this regard. The state also may impose regulatory or reporting requirements that limit organizational choice. In American history, a well-known example is antitrust laws that encouraged mergers rather than cartels.[35] In other cases, class may be crucial. William Roy has reinterpreted the rise of the corporation as an outcome of the structure of American law and the state. In a more traditionally Marxian vein, Martin Sklar has looked at the corporation as a social movement of capitalists out to promote their view of how the economy should be managed.[36]

The introduction of power and social relations are important steps in locating corporations in society. But there is a tendency in such work to revert to a form of functionalism. In this view, the capitalists ultimately get the structures they need, either through intentional action or as the unintended but functional consequence of their interests. The corporation in this case becomes the pet project of the capitalist class. Thus, unlike the rest of us, capitalists always know what they want and how to get it. But other work on institutionalization emphasizes the pre-conscious schemes and rules, the classifications and categories that are the tools of no one class, even if they serve a class interest.[37] This more discursive formulation engages culture as a contested terrain of meanings. Subjective interests, rather than being fixed – and hence the site of power struggles – are themselves formed and institutionalized historically.

Seeing the ways in which organizations and environment "constitute" each other has been perhaps the most innovative step in the sociological study of economic institutions. Instead of looking at social relations as a field around the organization, the organization itself is a social actor. It expresses intentions and interests, to be sure, but like any other actor it is also an artifact of rules, schemes, patterns, and history not of its own choosing. Organizations' structures and boundaries are not givens or logical responses to the environment, but rather flexible, open-ended, and constituted in the same process that shapes the political environment and the market. Part of the process of institutionalization is determining where lines are to be drawn – between public and private, market and organization – and what the rules are for legitimate business behavior. These rules and lines can vary depending on historical circumstances, experiences, political and cultural traditions, or the balance of power among contending groups. Different places and times would be expected to have different constitutive orders.

The constitutive view breaks most completely with the tradition of seeing institutionalization as at odds with technical notions of efficiency and rational action. Instead, it treats optimization, efficiency, and rationalization as socially constituted categories created by the interaction of individuals and organizations. As constructed categories, they are variable and far from universal. They are part of a contested terrain of meanings. Here, in this field of meanings, is where institutionalization takes place – as rules, perceptions, and values harden into unquestioned notions of how things are "best done." Corporations themselves may participate in this process, creating the rules, resources, and definitions they need. They do so, however, in contest with others. The arrival of the corporation in the field of meanings does not simply reflect "corporate power." Rather, power comes from the institutionalization of definitions and meanings in the discursive process of category formation.

This approach shifts emphasis somewhat away from causation and behavior to meanings and content. What matters about organizations is the larger moral order that they codify and express. What works in organizations are not formal rules and procedures, but the symbolic meaning and cultural content expressed by those rules and procedures. Similarly, what matters is not so much the influence of the environment on organizations, nor the underlying interaction of individuals in organizations, but the ways in which environments constitute individuals, who in turn express their values in organizations.[38] As values are formalized in organizations (as well as in law and politics), they take on an institutional status and become a naturalized, unquestioned component of everyday life.[39] In this view, the corporation no longer is simply a model of efficiency or a means of production. It becomes a model for society. It comes loaded with values that often are *expressed* in what seem to be objective and formal structures of efficiency and rationality.

THE CHAPTERS AHEAD

The chapters that follow move among these various theoretical positions, although they share the goal of reaching beyond narrow discussions of efficiency and shareholder value to explore the multiple ways that the corporation and society reverberate through each other. They take as their starting point the premise that the corporate form is just one solution to problems of production and management. They note the way in which the distribution of power, the structure of the state, and broader cultural values have affected business growth. Some look at how the corporation as an institution is built up from individual decisions. Others focus on the embeddedness of corporate structures in the larger social and cultural matrix. Still others consider how the corporation was institutionalized through engagement with the state. All recognize that there is no one best way or transcendent form that the corporation must take. At the same time, all are interested in explaining why business took the form it did in America.

The economic theory of organizations remains central in Naomi Lamoreaux's study of corporations and partnerships. Noting how the corporate form was used by many small firms long before it became identified with large-scale managerial enterprise, Lamoureaux shows how legal traditions and legal precedent more than economic theory defined the possible range of organizational structures in America. But law did not simply yield to pressure from interest groups. Rather, jurists were forced to wrestle with the meaning of corporate personhood, shifting among theories of the corporation as an artificial, state-created entity, an aggregation of individuals, and a real entity with civil rights. These legal definitions reflected in part the startling and troublesome political issues that big business itself created, as it adopted the corporate form at the end of the century.

Colleen Dunlavy continues the process of situating the early corporation in the American political economy. Her comparative statistics on shareholder voting rights starkly reveal a facet of corporate governance largely missed by historians and economists alike. Originally, the shareholder of the corporation was not merely an owner of capital, but also a member with democratic rights. At one time, members of corporations were entitled to one vote per person, not one vote per share, as is common today. Like Lamoreaux, Dunlavy notes the distinction that slowly emerged in law between corporations and partnerships, and the gradual erosion of minority voting rights that concentrated decision-making at the top of corporate hierarchies. Diverse American commentators, starting with Alexander Hamilton, warned against the concentration of power possible in the one-vote-per-share system. Yet that system still emerged in late nineteenth century America, in contrast to other nations.

Both Lamoreaux and Dunlavy point to the need for further investigations of the complex legal and political history of the corporate form and the institutions of corporate governance, both of which emerged and evolved in ways not predicted by transactions costs economics. Their chapters take exception to simple, linear historical models of business and institutional evolution, which portray organizations as emerging rather effortlessly in response to market or technical needs.

But why did the modern corporation take precisely the form that it did? The next two chapters consider this question in light of broader cultural and political trends in American history. Kenneth Lipartito notes how formal organization and organizational hierarchies were powerful cultural paradigms before they were concrete business forms. Their roots, he argues, go back to diverse sources, most notably an antebellum tradition of reform and utopian experimentation centered on questions of social order. This tradition often made use of the tools of bureaucratic organization to solve certain perceived social problems, tools that later would be adopted by large corporations to achieve control and order over their own environments. Utopian thought, with its visions of top-down planning and rational authority, provided one of the deep sources of legitimacy for the controversial business corporation of the late nineteenth century.

Although focused on regulation rather than business per se, Gerald Berk takes up the related theme of the political construction of the corporation. In a famous brief to the Interstate Commerce Commission, champion of small business and the worker Louis Brandeis argued that if railroads adopted the practices of scientific management they could save substantial money and operate at lower rates. Historians have puzzled over Brandeis' decision to embrace scientific management, a tool of the large corporations he so often opposed. Berk reveals that there was no contradiction here. Brandeis operated in the tradition of American pragmatism. He rejected the impossible quest for a clear line between public and private interests, as well as the futile search for some objectively "fair" rate of return on capital that obsessed judges working in a tradition of legal formalism and imbibing the new marginalist economics. Recognizing that the so-called hard facts of costs and technology were in reality social conventions, Brandeis promoted instead a public–private partnership that would have recognized the inescapable public nature of private corporations. But the American political tradition did not follow Brandeis' suggestion, with the result that railroad and other regulation went down a tortuous path to a dead-end. With Brandeis' alternative lost, judges and policy-makers constructed the modern, private, managerial authority of the corporation.

This first section of the volume looks at the construction of the corporation and the debates and alternatives that accompanied it. The chapters emphasize the close connections among politics, culture, and institutions, as well as the alternatives that might have been pursued. The next section looks at the consequences of corporation at high tide. In many ways, Louis Galambos' Chapter 5 picks up the story where Berk's leaves off. Following the formalist tradition of legal thought, antitrust law attempted to draw a bright line between abusive and acceptable corporate practices, particularly with the Rule of Reason in the Standard Oil case of 1911. As Galambos argues, however, antitrust only encouraged a trend toward oligopoly and restricted businesses' ability to reorganize in the face of technological and market changes. As might have been predicted by Louis Brandeis, this political economy – lacking the pragmatist notion of continual adjustments of regulation to shifting social and economic needs – eventually fell apart under its own weight. Quietly and with little public debate, antitrust was dropped in the Reagan era. The results, Galambos argues, have been greatly improved business performance through a wave of mergers and reorganizations to meet the challenges of globalization.

David Hart's Chapter 6 provides a similarly broad survey of state–business relations, concentrating on technology. He argues that technological innovation long has required a coordination of public and private efforts. Identifying four main areas where the state intersects with the corporation on technology, he shows how – through fiscal policy and regulation, and by purchasing products and setting the normative order – the state has played a crucial role in the creation of technological capabilities. In this domain, the government's record stands in stark contrast to the sort of problems that Galambos identifies with antitrust policy. Taken together, the two chapters map the terrain of business–government policy from its least to its most effective outcomes. Hart also challenges business historians to move beyond their focus on the firm, by considering the network of relationships and organizations that make for "corporate capabilities," although he admonishes sociologists and political scientists to remember that the firm remains the "heart" of modern capitalism.

David Sicilia's Chapter 7 shows the iterative relationship between the social order and big business in the post-Second World War era by exploring how three major industries – nuclear power, chemical manufacturing, and tobacco – sustained, and ultimately responded to, intense social, rhetorical, regulatory, and legal challenges to their profitability and even their legitimacy. Chronicling the nature and scope of the interest groups that lined up against these three industries as well as the corporate counter-strategies, Sicilia's chapter brings into high relief the highly changeable character of social–state–business relations. Initially, the state played a growing role through a wave of "new social regulation" that especially affected chemical manufacturing. But with the conservative political dismantling of the regulatory state in the 1980s and 1990s, industry adversaries increasingly turned to class action tort litigation to achieve social aims. For their part, the corporations under siege – confronted with rapid shifting political regimes – increasingly cultivated public relations capabilities in an effort to redefine their social role to fit better with a new postwar social order.

Taken together, these three chapters provide some evidence for what critics of corporate power have long believed: Big firms are often capable of shaping their political environment. But the chapters also show how the political strengths of the corporation vary with social conditions. Corporations have had to wait for policy changes that they could not control, and in several vital areas dealing with the basic function of innovation, corporations have been heavily dependent on the state. Politics has been crucial to modern business, to be sure, but the political relations of capitalism cannot be captured in a simple power elite or functional model that suggests corporations always get the politics they want. Corporations avoided the sort of pragmatic or "democratic" alternative that Dunlavy and Berk highlight, and thus, perhaps, circumvented certain limits on their autonomy; but they have adapted to changing political winds with a lag and have remained dependent on the state for important capabilities.

The final section of the volume turns to culture, like Lipartito's chapter on the early nineteenth century, and places the corporation in its twentieth and twenty-first century American milieu. In the classic Chandlerian account of the corporation, issues such as identity, ethnicity, and gender play virtually no role in the structures of management central to corporate behavior. All four of the chapters in this section challenge this assumption. Charles Dellheim begins by noting the important role in the American economy played by Jewish entrepreneurs. At first they, like other immigrants, operated outside of the corporate sector and drew on ethnic ties and cultural resources to prosper in distinct sectors of the economy. Excluded from "white shoe" corporations and professional practices, they prospered by marketing new consumer goods and cultural products, such as films, art, and antiques. In finance, they established new brokerage and investment houses alongside the established investment banks. In publishing, Jewish firms became the mediators of modern and classical European texts to the broad middle class, in contrast to established Anglo-Saxon publishers.

Taking note of these ethnic variations in the broader economy, Dellheim calls attention to the neglected role of identity in business strategy and management. He does so, however, not only by recounting the history of Jewish business, but also by reminding us that the management of corporations dominant in heavy manufacturing and mass retailing – which have been taken as models of bureaucratic enterprise – also had identities. These were the projects of the Anglo-Saxon elite, and they excluded Jews and other ethnic Americans for the first half of the twentieth century. Eventually, however, many businesses that started out as small family operations in the Jewish community grew to national and international scale. They became like other corporations.

Eventually, too, many Anglo-Saxon firms in industry and finance opened their doors to those of different religious and ethnic backgrounds. But as Juliet Walker shows, these changes did not mean a triumph of neutral organizational structures over personality and identity. In one case in particular, corporate America has been strongly resistant to full acceptance of difference. African-Americans remain woefully under-represented in large corporations, especially at the executive level. Like members of other minority groups, black Americans carved out their own economic niches, in the face of prejudice and hostility that excluded them from full participation in the white economy. Decades after desegregation and after a substantial rise in black income and educational attainment, however, the upper ranks of corporate management remain overwhelmingly white. African-Americans have thus been whipsawed between two trends. Black-owned businesses have lost their economic niches with desegregation. But black professionals and entrepreneurs have not risen through the ranks of corporate management. Only recently, Walker notes, have a small number of black entrepreneurs in media, sports, and entertainment had the capital to create their own large, diverse business operations. These enterprises often operate with strategic alliances to mainstream white-owned firms targeting black consumers. Although such alliances may threaten the identity of black businesses, they also provide greater opportunities for partnership across racial lines and widened opportunities for black employment.

The final two chapters in this volume investigate the role of identity and subjective experience in organization by taking account of gender. Like race and ethnicity, these facets of identity are largely ignored in treatments of business organization that emphasize strategy, structure, and bureaucratic systems. But those systems are, in fact, composed of people who do not lose their identities by walking through the doors to the executive suite. Melissa Fisher relates the changes in the post-Second World War financial markets to the experiences of women who entered financial services in the same period. As capital became more global and freed itself from restrictions enacted in the wake of the Great Depression, Wall Street firms finally began to open their doors to women in the 1970s and 1980s. Women's experience in finance, however, differed in certain crucial ways from those of men. Female brokers, traders, and analysts were often able to draw on their supposedly "feminine" characteristics to create relationships with clients, in ways that men had not. But femininity defined in this traditional way proved a double-edged sword on Wall Street. In an age of capital mobility, high risk, and huge market swings, women in finance often received the brunt of middle-class anxieties over economic change and instability. To some extent, like African-Americans, successful women financiers have been whipsawed between, on one hand, limitations that placed them in roles that involve less risk (and lower rewards), and on the other, social approbation when they took on traditionally high-risk male roles.

Our final contribution by Eric Guthey investigates a similar relationship between changes in business and representations of gender. In this case, though, the spotlight is on masculinity. Like Fisher, Guthey notes how the restructurings of once-stable industries and the release of new entrepreneurial energy during a moment of technological change called forth new images of the corporate man of action. In the rapidly changing businesses of information and communications, diverse figures such as Ted Turner, Bill Gates, and Jim Clark represented new types of businessmen for a "post corporate" age. They reinvigorated whole industries by adopting a self-consciously anti-bureaucratic ethos, even while using their images to gain control of very powerful corporations or to dominate entire industries. Such narratives, Guthey reminds us, tell us much more about the rhetorical projects of their creators than about their "real" business practices. But these projects are in many ways more salient for various stakeholders than is business practice. In these cases, image was as important for outcomes as any material factor.

Guthey's contribution carries us toward the opposite end of the spectrum illustrated early in this chapter (see Figure I.1), toward what might be called the "rhetorical corporation." At the opposite antipode sits the hyper-rational, efficient, functionalist, transaction-oriented corporation sharply delineated from its social order. Of course, neither ideal type exists in the practical world of business affairs. But in between lies a sprawling terrain of complexity, contingency, porous boundaries, and mutual social–business constitution. There you will find the corporations portrayed in this collection.

NOTES

1. See Alfred D. Chandler, Jr., Franco Amatori, and Takashi Hikino (eds.), *Big Business and the Wealth of Nations* (New York, 1997).

2. As measured by business receipts. See United States Bureau of the Census, *Statistical Abstract of the United States* (Washington, DC, 2001), table 711; Chandler *et al.*, *Big Business and the Wealth of Nations*; and Alfred D. Chandler, Jr. and Herman Daems (eds.), *Managerial Hierarchies: Comparative Perspectives on the Rise of the Modern Industrial Enterprise* (Cambridge, MA, 1980).

3. *New York Times*, Nov. 8, 1999, A-22; *Economic Report of the President*, 2001, 141; United States Bureau of the Census, *Statistical Abstract of the United States*, (Washington, DC, 2001), table 710; *Statistical Abstract of the United States* (2000), tables 864, 855, 866.

4. Oliver E. Williamson, *Markets and Hierarchies, Analysis and Antitrust Implications: A Study in the Economics of Internal Organization* (New York, 1975).

5. Alfred D. Chandler, Jr. *The Visible Hand: The Managerial Revolution in American Business* (Cambridge, MA, 1977).

6. The classic works on the American corporation are Chandler, *The Visible Hand*, and *Scale and Scope: The Dynamics of Industrial Capitalism* (Cambridge, MA, 1990). His recent arguments in favor of the American corporation are found in "The Enduring Logic of Industrial Success," *Harvard Business Review* 68 (Mar.–Apr. 1990), 130–4; and Chandler *et al.*, *Big Business and the Wealth of Nations*.

7. The important contrast between Chandler and others who emphasize managerial creativity, and the traditional view of industrial economics, is discussed in Neil Fligstein and Kenneth Dauber, "Structural Change in Corporate Organizations," *Annual Review of Sociology* 15 (1989), 73–96. The traditional economic view is represented in Richard Caves, *Structure, Conduct and, Performance* (New York, 1980), and William Baumol, *Business Behavior, Value, and Growth* (New York, 1959).

8. Ronald Coase, "The Nature of the Firm," *Economica* 4 (Nov. 1937), 386–405.

9. Williamson, *Markets and Hierarchies*; *The Economic Institutions of Capitalism* (New York, 1985); and "The Modern Corporation: Origins, Evolution, Attributes," *Journal of Economic Literature* 19 (1981), 1537–68.

10. Herbert Simon, *Administrative Behavior* (New York, 1945); James March and Herbert Simon, *Organizations* (New York, 1958).

11. Louis Galambos, "Technology, Political Economy, and Professionalization: Central Themes of the Organizational Synthesis," *Business History Review* 57 (1983), 471–93; "The Emerging Organizational Synthesis in Modern American History," *Business History Review* 44 (1970), 279–90.

12. Michael Jensen, "The Eclipse of the Public Corporation," *Harvard Business Review* 89:5 (1989), 61–74. Other important works in this vein are Michael Jensen and William Meckling, "The Theory of the Firm: Managerial Behavior, Agency Costs and Ownership Structure," *Journal of Financial Economics* 3 (1974), 305–60; Eugene Fama and Michael Jensen, "Separation of Ownership and Control," *Journal of Law and Economics* 26 (1983), 301–26, and "Agency Problems and Residual Claims," *Journal of Law and Economics* 26 (1983), 327–50; Armen A. Alchian and Harold Demsetz, "Production, Information Cost and Economic Organization," *American Economic Review* 62 (1972), 777–95.

13. Chandler, "The Enduring Logic of Industrial Success," 130–40.

14. Alfred D. Chandler, "Organizational Capabilities and the Economic History of Industrial Enterprise," *Journal of Economic Perspectives* 6 (Summer 1992), 81.

15. William Lazonick, *Business Organization and the Myth of the Market Economy* (Cambridge, MA, 1991).

16. Richard Nelson and Sidney Winter, *An Evolutionary Theory of Economic Change* (Cambridge, MA, 1982); Richard Nelson, "Recent Evolutionary Theorizing About Economic Change," *Journal of Economic Literature* 33 (1995), 48–91.

17. As Nathan Rosenberg puts it, an important source of success for capitalist economies may be their institutional capabilities, "their capacity [as a society] to initiate appropriate organizational changes in response to opportunities presented by large changes in size of markets, drastic improvements in resource availability or in the availability of new products and new production technologies." Nathan Rosenberg, "Comments on Robert Hessen, 'The Modern Corporation and Private Property: A Reappraisal,' " *Journal of Law and Economics* 26 (Jun. 1983), 295.

18. David Teece and Giovanni Dosi, "Organizational Competencies and the Boundaries of the Firm," in Richard Arena and Christian Longhi (eds.), *Markets and Organization* (Heidelberg and New York, 1998), 281–301; David Teece, Gary Pisano, and A. Shuen, "Dynamic Capabilities and Strategic Management," *Strategic Management Journal* 18 (1997), 509–25; Richard Langlois and Paul Robertson, *Firms, Markets and Economic Change: A Dynamic Theory of Business Institutions* (London, 1995); Richard Langlois, *Economics as a Process: Essays in the New Institutional Economics* (New York, 1986).

19. For a critique of functionalism and look at other approaches to social action, see John Elster, "Marxism, Functionalism, and Game Theory," in Sharon Zukin and Paul DiMaggio (eds.), *Structures of Capital: The Social Organization of the Economy* (New York, 1990), 87–118.

20. Neil Fligstein, *The Transformation of Corporate Control* (Cambridge, MA, 1990), and "The Structural Transformation of American Industry: An Institutional Account of the Causes of Diversification in the Largest Firms, 1919–1979," in DiMaggio and Powell (eds.), *The New Institutionalism*, 311–36; Jonathan Zeitlin, "Productive Alternatives: Flexibility, Governance, and Strategic Choice in Industrial History," in Franco Amatori and Geoffrey Jones (eds.), *Business History Around the World* (New York, 2002); Zukin and DiMaggio, *Structures of Capital*, 24, 45.

21. The history of the discipline is taken up by Louis Galambos, "Identity and the Boundaries of Business History: An Essay on Consensus and Creativity," unpublished paper. On Cochran, see David B. Sicilia, "Cochran's Legacy: A Cultural Path Not Taken," *Business and Economic History* 24 (1995), 27–39.

22. See, for example, Kenneth Lipartito, "Culture and the Practice of Business History," *Business and Economic History* 24 (1995), 1–41; Regina Blaszczyk, *Imagining Consumers: Design Innovation from Wedgwood to Corning* (Baltimore, 2000); Angel Kwolek-Folland, *Incorporating Women: A History of Women and Business in the United States* (New York, 1998); Juliet E. K. Walker, *The History of Black Business in America: Capitalism, Race and Entrepreneurship* (New York, 1998).

23. Paul DiMaggio and Walter Powell (eds.), "Introduction," in *The New Institutionalism*, 1–40; Ronald Jepperson, "Institutional Effects and Institutionalism," in DiMaggio and Powell (eds.), *The New Institutionalism*, 143–63.

24. Paul Lawrence and Jay Lorsch, *Organization and Environment* (Boston, 1967); and Jeffrey Pfeffer and G. Salancik, *The External Control of Organizations* (New York, 1978).

25. Philip Selznick, *The TVA and the Grass Roots: A Study in the Sociology of Formal Organization* (New York, 1949); Michel Crozier, *The Bureaucratic Phenomenon* (Chicago, 1964); Anthony Downs, *Inside Bureaucracy* (Boston, 1967).

26. J. Hannan and J. Freeman, "The Population Ecology of Organizations," *American Journal of Sociology* 82 (1977), 929–66.

27. Organizations are seen as conforming to "myths of rational action" in the now classic work by John Meyer and Brian Rowan, "Institutionalized Organizations: Formal Structure as Myth and Ceremony," *American Journal of Sociology* 83 (Sep. 1977), 340–63. We avoid the use of the term "myth" as too evocative and packed with multiple theoretical meanings. See also Marshall Meyer, "The Growth of Public and Private Bureaucracies," in Zukin and DiMaggio (eds.), *Structures of Capital*.

28. Walter Powell, "Expanding the Scope of Institutional Analysis," in DiMaggio and Powell (eds.), *The New Institutionalism*, 183–203; Neil Fligstein and Robert Freeland, "Theoretical and Comparative Perspectives on Corporate Organization," *Annual Review of Sociology* 21 (1995), 21–43.

29. Paul DiMaggio and Walter Powell, "The Iron Cage Revisited: Institutional Isomorphism and Collective Rationality in Organizational Fields," in DiMaggio and Powell (eds.), *The New Institutionalism*, 63–82.

30. Louis Galambos, with Jane Eliot Sewell, *Networks of Innovation: Vaccine Development at Merck, Sharp & Dohme, and Mulford, 1895–1995* (New York, 1995). Once again a parallel can be found in evolutionary economics. See Richard R. Nelson (ed.), *National Innovation Systems: A Comparative Analysis* (New York, 1993).

31. Mark Granovetter, "Business Groups"; and Walter Powell and Laurel Smith-Doerr, "Networks and Economic Life," in Neil J. Smelser and Richard Swedberg (eds.), *The Handbook of Economic Sociology* (Princeton, 1994).

32. Mark Granovetter, "Economic Action and Social Structure: The Problem of Embeddedness," *American Journal of Sociology* 91 (Nov. 1985), 481–510. Note that now markets and hierarchies are no longer opposed, as they are in the work of economists like Williamson. Both are forms of exchange and production that involve complex social relationships and are embedded in society.

33. Charles Perrow, "Economic Theories of Organization," in Zukin and DiMaggio (eds.), *Structures of Capital*, 132.

34. Robert Freeland, "The Myth of the M-Form? Governance, Consent and Organizational Change," *American Journal of Sociology* 102 (Sep. 1996), 483–526.

35. Tony Freyer, *Regulating Big Business: Antitrust in Great Britain and America, 1880–1990* (New York, 1992).

36. William Roy, *Socializing Capital: The Rise of the Large Industrial Corporation in America* (Princeton, 1997); Martin J. Sklar, *The Corporate Reconstruction of American Capitalism; 1890–1916: The Market, the Law, and Politics* (Cambridge, 1988); James Livingston, *Origins of the Federal Reserve: Money, Class and Corporate Capitalism, 1890–1913* (Ithaca, 1986); Charles Perrow, "Economic Theories of Organization," in Zukin and DiMaggio (eds.), *Structures of Capital*, 121–52.

37. It is still possible in this way to construct a functionalist model – capitalists receive benefits from a certain set of institutional arrangements, though they do not control those arrangements and the relationship between the maintenance of the arrangements and the benefit to the class is not recognized. This "weak" form of functionalism avoids some of the pitfalls of stronger versions, which can tend toward conspiracy theories, but it does not explain why the beneficial arrangements arise in the first place. John Elster, "Marxism, Functionalism, and Game Theory," 87–90.

38. Oliver Zunz, for example, has shown how the corporation helped to create a new class of middle managers, out of the rural and immigrant populations of nineteenth century America. Olivier Zunz, *Making American Corporate, 1870–1920* (Chicago, 1990). The corporation as a site of identity construction can borrow from practice theory. See Sherry Ortner, "Theory in Anthropology since the Sixties," in Nicholas Dirks, Geoff Ely, and Sherry Ortner (eds.), *Culture/Power/History: A Reader in Contemporary Social Theory* (Princeton, 1994); Karen Cerulo "Identity Construction: New Issues, New Directions," *Annual Review of Sociology* 23 (1997), 385–409.

39. Ronald Jepperson and John W. Meyer, "The Public Order and the Construction of Formal Organizations," in DiMaggio and Powell (eds.), *The New Institutionalism*, 204–31.

I

THE CORPORATE PROJECT

1

Partnerships, Corporations, and the Limits on Contractual Freedom in U.S. History: An Essay in Economics, Law, and Culture

Naomi R. Lamoreaux

There is general consensus that, by the end of the nineteenth century, corporations were critical to the task of mobilizing capital for large-scale industry. Partnerships, the main alternative form of business organization, had obvious limitations. In the first place, a partnership's continued existence depended on the lives and will of the people who made it up; consequently, there was a mismatch between the impermanence of the form and the long-lived capital investments that industrial enterprise required. Corporations, on the other hand, were legal persons whose existence was independent of their individual owners. Indeed, the identity of each and every one of a corporation's stockholders could change without affecting the continuance of the enterprise. A second important issue was liability. Typically, stockholders in corporations risked only their investments, an advantage that made it possible to raise capital on a large scale from passive investors. By contrast, the only way to invest

I am grateful to the many scholars who have read and commented on earlier drafts of this essay: Randolf Arguelles, Lucy Barber, Margaret Blair, Ruth Bloch, Cynthia Culver, Colleen Dunlavy, Michael Easterly, Stanley Engerman, Louis Galambos, Oscar Gelderbloom, Stephen Haber, Margaret Jacob, David Lamoreaux, Kenneth Lipartito, John Majewski, Gregory Mark, Chelsea Neel, Jean-Laurent Rosenthal, David Sicilia, Kenneth Sokoloff, Joseph Sommer, Lynn Stout, Tristan Traviola, John Wallis, and Mary Yeager. Thanks, too, to participants in seminars and conference sessions at the California Institute of Technology, Columbia University, the Georgetown Law Center, the Hagley Library, the National Bureau of Economic Research, Stanford University, the University of California, Davis, the University of Maryland, and the UCLA Law School. Research for this project was supported by fellowships from the National Endowment for the Humanities and the American Council of Learned Societies and grants from the Academic Senate of the University of California, Los Angeles.

in a partnership was to become a member of the firm; and because all partners were fully liable for their firm's debts, in general only investors who planned to play an active role in management could afford to take the risk.[1]

Today, any businessperson who so desires can organize a corporation by filling out a set of forms and paying a standard fee. In the early years of U.S. history, however, corporate charters could only be obtained by special act of the legislature and were generally reserved for projects deemed to be in the public interest. Scholars have devoted a great deal of attention to understanding how the corporation evolved from an instrument of public policy to a common business device, but they have focused almost exclusively on the use of the form by large-scale enterprises. As a result, their explanations have tended toward one of two alternative narratives. The first is a story of increasing efficiency in which technological change made possible the exploitation of new economies of scale, motivating governments to remove the legal constraints that impeded businesses from raising the necessary capital. The second is a story of power in which business groups exploited their political and economic muscle to secure the legal reforms they needed to entrench and extend their dominance. Although these two explanations have very different political slants, in other respects they are quite similar. Both portray corporate law as evolving more or less steadily toward its modern form as a result of the pressures exerted by self-interested businesses.[2]

Scholars have devoted comparatively little attention to the experience of small and medium-sized firms, even though these enterprises were numerically preponderant.[3] If, however, the focus of scholarly writing were to shift toward these smaller size categories, it would quickly become apparent that the history of the corporate form needs to be rewritten – that one must substitute for these unidirectional narratives of self-interest a more complex account replete with ironic twists and unintended consequences. Moreover, unlike the standard accounts, which implicitly treat the political and legal systems as responding flexibly to the demands of business, this rewriting would highlight both the elusiveness of self-interest and the inherent conservatism of the law in the face of dramatic economic change.

The need for revision is apparent even for the early history of the corporation – before the rise of big business in the late nineteenth century. As the first section of this chapter shows, there was initially considerable variation in the attributes of the corporate form, a pattern that is not at all surprising given that each charter was the product of a special legislative act. It is well known that Jacksonian opposition to the favoritism inherent in this system of granting charters ultimately led to the passage of general incorporation laws that democratized access to the corporate form. What is less well known, however, is that the same political pressures that forced legislatures to liberalize the chartering process induced them to make the form more uniform as well. Hence, businesspeople seeking such corporate advantages as limited liability increasingly had to accept, in addition, centralized management based on majority rule and one vote per share, whether they wanted to organize their enterprises in this way or not.[4]

So long as scholars were mainly preoccupied with the rise of big business, there was no need for them to concern themselves with this enforced uniformity, for the standard constellation of features posed no problems (and indeed may have been highly desirable) for large-scale enterprises. As the second section of this chapter demonstrates, however, these uniform rules imposed potentially significant costs on firms in the smaller size categories. Using the case of the Corliss Steam Engine Company as an example, I show that majority-rule governance, in combination with the greater permanence of the corporate form, exposed minority shareholders in closely held firms to the threat of exploitation. Members of smaller firms would probably have been better off if they could have mixed and matched attributes of the partnership and corporate forms as suited to their needs, combining, for example, limited liability with governance rules based on consensus and ability to exit. For most of U.S. history, however, firms that attempted to exercise their contractual freedom in this way faced considerable risk that their agreements would not be upheld by courts intent on maintaining a clear line between partnerships and corporations.

This is not to say that the boundary between partnerships and corporations was never contested. To the contrary, as I will show in middle sections of this chapter, the distinctions between these two organizational forms were an important source of tension from the early nineteenth century on. At the heart of this conflict was the idea of personhood. From the beginning, corporations and partnerships had very different statuses at law. Partnerships could be formed freely, but were not legal persons. Corporations could not be organized without a grant from the state, but were legal persons. As creatures of government, however, corporations were artificial persons, possessing only those attributes of natural persons that they were explicitly granted by their creators. This distinction did not pose a problem so long as use of the corporate form was severely restricted. But once ordinary businesses could readily choose this organizational form – once firms that would otherwise have organized as partnerships could cross over and become corporations – all kinds of new economic and legal problems arose, and the boundary between the two forms correspondingly blurred. Partnerships came to be seen more like corporations and vice versa in law and also, as we shall see, in common parlance, and both forms came to be seen more like natural persons.

These developments, however, ultimately had little consequence for the menu of organizational choices available to small and medium-sized enterprises. Indeed, early twentieth-century businesspeople still basically had the same two starkly differentiated options that had emerged a century ago. Why there was so little change, I argue, had much to do with the nature of the common law. Although the law can and does evolve in response to economic and political pressures, its broad sweep and the responsiveness of its judicial interpreters, both to political pressures and to larger cognitive patterns in the general culture, mean that change can easily be derailed. Ironically, it was the revival at the turn of the century of artificial-entity theories of the corporation in response to outrage over the growing power of big business that made the situation of minority stockholders in small corporations more precarious.

In combination with cultural trends that made it increasingly difficult to conceptualize the differences between small and large businesses, this revival stalled the move toward greater contractual freedom.

THE EMERGENCE OF A STANDARD CORPORATE FORM

According to the classic definition offered in Stewart Kyd's 1793 *Treatise on the Law of Corporations*, a corporation was a group of individuals united "in one body" that was "vested by the policy of the law, with a capacity of acting, in several respects, as an individual, particularly of taking and granting property, contracting obligations, and of suing and being sued." Chief Justice John Marshall underscored the importance of this attribute of personhood in his famous 1819 *Dartmouth College* decision, pointing out that it was "chiefly for the purpose of clothing bodies of men, in succession, with these qualities and capacities, that corporations were invented, and are in use."[5]

The most important initial difference between corporations and partnerships, therefore, was that the former were legal persons but the latter were not. In other respects, the two forms were much more similar at the beginning of the nineteenth century than they would become over time. Many early corporations did not have perpetual life, but rather were chartered for finite periods; shareholders often were fully liable for their corporation's debts, just like members of partnerships; moreover, corporations frequently operated according to voting rules that granted each shareholder one vote or imposed some kind of graduated scale rather than one vote per share.[6]

Even the personhood difference was not absolute. A corporation was not a natural person, but a creation of the state. It was "an artificial being, invisible, intangible," to use Marshall's words, "existing only in contemplation of law," and as such, "possesse[d] only those properties which the charter of its creation confer[ed] upon it, either expressly, or as incidental to its very existence."[7] Although, for example, an individual was free to enter into any contract that was not contrary to law, a corporation not only could "make no contracts forbidden by its charter, . . . but in general [could] make no contracts which [were] not necessary either directly or incidentally" to fulfill the purpose of its charter. More generally, unlike a natural person, a corporation could not "be deemed a moral agent, subject to moral obligation." Neither could it "be subject to personal suffering," nor participate, like an ordinary citizen, "in the civil government of the country."[8]

During the first quarter century or so following the American revolution, state legislatures chartered corporations – that is, created these special types of legal persons – with the primary aim of encouraging investment in infrastructure projects that they could not, either for economic or political reasons, undertake with government funds. The principal that the power to charter corporations should be used for the public good was not, however, incompatible with the expectation that these projects would earn money for their investors. Quite the contrary, the idea was that private citizens would be encouraged by the lure of profits to channel their savings into socially useful projects, and, in order to make such investments more attractive, states often included in the charters additional privileges, like limited liability, that are now generally associated with the corporate form.[9]

Although many early corporations were not, in fact, profitable, the privileges that charters conferred on those who secured them became a source of heated political controversy.[10] Because the grant of a corporate charter required a special legislative act, critics charged that only those who were politically well connected could obtain them. Even worse, they worried that those who secured charters might use the resulting privileges to the detriment of those who were less well connected. Banks were particular objects of criticism – both because they often lent substantial proportions of their funds to their own officers and directors, and because the currency which they alone were allowed to issue appeared to give them power over the community's money supply – but similar complaints extended to corporations in general.[11]

The most extreme critics of corporations proposed abolishing them entirely, but other opponents advocated liberalizing the granting process so as to make charters freely available to all who wanted them. Depending on the relative political strength of these critics (and the particular remedy they favored), state legislatures sometimes made it easier for petitioners to obtain special charters, but sometimes made it very difficult. They also swung between extremes in the details of the charters they granted; sometimes insisting on unlimited liability but at other times limiting shareholders' risk to the amount of their investments, sometimes restricting the life of charters to fixed periods of time but other times granting corporations perpetual life, and sometimes limiting large shareholders' voting rights, but other times allowing them to dominate their firm's governance.

In the end, however, the more liberal tendencies won out – in part, because there was broad support for economic development and interest in participating in corporate ventures, and in part because incorporation fees were so lucrative that states that chartered large numbers of corporations could reduce the property-tax burden on their citizens.[12] By the middle of the century, therefore, most states had regularized the process of granting charters by passing general incorporation laws. These laws enabled any group of businesspeople that paid a fee and met specified requirements (such as minimum capitalization) to take out a corporate charter. Initially, they applied only to designated industries and were quite restrictive in their provisions. Over time, however, the range of businesses that could be incorporated widened and the terms on which charters were granted became more attractive.[13]

Even after corporate charters became routinely available, it was often still possible for entrepreneurs who wished to secure more desirable provisions than those available under general laws to petition their legislatures for special charters. Hence, the controversy over corporations as vehicles of privilege continued, and the upshot, during the third quarter of the century, was that many states added provisions to their constitutions forbidding the chartering of corporations by special legislative act.[14] Even before the passage of these amendments, it had become increasingly common for legislatures to insist on applying standard templates in writing charters for corporations in sectors such as manufacturing and banking. After the amendments, the extent of variation was further reduced. Although there were still some differences across states and sectors of the economy, certain features of the corporate form became increasingly standard. These included not only perpetual life and limited liability, but also governance features such as centralized management based on majority rule and one vote per share.[15] In other words, in order to secure corporate advantages such as limited liability, businesspeople increasingly had to agree to a particular set of organizational rules.

As state legislatures made it easier for firms to obtain these now more standard charters, the number of corporations increased dramatically. For example, between 1826 and 1835 New Jersey authorized on average eleven corporations per year using a special charter system; between 1846 and 1855 it granted on average forty-five per year through a combination of special and general incorporation; between 1866 and 1875, 145 per year under a similar combination; and between 1886 and 1895, 820 per year using general incorporation alone. Although New Jersey was a leader in chartering corporations by the end of the nineteenth century, the growth pattern in other states was similar. By the time of the first federal income tax in 1916, there were more than 300,000 corporations active across the United States.[16]

Although most large firms now routinely incorporated their businesses, the vast majority of enterprises that took out corporate charters were small and medium-sized firms. To use the example of New Jersey again, 42 percent of the 4,300 plus corporations chartered during the 1870s and 1880s were capitalized at less than $100,000 and 88 percent at less than $1,000,000. Even during the Great Merger Movement of 1895–1904, when many giant combines took out New Jersey charters in order to benefit from the state's liberal incorporation laws, 40 percent of the approximately 16,500 corporations formed had less than $100,000 capital and 90 percent less than $1,000,000.[17]

These small and medium-sized business enterprises chose the corporate form in preference not only to partnerships, but also to other available forms – most notably limited partnerships. Legislation permitting this type of organization was first passed by the New York and Connecticut legislatures in 1822, and then by most other states over the next couple of decades, as part of the effort to respond both to opponents of the corporation and to the demand for broader access to privileges like limited liability. Limited partnerships consisted of two types of partners: general partners, who ran the company and had unlimited liability for its debts; and special partners, who had no managerial authority but whose liabilities were limited to their investments. From the standpoint of a general partner, the limited partnership functioned much like an ordinary partnership, but afforded greater possibilities for tapping external sources of capital. From the standpoint of a special partner, the form created the possibility of greater gains than could be obtained from a simple loan contract (especially given usury restrictions) without the risks that an ordinary partnership entailed.[18]

What is most interesting about the limited partnership form, however, is how rarely it was used, despite the advantages it would seem to offer over ordinary partnerships in raising capital. During the early 1930s, for example, Stanley Howard searched records for five New Jersey counties (representing about a third of the population of the state) over the preceding century and found that only 142 limited partnerships had been formed.[19] Although there were problems with the way the legislation in New Jersey and other states was written that, by exposing special partners to unlimited liability under certain circumstances beyond their control, reduced the attractiveness of the form, these statutory deficiencies should have been easy to remedy. There was little effort to do so, however, the most likely reason being the strong preference that businesspeople exhibited for the corporate form.[20]

THE CORLISS CASE: DISCOVERING THE POTENTIAL COSTS OF PERSONHOOD

Why so many small and medium-sized firms preferred the corporate form of organization is not clear. The main advantage of incorporation was the ability to raise capital from a broad pool of investors, but typically the stock in these firms was closely held and not bought or sold.[21] Although limited liability undoubtedly reduced the risks that each firm's small numbers of equity holders faced, it could also increase the cost of borrowing – an important consideration given that whatever funds these firms raised on the outside typically took the form of debt rather than equity. Indeed, stockholders of small firms often found that they had to endorse personally their companies' debts in order to secure loans at affordable rates.[22] Some businesspeople may have chosen the corporate form because it offered an easy way to pass their enterprise on to heirs when they died, but the greater permanence of the corporation was not an unalloyed advantage either. The case of the Corliss Steam Engine Company, the firm that designed the famous engine that powered the Philadelphia Centennial Exposition, serves as an excellent example.

The Corliss firm had been in business for more than ten years when, on August 1, 1857, it was reorganized as a Rhode Island corporation with a capital stock of $300,000. Since 1850 it had been operating under the name Corliss & Nightingale, a partnership with two equal partners, George H. Corliss and Edwin J. Nightingale. Although both men had mechanical backgrounds, the steam engine for which the firm was famous was Corliss' invention, and it was Corliss who controlled the resulting patents.[23]

When they reorganized their firm as a corporation, Corliss and Nightingale divided the bulk of the stock between them. They also brought in three new people as stockholders – G. Wood, J. H. Clark, and S. A. Smith. These men held managerial positions in the firm and together owned less than 10 percent of the shares.[24] Otherwise, as far as it is possible to tell from the rather sparse historical record, nothing much changed when the firm was reorganized as a corporation. Day-to-day operations appear to have continued as before, the main difference being that Corliss now had the title president and Nightingale treasurer.

More important, there is evidence that the principals still thought of their enterprise in much the same way as they had when it was organized as a partnership. The decision to sell small amounts of stock to the three managers followed the long-standing practice of making valued employees junior partners in a concern. When these men left the firm shortly thereafter, they sold out their holdings to Corliss and Nightingale – just as they would have if the firm were still a partnership – and the men who replaced them (one of whom was Corliss' brother William) were gradually given ownership stakes.[25] Even more intriguing, this series of transactions was discussed in the language of partnership, as the following account of Smith's departure from William Corliss' diary suggests:

Went to the works twice today. Mr. Clark is no longer a member of the C.S.E. Co. and it seems pretty generally understood that I shall soon be one of the concern. I think Scott has made a great mistake and I believe he himself begins to think so – for he observed that this dissolution would be a good thing for me.[26]

The use of the word "dissolution" is the tip-off. When a shareholder of a corporation sold all of his or her stock and ceased to be a "member" of the company, the firm did not thereby dissolve. When, however, a member of a partnership sold out to the other members, the partnership had to be dissolved and a new firm consisting of the remaining parties (and any additional members) had to be organized. The use of the word dissolution by William (and Scott) is good evidence that the parties involved continued to think of their firm in much the same way as they had when it was a partnership.

Nonetheless, the change in organizational form altered the nature of the firm in significant ways, as the Corlisses discovered to their great distress several years later when another important employee (Frederick Grinnell) applied to become a stockholder, and George Corliss sought to accommodate him and, at the same time, increase William's interest in the firm. Up to that point, Corliss and Nightingale had maintained an even balance in their shares by selling equal amounts of their stock to managers they wished to reward with an ownership stake. But now Nightingale refused to continue the practice, probably because he slowly had come to understand that the shift to the corporate form of organization had subtly altered power relations within the firm and that, by admitting more "members" in this way, he was losing control of the company. The Corliss Steam Engine Company's charter specified that stockholders had one vote for each share of stock they owned. William and Grinnell were

George's men, and in combination with them George would control a majority of the shares.

If the firm had still been a partnership, Nightingale would not have suffered any loss of authority from admitting more partners – even if they were George's people. His ownership rights would not in any respect have been diminished, and he would have retained the power to act on behalf of the firm. The corporate form of organization, however, concentrated management in the hands of officers elected by the stockholders. No matter how many shares they owned, members who were not empowered by such a vote could not act as agents of the firm. If Nightingale reduced his shareholdings as George proposed, his position in the firm might have become increasingly marginalized.[27]

George was furious at this turn of events, but the shift to the corporate form also limited his options for dealing with Nightingale's refusal. If the firm had still been a partnership, George could have responded to Nightingale's obstinacy by moving unilaterally to dissolve the company, but the corporation could not easily be dissolved, especially not without Nightingale's agreement.[28] The only solution, as George saw it, was to force Nightingale to sell out. George still retained control of the important steam engine patents, and he threatened to license other engine manufacturers to use his patents on favorable terms.[29] This was a strategy of desperation, however, because if forced to carry it out, George would have undermined the competitive position of his firm. William thought the threat was real (he wrote in his diary that "George talks about 'winding up the Concern' and 'getting out of business'"), and Grinnell took it so seriously that he sold back his shares, stating "that in view of the present prospects of the Company he felt unwilling to borrow money for the investment."[30]

Because George owned such valuable patents, however, Nightingale was forced to give in.[31] Later investors in corporations would not make Nightingale's mistake; they would force inventors to assign their patent rights to the company. But the more general point to make here is that Corliss was able to vanquish Nightingale only because he retained a key property right as an individual. If that right had been transferred to the company, he would have been in a much more difficult position as a result of the shift to the corporate form. Unless Nightingale put a high value on George's continued active participation in the firm, Corliss probably would not have been able to force Nightingale to sell out his interest or even to increase his brother's ownership stake in the firm.[32]

The important lesson to draw from this example is that partnerships and corporations offered very different degrees of protection against what economists call "hold-up" – that is, pressure to accept less favorable terms once capital is sunk in an investment. As Oliver Williamson has shown, whenever parties must make investments that are highly specific to a particular transaction, they are susceptible to this kind of extortion because the resulting assets cannot readily be used for other purposes – that is, their value outside the relationship is much less than it is within it. It is very difficult to write arm's-length contracts that can eliminate this risk, and so, Williamson argued, parties can most easily resolve the problem and elicit the desired investment by integrating vertically, so as to bring the transaction within the bounds of a single firm.[33]

As the Corliss case suggests, however, the particular organizational form employed affects the workability of this solution. Partnerships offer greater protection against hold-up than ordinary contracts because, if one partner tries to extort income from another, the aggrieved party can threaten to dissolve the enterprise and force the exploiter either to buy him out or to bear proportionately the costs of liquidating firm-specific assets. The ability to exit thus provides an incentive for partners to resolve their differences in a mutually satisfactory way. This incentive does not exist, however, in the case of corporations. As Nightingale realized belatedly, if majority stockholders pursue their own interests to the detriment of other shareholders, there is little that the minority can do to remedy the situation. Minority shareholders do not have the votes to force management to change course; nor can they unilaterally dissolve the enterprise.[34]

Of course, the partnership form of organization also entailed costs. Unlimited liability meant that partners risked their personal assets as well as those that they placed into the firm, a risk that was heightened by the principal-agent problems that each partner faced vis-à-vis the others.[35] But the Corliss case suggests that at the same time the corporate form eliminated this source of danger by granting members of the firm limited liability, it substituted a new one in its place – the possibility that majority stockholders would use their powers of control to hold up the minority and reduce its share of the firm's income. This danger was not a serious one for large firms whose securities found a ready market on the exchanges because dissatisfied shareholders could exit by selling off their stock. Minority shareholders in small corporations did not have this ready escape option, however, and would likely find it especially difficult to sell their shares when the majority behaved exploitatively. Presumably, members of small firms would be better off if they could mix and match attributes of the partnership and corporate forms as best suited their needs, say by combining limited liability with a governance structure more like that of a partnership.[36] But, as I will show, such solutions did not become readily available until the late twentieth century.

LEGAL PERSONHOOD AND THE BOUNDARY BETWEEN PARTNERSHIPS AND CORPORATIONS

As the Corliss example suggests, during this early period in the history of American business, people who switched from the partnership to the corporate form did not always understand the ramifications of the change. Indeed, throughout the nineteenth century, the courts adjudicated a steady stream of cases involving incorporated businesses whose proprietors continued to operate in the more informal manner of partnerships, only confronting the constraints that the form imposed when things began to go wrong with their relationships. Although the more savvy might avoid the legal troubles that such neglect of proper procedure could entail by writing into their charter or bylaws provisions that made the corporation function more like a partnership, there was considerable risk that such arrangements would not be upheld in court.[37]

The problem was that there were conflicting traditions in the case law. On the one hand, for a variety of reasons, including desire to protect creditors, judges attempted to draw a clear line between partnerships and corporations. On the other, in a number of concrete situations they were forced to recognize that the incorporation of large numbers of ordinary businesses had blurred the distinction between the two forms. Although the latter body of cases appeared for a time to point the way toward greater contractual freedom for those forming small corporations, in the end this trend did not dominate. Indeed, if anything, by the early twentieth century the courts were enforcing the requisites of the standard corporate form more rigidly than ever.

Some of the cases in which judges attempted to maintain a distinction between partnerships and corporations turned on the issue of personhood. A good example was *Pratt* v. *Bacon*, an 1830 Massachusetts case involving the Merino Wool Factory Company, a corporation whose stock was held by just three shareholders.[38] One of the three, Elijah Pratt, claimed that he had been victimized by the other two. He accused the majority of expropriating the firm's property, selling it off, and refusing to account to him for his share or give him access to the firm's records. To secure redress, he entered a plea in equity. The Massachusetts legislature had passed a statute in 1823 granting the state's courts equity jurisdiction in disputes involving partners, joint-tenants, and tenants in common. The legislation was controversial because at the time there was a great deal of distrust of the broad discretionary authority that judges exercised in equity, and the courts sought to construe the statute narrowly.[39]

The 1823 law did not mention corporations, but Pratt's lawyer argued that the jurisdiction should be extended to corporations like the Merino Wool Factory Company, which were "not like those to which some exclusive privileges are given," but rather differed "from partnerships only in possessing greater facilities to manage their affairs." Although the court agreed that "there is certainly some resemblance between a corporation and a partnership," it dismissed the bill on the grounds that "the difference between the relative rights and duties, the legal qualities and characteristics of the members of a manufacturing corporation, and copartners and tenants in common, is obvious and strongly marked." A corporation, unlike a partnership, was a legal person. It was "an ideal body, subsisting only in contemplation of law" and "deemed, for useful purposes, to have an existence independent of that of all the members of which it is composed." Because corporations had this quality of personhood, their members "in their legal relations to each other, differ[ed] essentially and radically from partners." Therefore, the judges announced, "by no reasonable construction of the statute" could the equity jurisdiction be extended to them.[40] Justice Putnam elaborated the point in a similar case three years later: "One great reason for giving a remedy in equity in the case of partners, was the inadequacy of the legal remedies which existed." Partners could not sue their partnership, because the firm did not exist as an entity independent of its members. Hence, to sue one's partnership was in essence to sue oneself. "But the corporation, the artificial being, may be sued by a corporator, as well as by a stranger" and so there was no need for this extraordinary remedy.[41]

In other states, access to equity courts for small corporations was not an issue, but judges worried that if firms operating for all practical purposes as partnerships were allowed to exercise corporate privileges like limited liability, the result would be, in the words of a New Jersey chancellor, to perpetrate "a fraud upon the community." In the case at issue (another example of a minority shareholder fighting victimization), two shareholders had unequally divided all of the stock of the New England Manufacturing Company, excepting four shares, "which were put in the names of four other persons, merely for the purpose of having a sufficient number of stockholders to organize the company in the manner directed by the act of incorporation." After incorporation, the two major owners continued to run their business "as before . . . , by and between themselves as individuals, the company not acting by its board." In the chancellor's view, the business was "in reality but an ordinary partnership." Therefore, either the members of the firm "must be held to conduct their business as a corporation, and be governed by the law of corporations," or they "should be liable to debts to the whole amount of their property."[42]

In other early cases, however, courts found it useful to exploit practical similarities between the two forms of organization. As the number of ordinary private businesses using the corporate form increased, the number and kinds of disputes involving corporations inevitably increased as well. In many instances, judges did not have precedents in corporate law on which to base their decisions, and so they turned for assistance to other bodies of law, including cases involving partnerships. For example, in his 1807 opinion finding that a stockholder in the Portland Bank had been wrongly prevented by the bank's directors from buying additional shares of the corporation's stock, Justice Sedgwick of Massachusetts declared that "all the stockholders of the bank were *partners*." His decision followed from this premise, for "whenever a partnership adopts a project, within the principles of their agreement, for the purpose of profit, it must be for the benefit of all the partners, in proportion to their respective interests in the concern."[43] Similarly, in an 1812 Connecticut case, Justice Ingersoll upheld a corporate bylaw that permitted proxy voting on the grounds that in any business association a person may authorize a representative "to act for him in his absence, in all matters relative to the subject matter of the association." Pointing out that "all trading companies and joint partnerships stand on this ground," the judge asked rhetorically, "[i]s it not, then, very absurd to say, that these rights are all taken away, the moment that an incorporation takes place?"[44]

To give a later example, in 1860 the New York Court of Appeals used the analogy between partnerships and corporations to block an effort by a railroad corporation to escape liability for a crash. Lawyers for the railroad had argued that the corporation was not authorized by its charter to operate that segment of track and could not be held liable for the consequences of such *ultra vires* activities. The court countered that "a private or trading corporation is essentially a chartered partnership." Whereas "in a well regulated unincorporated partnership" associates use their copartnership contract to specify "the objects of their association," in a corporation the charter serves essentially the same purpose. If the managers of a corporation engage in activities that are beyond the scope of the charter, these activities are *ultra vires* in the same sense that activities beyond the scope of a partnership agreement would be. Hence, corporations are no less liable than partnerships for the consequences of such activities.[45]

These kinds of decisions, in which judges exploited the analogy with partnerships to resolve disputes involving corporations, increased in number and type over the course of the nineteenth century. Corporate law, as a result, grew in many ways more similar to partnership law, and corporations increasingly were treated as contracts into which their members entered just as they might any other kind of business contract. For example, although corporations made decisions by majority votes about important matters such as who was able to act on behalf of the firm, by the mid-nineteenth century the courts had established the principle that any non-trivial change to a corporation's charter required stockholders' unanimous consent. The analogy to partnerships in these cases was explicit. As Chancellor Bennett of Vermont pointed out in *Stevens v. Rutland and Burlington Railroad Company*, partnerships and joint stock associations "cannot by a vote of the majority change or alter their fundamental articles of copartnership or association, against the will of the minority, however small, unless there is an express or implied provision in the articles themselves that they may do it." The same principle must hold for corporations. To find otherwise would undermine the sanctity of contract, because when an individual purchased a share in a corporation, he or she invested "for the purpose specified in the charter, . . . and there was at the same time a trust created, and an implied assumption on the part of the corporation, to apply it to that object, and none other." Altering the charter without the individual's consent violated his or her rights, for as Bennett put it, "no one can suppose, that upon the payment of his subscription, the personal identity of the plaintiff was merged in the corporation, or that he ceased to have distinct and independent rights."[46]

The growing body of decisions that treated corporate charters as ordinary business contracts had a subtly corrosive effect on the idea that the fundamental difference between corporations and partnerships was that the former were legal persons and the latter were not. Indeed, these cases provided the basis for the emergence during the late nineteenth century of a new "aggregate theory" of the corporation that denied that corporations could be distinguished from the natural persons who made them up. The most notable proponent of this view, Victor Morawetz, began his *Treatise on the Law of Private*

Corporations with a critique of Marshall's definition of a corporation as an artificial being. "It is evident," he countered, that the corporation cannot be "in reality a person or a thing distinct from the corporators who compose it." As a result, "when it is said that a corporation is itself a person, or being, or creature, this must be understood in a figurative sense only."

> Although a corporation is frequently spoken of as a person or unit, it is essential to a clear understanding of many important branches of the law of corporations to bear in mind distinctly, that the existence of a corporation independently of its shareholders is a fiction; and that the rights and duties of an incorporated association are in reality the rights and duties of the persons who compose it, and not of an imaginary being.[47]

For Morawetz, "the ultimate object" of "every ordinary business corporation" was "the pecuniary profit of the individual members," who came together voluntarily to pursue some particular business purpose.[48] From this basic assumption, he attempted to derive most of the important principles of corporate law. For example, he argued that corporations were forbidden to enter into contracts that were contrary to their charters (*ultra vires*), not because they were artificial creatures of the state, but because the charter delimited the boundaries of the business on which the incorporators themselves had decided when they formed the enterprise: "Those who become members of a corporation for purposes of pecuniary profit evidently intend that the object of their company shall be to prosecute the enterprise expressly set forth in their charter or articles of association; and they evidently do not intend to join in any speculation which is not in pursuance of the purposes thus indicated."[49]

Morawetz also sought to counter the view that corporations were privileged entities that could only be created by permission of the state. As he saw it, the "assumption of the privilege of acting in a corporate capacity [did] not involve an infringement of the rights of other persons." There were no insurmountable problems, for example, with allowing individuals to contract for corporate attributes such as limited liability, for creditors could easily be protected "by requiring due notice of the corporate organization to be given to the world." Moreover, the states had already gone a long way in this direction by passing general incorporation laws that effectively "repeal the prohibition of the common law, and leave the right of forming a corporation and of acting in a corporate capacity free to all, subject merely to such limitations and safeguards as are required for the protection of the public."[50] As he saw it, the requirement of state permission for forming a corporation had become, in actual practice, little more than a formality.

Morawetz's contractual view of the corporation was increasingly influential in the late nineteenth century,[51] and indeed his argument that state permission had, in effect, become perfunctory would seem to have been confirmed by a new wave of general incorporation laws passed in the wake of an 1888 New Jersey act permitting corporations to purchase and hold stock in other corporations. The new statutes repealed earlier restrictions that states had imposed on the business activities, securities issues, and capitalization of corporations and ostensibly greatly increased the contractual freedom with which incorporators could draft articles of association.[52] As I will show, however, in practice the ultimate effect of the new laws was to undermine the aggregate theory of the corporation. By facilitating the emergence of business enterprises that operated on an unprecedentedly large scale, the laws provoked a strong defensive reaction that breathed new life into the artificial theory of the corporation. At the same time, as I will also show, the laws decreased the power of individual stockholders vis-à-vis corporate boards, a development which, in combination with the revival of artificial theory, had the ironic consequence of making it more difficult for shareholders in small firms to modify the corporate form to suit their needs.

THE CULTURAL DIMENSION OF PERSONHOOD

Before turning to these issues, however, it is useful to discuss another trend that operated to obscure the differences between partnerships and corporations. At the same time that the common law was evolving to make corporations seem in some ways more like partnerships, Americans were experiencing a sea change in their way of perceiving the world that led them to consider partnerships increasingly like corporations. At the heart of this shift was a major transformation in the way Americans understood collective human activity of all types, not just business organizations: an increased tendency to think about groups, regardless of size or function, as being more than the sum of their parts, as having identities, indeed personalities, that were distinct from those of the individuals who made them up.

Gregory Mark, Morton Horwitz, and others have written about this phenomenon, but they have focused their attention on only one of its manifestations – the promotion of the natural-entity theory of the corporation by a segment of the intellectual elite. According to these scholars, the idea that corporations developed their own personalities originated in Germany during the second half of the nineteenth century as part of a philosophical project stimulated by, and in reaction to, the growth of the modern nation state. The writings of these German thinkers, the most influential of whom was Otto Gierke, were first introduced to America at the turn of the century, where they immediately appealed to intellectuals seeking to understand, and often to legitimate, the giant corporations that were mushrooming up around them. These ideas, Horwitz and Mark have argued, provided the intellectual raw material that a new generation of legal theorists needed for their own project – reinterpreting corporations as natural entities which existed in a Lockean sense prior to the state, which the law could "no more create . . . than it [could] a house out of a collection of loose bricks."[53]

This new way of thinking was not merely a German import, however, but rather part of a broader reorientation of American culture that scholars have dubbed the organizational revolution.[54] Although this transformation reached its apogee during the first couple of decades of the twentieth century – when the vanguard of a new, professional middle class promoted the superiority of formal hierarchical structures in business, government, the professions, and even labor – it was long in the making and already had taken deep root in the language with which Americans described their world. Thus Harold J. Laski, one of the proponents of the natural-entity view of corporations, observed in the *Harvard Law Review* in 1916 that there was a general tendency in the vernacular to personalize associations – to treat them grammatically as individuals, expressing their actions with singular verbs and their relationships with singular possessive pronouns. Laski argued that this usage expressed a deeper truth. "Clearly," he asserted, "there is compulsion in our personalising. We do it because we must. We do it because we feel in these things the red blood of a living personality. Here are no mere abstractions of an over-exuberant imagination. The need is so apparent as to make plain the reality beneath."[55]

Although it is beyond the scope of this paper to map this cultural transformation in any systematic way, its broad outlines can be sketched at least crudely by pursuing Laski's insight and observing the changes that occurred over time in the grammatical constructions that judges used in their opinions.[56] During the early nineteenth century, for example, judges invariably referred to partnerships in ways that focused attention on the people who made them up rather than on the enterprises as entities. Although collective nouns like partnership and firm took singular verbs and pronouns when judges wrote about them in the abstract (as in "A partnership between attorneys *is* admitted to be lawful. Like other partnerships, *it* may be composed of two or more individuals . . ."[57]), when writing about actual firms judges generally used plural verbs and pronouns (as in "the firm held the mortgage, *they* were agents for the plaintiff for all above *their* own debt, *they* have extinguished the whole mortgage, as I will presume, without receiving the money, and, therefore, *are* liable in this action to *their* principal . . . "[58] or "With the confidence which Cochran, Addoms & Co. had in the prisoner, and of which he could not be ignorant, the false pretenses thus put forth were well calculated to impose upon *them*, and accomplish the cheat and fraud intended."[59])

During this early period, judges often referred to corporations in the same way they did partnerships. Compare, for example, the abstract statement, "A corporation *has* been said to have no soul; and surely *it has* no corporeal body,"[60] with the more specific "The construction contended for by the plaintiff would give to the provisions of the charter, as far as the Corporation *are* concerned, an effect and operation nearly tantamount to a virtual repeal of the Statute against Usury . . . "[61] From early on, however, judges also found it necessary to distinguish individual corporations from their constituent shareholders and, to make their meaning clear, referred to corporations with singular verbs and pronouns:

This court decided, on the former appeal . . . that the Company *was* dissolved, and that the respondents were chargeable with the debt due from the Company to the appellant, to the extent of their respective shares of stock in the Company. I perceive no escape from the conclusion that the respondents are individually liable to the same extent that the Company *was* liable.[62]

Over time, this latter pattern came to dominate, and the plural constructions that typified the first half of the century gradually disappeared.[63] Not only was it much more common for words like corporation to be associated with singular pronouns and verbs, but the particular verbs used often implied that the entities had human capacities or qualities. For example, in one case, "*the plaintiff was a company* engaged in the manufacture of cutlery at Greenfield, Massachusetts, having an agency in the city of New York for the sale of its products. [F]or some years previous to the occurrence, out of which this action arose, *it had been in the habit of sending its products to its agent* at New York."[64] Even more striking is another example in which a judge used language that attributed human characteristics to a corporation in order to justify holding it to a higher legal standard than he would an individual:

In undertaking to adopt regulations to operate upon the public in detail affected by *its* actions, it had the opportunity from *its character as a corporation, to determine at its leisure, its policy; and could not well claim to be excused for hasty and illegal conduct.* If the result of such determination was the establishment of rules, either to compel the passenger availing himself of his legal right to travel in *its* cars, to pay an unwarranted and illegal exaction, or be compelled to submit to his expulsion therefrom by force, though *its* subordinates, through all the attendant indignity; *it thereby assumed the hazard of subjecting itself* to the highest measure of damages, *for the deliberation and force accompanying its illegal conduct.*[65]

Interestingly enough, the spread of this kind of usage occurred at the very time that corporate law was developing along lines that were increasingly similar to partnership law. Indeed, the aggregate theorists themselves employed it, enmeshing themselves in a kind of linguistic contradiction that would enable proponents of the natural-entity view to cite their work as if its underlying message was identical to their own. Morawetz, for example, invariably used singular verbs and pronouns to refer to corporations. Moreover, as he himself noted, the tendency to anthropomorphize corporations was spreading to other forms of collective human activity. In a passage that natural-entity theorists would later repeatedly quote, he observed that "in numberless . . . instances, associations which are not legally incorporated are considered as personified entities, acting as a unit, and in one name; for example, political parties, societies, committees, courts, newspapers." He also remarked that "the popular conception of a copartnership is essentially that of a corporation."[66]

In the case of partnerships, however, the grammatical change was more subtle than Morawetz's observation would seem to indicate. Indeed, throughout the early twentieth century, one continues to find enterprises that took the form of partnerships paired with plural verbs and pronouns (as in "said firm entered into a composition agreement with certain of *their* creditors"[67]). But the use of single verbs and pronouns also became more common ("The firm of Whitney & Kitchen *was* also liable thereon to the same extent, and *its* assets having been distributed and found insufficient to pay appellant's claim in full . . ."[68]), and there was a growing tendency to make firms not partners the subjects of sentences:

> It is, then, alleged that the *firm* of F. J. Lisman & Co. of New York city *controlled* the conduct of the affairs and business of the Iron Railway Company, through ownership and control of the capital stock, and *arranged* the terms of the contract of sale, which has been referred to; that the said *firm* of F. J. Lisman & Co., *purporting to act on behalf of* the railway company, *received* in New York city the said sum of $ 600,000, and interest thereon, and, thereupon, and in accordance with the provisions of said contract, *paid* the same in said city to certain firms named . . .[69]

These changes, although subtle, were nonetheless indicative of a significant shift in the way small businesses, as well as large, were conceptualized. Further evidence of this shift comes from an early twentieth-century movement to make partnerships as well as corporations legal persons. When the Conference on Uniform State Laws (a Progressive-Era effort to standardize legal practice across states) directed its Committee on Commercial Law to draft a uniform law of partnerships in 1902, the Committee initially delegated this task to James Barr Ames, Dean of the Harvard Law School. Ames was a proponent of the new ideas about the personality of associations, and the bill he drafted assumed that partnerships were real entities and therefore should have the status of legal persons. The choice of Ames was deliberate; there was widespread support in the legal community for a revision of partnership law along these lines. However, at least some members of the Committee must have had doubts about the utility of Ames' approach because, after his untimely death, the Committee turned to William Draper Lewis of the University of Pennsylvania School of Law, and asked him to prepare two drafts – one on the basis of real-entity theory, as Ames had done, and the other on aggregate theory. When Lewis finished his work, the Committee held a conference attended by a number of experts in partnership law. Although the participants in the conference originally had, virtually all, supported the real-entity view, they changed their minds after studying the two drafts, and the consensus of the meeting was that the effort to rewrite partnership law on entity-theory terms should be abandoned. The Committee asked Lewis to write yet another version of the draft based on the aggregate theory. This Lewis did, and after further discussion the bill was accepted by the Committee and introduced in (and passed by) a number of state legislatures.[70]

The strongest proponents of real-entity theory were not satisfied, however. In a scathing critique published in the *Harvard Law Review*, Judson A. Crane argued that Lewis' bill was confused. Although Lewis claimed that his draft was consistent with aggregate theory, according to Crane it actually muddied the law by intermixing aggregate with entity theory. It did so, moreover, because of "the difficulty, if not impossibility, . . . of writing and talking about the partnership . . . without treating it as a legal person." Crane lambasted Lewis for refusing to recognize the extent to which both Americans' perceptions of partnerships and the relevant common law had already evolved in the direction of entity theory. Careful attention to the wording used by judges in deciding partnership cases, he claimed, showed that, "consciously or unconsciously," they were already treating partnerships as legal persons.[71]

Crane's assertion seems somewhat disingenuous, however, for if the change in the law really were as evident as he claimed, there would have been little need for the statutory reforms he and his colleagues were advocating. To the contrary, the experts attending the conference had backed away from the idea of a law based on entity theory because, when faced with a concrete draft, the proposal suddenly seemed too radical. Participants worried that the change might have the undesirable consequence of weakening the partners' sense of moral responsibility for their business dealings. More important, they worried that it would effectively overturn much of the existing case law and result in legal chaos. As Samuel Williston explained in an address to the Law Association of Philadelphia, "we can not escape from our past legal history satisfactorily by a legislative *fiat*. We may trim and pare excrescences . . . but in subjects with a long past, experience seems to show that it is difficult to adopt fundamentally new ideas."[72]

THE RISE OF BIG BUSINESS AND INCREASING FORMALISM

Included in the version of the uniform partnership act that Ames drafted based on entity theory was a provision requiring partnerships to register with local authorities. By ensuring that information about firms was publicly available, this requirement would likely have opened the door to greater flexibility in the way people organized their businesses.[73] As we have seen, however, fear that such a bill would wreak havoc with the large body of law based on aggregate theory caused experts to back away from the draft, and the move toward greater contractual freedom was stalled.

Common law precedents had a similar inhibiting effect on the evolution of the corporate form, disrupting the courts' growing tendency (applauded by Morawetz and other aggregate theorists) to view corporate charters as contracts into which business people entered freely just as they did any other organizational device. In this case, however, the source of the problem was the new wave of liberal incorporation laws that states began to pass in the late nineteenth century – statutes that appeared at least on the surface to be logical extensions of this trend in interpretation. General incorporation laws passed earlier in the century had imposed all kinds of restrictions on corporations, forcing them to secure new or amended charters in order to merge with other firms, expand into new areas of business, or even increase their capital beyond the authorized limit. Beginning with New Jersey's 1888 law permitting corporations to own stock in other enterprises, the new statutes removed virtually all restrictions on the size and scope of the activities in which corporations could engage. As a committee appointed by the governor of Massachusetts to recommend new laws on the subject reported in 1902, the principle underpinning this wave of legislation was, "that, in the absence of fraud in its organization or government, an ordinary business corporation should be allowed to do anything that an individual may do."[74]

As quickly became apparent, the new laws made possible the formation of businesses operating on an unprecedented scale. Beginning in the late 1880s and early 1890s and then accelerating around the turn of the century, firms began to merge into giant consolidations under charters from New Jersey or other states (like Delaware) that had passed similarly permissive laws. Many of these combines controlled (for a time at least) major shares of the markets in which they bought and sold, and, as the specter of monopoly power grew, Americans demanded that their governments protect them. State officials moved to take action, asserting their authority under the artificial theory of the corporation by filing *quo warranto* and similar lawsuits challenging the legality of the mergers, and the courts proved receptive to these actions.[75] In 1892, for example, the New Jersey chancellor supported an attempt by the state's attorney general to overturn a leasing arrangement among railroads that tended "to create a monopoly of the anthracite coal trade within the state" by invoking the artificial-entity theory that "a corporation created by statute can exercise no power and has no rights except such as are expressly given or necessarily implied," which he dubbed "a cardinal rule of the law of corporations."[76]

Although, from the standpoint of artificial-entity theory, the power to charter corporations gave states the authority to determine the very conditions under which their "creations" could do business, the giant firms that emerged during this period could respond to efforts to regulate their behavior by closing down their operations in a state or by obtaining a charter from a more friendly jurisdiction. In reality, only the federal government could effectively regulate corporations whose operations were national in scope and who could pick and choose among states, escaping oversight by locating in areas where the laws were most lenient. As a result, after a brief flurry of antitrust activity during the late 1880s and early 1890s, state initiatives waned, and the locus of policy shifted of necessity to the federal government.[77]

However weak the states' charter powers now were in practice, they nonetheless hamstrung the federal government in its efforts to fill the power vacuum. The main legal tools that national authorities had to regulate giant corporations were the common law prohibitions against restraint of trade and attempts to monopolize that had been embodied in the Sherman Antitrust Act of 1890. Although prosecutors found it relatively easy to wield these tools against pools and similar collusive agreements that involved more than one firm, they found it much more difficult to use them against combinations that took the form of state-chartered corporations and whose existence, therefore, had seemingly received state sanction. Hence, the central questions in antitrust law during the first decade of the twentieth century became, first, how the federal government could assert regulatory authority over corporations operating in interstate commerce without undermining states' powers over corporations and, second, how the special status of corporations as creatures of the states could be used to bolster the federal government's otherwise weak position.[78]

The ultimate solution to the first of these problems was the "rule of reason," articulated by the Supreme Court's Chief Justice Edward Douglass White in 1911 in the *Standard Oil* and *American Tobacco* decisions. White classified combinations into two distinct categories, for which two different tests of restraint of trade were required. First were those contracts or combinations whose "inherent nature or effect" was to restrain trade. This category included combinations involving more than one individual or corporation, such as gentlemen's agreements, pools, and other types of cartels. These combinations were illegal per se; that is, the Sherman Act applied literally to them. Combinations formed by merger, however, did not fall into the category of agreements whose "inherent nature or effect" was to restrain trade. In order to find combinations in violation of the Sherman Act, the Court must have proof that the "evident purpose" of the combination was to restrain trade. If this proof was available, it did not matter that the combination took the form of a state-chartered corporation because states did not have the right to charter corporations whose purpose was to violate federal law.[79]

Demonstrating such purpose, however, was highly dependent on the continuing power of the artificial theory of the corporation, as an earlier Supreme Court decision involving one of the companies implicated in the *American Tobacco* case had demonstrated. The government had subpoenaed records of a number of firms for evidence of anticompetitive activity. The secretary–treasurer of one of these companies had refused to produce the requested documents on a number of grounds, among them that by doing so he would violate the corporation's rights under the Fifth Amendment to the Constitution. Writing for the majority of the Court, Justice Henry B. Brown rejected the corporation's claim to Fifth-Amendment protection. The corporation, he pointed out, "is a creature of the State."

It is presumed to be incorporated for the benefit of the public. It receives certain special privileges and franchises, and holds them subject to the laws of the State and the limitations of its charter . . . Its rights to act as a corporation are only preserved to it so long as it obeys the laws of its creation. There is a reserved right in the legislature to investigate its contracts and find out whether it has exceeded its powers.[80]

Brown acknowledged that an individual "may lawfully refuse to answer incriminating questions unless protected by an immunity statute." But, he asserted, "it does not follow that a corporation, vested with special privileges and franchises, may refuse to show its hand when charged with an abuse of such privileges." Indeed, it would be "a strange anomaly" if a state could not, after chartering a corporation and granting it certain privileges, "demand the production of the corporate books and papers" to ensure that these privileges were legally employed. Because such privileges "must also be exercised in subordination to the power of Congress to regulate commerce," the federal government "may also assert a sovereign authority" over the corporation to make sure that its laws were being upheld. Thus Brown put the state's charter powers in service of the federal government: "The powers of the General Government . . . are the same as if the corporation had been created by an act of Congress."[81]

Perhaps because it was so difficult for Americans at this time to differentiate conceptually between small and large firms, all of whom were perceived to be collectivities with their own well-developed personalities, the resurgence of artificial-entity theory had important implications for small corporations as well as for the giant combines who were the target of antitrust prosecutions.[82] Indeed, this resurgence, in combination with the liberal incorporation statutes of the late nineteenth century, had the perverse effect of making it more difficult for members of small firms to build into their incorporation agreements provisions that would help protect them against hold-up. As part of the effort to remove restrictions on the business activities of corporations, the new legislation had included provisions that reduced the ability of individual stockholders to block managerial decisions by increasing the relative power of boards of directors and making majority (or occasionally super-majority) votes of stockholders sufficient for major changes, even amendments to the articles of associations or resolutions that effectively disposed of all the assets of the enterprise. The result, as one legal writer put it, was to place the individual stockholder "in the position of holding a 'pig-in-a-poke' " – to make him or her "more dependent with each new statute upon the desires of the management and the majority which often is only another name for the management."[83]

Although incorporators of small businesses might write into their agreements provisions that bolstered the power of minority shareholders, the courts were increasingly reluctant to enforce such agreements whenever they came into conflict with the general statutes. A good example is the case of *Jackson* v. *Hooper*, decided by the New Jersey Appeals Court in 1910. Several years earlier, Walter M. Jackson and Horace E. Hooper had organized two corporations, one in Britain and one in the United States, to publish and distribute the *Encyclopedia Britannica*. Jackson and Hooper divided the stock of the corporations equally between them and also contracted between themselves to run the two businesses as a partnership. They agreed that all decisions were to be made by mutual assent, and they bound the other directors, whose positions were merely nominal, to ratify whatever actions they took. By 1908, however, the two men had a falling out. Hooper, with the support of the dummy directors, effectively stripped Jackson of his power in the enterprise, and Jackson sued in equity to enforce the partnership agreement.

Although Jackson initially secured an injunction to enforce his partnership rights, the order was reversed on appeal. The court adamantly declared that partnerships and corporations were different legal forms and that businesspeople could not "Proteus-like" become "at will a co-partnership or a corporation, as the exigencies or purposes of their joint enterprise may from time to time require."

If the parties have the rights of partners, they have the duties and liabilities imposed by law, and are responsible in solido to all their creditors. If they adopt the corporate form, with the corporate shield extended over them to protect them against personal liability, they cease to be partners, and have only the rights, duties, and obligations of stockholders.[84]

The subtext for this decision was the tremendous importance that the states' charter powers had acquired as a result of the rise of big business. To allow the partnership agreement among Jackson and Hooper to stand, the court declared, would render "nugatory and void the authority of the Legislature . . . in respect to the creation, supervision, and winding up of corporations," a result, the court declared, that could not "be tolerated."[85]

Subsequent decisions echoed this concern for maintaining the power of the state over corporations.[86] As late as 1945, for example, in *Benintendi* v. *Kenton Hotel*, the New York Court of Appeals struck down a bylaw requiring stockholders' unanimous consent for the election of directors on the grounds that it was "obnoxious to the statutory scheme of stock corporation management."

The State, granting to individuals the privilege of limiting their individual liabilities for business debts by forming themselves into an entity separate and distinct from the persons who own it, demands in turn that the entity take a prescribed form and conduct itself, procedurally, according to fixed rules.[87]

In language that had changed remarkably little from the early nineteenth-century case of *Pratt* v. *Bacon*, the court insisted that legal personhood was not something for which businesspeople could freely contract. Rather, it was a privilege granted by the state, and those who obtained it had to submit to the forms the state prescribed.

EPILOGUE AND CONCLUSION

Despite this conservative outcome, *Benintendi* v. *Kenton Hotel* was, in an important sense, a turning point. It was a split (four-to-three) decision, and the three justices in the minority offered a vigorous dissent formulated along aggregate-theory lines. So long as creditors' interests were unaffected, the dissenting justices declared, stockholders should be able to govern their enterprises however they wished, and "they may by agreement waive or relinquish as between themselves statutory rights where such waiver or abandonment is not contrary to the public interest."[88] More important, the New York legislature responded to the decision by passing legislation that ratified the dissenting judges' view, granting stockholders liberty to set high voting and quorum requirements for corporate decisions.[89]

Until this point, general incorporation laws had always had a one-size-fits-all character. New York's action signaled the beginning of a new recognition on the part of state legislatures that the needs of small businesses might differ from those of large. The first real break with the past, however, occurred in North Carolina in 1955. Embedded in that state's new Business Corporation Act were several provisions aimed specifically at small, closely held firms, including one declaring that agreements among all the shareholders of such corporations shall not, regardless of their form or purpose, "be invalidated on the ground that [their] effect is to make the parties partners among themselves."[90]

A few others states passed similar statutes over the next decade or so, after which the trickle grew into a flood. From the late 1960s into the 1980s there were at least two major waves of legislation, the first creating, in most jurisdictions, a separate legal status for close corporations and the second defining (and establishing legal remedies for) "corporate oppression" and other similar torts.[91] The reform impulse next spread to partnership law. In 1987 the American Bar Association appointed a drafting committee to begin the process of rewriting the Uniform Partnership Act. The end result, the Revised Uniform Partnership Act (RUPA) of 1992, reversed the tack taken at the turn of the century and declared partnerships to be legal entities in the same sense as Kyd's corporations – that is, they had the right to hold property and sue and be sued like an individual.[92] Around the same time, states also began to pass legislation increasing the available menu of organizational choices. The first wave of statutes made possible the formation of Limited Liability Companies (LLCs); the second created Limited Liability Partnerships (LLPs). The latter innovation was particularly significant because it made it possible for every member of an ordinary partnership to limit their liability for the firm's future debts simply by filing the appropriate notice.[93] The result of all these changes, therefore, was to increase in a sudden and dramatic way the contractual freedom of businesspeople involved in small and medium-sized firms, so that they both could secure limited liability and choose among a broad range of governance structures.

Before this late twentieth-century wave of statutory reform, the options available to firms in these size categories were, as we have seen, much more limited. Businesspeople could organize their enterprises as partnerships, or they could take out corporate charters. In either case, they had little leeway to modify the standard terms associated with these organizational forms. By 1920 there were approximately 314,000 corporations in the United States compared with about 241,000 partnerships.[94] These numbers suggest that many ordinary businesspeople perceived the corporation to be superior, at least marginally, to the partnership. As we have also seen, however, there were potential costs associated with this choice, particularly the possibility that majority shareholders would "hold up" minority owners. Although it is impossible to estimate the magnitude of these costs, the large number of suits involving members of close corporations that reached the appeals-court level throughout U.S. history suggests that the number of firms affected by such problems was likely to be high.[95]

Attention to the experience of small and medium-sized firms thus forces us to revise the standard unidirectional history of the corporate form. Rather than a more or less steady evolution toward greater contractual freedom in response to businesses' needs, there was no clear trend for most of American history. Indeed, during the first half of the twentieth century, judges were just as likely as they had been a hundred years before to invoke the principle that corporations were creations of the state and could do only what their creators allowed them to do. They even cited early nineteenth-century precedents to buttress their decisions.[96]

When change finally came, moreover, it was both sudden and revolutionary. Although it is beyond the scope of this chapter to explain the dramatic reversal of the late twentieth century, it is unlikely that the shift was propelled by accumulated discontent with the rigidities of the standard corporate form. The explanation most often offered in literature attributes causal importance to the burdensome income tax. High tax rates on personal relative to corporate income had encouraged a shift toward the corporate form in the years after the Second World War, but the tax reform act of 1986 moved things in the opposite direction again, spurring business groups to seek out ways of enjoying corporate advantages without subjecting themselves to the corporate income tax. For example, Wyoming had passed enabling legislation for LLCs as early as 1977, consciously designing the form so as to allow firms to acquire the privilege of limited liability without losing the tax status of partnerships. Few states followed Wyoming's lead, however, until 1988 when the IRS confirmed the tax advantages of the new form. Many states then moved quickly to pass statutes, establishing not only the LLC as a legal form of organization but also the LLP.[97] It is likely that there were also more general cultural trends behind this statutory revolution,[98] but even if tax avoidance is the main story, the rapidity with which the legal system responded after more than a century of stasis raises the intriguing question of why some kinds of economic interests become rallying points for change whereas others generate little in the way of action.

This is not to say that there was no change at all from the mid-nineteenth to the mid-twentieth century. The language that the dissenters used in *Benintendi* had its roots in the late nineteenth-century aggregate theory of the corporation, which in turn grew out of a long line of cases that exploited analogies between the partnership and corporate forms. The difficulties that businesspeople experienced in adapting the corporate form to their needs led frequently to complicated litigation that judges found partnership law to be useful in resolving. Encouraged by this instrumental use of precedents from partnership cases, theorists developed the view that corporate charters were contractual arrangements that were fundamentally similar to common law business forms. During the late nineteenth and early twentieth centuries, moreover, this idea received reinforcement from a transformation in the way Americans perceived human associations of all kinds, a transformation that led them to view both partnerships and corporations as the equivalent of natural persons and not dependent on governmental authority for their existence.

This movement to see corporations as no different from other private businesses stalled, however. The proximate cause was the rise of big business, the reaction against which breathed new life into the artificial theory of the corporation. Although there was nothing foreordained about this particular turn of events, I would like to suggest that such reversions are characteristic of the common law. Not only does the weight of precedent have a conservative effect that can inhibit significant change (even in the form of statutory law, as the example of the uniform partnership act demonstrated), but, because of its broad sweep, the common law often evolves simultaneously along very different tracks. The result can be strands of the case law that are fundamentally inconsistent with each other. Moreover, these inconsistencies can and do persist for long periods of time. When issues arise that cause the conflicting bodies of law to intersect, as happened at the turn of the last century in the antitrust arena, the contradictions must be confronted – with ramifications that are typically broader than the issues immediately at hand. Thus, the revival of artificial-entity theory in antitrust law had profound consequences beyond the large firms that were its targets, affecting in particular the ability of small and medium-sized firms to write contracts that reduced some of the disadvantages of the corporate form.

Even if our concern is primarily with large-scale enterprises, these considerations should induce us to move beyond the standard histories of the corporate form. As we have seen, the trend toward ever more liberal incorporation laws is really only part of the story, for the backlash generated by the rise of big business led to the revival of older conceptions of the corporation in order to justify the new regulatory powers of the federal government. But this revival of artificial-entity theory is not the whole story either, for alternative views of the corporation survived in different areas of case law. Indeed, they persist to the present day, intersecting from time to time to shape the response of policymakers and the courts to such politically charged issues as hostile takeovers of businesses by conglomerates, plant closures in communities highly dependent on these sources of employment, or reparations for crimes against humanity in the past.[99]

NOTES

1. Although it was possible to write contracts that gave the partnership form greater permanence (joint-stock companies are a good example), it was much more difficult to contract for unlimited liability. See Edward H. Warren, *Corporate Advantages without Incorporation* (New York: Baker, Voorhis & Co., 1929). In Europe, firms often used an intermediate form, the *commandite* or limited partnership. Although available in the United States, this device was not much used (see below).

2. For the efficiency story, see Nathan Rosenberg and L. E. Birdzell Jr., *How the West Grew Rich: The Economic Transformation of the Industrial World* (New York: Basic Books, 1986), pp. 189–241. For the power story, see William G. Roy, *Socializing Capital: The Rise of the Large Industrial Corporation in America* (Princeton: Princeton University Press, 1997). For an account that combines elements of both, see James Willard Hurst, *The Legitimacy of the Business Corporation in the Law of the United States*, 1780–1970 (Charlottesville: University of Virginia Press, 1970).

3. Philip Scranton has done more than any other historian to try to move these firms to center stage. See especially *Proprietary Capitalism: The Textile Manufacture at Philadelphia, 1800–1885* (New York: Cambridge University Press, 1983); and *Endless Novelty: Specialty Production and American Industrialization, 1865–1925* (Princeton: Princeton University Press, 1997).

4. See especially Colleen A. Dunlavy, "From Citizens to Plutocrats: Nineteenth-Century Shareholder Voting Rights and Theories of the Corporation," Chapter 2 in this volume.

5. Kyd quoted in Joseph K. Angell and Samuel Ames, *A Treatise on the Law of Private Corporations Aggregate* (Boston: Hilliard, Gray, Little & Wilkins, 1832), p. 1; *Trustees of Dartmouth College* v. *Woodward*, 17 U.S. 518 at 636 (1819).

6. See Edwin Merrick Dodd, *American Business Corporations until 1860: With Special Reference to Massachusetts* (Cambridge, MA: Harvard University Press, 1954), pp. 365–437; Oscar Handlin and Mary Flug Handlin, "Origins of the American Business Corporation," *Journal of Economic History* 5 (May 1945), 8–17; Shaw Livermore, "Unlimited Liability in Early American Corporations," *Journal of Political Economy* 43 (Oct. 1935), 674–87; Edwin J. Perkins, *American Public Finance and Financial Services, 1700–1815* (Columbus: Ohio State University Press, 1994), pp. 373–6; and Dunlavy, "From Citizens to Plutocrats."

7. *Dartmouth College* v. *Woodward*, 17 U.S. 518 at 636.

8. Angell and Ames, *Law of Private Corporations*, pp. 2–3, 139. The last quotation was from Marshall, who qualified it with the phrase "unless that be the purpose for which it was created," pointing again to the importance of the specific provisions of the charter – that is, the specific aspects of personhood granted to the corporation by the state. On this "artificial entity" theory of corporations, see Gregory A. Mark, "The Personification of the Business Corporation in American Law," *University of Chicago Law Review* 54 (Fall 1987), 1447–55. Herbert Hovenkamp uses Marshall's declaration that a corporation was not a citizen under the Constitution in *Bank of the United States* v. *Deveaux* to argue that Marshall held an "associational" view of the corporation, but it makes more sense to view this decision as consistent with the view that corporations were artificial persons in the limited sense provided for by their charters. See *Enterprise and American Law, 1836–1937* (Cambridge, MA: Harvard University Press, 1991), pp. 14–16.

9. Hurst, *Legitimacy of the Business Corporation*, pp. 17–18, 22–5.

10. On the meager returns earned by many early transportation companies, see John Majewski, *A House Dividing: Economic Development in Pennsylvania and Virginia Before the Civil War* (New York: Cambridge University Press, 2000).

11. See Hurst, *Legitimacy of the Business Corporation*, pp. 30–45; Louis Hartz, *Economic Policy and Democratic Thought: Pennsylvania, 1776–1860* (Cambridge, MA: Harvard University Press, 1948), ch. 2; Oscar Handlin and Mary Flug Handlin, *Commonwealth: A Study of the Role of Government in the American Economy: Massachusetts, 1774–1861* (Rev. edn.; Cambridge, MA: Harvard University Press, 1969); Pauline Maier, "The Revolutionary Origins of the American Corporation," *William and Mary Quarterly* 50 (Jan. 1993), pp. 51–84. On banks, see Naomi R. Lamoreaux, *Insider Lending: Banks, Personal Connections, and Economic Development in Industrial New England* (New York: Cambridge University Press, 1994), pp. 31–51.

12. On this latter point, see John Joseph Wallis, Richard E. Sylla, and John B. Legler, "The Interaction of Taxation and Regulation in Nineteenth-Century U.S. Banking," in Claudia Goldin and Gary D. Libecap (eds.), *The Regulated Economy: A Historical Approach to Political Economy* (Chicago: University of Chicago Press, 1994), pp. 121–44.

13. Hurst, *Legitimacy of the Business Corporation*, pp. 13–57; Maier, "The Revolutionary Origins of the American Corporation." There are a number of studies of this process in different states, but see especially Handlin and Handlin, *Commonwealth*; Hartz, *Economic Policy and Democratic Thought*; John W. Cadman Jr., *The Corporation in New Jersey: Business and Politics*, 1791–1875 (Cambridge, MA: Harvard University Press, 1949); and Ronald E. Seavoy, *The Origins of the American Business Corporation, 1784–1855: Broadening the Concept of Public Service during Industrialization* (Westport: Greenwood Press, 1982).

14. For a summary of such constitutional provisions, see George Heberton Evans Jr., *Business Incorporation in the United States*, 1800–1943 (New York: National Bureau of Economic Research, 1948), p. 11. All the major industrial states outside New England passed such amendments during this period.

15. John Wallis, "Market Augmenting Government? The State and the Corporation in Nineteenth-Century America," in Omar Azfar and Charles Cadwell (eds.), *Market Augmenting Government: The Institutional Foundations of Prosperity* (Ann Arbor: University of Michigan Press, 2003), pp. 223–67; Hurst, *Legitimacy of the Business Corporation*, pp. 27–30; Perkins, *American Public Finance*, pp. 373–6; Morton J. Horwitz, *Transformation of American Law*, 1870–1960: *The Crisis of Legal Orthodoxy* (New York: Oxford University Press, 1992), p. 94; Dunlavy, "From Citizens to Plutocrats."

16. See Evans, *Business Incorporations in the United States*, for the figures for New Jersey (pp. 15, 126–7) and a number of other states. In 1920 approximately 314,000 active corporations filed federal tax returns. See U.S. Treasury Department, Internal Revenue Service, *Statistics of Income From Returns of Net Income for 1920* (Washington, DC: Government Printing Office, 1922), pp. 8–10.

17. On the number of corporations of different sizes chartered in New Jersey and other states during the late nineteenth and early twentieth century, see Evans, *Business Incorporations in the United States*, appendix 3. According to Internal Revenue Service data, as late as 1931, about 56 percent of the more than 300,000 U.S. corporations filing balance sheets with their tax returns had assets of less than $50,000, whereas only about 7 percent had assets of $1 million or more. Because large firms were more likely to file balance sheets than small, these figures understate the proportion of corporate charters held by the smallest size classes of firms. See U.S. Bureau of the Census, *Historical Statistics of the United States, Colonial Times to 1970* (Washington, DC: Government Printing Office, 1975), series V182.

18. See Stanley E. Howard, "The Limited Partnership in New Jersey," *Journal of Business of the University of Chicago* 7 (Oct. 1934), 296–301; and William Draper Lewis, "The Uniform Limited Partnership Act," *University of Pennsylvania Law Review and American Law Register* 65 (June 1917), 716.

19. Howard, "Limited Partnership in New Jersey," pp. 309–12. Businesspeople organizing limited partnerships were required by law to announce the formation of their firms in local newspapers. My own work in nineteenth-century newspapers in Boston and New York City confirms Howard's claim that the form was rarely used.

20. On the deficiencies of the statutes and the lack of effort to remedy them, see Howard, "The Limited Partnership in New Jersey"; Lewis, "The Uniform Limited Partnership Act," pp. 718–21; Warren, *Corporate Advantages without Incorporation*, pp. 306–10. Another form that fell into relative disuse during this period was the joint-stock company, whose members had unlimited liability. See Hurst, *Legitimacy of the Business*

Corporation, p. 14. However, as Kenneth Lipartito shows in "The Utopian Corporation," Chapter 3 in this volume, the joint-stock company was the organizational form favored by utopian societies.

21. Thomas R. Navin and Marian V. Sears, "The Rise of a Market for Industrial Securities, 1887–1902," *Business History Review* 29 (June 1955), 105–38.

22. See Hurst, *Legitimacy of the Business Corporation*, p. 28; and *Law and Economic Growth: The Legal History of the Lumber Industry in Wisconsin, 1836–1915* (Cambridge, MA: Harvard University Press, 1964), pp. 414 and 862, note 104; Susan E. Woodward, "Limited Liability in the Theory of the Firm," *Journal of Institutional and Theoretical Economics* 141 (Dec. 1985), 601–11; and Kevin F. Forbes, "Limited Liability and the Development of the Business Corporation," *Journal of Law, Economics, and Organization* 2 (Spring 1986), pp. 163–77. For this reason, the R. G. Dun credit reports typically assessed the creditworthiness of major stockholders of a small corporation as well as the firm itself, with the former positively or negatively affecting the latter. See, for example, the Dec. 2, 1869 entry for the Gorham Manufacturing Co. in Rhode Island: "Since the Senior Gorham's death + the consequent deprivation of his endorsement their credit has been weakened." Rhode Island vol. 9, R. G. Dun & Co., Baker Library, Harvard Graduate School of Business Administration.

    Even if stockholders had to assume responsibility for their corporation's debts, however, limited liability might still bring advantages. It helped to resolve the principal-agent problem that partners faced vis-á-vis each other by eliminating the possibility that one member of a firm could unilaterally encumber the enterprise with debts that the others might have to repay out of their own assets. Moreover, stockholders also benefited from limited liability in the case of tort actions against the firm.

23. The extant records are silent on the motives for incorporation, but they show that the firm received a special charter from the Rhode Island legislature in May, 1856. See Rhode Island, General Assembly, *Acts and Resolves Passed at the May Session* (Providence: A. Crawford Greene & Brother, 1856), pp. 94–7. For the organizational history of the firm, see "Memorandum of an Arrangement," Dec. 10, 1846, Box 4, Folder 1, and "Business from 1847 to 1861," Box 4, Folder 6, George H. Corliss Papers, Ms. 80.3, The John Hay Library, Brown University. For background information on Corliss and his inventions, see Robert Stowe Holding, *George H. Corliss of Rhode Island, 1817–1888* (New York: Newcomen Society, 1945); and Robert W. Kenny, "George H. Corliss: Engineer, Architect, Philanthropist," *Rhode Island History* 40 (May 1981), 48–61.

24. "Business from 1847 to 1861," Box 4, Folder 6, George H. Corliss Papers.

25. As William noted the arrangement in his diary, "Bro George and Nightingale talked over my affairs today and decided to give me a salary of $450 for my services during the year 1857 – $1000 for year 1858 $1000 for the year 1859 – and to continue henceforth at $1000 – And I shall take stock on the 1st of January 1860 for balance due – which will be about $1200 or $1400 and they will let me have enough more stock and take my note at 6 pr cent pr annum to make my share $5000." Entry of Nov. 23, 1859, William Corliss Diaries, Ms. 80.4, John Hay Library, Brown University.

26. Entry of Apr. 1, 1859, William Corliss Diaries.

27. Rhode Island, General Assembly, *Acts and Resolves* (1856), p. 95. Nightingale attempted to mollify George (unsuccessfully) by writing him a check for $2000, and George went ahead and sold Grinnell some of his own shares. Mar. 19, 1863, William Corliss Diaries.

28. At this point in time, it was not even clear that the majority had a right to wind up the affairs of a solvent corporation without both unanimous approval of the stockholders and authorization by the legislature. See Dodd, *American Business Corporations Until* 1860, pp. 139–40, 184–5, 191–2, 361.

29. Entries of Mar. 20, June 1, June 8, and June 24, 1863, William Corliss Diaries.

30. See entries of June 1, 8, and 24, 1863, William Corliss Diaries.

31. To make matters worse for Nightingale, one of the managers to whom he had earlier sold some of his stock transferred his entire interest to George Corliss, giving the latter control of a slight majority of shares. See entry of Mar. 28, 1863, William Corliss Diaries.

32. Thomas Edison, for example, found himself in just this difficult position later in the century. He had assigned his phonographic patents to Edison United Phonograph Company in exchange for half of the firm's stock. Later, when he found himself in disagreement with the policies pursued by the firm's management to exploit these inventions, there was little he could do because a large majority of the firm's directors disagreed with him. Frustrated, he sued in equity to try to force the dissolution of the firm, but the court refused to intervene. See *Edison et al.* v. *Edison United Phonograph Co. et al.*, 29 A.H. 195 (1894). Edison encountered similar problems with the company formed to exploit his light-bulb invention. This time he waged a costly proxy fight in order to force managers to pursue his vision of the firm's future. See Patrick McGuire, Mark Granovetter, and Michael Schwartz, "Thomas Edison and the Social Construction of the Early Electricity Industry in America," in Richard Swedberg (ed.), *Explorations in Economic Sociology* (New York: Russell Sage Foundation, 1993), pp. 213–46.

33. See Williamson, *The Economic Institutions of Capitalism* (New York: Free Press–Macmillan, 1995); and "The Modern Corporation: Origins, Evolution, Attributes," *Journal of Economic Literature* 19 (Dec. 1981), 1537–68.

34. If the majority's actions became too exploitative, the minority might be able to secure redress in court. The legal hurdles such cases had to pass were relatively high, however, until the last half of the twentieth century. See J. A. C. Hetherington and Michael P. Dooley, "Illiquidity and Exploitation: A Proposed Statutory Solution to the Remaining Close Corporation Problem," *Virginia Law Review* 63 (Feb. 1977), 1–62; Robert W. Hillman, "The Dissatisfied Participant in the Solvent Business Venture: A Consideration of the Relative Permanence of Partnerships and Close Corporations," *Minnesota Law Review* 67 (Oct. 1982), 1–88; See also Lawrence E. Mitchell, "The Death of Fiduciary Duty in Close Corporations," *University of Pennsylvania Law Review* 138 (June 1990), 1675–731.

35. Of course, the dissolution process could itself be used in an attempt to hold up other members of a partnership, but victims of such squeezes (unlike minority shareholders who claimed their income was being expropriated by the majority) had routine access to the equity courts.

36. This is not to say that such arrangements would be desirable in all situations. The ability to lock in minority shareholders can have benefits. For example, venture capitalists who finance entrepreneurial enterprises take extraordinary risks in exchange for assurances that they will be able to profit from their investments once the enterprise is successful. On this point, see Edward B. Rock and Michael L. Wachter, "Waiting for the Omelet to Set: Match-Specific Assets and Minority Oppression in Close Corporations," in Randall K. Morck (ed.), *Concentrated Corporate Ownership* (Chicago: University of Chicago Press, 2000), pp. 201–42.

37. Writing about the problem as late as 1929, Joseph L. Weiner asserted that the pitfalls awaiting attorneys who constructed such agreements reminded him of piece of doggerel:

There's a great text in Galations
Once you trip on it, entails
Twenty-nine distinct damnations
One sure, if another fails.

See "Legislative Recognition of the Close Corporation," *Michigan Law Review* 27 (Jan. 1929), 275.

38. *Elijah Pratt* v. *Jephthah Bacon et al.*, 27 Mass. 123, 27 Pick.123 (1830).

39. See Peter Dobkin Hall, "What the Merchants Did with Their Money: Charitable and Testamentary Trusts in Massachusetts, 1780–1880," in Conrad Edick Wright and Katheryn P. Viens (eds.), *Entrepreneurs: The Boston Business Community, 1700–1850* (Boston: Massachusetts Historical Society, 1997), pp. 368, 371–6; William J. Curran, "The Struggle for Equity Jurisdiction in Massachusetts," *Boston University Law Review* 31 (June 1951), 269–96. Equity courts, of course, would become important forums for resolving disputes involving corporations.

40. *Pratt* v. *Bacon*, 27 Mass. 123.

41. As Putnam noted, "the equity jurisdiction was intended to be given with great caution." *Joseph Russell* v. *Isaac M'Lellan*, 31 Mass. 63, 31 Pick. 63 (1833).

42. *Frederick A. Vandyke, Jr.*, v. *David S. Brown and others, and the New England Manufacturing Co.*, 4 Halstead 657 at 670 (N.J. Eq. 1852).

43. *William Gray, Jun.*, v. *The President, Directors and Company of the Portland Bank*, 3 Mass. 364, Tyng 364 (1807). Justice Sewall, who also delivered an opinion in the case, exploited the analogy between corporations and trusts as well as between corporations and partnerships.

44. *State of Connecticut, ex rel. Freeman Kilbourn against Samuel Tudor, jun.*, 5 Day 329 (1812).

45. *Bissell* v. *The Michigan Southern and Northern Indiana Railroad Companies*, 22 N.Y. 258 at pp. 270–1 (1860).

46. The court also used the partnership analogy to justify its remedy, an injunction blocking the extension of the railroad. *Byron Stevens* v. *The Rutland and Burlington Railroad Company and Others*, 29 Vt. 545 (1851). For discussions of other cases, see Dodd, *American Business Corporations Until 1860*, pp. 134–48; and Victor Morawetz, *A Treatise on the Law of Private Corporations Other than Charitable* (Boston: Little, Brown, and Company, 1882), pp. 47–9. William J. Carney has shown that this unanimity rule was seriously weakened in the second half of the century as courts permitted firms effectively to liquidate and reorganize in order to bypass recalcitrant shareholders. But I would argue that this change, too, was consistent with partnership law. In a partnership, if one member disapproved of a new direction for the firm, the likely outcome was dissolution of the old firm and formation of a new one. The change, moreover, resolved a hold-up problem which the incomplete application of partnership principles to corporate law had created. See Carney, "Fundamental Corporate Changes, Minority Shareholders, and Business Purposes," *American Bar Foundation Research Journal* 1980 (Winter 1980), 69–132.

47. Morawetz, *Treatise on the Law of Private Corporations*, pp. 1–2. On the rise of the aggregate theory of corporations, see Horwitz, *Transformation of American Law*, pp. 90–3; and Mark, "Personification of the Business Corporation," pp. 1455–64.

48. Morawetz, *Law of Private Corporations*, p. 346.

49. Morawetz, *Law of Private Corporations*, p. 148.

50. Morawetz, *Law of Private Corporations*, pp. 24–25.

51. As Gregory Mark and Morton Horwitz have convincingly argued, this type of theory provided the logic that underpinned the U.S. Supreme Court's famous *Santa Clara* decision in 1886 – the first decision that extended Fourteenth-Amendment protection against discriminatory legislation to corporations. See Mark, "The Personification of the Business Corporation," pp. 1460–4; and Horwitz, *The Transformation of American Law*, pp. 66–70. See also Hovenkamp, *Enterprise and American Law*, pp. 43–7.

52. Wiley B. Rutledge Jr., "Significant Trends in Modern Incorporation Statutes," *Washington University Law Review* 22 (April 1937), 305–43.

53. Arthur W. Machen Jr., quoted in Horwitz, *Transformation of American Law*, p. 103. See also Horwitz, pp. 71–4, 100–5; and Mark, "The Personification of the Corporation," pp. 1464–78. For an alternative view of the political motives of these intellectuals, see Mark M. Hager, "Bodies Politic: The Progressive History of Organizational 'Real Entity' Theory," *University of Pittsburgh Law Review* 50 (Winter 1989), 575–653.

54. For an early survey of this literature, see Louis Galambos, "The Emerging Organizational Synthesis in Modern American History," *Business History Review* 44 (Autumn 1970), 279–90. Key works in this tradition include Robert Wiebe, *The Search for Order, 1877–1920* (New York: Hill & Wang, 1967); Alfred D. Chandler Jr., *Strategy and Structure: Chapters in the History of the Industrial Enterprise* (Cambridge, MA: Harvard University Press, 1962); and Samuel P. Hays, *The Response to Industrialism, 1885–1914* (Chicago: University of Chicago Press, 1957). For later works, see Galambos, "Technology, Political Economy, and Professionalization: Central Themes of the Organizational Synthesis," *Business History Review* 57 (Winter 1983), 471–93.

55. "The Personality of Associations," *Harvard Law Review* 29 (Feb. 1916), 404–5. Contemporary sociologists also observed the change and used it to justify the redefinition of their discipline around the study of groups. See, for example, Charles A. Ellwood, "The Psychological View of Society," *American Journal of Sociology* 15 (May 1910), 596–618; and Walter B. Bodenhafer, "The Comparative Role of the Group Concept in Ward's Dynamic Sociology and Contemporary American Sociology," *American Journal of Sociology* 26 (Nov. 1920), 273–314; (Jan. 1921), 425–74; (Mar. 1921), 588–600; and (May 1921), 716–43.

56. The emphases in the following quotes are mine. For this sketch I supplemented the cases collected for this article with a search (generated by keying on the words partnership, firm, company, and corporation) in the Lexis-Nexis database of New York cases for a scattered set of years. Of course, judges were not representative of the general population, and justices of higher courts especially might be expected to be more highly educated. One might expect, as a result, that they would be more attentive in their writing to formal grammatical rules and that, as a result, their usage would change more slowly than that of the population of the whole. A cursory comparison of the language used by judges and that found in the material written by others at the front of each case (headnotes, syllabi, summaries of arguments of counsel, etc.) appears to confirm this expectation. In "The Corporation is a Person: The Language of a Legal Fiction," Sanford A Schane argued that the real-entity theory of the corporation had a basis in linguistic practice, but he did not attempt to explore the history of this practice, *Tulane Law Review* 61 (Feb. 1987), 563–609.

57. *Warner & Post* v. *Griswold*, 8 Wend. 665 (NY 1832).

58. *Gilchrist* v. *Cunningham*, 8 Wend. 641 (NY 1832).

59. *The People* v. *Haynes*, 11 Wend. 557 (NY 1834).

60. *Bank of Ithaca* v. *King*, 12 Wend. 390 (NY 1834).

61. *Macomber* v. *Dunham*, 8 Wend. 550 (NY 1832).

62. *Slee* v. *Bloom*, 20 Johns. 669 (NY 1822).

63. As late as the 1870s, however, one observes an occasional throwback, such as "The company *was* organized June 14, 1851. In August, 1852, *they* made an assessment for alleged losses, in which the defendant was assessed on the said premium note $132." *Sands* v. *Hill*, 55 N.Y. 18 (1873). British English never experienced the same grammatical change, but then British businesses did not function as entities to the same degree that American firms did. See Tony Freyer, *Regulating Big Business: Antitrust in Great Britain and America, 1880–1990* (Cambridge: Cambridge University Press, 1992).

64. *J. Russell Manufacturing Company* v. *New Haven Steamboat Company*, 50 N.Y. 121 (1872).

65. *Baltimore and Yorktown Turnpike Road* v. *Boone*, 45 Md. 344 (1876).

66. Morawetz, *Law of Private Corporations*, p. 24. Morawetz used this similarity as evidence to bolster his claim "that the idea of a corporation does not necessarily imply a grant of corporate power by statute," a point he thought was essential to justify his contractual view of the corporation. But where Morawetz conceptualized corporations as essentially similar to partnerships, others used his evidence to make just the opposite point – that partnerships were essentially similar to corporations in that both were real entities. See, for example, Arthur W. Machem Jr., "Corporate Personality," *Harvard Law Review* 24 (Feb. 1911), 253–67, and (Mar. 1911), 347–65.

67. *Straus* v. *Cunningham*, 159 A.D. 718, 144 N.Y.S. 1014 (1913).

68. *In the Matter of the Accounting of Bayard L. Peck, as Assignee for Creditors of Girard N. Whitney, Respondent. John F. McIntyre, Appellant*, 206 N.Y. 55, 99 N.E. 258 (1912). One also finds more mixed constructions, such as "the firm of Gugino Brothers, composed of Carmelo and Natale Gugino, *was* engaged in the manufacture and sale of macaroni in the city of Buffalo. *They* had a plant, machinery and stock worth about $ 10,000, of which Carmelo owned two-thirds and Natale one-third." *Watson* v. *Gugino*, 204 N.Y. 535, 98 N.E. 18 (1912).

69. *Trotter et al.* v. *Lisman et al.*, 209 N.Y. 174, 102 N.E. 575 (1913). There is an ambiguity in the English language in that for verbs in the past tense the third-person singular and plural are identical. Readers could interpret these sentences differently depending on whether they conceived of firms as aggregates or entities.

70. William Draper Lewis, "The Desirability of Expressing the Law of Partnership in Statutory Form," *University of Pennsylvania Law Review* 60 (Nov. 1911), 93–102; Samuel Williston, "The Uniform Partnership Act, with Some Remarks on Other Uniform Commercial Laws," *University of Pennsylvania Law Review* 63 (Jan. 1915), 206–13; Lewis, "The Uniform Partnership Act – A Reply to Mr. Crane's Criticism," *Harvard Law Review*, 29 (Dec. 1915), pp. 159, 162–74.

71. Judson A. Crane, "The Uniform Partnership Act: A Criticism," *Harvard Law Review* 26 (June 1915), 768–71.

72. Williston, "The Uniform Partnership Act," pp. 206–13. The quote is from pp. 207–8. See also Lewis, "The Uniform Partnership Act – A Reply," pp. 162–74.

73. In France, for example, the requirement of notification allowed partners to structure their firm's governance so as to limit each other's ability to incur debts on behalf of

the firm. See Naomi R. Lamoreaux and Jean-Laurent Rosenthal, "Organizational Choice and Economic Development: A Comparison of France and the United States during the Mid Nineteenth Century," unpublished paper, 2001.

74. Quoted on p. 35 of E. Merrick Dodd Jr., "Statutory Developments in Business Corporation Law, 1886–1936," *Harvard Law Review* 50 (Nov. 1936), 27–59. See also Rutledge, "Significant Trends in Modern Incorporation Statutes." Roy has argued that in actuality these statutes gave corporations powers that individuals did not have. See *Socializing Capital*, pp. 144–75.

75. Charles W. McCurdy, "The *Knight* Sugar Decision of 1895 and the Modernization of American Corporation Law, 1869–1903," *Business History Review* 53 (Autumn 1979), 304–42.

76. *John P. Stockton, Attorney-General of New Jersey, v. The Central Railroad Company of New Jersey et al.*, 5 Dickinson 52 (N.J. Eq. 1892) at pp. 53, 65.

77. See McCurdy, "The *Knight* Sugar Decision of 1895," pp. 306–7, 336–40; and Roy, *Socializing Capital*, pp. 144–258. An exception to the rule of state governmental weakness was Texas, which was able to use its control of vital petroleum resources to assert regulatory authority in that industry. See Joseph A. Pratt, "The Petroleum Industry in Transition: Antitrust and the Decline of Monopoly Control in Oil," *Journal of Economic History* 40 (Dec. 1980), 815–37.

78. McCurdy, "*Knight* Sugar Decision"; Naomi R. Lamoreaux, *The Great Merger Movement in American Business, 1895–1904* (New York: Cambridge University Press, 1985), pp. 159–86; Freyer, *Regulating Big Business*, pp. 61–8, 90–102. One manifestation of this concern was the attempt to secure a federal incorporation law during the first decade of the twentieth century. For the legislative history, see Martin J. Sklar, *The Corporate Reconstruction of American Capitalism, 1890–1916: The Market, the Law, and Politics* (New York: Cambridge University Press, 1988), pp. 203–85.

79. *Standard Oil Co. v. United States*, 221 U.S. 1 (1911); *United States of America v. American Tobacco Co.*, 221 U.S. 106 (1911); Lamoreaux, *Great Merger Movement*, pp. 159–86.

80. *Hale v. Henkel*, 210 U.S. 43 (1906) at pp. 74–6. The corporation also claimed Fourth-Amendment protection against unreasonable searches and seizures. Brown found this argument much more difficult to dismiss (mainly on aggregate-theory grounds), but he, nonetheless, found the corporation in contempt. Horwitz has called this decision "the first Supreme Court natural entity opinion," but this view is not supported by a reading of the case. There were four separate written opinions (the opinion that Brown wrote for the court, two concurring opinions, and one dissent), none of which were based on natural-entity theory. Horwitz, *Transformation of American Law*, p. 73.

81. In his dissenting opinion, Justice David J. Brewer opposed this attempt to harness the states' charter powers in service of the federal government, countering that such a supervisory authority belonged only "to the creator of the corporation" – which in the case at hand was a state, not the federal, government. *Hale v. Henkel*, 210 U.S. 43, at pp. 83–9.

82. When Arthur W. Machen Jr., sought to make the case that all businesses should be considered legal persons, he asked rhetorically whether a house was "merely the sum of the bricks that compose it?" The answer obviously had to be no, because one could "change many of the bricks without changing the identity of the house." He then went to argue that any "sensible business man" would understand that when a senior partner gave his son "on attaining majority a small interest in the

firm," this act did not create "an entirely new firm." Only those learned in the law could make such a mistake; "the ordinary layman has the conception of the firm as an entity." To the modern reader this argument seems disingenuous – after all, if the son actually replaced his father, the firm might very well be perceived as fundamentally different – but it is likely that Machen made the claim in all sincerity. The idea that when individuals combined their skills and energies they created something that was more than the some of its parts was so powerful at this time that it often blinded partisans to issues of scale. See "Corporate Personality," *Harvard Law Review* 34 (Feb. 1911), pp. 259–60.

83. Rutledge, "Significant Trends in Modern Incorporation Statutes." The quotes are from pp. 312 and 337.

84. *Jackson v. Hooper et al.*, 76 N.J. Eq. 592, 75 Atl. 568 (1910).

85. *Jackson v. Hooper* 75 Atl. 571. F. Hodge O'Neal later blamed this resurgence of artificial theory for the plight of small corporations: "A great number of our present judges and legislators are part of a legal generation which grew up in an atmosphere of corporate theory. . . under which the corporation is viewed as an artificial, fictitious being, and a corporate charter as a grant from the sovereign giving 'life' to a new legal entity. Small wonder it is that such a generation is slow to approve unorthodox arrangements among shareholders which imply that a corporation is simply a group of businessmen voluntarily associating together, with freedom within broad bounds to determine by contract their relations among themselves." *"Squeeze-Outs" of Minority Shareholders: Expulsion or Oppression of Business Associates* (Chicago: Callaghan & Co., 1975), pp. 577–8.

86. For discussions of the case law, see Joseph L. Weiner, "Legislative Recognition of the Close Corporation," *Michigan Law Review* 27 (Jan. 1929), 273–8; Edward R. Schwartz, "The Limited Partnership Association – An Alternative to the Corporation for the Small Business with 'Control' Problems?" *Rutgers Law Review* 20 (1965), 29, 64–76; George D. Hornstein, "Stockholders' Agreements in the Closely Held Corporation," *Yale Law Journal* 59 (May 1950), 1040–56; Hornstein, "Judicial Tolerance of the Incorporated Partnership," *Law and Contemporary Problems* 18 (Autumn 1953), 435–50; William L. Cary, "How Illinois Corporations May Enjoy Partnership Advantages: Planning for the Closely Held Firm," *Northwestern University Law Review* 48 (Sept.–Oct. 1953), 427–41; F. Hodge O'Neal, *Close Corporations: Law and Practice* (Chicago: Callaghan & Co., 1958), 2 vols.

87. *James Benintendi et al. v. Kenton Hotel and John B. Dondero et al.*, 294 N.Y. 112 at p. 118; 60 N.E.2d 829 (1945).

88. *Benintendi v. Kenton Hotel*, 294 N.Y. 112 at p. 129.

89. F. Hodge O'Neal, "Close Corporations: Existing Legislation and Recommended Reform," *The Business Lawyer* 33 (Jan. 1978), p. 874.

90. The North Carolina law also contained a provision that made it possible for any shareholder to precipitate a judicial dissolution if the corporation's charter or any other written agreement among all the shareholders entitled "the complaining shareholder to liquidation or dissolution of the corporation at will or upon the occurrence of some event which has subsequently occurred." F. Hodge O'Neal, "Developments in the Regulation of the Close Corporation," *Cornell Law Quarterly* 50 (Summer 1965), 646–8.

91. O'Neal, "Close Corporations," pp. 873–80; Hillman, "The Dissatisfied Participant in the Solvent Business Venture," 38–55; Mitchell, "The Death of Fiduciary Duty in Close Corporations," 1680–1.

92. See Donald J. Weidner, "Three Policy Decisions Animate Revision of Uniform Partnership Act," *The Business Lawyer* 46 (Feb. 1991), 427–8.

93. See Carter G. Bishop, "Unincorporated Limited Liability Business Organizations: Limited Liability Companies and Partnerships," *Suffolk University Law Review* 29 (Winter 1995), 985–1058; Larry E. Ribstein, "Possible Futures for Unincorporated Firms," *University of Cincinnati Law Review* 64 (Winter 1996), 319–68; and Fallany O. Stover and Susan Pace Hamill, "The LLC Versus LLP Conundrum: Advice for Businesses Contemplating the Choice," *Alabama Law Review* 50 (Spring 1999), 813–47.

94. These figures undoubtedly understate the number of partnerships relative to corporations because all corporations were required to file tax returns, whereas partnerships would file only if they had taxable income. The more general point holds, however: a very large number of people involved in small-scale businesses chose the corporate form over the partnership. See Internal Revenue Service, *Statistics of Income for 1920*, pp. 8–10.

95. Of course, there would have been some costs and potential hold-up problems if members of small corporations had the same right as partners to force a dissolution. The problem of estimating their relative magnitude is analogous to the problem of estimating the costs of allowing divorce versus forcing couples to remain in bad marriages. Even if we could calculate the former, the latter would remain elusive. The records of "bad firms" only occasionally survive, but they are suggestive. For example, disagreements over the proper course of business for the Lee Arms Company led to protracted conflict between James P. Lee and other principals in the firm. Fighting Lee's ultimately unsuccessful attempt to revoke his assignment of gun patents to the company absorbed much of the firm's energy and resources for several years and left it in a weak competitive position. See Exhibit A, New York Supreme Court, General Term – Fourth Department – The People of the State of New York against E. Remington & Sons, in the Matter of the Claim of the Lee Arms Company: Papers on Appeal from Order, Box 2, and "The Lee Arms Company," Folder 1896, Box 3, Arthur S. Winchester, Correspondence & Papers, 1871–1901, Ms. 73843, Connecticut Historical Society. Similarly, Box 1 of the same manuscript collection includes a letter dated Dec. 31, 1887 to Winchester from J. W. Frazier, Agent of the Spencer Arms Co., referring to an unrelated case of hold-up: "I sold out yesterday my entire interest in the Spencer Co. except the guns on hand – These I retained because I thought I could make a profit instead of a loss – The squeeze was complete; but still I do not regret it as I think I will get rid of . . . the annoyance of doing business with a gang that would ruin any industry with which they were connected."

96. For example, both *Pratt* v. *Bacon* (1830) and *Russell* v. *M'Lellan* (1833) were cited as key precedents by the New Jersey appeals court in *Jackson* v. *Hooper* in 1910.

97. The impact of the reversal that occurred during the administration of Ronald Reagan in the relative burden of personal and corporate tax rates on businesspeople's organizational choices was to some extent counteracted, however, by legislation liberalizing the rules under which small corporations could claim Subchapter S status, which essentially allowed them to be taxed as partnerships. Thomas B. Petska and Robert A. Wilson, "Trends in Business Structure and Activity, 1980–1990," *SOI Bulletin* 13 (Spring 1994), 27–72; Petska, "Taxes and Organizational Choice: An Analysis of Trends, 1985–1992," *SOI Bulletin* 15 (Spring 1996), 86–102. For the general postwar trends in tax rates, see W. Elliot Brownlee, *Federal Taxation in America: A Short History* (New York: Cambridge University Press, 1996), pp. 89–129. On the LLC, see Wayne M. Gazur and

Neil M. Goff, "Assessing the Limited Liability Company," *Case Western Reserve Law Review* 41 (1991), 387–501, 389–93. Although the initial Texas legislation creating the LLP form was apparently "a response to astronomical losses threatening lawyers and accountants as a result of their partners' involvement in the savings and loan crises of the late 1980s," the rapid spread of the form to other states owed more to tax considerations. See Stover and Hamill, "The LLC Versus LLP Conundrum, 815–16.

98. Intriguingly, for example, the wave of legislation recognizing and providing remedies for oppression within small corporations coincided temporally with the wave of legislation recognizing and providing remedies for oppression within marriage.

99. On the persistence and importance of alternative theories of the corporation, see William T. Allen, "Our Schizophrenic Conception of the Business Corporation," *Cardozo Law Review* 14 (Nov. 1992), 261–81; and Margaret M. Blair, *Ownership and Control: Rethinking Corporate Governance for the Twentieth Century* (Washington, DC: Brookings Institution, 1995).

From Citizens to Plutocrats: Nineteenth-century Shareholder Voting Rights and Theories of the Corporation

Colleen A. Dunlavy

INTRODUCTION

Although corporate governance attracts widespread interest in business circles today,[1] its history before the twentieth century remains largely unexplored.[2] Much of what we know about nineteenth-century American corporations yields an exterior, not an interior, view. In one line of research, historians have charted changes in the process by which corporations were created, highlighting the shift from incorporation by special acts of the state legislatures to "free" or general incorporation, a bureaucratic procedure governed by statute law.[3] A second line of research has centered on theories or conceptions of the corporation.[4] Yet, these two strands of scholarship tell us virtually nothing about the goings-on in the interior of the corporation.

This chapter is based on research for a history of nineteenth-century corporate governance in the United States, Britain, France, and Germany, tentatively entitled *Shareholder Democracy: The Forgotten History*. I am grateful to a team of research assistants, especially Cynthia Poe, for their unflagging energy and to the Alfred P. Sloan Foundation, the Center for World Affairs and the Global Economy and the Graduate School of the University of Wisconsin, the Russell Sage Foundation, and the German Marshall Fund of the United States for financial support. Many thanks to the conference participants (especially Naømi Lamoreaux) as well as to Alfred Chandler, Shane Hamilton, Gregory Mark, and Cynthia Poe for constructive criticism; the remaining deficiencies are mine. A very early version of the third through fifth sections appeared as "Corporate Governance in Late 19th-Century Europe and the U.S.: The Case of Shareholder Voting Rights," in Klaus J. Hopt, Hideki Kanda, Mark J. Roe, Eddy Wymeersch, and Stefan Prigge (eds.), *Comparative Corporate Governance – the State of the Art and Emerging Research* (Oxford: Clarendon Press, 1998), pp. 5–39.

To complicate matters, Alfred Chandler's enormously influential work on the rise of managerial capitalism, paradoxically, has diverted attention away from the corporation.[5] His historical typology of capitalisms moves from entrepreneurial or *family capitalism*, in which firms were controlled personally by proprietors; to *financial capitalism*, in which representatives of financial institutions wielded power; to *managerial capitalism*, in which manager-led firms predominated.[6] Shareholders are absent. Missing, even as a logical possibility, is *shareholder capitalism*, in which the shareholders collectively controlled firms. This is not an oversight on Chandler's part, for he distinguishes carefully in *The Visible Hand* between the rise of the corporation and the rise of managerial capitalism. Although he regards the emergence of the corporation as "the most significant institutional development" in American business to the 1840s, it did not mark a turning point in the rise of managerial capitalism, because, in his words, it "did not lead to new ways of doing business between or within enterprises."[7] His focus is on the enterprise, in other words, whether organized as a partnership or a corporation. Its legal status matters little and is often difficult to discern in his work. In this sense, the Chandlerian paradigm invites historians to overlook the corporation and its constituents, the shareholders.

Lacking concrete knowledge of corporate governance in the nineteenth century, historians rely on assumption rather than fact. Nearly every historian, I suspect, takes it for granted that the power of individual shareholders has always been proportional to their investment and, therefore, that large shareholders have always had more power and small shareholders, less. The assumption underlying this (usually unarticulated) view is that large shareholders held the preponderance of power because American corporate governance has always been based on one vote per share.

This essentially timeless view of the distribution of power among shareholders, as this chapter shows, is simply wrong. Shareholder power was not always "plutocratic," that is, directly proportional to the amount of investment. Through the early decades of the nineteenth century, corporate governance was much more "democratic" than it came to be by the end of the century. Early norms put relatively little weight on the amount a shareholder had invested, and instead they tended to treat shareholders more like citizens in a relatively egalitarian polity. It was only at mid-century that democratic norms began to be pushed aside in the United States (but not elsewhere) by the modern practice of apportioning power among shareholders on the basis of their investment. This essentially historical process was an indispensable prelude to the great concentration of control that marked American corporations in the era of financial capitalism at the end of the century. In overlooking it, historians have inadvertently naturalized a particular, twentieth-century, and distinctively American form of corporate governance.[8]

This tendency to treat plutocratic governance as natural, moreover, has impoverished our understanding of nineteenth-century debates about corporations. A good case in point, explored in detail below, is the dramatic transformation in thinking about the nature and origins of corporations that occurred in the last two decades of the century. The transformation remains poorly understood, in part, I suggest, because historians have overlooked these very real changes inside corporations, which preceded and deepened the intellectual turmoil of the late nineteenth century. Viewed from the interior, in other words, corporations and shareholders had *become* something very different by the 1880s. Appreciating this change and its timing helps to explain more persuasively why theories of the corporation underwent dramatic change in the 1880s and 1890s.

The argument unfolds in four steps. The next section lays out the now-conventional understanding of this transformation in theories of the corporation and probes its weaknesses. The third section offers an analytical perspective on the spectrum of voting rights found in corporate charters in the antebellum period. These ranged from democratic (one vote per person) to plutocratic (one vote per share), while the middle portions of the spectrum were occupied by what I call prudent-mean voting rights. The fourth section draws on a database of corporate charter provisions to show that the preponderance of shareholder voting rights fell on the democratic-to-prudent-mean end of the spectrum in the early to mid-antebellum period. The fifth section documents the shift toward plutocratic voting rights that became visible in the U.S. in the 1850s. This signaled the demise of the shareholder as citizen of the corporation and ushered in the plutocratically governed corporation, thus fundamentally altering the nature of the corporation on the eve of a thoroughgoing transformation in thinking about its nature and origins. Why this change took place in the United States is a question beyond the scope of this chapter,[9] but, in order to underline the specific, historical nature of this transformation in American corporate governance, the section demonstrates briefly that more democratic forms of governance persisted in Britain, France, and Germany as American practice took a plutocratic turn.

PROBING THE CONVENTIONAL UNDERSTANDING

As Morton J. Horwitz, Gregory A. Mark, and others have argued,[10] the early American business corporation was understood as a "body politic" or "political person."[11] As the legal terms suggest, it enjoyed a quality of "personhood" distinct from that of the shareholders who composed it. It was viewed an "artificial entity" – in Mark's words, as inherently "unnatural." Brought into being by a special act of a state legislature, moreover, it was regarded as a state-created entity, which, after *Dartmouth College* v. *Woodward* (1819), was understood to enjoy only the rights specified in its charters (e.g. to hold certain kinds of property, to sue and be sued, and so on).[12] In short, the early corporation was a state-created, legal "person" with well-defined powers. In the famous words of Chief Justice Marshall in the Dartmouth College case: "A corporation is an artificial being, invisible, intangible and existing only in contemplation of law."[13]

Its shareholders, finally, were regarded not as passive investors (as they would be later) but as active owners or "members" of the corporation, trustees of its capital. This conception of the nature of the corporation, its origins, and its shareholders dominated thinking through the middle decades of the nineteenth century.

Then, in the last two decades of the nineteenth century, a momentous change occurred: the corporation came to be regarded, on the one hand, as intrinsically private – that is, as arising not out of state action but out of the private actions of individuals – and ultimately, on the other hand, as a "natural person." Two new theories of the corporation surfaced in succession, both rejecting altogether the notion of a state-created entity and instead envisioning the corporation as arising naturally out of private economic relations. On its inherent "personhood," however, they differed. An "aggregate" or partnership theory in the 1880s retained the earlier conception of members, now conceiving of the corporation as nothing more than an aggregation of those members – "as a creature of free contract among individual shareholders," in Horwitz's words, "no different, in effect, from a partnership." Then in the 1890s an opposing view – the natural-entity or natural-person theory – challenged the partnership view. This theory also regarded the corporation as the outcome of private action but envisioned it to have the attributes of "a real person," in Mark's words, the character of "an autonomous, self-directed entity in which rights adhered."[14] These competing views of the corporation also implied radically different conceptions of the shareholder. The partnership theory clearly carried forward the traditional view of the shareholder as an active member of the corporation. But alongside of – and validated by – the natural-person theory of the corporation, Horwitz suggests, a new vision of the stockholder arose: the once active member became merely a passive investor in the corporation, while the power of action now largely inhered in the board of directors. The natural-person theory, with its associated conception of shareholders as passive investors, ultimately triumphed and went on to dominate thought about the corporation through the early decades of the twentieth century.[15]

Why did this momentous, multifaceted transformation in thinking about the nature of corporations and shareholders occur? A two-stage explanation emerges from the literature. The first centers on the shift from special to general incorporation and its consequences for theories of the origin of corporations. By the 1870s, the practice of chartering corporations by special legislative act had largely given way to "general" or "free" incorporation, which enabled private parties to incorporate merely by meeting general requirements set in statute law. "Gradually," Horwitz writes, "by making the corporate form universally available, free incorporation undermined the grant [or state-creation] theory." The advent of general incorporation – so his story goes – made it increasingly difficult to maintain the notion that incorporation was "a special state-conferred privilege."[16] General incorporation, thus, opened up conceptual space for the corporation as the partnership and natural-entity theories viewed it: as essentially private in nature. This was the conceptual terrain on which advocates of the partnership and natural-person theories sparred over the nature of corporations in the 1890s.

A second stage of change, itself two-sided, made the partnership theory increasingly less tenable, giving the edge to the natural-person theory and its associated conception of shareholders as passive investors. On the one side, the rise of a national market for industrial securities reinforced a long-term process by which the courts had eroded the trust-fund doctrine; that is to say, as stock ownership became increasingly dispersed, it became correspondingly more difficult to regard individual stockholders as trustees of the corporation's capital. On the other side, as stockholding became fragmented, turn-of-the-century corporate boards of directors, supported by the courts, assumed increasing power.[17] And, as the corporation came to resemble, in the words of the legal scholar Ernst Freund in 1897, more "an aggregation of capital than an association of persons,"[18] the stockholder, by extension, became more an owner of a portion of its capital than a member of the corporation; or, as Mark puts it: "The reality of the corporation apart from its members was becoming clearer as the relationship of the shareholders to the operations of the business became increasingly distant."[19]

On closer inspection, however, neither stage in this two-stage explanation is entirely persuasive. In explaining how the nature of the corporation was thrown open to redefinition in the 1880s, Horwitz gives great causal weight to the shift from special to general incorporation, but his argument seems to be based largely on inference; he cites no evidence.[20] Why incorporation under general acts should somehow not count as "state creation" is simply unclear. As David Millon observes, "the switch to general incorporation statutes during the last third of the nineteenth century could have been interpreted as a continuation of the states' traditional constitutive and regulatory role in the creation of corporations." [21] After all, incorporation still required a charter from the state, even though it was now granted administratively rather than legislatively, and this, he notes, "continued to reinforce the idea that corporations (in contrast to unincorporated business associations such as general partnerships) were artificial creations of the state." Citing J. Willard Hurst's work, moreover, he points out that general-incorporation statutes through the 1880s imposed significant restrictions on corporations.[22] The general statutes, rather strictly enforced by the courts, continued to define corporate purposes and powers, limiting, for example, the corporation's ability to hold stock in other corporations, its total capitalization or the value of the assets it could hold, and the duration of its life.[23] "The pervasive adoption of general incorporation statutes by many states during the latter half of the 19th century," Millon maintains, "did not signal abdication of the regulatory notion of corporate law."[24]

Instead, both Hurst and Millon locate the crucial change not in the shift from special to general incorporation but in New Jersey's holding-company laws in the late 1880s. These, Hurst writes, constituted "[t]he first signal of a new trend" that would reach maturity in the 1930s. New Jersey's laws and those that followed in Delaware and elsewhere permitted the corporation's structure and business to be largely self-defined, "in effect" deeming the corporation to be essentially private in nature.[25] Citing New Jersey in particular, Millon, too, sees the turning point in "the last years of the 19th century, [when] state legislatures eliminated several significant restrictions" in general-incorporation laws. But if the legal changes that opened up conceptual space to redefine the corporation as private occurred, not in the widespread shift to general incorporation in the 1870s, but in the laxer laws of the late 1880s and 1890s, what prompted the intellectual turmoil of the 1880s?

The second stage of the explanation, which locates the emergence of the shareholder as passive investor at the turn of the century, also proves to have a timing problem, though subtler in nature. The critical step in this stage of the explanation centers on the emergence of the national market for industrial securities, which Horwitz emphasizes repeatedly. "[D]uring the 1880s," he writes, "it was beginning to become clear that the managers, not the shareholders, were the real decision makers in large, publicly owned enterprises."[26] "[T]he rise of a national stock market," he argues, "definitively converted shareholders into impersonal investors," thus encouraging the "courts beginning in the 1890s [to] gradually [erode] the trust fund doctrine."[27] Trading of industrial securities expanded dramatically during the turn-of-the-century merger movement, he observes: "It is perhaps at this point that we can clearly identify the beginning of the shift away from 'the traditional point of view' of shareholders as 'the ultimate owners, the corporate equivalent of partners and proprietors.' "[28] Again: "The root of the problem was that the relationship of the shareholder to the corporation had begun to change fundamentally during the 1890s."[29]

Lurking behind these statements is the growing separation of ownership from control that marked "managerial capitalism" and would agitate public debates in the 1930s. In suggesting why the aggregate theory did not take hold in the late nineteenth century, Millon is more explicit on this point:

Growth in the size of corporations and dispersal of share ownership resulted in the phenomenon later described as the separation of ownership and control in Adolf Berle and Gardner Means' famous book, *The Modern Corporation and Private Property*. One of the most salient features of this development was the prevention of active participation by shareholders in the management of the business. As a practical matter, dispersed share ownership, small individual holdings, and increasingly complex operations transformed shareholders from entrepreneurs into passive investors who placed their economic interests in the hands of professional managers.

"[R]ender[ing] the partnership analogy untenable" and the natural-person theory more plausible, these changes "in the internal relationship between management and shareholders," he argues, turned the shareholder into a passive investor.[30]

The problem with this explanation lies in the erroneous assumption that professional managers, not shareholders, sat on boards of directors by the 1890s. In fact, routinely with the very important exception of railroads, boards of directors did not succumb to managerial control this early – certainly not in the 1880s and not even when great horizontal combinations initially formed during the "Great Merger Movement" (1895–1904). The new techniques of managerial capitalism were first worked out by the new vertically integrated firms of the 1880s and 1890s in the ranks of *middle* management. Because their growth was largely internally financed, according to Chandler, they remained "entrepreneurial enterprises" – that is, firms owned by single proprietors or by partnerships.[31] At the uppermost levels of the corporation, as he explains in a separate chapter in *The Visible Hand* on "Top Management," it was the great horizontal combinations that begot separation of ownership and control by putting salaried managers on their boards – but they did so only after the turn of the century, when they began to integrate forward and backward. "The shift in strategy from horizontal combination to vertical integration," in Chandler's words, "first brought the managerial *enterprise* to American industry."[32] Through the turn of the century, all but a handful of boards of directors (again, excepting railroads) continued to be dominated by shareholders. Why, then, did shareholders generally come to be seen as passive investors by the 1890s?

Both the roiling debates about the nature of the corporation of the 1880s and the growing perception of shareholders as passive investors in the 1890s need to be reconsidered in light of prior changes in the balance of power among shareholders. The remaining sections outline the key change in corporate governance – a shift from democratic to plutocratic voting rights – that put in place radically new power relations in the corporation, centralizing control in boards of directors dominated by the largest shareholders and turning the mass of smaller shareholders into mere investors by the 1870s.

SHAREHOLDER VOTING RIGHTS – THE ANTEBELLUM SPECTRUM

An antebellum shareholder's voting rights depended on the provisions of the corporation's charter or, failing an explicit provision or generic legislation regarding voting rights they were determined by the common law. The vast majority of American corporate charters, as noted earlier, were granted in special acts of legislation passed by the state legislatures and published along with other laws.[33] By the 1830s and 1840s these special acts frequently subordinated newly created corporations to generic laws, whose boilerplate provisions offered a means of streamlining charters. As reliance on general incorporation became widespread in the 1870s, finally, corporations could be formed simply by means of an administrative process as long as one met the statutory requirements and paid the necessary fees.[34] Special acts and generic legislation almost always included detailed provisions regarding the governance of the corporation. Only during the era of general incorporation did it become common for the legislatures to permit corporations to determine their own rules of governance, although this, too, required explicit provision. In the absence of a provision, the common law set the default.

Though remarkably diverse in practice, shareholder voting rights in the antebellum period may be arrayed along a spectrum ranging from democratic to plutocratic. A description of shareholder voting rights in overtly political terms may jar the modern reader, accustomed to thinking of corporations in economic terms, but doing so is consistent with antebellum practice. At a time when Americans still thought in terms of political economy, thinking of the corporation as a polity came easily. Thus, as Pauline Maier notes, "[corporate] charters and constitutions were understood as essentially the same." Debates about the governance provisions of corporate charters, she suggests, had much in common with debates about the governance provisions of state and federal constitutions.[35] Americans discussed them within a common framework of understanding.

Thinking about shareholder voting rights in terms of democracy and plutocracy would also have accorded well with nineteenth-century practice. Writing in 1837, the Prussian railroad promoter David Hansemann defined the endpoints of a spectrum in virtually the same terms: "The two extremes, giving each shareholder one vote and giving each share one vote, stand in relation to one another like democracy and aristocracy."[36] But "aristocracy" could include systems of hereditary power, so "plutocracy" seems a more accurate description. The term came into wider use in the U.S. after mid-nineteenth century, moreover, just as one vote per share was becoming more common. One of the grounds on which the abolitionist minister Henry Ward Beecher condemned slavery in 1863, for example, was its tendency to concentrate wealth and therefore power, in the hands of a few. "Slavery makes not only aristocracy, but plutocracy," he wrote, "which is the most dangerous kind of aristocracy . . . What would you think of voting, if one man could cast a thousand votes? . . . Where this disproportioned power exists, even in the Free States, it is dangerous."[37] Since shareholder voting rights based solely on the number of shares one owned yielded a similarly "disproportioned power," plutocracy and its counterpoint, democracy, seem apt descriptions of the two extremes of antebellum voting rights.

The American common law, which required fully equal voting rights, defined the democratic end of the spectrum. In the absence of an explicit provision, shareholders were treated like citizens, entitled to only one vote each, no matter how much they invested. This tradition, which has largely escaped historical memory,[38] derived from seventeenth-century Britain. As Pauline Maier explains, British tradition regarded the shareholder not as the owner of a portion of capital, but as a "member" of the corporation and therefore as an equal among equals. This was the model embodied in the English trading company. "Voting in early English profit-seeking corporations such as the East India Company," Maier writes, "allowed all shareholders single votes since 'the units of which the corporation was composed were still considered to be the members, as is the case in municipal corporations and guilds,' not shares."[39] Linking suffrage to human beings rather than to an amount of capital, the common law prescribed the most democratic form of shareholder voting rights.

The democratic default could be overridden in legislation and, as will become evident, usually was, but even then the common law could still have significant scope. It all depended on how the provisions were worded. If voting rights were described as applying specifically in the election of directors, then the common law continued to govern other decision-making processes. In such cases, when the shareholders made strategic decisions, they did so democratically: each shareholder, large and small alike, cast only one vote. This practice can be discerned between the lines, so to speak, of the minutes of shareholders' meetings. The minutes usually reported events in very terse terms, noting merely that this or that action was "resolved." But decision by ballot always required the appointment of a committee to determine who was entitled to how many votes, to examine proxies, to collect the ballots, and to report the results. All this was duly noted in the minutes and often required adjournment during the balloting. Thus, when decisions were made without appointing such a committee, they were clearly being made on the basis of a voice vote or a show of hands – necessarily one vote per person. In the terminology of the day this was known as a "vote by acclamation," in contrast to a "stock vote," that is, a vote according to the prescribed voting rights.[40]

The other end of the spectrum was defined by the modern, plutocratic practice of granting one vote per share. In the late eighteenth and early nineteenth century, distributing power among shareholders in direct proportion to their investment was widely viewed as an unwise, if not dangerous, practice. Critics of the one-vote-per-share rule stressed the political as well as economic dangers of permitting the concentration of control in the hands of the largest shareholders. As Maier and others have shown, "anti-corporate" sentiment was rampant in the antebellum period and centered on fears that corporations, necessarily privileged in some degree and widely viewed as a remnant of monarchical privilege, posed a threat to the republican nature of American society. At the same time, critics of plutocratic voting rights feared that large shareholders, left to their own devices, would attend only to their own financial interests, thereby undermining the general welfare of the enterprise.[41] Early corporations, it should be noted, were usually assumed to provide a public service, and some (especially in transportation) attracted considerable public investment. Manufacturing was an exception and perhaps for this reason New York's 1811 general incorporation law for manufacturing permitted plutocratic voting rights – "Each stockholder," it declared, "shall be entitled to as many votes as he owns shares of stock in said company.[42] But, as the next section shows, plutocratic voting rights were exceptional.

Occupying the middle portion of the spectrum was a great variety of voting-rights schemes that struck a balance between democracy and plutocracy by limiting the power of larger investors. Some charters, for example, limited a shareholder's total votes to a certain number or to a certain proportion of the total votes cast (e.g. one-tenth). More common, however, were graduated voting scales that diminished voting power relative to shareholdings as shareholdings increased. One of the more elaborate was that of the first Bank of the United States (BUS), chartered in 1791:

The number of votes to which each stockholder shall be entitled, shall be according to the number of shares he shall hold, in the proportions following, that is to say: For one share, and not more than two shares, one vote; for every two shares above two, and not exceeding ten, one vote; for every four shares above ten, and not exceeding thirty, one vote; for every six shares above thirty, and not exceeding sixty, one vote; for every eight shares above sixty, and not exceeding one hundred, one vote; and for every ten shares above one hundred, one vote; but no person, co-partnership, or body politic, shall be entitled to a greater number than thirty votes.[43]

The scale apportioned votes over six, increasingly wider steps, ending with one for every ten shares. Graduated scales could also be combined with a cap on total votes, as this one was; no BUS shareholder could cast more than thirty votes. This provision was carried over to the 1816 charter of the second BUS, except that its use was restricted explicitly to "voting for directors," which meant that the common law default would have applied to other decisions.[44]

Following Alexander Hamilton, I call these "prudent-mean" voting rights. As Secretary of the Treasury, Hamilton laid out his thoughts about the proper organization of a national bank in 1790. Pondering whether Congress should create a new institution or renovate the Bank of North America (BNA), he raised a series of objections to the constitution of the BNA, one of which centered on its shareholder voting rights. Its Congressional charter of 1781, he noted, called for "a vote for each share," which he deemed an "improper rule." The company's 1787 Pennsylvania charter, on the other hand, said nothing about voting rights. "[T]he silence of it, on that point, may signify that every stockholder is to have an equal and a single vote," but this he regarded as "a rule in a different extreme, not less erroneous." Instead, the voting-rights provision should be explicit and "a proper one," he declared. In arriving at a proper rule, he reasoned on the following lines:

A vote for each share renders a combination of a few principal stockholders, to monopolize the power and benefits of the bank, too easy. An equal vote to each stockholder, however great or small his interest in the institution, allows not that degree of weight to large stockholders which it is reasonable they should have, and which, perhaps, their security and that of the bank require. A *prudent mean* is to be preferred.[45]

As a "prudent mean" for a national bank, he went on to suggest exactly the graduated voting scale that appeared in the charter of the first BUS the following year. "Prudent-mean" is used here in a Hamiltonian spirit for voting rights that accorded some weight to the amount that a shareholder invested, but also limited the power of large shareholders.

To understand how these three types of shareholder voting rights – democratic, prudent-mean, and plutocratic – affected voting power, they may be represented graphically, as in Fig. 2.1. Along the x-axis is the number of shares; along the y-axis, the number of votes. The horizontal line represents democratic voting rights – always and only one vote, no matter how many shares one owned. The diagonal line represents plutocratic voting rights, in which the number of votes exactly equals the number of shares. The slightly curved line represents Hamilton's graduated scale for the first BUS, while the line that crosses it represents a straight linear scale (one vote for every five shares). As a glance easily confirms, the use of a prudent-mean voting scale,

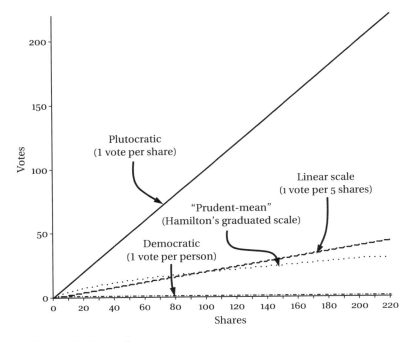

Fig. 2.1. Types of voting rights

whether a graduated scale like that of the BUS or a simple linear scale, shifted the shareholders' voting rights visibly towards the democratic side of the spectrum.

It is worth emphasizing that this insight applies only to formal voting rules. How votes played out in practice, of course, may have been another matter altogether. Rational-choice theorists who study voting rights would point out that the effective power of a vote can vary widely, depending on the overall configuration and balance of interests. Consider the simplest of scenarios: if two shareholders each had forty-nine votes and a third had only two, formation of a winning coalition would obviously depend on the shareholder with two votes, who therefore could be said to wield the most power.[46] Nonetheless, analysis of formal voting rights establishes a baseline for understanding real voting power. It seems fair to think that prudent-mean voting rights established an initial distribution of power among shareholders that was broader – hence, more democratic – than did plutocratic voting rights, and this is what the graphic representation illustrates.

AMERICAN SHAREHOLDER VOTING RIGHTS, 1825–35

In what proportions were these various kinds of voting rights actually used in the antebellum period? Some conclusions may be drawn from the corporate charters that were granted by special act from 1825 to 1835. The data reported

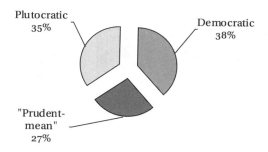

Plutocratic
35%

Democratic
38%

"Prudent-
mean"
27%

Fig. 2.2. Voting rights, 1825–35, $N = 1,233$

here encompass all charters granted by all states in 1825, by seven states from 1826 through 1834 (Connecticut, Massachusetts, New Jersey, Virginia [except for 1829 and 1831–33], South Carolina, Louisiana, Ohio), and by all states in 1835.[47] Altogether they totaled 1,233: eighty-six corporations chartered in nineteen states in 1825, 790 in the seven states from 1826 through 1834, and 357 in nineteen states in 1835.

The voting-rights provisions in these 1,233 charters are classified in Fig. 2.2 according to the three types of voting rights described above – plutocratic, prudent-mean, and democratic. The plutocratic group includes only those charters that granted shareholders one vote per share without any limit on the total number of votes that they could cast. In the prudent-mean group fall those that specified graduated scales with or without an absolute or proportional cap on total votes, linear scales with or without a cap, and one vote per share with an absolute or proportional cap on total votes. Classified as democratic, finally, are those instances in which the charter said nothing about voting rights, since the common law would have required equal votes, as well as seven cases in which the charter explicitly permitted only one vote per person.

As the data clearly demonstrate, the state legislatures did not routinely grant plutocratic voting rights between 1825 and 1835. They did so for little more than one-third of these corporations (35 percent). Much more commonly – in two-thirds of the cases – charters specified some kind of limitation that shifted voting rights towards the prudent-mean side of the spectrum, or they said nothing at all, which put them in the domain of the common law. Year to year, moreover, the proportions fluctuated (see Fig. 2.3) but without a clear direction of change. The traditional limitations on the power of large shareholders, in short, remained the norm in American corporate governance through the middle 1830s.

The common-law default, moreover, received a ringing affirmation from the New Jersey Supreme Court in 1834. In *Taylor v. Griswold*, shareholders of a bridge company asked the court to set aside the results of an election of directors two years earlier. Among other things, they charged, those in charge of

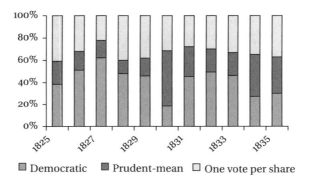

☐ Democratic ■ Prudent-mean ☐ One vote per share

Fig. 2.3. Types of voting rights, 1825–35

the election had "erred, in allowing to each stockholder but one vote, instead of a vote for each share owned by him." In fact, the company's 1797 charter was silent on voting rights, but even before incorporation the company had adopted a bylaw that gave each shareholder one vote per share on all decisions. Contrary to established practice, however, the election inspectors in 1833 had suddenly allowed each shareholder only one vote each in the disputed election.[48]

Chief Justice Joseph Hornblower found this issue not the least bit troublesome: "To my mind," he wrote, "the answer to this question is perfectly plain, whether it is considered upon general and common law principles, or upon the terms of the charter itself." On both counts, he found the bylaw granting one vote per share to be void. As a general rule, he argued, "[e]very corporator, every individual member of a body politic, whether public or private, is, *prima facie*, entitled to equal rights." Even if the charter did not specify one vote per person, "yet in its spirit and legal intendment," Justice Hornblower maintained, it "gives each member the same rights, and consequently, but one vote." He elaborated in the following terms:

a by-law excluding a member from office, or from the right to vote at all, unless he owns five, or ten, or twenty shares, would not be a more palpable, though it might be a more flagrant violation of the charter. A man with one share, is as much a *member* as a man with fifty; and it is difficult to perceive any substantial difference between a by-law, excluding a member with one share from voting at all, and a by-law reducing his one vote to a cipher, by giving another member fifty or a hundred votes.[49]

Clinching the matter, in Justice Hornblower's view, were "the very terms of the charter" itself. Following common practice, the charter incorporated individuals by name and spoke of them and their successors as "collectively constitut[ing] 'the corporation,' 'the body,' politic and corporate." And to what did "that 'body' " refer, Justice Hornblower queried? "The aggregate amount of property? or the collective number of individual proprietors who were incorporated? Manifestly the latter." By this route he reached the same conclusion – reluctantly, because he hesitated to overturn the company's long-established practice of allowing one vote per share – that he had on general principles: "There is nothing then in this charter to change the common law rights and relative influence of the individual corporators." In fact, he went further, cautioning that such a bylaw might have pernicious effects, whether intended or not. "[T]he tendency, at least, the *apparent* tendency, of the by-law in question," he maintained, "is to encourage speculation and monopoly, to lessen the rights of the smaller stockholders, depreciate the value of their shares, and throw the whole property and government of the company into the hands of a few capitalists; and it may be, to the utter neglect or disregard of the public convenience and interest."[50]

The sentiments expressed in this New Jersey Supreme Court decision, one of few pieces of surviving evidence in which shareholder voting rights were discussed explicitly,[51] seem entirely consistent with the evidence gleaned from the corporate charters themselves. In specific instances, the state legislatures granted one vote per share, but this was not at all the norm and many corporations, it seems, remained subject to the common-law default that Justice Hornblower and his colleagues defended so vigorously.

FROM DEMOCRACY TO PLUTOCRACY

Within a few years, however, state legislation trumped the New Jersey Supreme Court's decision in *Taylor* v. *Griswold*, signaling that a transformation in the norms of corporate governance was underway. In 1841 the New Jersey legislature passed an act that substantially overruled the common-law default of one vote per person, at least in company elections. "[U]nless otherwise expressly provided in their respective charters," the act declared, "at every such election [of managers or directors] each stockholder shall be entitled to one vote for each share . . . held by him or her."[52] Five years later, the legislature acted again. This time, in authorizing general incorporation of manufacturing companies, it permitted them to determine their own voting rules, entirely privatizing the matter. In 1849 the legislature extended this practice to other lines of business (any kind of manufacturing, mining, mechanical, agricultural, or chemical business as well as inland navigation).[53]

New Jersey's action was not without precedent; rumblings of change had been heard earlier elsewhere. The 1811 New York law permitting "free" or general incorporation of manufacturing companies, as mentioned earlier, specified one vote per share. The Massachusetts *Revised Statutes* of 1836 retained various caps on the voting power of shareholders in railroad, banking, and insurance corporations, but manufacturing corporations were permitted to set their own voting rights in their bylaws.[54] In 1837, the Connecticut legislature passed a general incorporation law for mining and manufacturing that entitled shareholders to one vote per share.[55]

In the late 1840s and early 1850s, the New York legislature endorsed plutocratic voting across the board. Between 1847 and 1855, it passed general incorporation laws for most organizations, from villages and benevolent societies through toll bridge and chemical companies to railroads. Where applicable, it was "characteristic" of these laws, Ronald Seavoy writes, that "[e]ach share had one vote."[56] Indeed, plutocratic voting rules had become the norm in New York State by then. As A. B. Johnson, president of the Ontario (Branch) Bank, noted in an 1850 article,

The early corporations of our State [New York] attempted to guard against the dangers of so alarming a power [i.e., control by large shareholders], by according to large share-holders a smaller ratio of elective efficiency than was accorded to smaller stockholders; but the guard is abandoned in modern corporations from indifference to the consequences on the part of Legislatures, or from an opinion that every guard can be easily evaded, and that stockholders had better be presented with a known evil, than deluded with a fallacious remedy.[57]

Whether Johnson was right in the reasons he cited, the prevailing norms were clearly in the midst of a transformation.

New York was not alone in coupling general incorporation with one-vote-per-share voting rights, if not privatizing voting rights altogether. Louisiana took the latter route in 1848, having pioneered three years earlier in adopting a constitutional prohibition on special charters.[58] California passed a comprehensive general corporation law in 1850, according to which shareholders in insurance, manufacturing, mining, mechanical, chemical, and steam navigation companies were entitled to one vote per share. All other companies could determine their voting rules themselves in their bylaws. In 1853, further acts affirmed one vote per share in elections of directors of corporations engaged in a broad range of businesses.[59] The state of Ohio also passed a comprehensive general incorporation law in 1852, authorizing one vote per share for transportation and utility companies but permitting manufacturing and magnetic telegraphic companies to determine their own voting rights.[60]

Yet, through the 1850s, change proceeded unevenly and in piecemeal fashion. Some corporations apparently tried to buck the trend emerging elsewhere. It is probably significant that five of the seven charters granted between 1825 and 1835 that explicitly gave each shareholder only one vote were granted not in the early years but at the end of the period (in 1835 – one in Kentucky, four in Ohio). Since these provisions merely recapitulated the common-law default, their existence may be read as a sign that it could no longer be taken for granted. Writing the common-law rule explicitly into a charter would have served to quiet any looming uncertainty.

The general thrust of Virginia's chartering policy for many years, moreover, was to limit the power of the largest investors by means of graduated voting scales. A Virginia law of 1837 regulating all manufacturing corporations specified a voting scale that was relatively flat (i.e., democratic). It gave one vote for each share up to fifteen, one additional vote for every five shares from sixteen to 100, and one vote for each increment of twenty shares above 100. Under legislation passed in the same year, railroad shareholders in Virginia were allowed one

Table 2.1. *Voting scale adopted by the State of Virginia for all corporations, 1849*

Shares	Votes
1–20	1 per share
21–200	1 for every 2 shares
201–500	1 for every 5 shares
501+	1 for every 10 shares

Source: Virginia Code, Title 18, ch. 57, sec. 10 (1849).

vote for each share up to ten shares and then one vote for every ten additional shares.[61] A dozen years later, the state legislature approved a standard voting scale (Table 2.1) for all joint-stock companies. For shareholdings under 200, this was a more plutocratic scale than those adopted in 1836 and 1837, but it was more democratic at higher levels of shareholding. This scale remained in place until the eve of the Civil War.

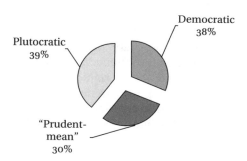

Plutocratic 39%

Democratic 38%

"Prudent-mean" 30%

Fig. 2.4. Voting rights, 1855, $N = 130$

Interestingly, another arena where evidence of substantial change does not emerge is in the special acts of incorporation that some states continued to grant. Of the seven states included in Fig. 2.3 for the years 1826–34, five were still granting special charters in 1855. Together, they incorporated 130 companies by special act that year. As Figure 2.4 shows, the proportions of voting rights in 1855 fell within the range of the earlier period. Thirty-nine percent specified plutocratic voting rights, but 61 percent still placed some limitation on the power of large shareholders, virtually the same as in 1825 and 1828.

Evidence that the turn to plutocracy proceeded very unevenly also surfaced in the shareholder meetings of existing companies (although this kind of evidence is scarcer). In 1847 the shareholders of the Greenville and Columbia

Railroad met in Columbia, South Carolina. The company's 1845 charter contained an elaborate voting scale of eleven steps to apply in the election of officers, in amending bylaws, and "in determining on measures involving the interests of the Company." This was the first official meeting of the stockholders, apparently called at that time because the company had only just attracted sufficient stock subscriptions to permit it to organize. Among the first set of resolutions offered for consideration was one that read: "*Resolved*, That until otherwise ordered, the vote on all questions before this meeting be taken by acclamation or count." The proposal to vote by voice or show of hands, according to the proceedings, gave rise to "some explanations" among the shareholders. After discussion, however, they approved the resolutions unanimously – "by acclamation or count," apparently, since a committee was formed to verify proxies and collect ballots only later in the meeting.[62] In this case, then, the shareholders agreed among themselves to ignore their charter provision and to proceed under the common-law rule.

A similar incident occurred in Vermont in 1852, but with the opposite outcome. In May of 1852 the shareholders of the Vermont Central Railroad met to confront a recently erupted scandal: their treasurer, the well-connected Boston citizen Josiah Quincy, had pledged the company's bonds to settle his private debts. According to the company's 1835 charter, shareholders enjoyed one vote per share specifically in the election of directors, and their practice had apparently been to make other decisions – such as what to do about Josiah Quincy – on the basis of one vote per person. Yet, when a disagreement emerged at the outset of the meeting, one of the shareholders, W. H. Gregerson of Boston, "called for a stock vote." Another, G. W. Benedict of Burlington, objected "that a stock vote cannot be called as a matter of right, under the charter, except upon the election of Directors." But the president demurred: "according to common usage, and to the rule established, as he conceived, by the charter, the call for a stock vote must be sustained." Benedict again protested, the question was put to a vote – one vote per person, it must be assumed – and the shareholders upheld the president: the decision would be made on the basis of a stock vote. In this instance, plutocratic governance won out, having already, in the president's view, come into "common usage."[63]

During and after the Civil War, the movement that would soon make one vote per share the norm accelerated at the national and the state level. Congressional charters granted to the transcontinental railroads in the 1860s and early 1870s specified one vote per share.[64] So, too, did Congressional legislation creating a national currency and nationally chartered banks. In elections of directors and at all their meetings, shareholders of the national banks were to have one vote per share.[65] Most states that had not done so earlier now followed suit. Virginia had simplified its mandated scale in 1860, giving one vote to each share up to ten and an additional vote to every four shares above ten.[66] Then in 1871 it abolished graduated voting scales for certain corporations – those chartered via a judicial process, a form of general incorporation that it had established in the mid-1850s. Finally, in 1886, the legislature mandated one vote per share for all corporations chartered "heretofore and hereafter."[67] The South Carolina legislature endorsed plutocratic voting rights in the same year, mandating one vote per share in its general incorporation law of 1886.[68]

One of the last states to come around was Massachusetts, which had been an early and energetic incorporator. Its manufacturing corporations, as noted earlier, were allowed to determine their own voting rights from the 1830s, but the state continued to restrict the voting power of individual railroad investors to one-tenth of the total votes. This restriction was carried forward in the Revised Statutes of 1860 (ch. 63, sect. 5), and a general revision in 1881 also left it intact. But the latter permitted municipalities, the Commonwealth, and other railroad corporations to vote the whole number of shares that they owned.[69] For individual railroad investors, voting rights were limited to one-tenth of all votes through the turn of the century.

Massachusetts was clearly exceptional in the 1880s, for legal scholars regarded plutocratic voting rights as the norm by then. In an 1884 treatise, Henry O. Taylor noted the old common-law rule, then stressed that it no longer applied to "stock corporations": "by statute and by-laws, and by custom so general, as to amount to accepted law, a shareholder is entitled to as many votes as he holds shares."[70] Three years later, William W. Cook took the same position. The old common-law rule, he noted, had been "[a]lmost universally" superseded by the provisions of individual charters, statutes, or state constitutions. "[A]t the present day," in his judgment, "it is probable that no court, even in the absence of any such provision, would uphold a rule which disregards, in the matter of voting, the number of shares which the shareholder holds in the corporation."[71]

Indeed, the transformation had progressed so far by then that plutocratic voting rights came to seem natural, fair, and right. This is the conception that one G. J. Greene voiced in an entirely different context – an expression noteworthy precisely because it was not concerned with *corporate* governance at all, but merely drew analogies with what he understood as the common practice in American corporations. In a letter on recent election frauds published in the *Keowee Courier* in Walhalla, South Carolina, in 1882, Greene proposed "A New Plan to Govern South Carolina." Declaring himself "a Republican outright, downright," and therefore "opposed to universal suffrage, that is, Democracy," he also argued against an electoral system organized along racial lines. (His reasons were surprisingly pragmatic: "It is so difficult with us to tell just where the negro begins and the white man ends." He also feared that it would put South Carolina in a bad light abroad.) Instead, he wanted to see representation organized "in an honest, just and impartial way" that would simultaneously ensure white control. In words worth quoting at length, he explained why he thought the large corporation offered an appropriate model:

I would govern South Carolina on the same principle on which all great corporations are governed. I would give to each man, white or black, precisely that power in the government of the State that each individual stockholder in a great corporation possesses, for what else is the State of South Carolina but a great corporation, with a taxable capital of say $100,000,000. How is a corporation governed? By the stock or capital being divided out among a large number of people in various amounts, from a single share to many thousands, and in the management of that corporation *each individual exercises precisely the power that his interest in or ownership of such shares entitles him to.* If he has one share he casts one vote. If he has ten shares he casts ten votes, and so on, according to the number of shares he holds. He has a vote for every share he owns. *Nothing could be fairer.* Nobody denies him this right. Everybody will admit that this is right and the law guarantees it to him.[72]

In the half-century since Chief Justice Hornblower of the New Jersey Supreme Court had so adamantly defended the common-law understanding of a democratic corporate governance, American practice had turned thoroughly plutocratic.

That this was a distinctively American, not a universal or natural, movement toward plutocracy is worth emphasizing. In the antebellum period, voting rights were at least as likely to limit the power of large shareholders in the European industrial powers as they were in the United States but, unlike in the United States, this seems to have held true throughout the century.[73] Indeed, plutocratic voting rights were virtually unknown in France and quite rare in the German states until late in the century. In a generous sample of French charters granted from 1825 through 1835 (74 out of a total of 107 companies chartered), only 3 percent had plutocratic voting rights; nearly complete samples for 1845 (twenty-six of twenty-eight) and 1855 (seventeen of eighteen) show no plutocratic voting rights at all. A general incorporation law adopted in 1867, moreover, officially limited a shareholder's total votes to ten; this restriction remained in place through the turn of the century. A sample of German corporations chartered from 1825 through 1870 (207 of 638 known corporations) yields a similar result: only 2 percent had plutocratic voting rights. A major revision of German law in 1884 endorsed the one-share, one-vote rule in principle, but it noted explicitly that voting rights could be limited by capping total votes or with graduated scales. Because of the "freedom" it gave companies to adopt limitations on voting rights, legal expert Viktor Ring emphasized in 1886, this provision of the new law left ample room to preserve the "personal element" in the corporation.[74] Although legal experts emphasized a large gap between theory and practice by the early twentieth century they, nonetheless, regarded German corporate law to be exceptionally "democratic," particularly in the powers it accorded to the shareholders' assembly and by comparison with American law.[75]

Shareholder voting rights in Britain, in contrast, more closely resembled those in the United States in the antebellum years, but certain features of British practice appear to have staved off a wholesale turn to plutocracy later in the century. A preliminary sample of charters granted under general incorporation laws between 1845 and 1865 suggests a pattern much like in the United States: 35 percent specified plutocratic voting rights.[76] But from 1845, the government offered a simple graduated scale that served as a default if a company's articles of association did not provide differently.[77] This provision remained in force through a revision of company law in 1900 and seems to have been widely adopted. In 1883, one Norman Pearson, like G. J. Greene of South Carolina, found in the corporate world what he regarded as a serviceable model for political suffrage – but a different model than Greene's. A declared opponent of universal manhood suffrage, he thought voting power should be distributed as he understood it to be in British corporations. Everyone with at least a minimal income should have one vote; no one should have more than twenty votes; and "the intermediate votes should be distributed on the same principle" as in the default provision. This clause "is very generally adopted by limited companies," he noted, "is specially designed for the protection of small shareholders, is found to work extremely well, and I do not see why its principle should not be applied with equal success to the franchise."[78] As late as 1894, C. E. H. Chadwyck-Healey's manual on incorporation recommended a graduated voting scale similar to the default scale. A footnote indicated that incorporators should opt for one vote per share if they wanted to give power to the "largest proprietors," but even then it added that total votes could be capped at a specific number. By the turn of the century, however, British corporations were apparently making greater use of plutocratic voting rights; a company-law expert reported in 1901 that companies "[v]ery commonly," though not exclusively, adopted one vote per share.[79] In 1906, the government finally revised its default provisions to specify one vote per share.[80] (see Table 2.2).

Even so, another feature of British governance continued to ensure a strongly democratic thrust. This was the common-law practice of requiring that all votes at shareholder meetings be taken by a show of hands unless at least five shareholders (later reduced to three) demanded a "poll" – the equivalent of a "stock vote" in the United States. Only then did the shareholders vote according to their prescribed voting rights. This manner of proceeding was included in the default regulations from at least 1856 on. When the graduated scale was eliminated as the default in 1906, the new wording read: "On a show of hands every member present in person shall have one vote. On a poll every member shall have one vote [in person or by proxy] for each share of which he is the holder." A 1911 manual with a practical bent advised matter-of-factly: "Unless the articles otherwise provide, questions arising at a general meeting are to be decided, in the first instance, by a show of hands. This is the common law rule

Table 2.2. *Default voting scale in Britain, 1845-1905*

Shares	Votes
1-10	1 per share
11-100	1 for every 5 shares
101+	1 for every 10 shares

Sources: 8 & 9 Vict. 16 (1845), 19 & 20 Vict. c. 47 (1856), 25 & 26 Vict. c. 89 (1862).

which, unless excluded, applies automatically." The author acknowledged that a poll often conveyed a better sense of "the wishes of the whole constituency of the company," but he gave no indication that a show of hands "in the first instance" had fallen into disuse.[81]

Although the difference may have been a matter of degree, not of kind, corporate governance in Britain, France, and Germany did not move as sharply towards plutocracy in the late nineteenth century as it did in the United States. Plutocratic corporate governance was not a natural consequence of industrial growth; in short, it was a distinctively American way of distributing power in the corporation.

CONCLUSION

As plutocratic voting rights superseded prudent-mean and democratic voting rights in the United States, the power of the small shareholder inevitably declined, turning him (or her) into a passive investor. Only after this had happened did the concentration of power in the hands of large shareholders – a precondition of the rise of financial and managerial capitalism at the turn of the century – become possible.

In the process, it seems reasonable to think, the spread of plutocratic voting rights – and the consequences that followed – may well have encouraged the notion that corporations were essentially private in nature. Foremost among the corollaries of plutocratic voting rights was the all-powerful board of directors. With large enough holdings, the largest investors could handily control the board of directors and turn this power to their advantage, just as Alexander Hamilton feared in the late eighteenth century. The premier example of this immediately after the Civil War was surely the Erie Railroad. As one observer, urging action by the New York legislature (or "Chamber of Commerce," as he called it), observed in 1868:

The present theory of the railroad law of this State is that the directors are not agents at will, and subject to consultation and instruction from their principals the stockholders, but that, for the period of their office, they are, with but slight qualification, absolute masters of affairs. Without the consent of the stockholders they can buy property or roads, lease other lines, guarantee the loans of other companies, extend the road, make what they may deem improvements at discretion, contract loans upon their own terms, and increase the capital stock through the issue of convertible bonds. What more absolute powers could be conferred upon them? That such prerogatives are dangerous to the interests of the corporation and of stockholders is too evident from the recent doings of directors in cases which have attracted much public attention.[82]

The same year another commentator, writing in the popular periodical *Hours at Home*, described the overweening power of boards of directors in more colorful terms:

[The stockholders'] rights in the management, control and even to the profits of the very works which his own capital has created have, in various ways, come to be, in practice at least, not only essentially restricted, abridged and fettered, but even threatened at last with virtual extinction . . . the Stockholder is fast becoming only an embarrassing recollection to ambitious, scheming and self-willed Boards of Directors . . . Stockholders' rights are no more considered by the managers of some of our colossal railway corporations than the squeezed rind of the lemon whose juice has given a passing flavor to the fluid which stands in the Directors' private room.[83]

Or as Charles F. Adams Jr. put it more sedately in 1871, "the idea of [corporate] management through representation has already given way to the one-man power."[84] This state of affairs – the concentration of great power in boards of directors – made the post-Civil War corporation into an entity very different from its antebellum counterpart.

In such circumstances – when plutocratic voting rights had enabled the largest shareholders to control boards of directors, when small shareholders had been reduced to "ciphers," as Chief Justice Hornblower feared, when colossal corporations seemed to be "as masters of affairs" – is it too much to think that the corporation appeared more private than public and that the multitude of stockholders seemed more like passive investors than citizens of the corporate polity?

NOTES

1. For a cross-national introduction, see Hopt *et al.*
2. Important exceptions are John W. Cadman Jr., *The Corporation in New Jersey: Business and Politics, 1791–1875* (Cambridge, MA: Harvard University Press, 1949), pp. 301–26; Edwin Merrick Dodd, *American Business Corporations until 1860: With Special Reference to Massachusetts* (Cambridge, MA: Harvard University Press, 1954), pp. 65–122, 188–94; and selected essays in Norbert Horn and Jürgen Kocka (eds.), *Recht und Entwicklung der Großunternehmen im 19. und frühen 20. Jahrhundert: Wirtschafts-, sozial- und rechtshistorische Untersuchungen zur Industrialisierung in Deutschland, Frankreich, England und den USA (Law and the Formation of Big Enterprises in the 19th and Early 20th Centuries: Studies in the History of Industrialization in Germany, France, Great Britain and the United States)* (Göttingen: Vandenhoeck & Ruprecht, 1979). Lawrence M. Friedman, *A History of American Law* (New York: Simon and Schuster/Touchstone, 1973), pp. 168–9, also touches on the subject, as does Pauline Maier, "The Revolutionary Origins of the American Corporation," *William and Mary Quarterly* 3rd ser. 50 (1993), 76–79.
3. Classic works include George Heberton Evans Jr., *Business Incorporations in the United States, 1800–1943* (New York: National Bureau of Economic Research, Inc., 1948); and J. Willard Hurst, *The Legitimacy of the Business Corporation in the Law of the United States, 1780–1970* (Charlottesville: University Press of Virginia, 1970). For a useful analysis of the literature, see Gregory A. Mark, "The Role of the State in Corporate Law Formation," *International Corporate Law Annual* 1 (2000), 5–9.
4. R. Kent Newmyer, "Justice Story's Doctrine of 'Public and Private Corporations' and the Rise of the American Business Corporation," *Depaul Law Review* 25 (1976), 825–41; Herbert Hovenkamp, *Enterprise and American Law, 1836–1937*

(Cambridge, MA, and London: Harvard University Press, 1991); Gregory A. Mark, "The Personification of the Business Corporation in American Law," *University of Chicago Law Review* 54 (1987), 1441–83; and Morton J. Horwitz, *The Transformation of American Law, 1870–1960: The Crisis of Legal Orthodoxy* (New York: Oxford University Press, 1992), pp. 65–107. Horwitz's chapter was originally published as "*Santa Clara* Revisited: The Development of Corporate Theory," *West Virginia Law Review* 88 (1985), 173 *ff*. For further discussion, see below.

5. Alfred D. Chandler Jr., *The Visible Hand: The Managerial Revolution in American Business* (Cambridge, MA: Harvard University Press/Belknap Press, 1977); and idem, *Scale and Scope: The Dynamics of Industrial Capitalism* (Cambridge, MA: Harvard University Press, 1990). On Chandler's influence, see Richard R. John, "Elaborations, Revisions, Dissents: Alfred D. Chandler Jr.'s, *The Visible Hand* After Twenty Years," *Business History Review* 71 (Summer 1997), 151–200.

6. Chandler, *The Visible Hand*, 9–10. *Scale and* Scope, his comparative study of industrial capitalism, is oriented around personal capitalism (Britain) and two variants of managerial capitalism, competitive (U.S.) and cooperative (Germany).

7. Chandler, *The Visible Hand*, 48.

8. A growing literature that seeks, like this chapter, to denaturalize the "big business" model of American business history includes: Charles Sabel and Jonathan Zeitlin, "Historical Alternatives to Mass Production: Politics, Markets and Technology in Nineteenth-Century Industrialization," *Past and Present* 108 (August 1985), 133–76; Gerald Berk, *Alternative Tracks: The Constitution of American Industrial Order* (Baltimore: Johns Hopkins University Press, 1994); Colleen A. Dunlavy, *Politics and Industrialization: Early Railroads in the United States and Prussia* (Princeton: Princeton University Press, 1994); Mark J. Roe, *Strong Managers, Weak Owners: The Political Roots of American Corporate Finance* (Princeton: Princeton University Press, 1994); Charles F. Sabel and Jonathan Zeitlin (eds.), *World of Possibilities: Flexibility and Mass Production in Western Industrialization* (New York: Cambridge University Press, 1997); and Philip Scranton, *Endless Novelty: Specialty Production and American Industrialization, 1865–1925* (Princeton: Princeton University Press, 1998).

9. Dunlavy, *Shareholder Democracy*, will take up this question.

10. Except as noted otherwise, the following account relies on two standard sources on the nineteenth and early twentieth centuries – Horwitz, *Transformation*, 65–107; and Mark, "Personification" – as well as on David Millon, "Frontiers of Legal Thought I: Theories of the Corporation," *Duke Law Journal* (1990) 201–51, which brings the story into the 1980s.

11. Joseph K. Angell and Samuel Ames, *A Treatise on the Law of Private Corporations Aggregate* (Boston: Hilliard, Gray, Little & Wilkins, 1832), pp. 1, 3 (quoting Mr. Kyd). The term "body politic" appeared in most American (special) charters, which may be consulted in the published laws of the states.

12. Early corporations were often characterized as public rather than private, but the public–private dichotomy has been used in so many different senses (see, for example, Newmyer; Horwitz, *Transformation*, 206–8; and Millon, 201–2) that I prefer to avoid it. Business corporations were a subset of the broader class of corporations that also included municipal, educational, religious, and charitable corporations; see Friedman, 459–63; Ronald E. Scavoy, *The Origins of the American Business Corporation, 1784–1855: Broadening the Concept of Public Service During Industrialization.* (Westport, CT, and London: Greenwood Press, 1982), pp. 9–38, 231–6; and Maier, 53–73.

13. Quoted in Angell and Ames, 2.
14. Mark, "Personification," 1442.
15. This literature, it should be noted, ignores an alternative conception of corporations that continued to regard them as inherently the creation of public policy. See Colleen A. Dunlavy, "How Did American Business Get So Big?" *Audacity, The Magazine of Business Experience* (Spring 1994), 41–9. For a similar, contemporary viewpoint, see Lawrence E. Mitchell (ed.), *Progressive Corporate Law* (Boulder: HarperCollins/Westview Press, 1995).
16. Horwitz, *Transformation*, 73. See also Mark, "Personification," 1453–7.
17. Horwitz, *Transformation*, 106, also emphasizes the functional attractions of the natural-person or entity theory for the new industrial combinations at the turn of the century.
18. Ernst Freud, *The Legal Nature of Corporations* (Chicago: University of Chicago Press, 1897), 60, quoted in Horwitz, *Transformation*, 100.
19. Mark, "Personification," 1472.
20. Horwitz, *Transformation*, 73, 75.
21. Millon, 211.
22. Millon, 206.
23. Millon, 208–210; Hurst, 44–45, 69–70.
24. Millon, 208.
25. Hurst, 69–71. Hurst's phrase "in effect" is significant, for it signals that he is drawing a conclusion (as he does throughout the book) based on the outcome rather than on evidence of intention.
26. Horwitz, *Transformation*, 93.
27. Horwitz, *Transformation*, 94.
28. Horwitz, *Transformation*, 95.
29. Horwitz, *Transformation*, 96.
30. Millon, 214–15. See also Horwitz, *Transformation*, 93.
31. Chandler, *The Visible Hand*, 381. On turn-of-the-century mergers, see Naomi Lamoreaux, *The Great Merger Movement in American Business, 1895–1904* (Cambridge: Cambridge University Press, 1985).
32. Chandler, *The Visible* Hand, 415 (emphasis added). His case studies in this chapter are Standard Oil, General Electric, United States Rubber, and Du Pont. Of these, Standard Oil was the earliest trust, but its trust certificates did not circulate publicly. Thomas R. Navin and Marian V. Sears, "The Rise of a Market for Industrial Securities, 1887–1902," *Business History Review* 29 (1955), 113. The trust was declared illegal and dissolved in 1893; it incorporated as a New Jersey holding company only in 1899.
33. Congressional charters granted to the Bank of North America and to the first and second Bank of the United States constituted the major exceptions in the antebellum period; the federal government did not charter corporations again until the transcontinental railroad and national banking acts in the 1860s. An early exception to the practice of incorporating by special acts occurred in New York State, which made general incorporation available to manufacturing corporations in 1811 (ch. 67, 1811 N.Y. Laws 111).
34. During the middle decades of the century, some states permitted chartering both by special act and under general incorporation laws. On New Jersey, for example, see Cadman, 111–82.
35. Maier, 79.

36. David Hansemann, *Die Eisenbahnen und deren Aktionäre in ihrem Verhältniß zum Staat* (Leipzig and Halle: Renger'sche Verlagsbuchhandlung, 1837), 116.

37. Henry Ward Beecher, *Freedom and War. Discourses on Topics Suggested by the Times* (Boston: Ticknor and Fields, 1863), 380–1.

38. Though legal scholars are aware of the common law on voting rights (see Jeffrey Kerbel, "An Examination of Nonvoting and Limited Voting Common Shares – Their History, Legality, and Validity," *Securities Regulation Law Journal* 16, no. 1 [Spring 1987], 47), business historians are largely unaware of it. One exception is Cadman, 307.

39. Maier, 77n, quoting Samuel Williston, "History of the Law of Business Corporations before 1800," *Harvard Law Review* 2 (1888), 156.

40. This description is based on a reading of minutes of shareholders' meetings, for example, those of the Boston and Worcester Railroad in the Boston and Albany Archive, Historical Collections, Baker Library, Harvard Business School. For a published reference to the practice, see *Proceedings of the Stockholders of the Vermont Central Railroad, at a Special Meeting Holden at Northfield, Vermont, May 4, 5, 1852: Printed by Order of the Corporation* (Montpelier, VT.: E. P. Walton & Son, 1852), p. 4. This case is discussed further below.

41. On anti-charter agitation regarding business corporations, see Maier, 64–81. The idea that shareholders could have different interests is squarely at odds with contemporary law. In practice and theory today, as Daniel J. H. Greenwood writes, "the shareholder is reduced to the shares" – becomes, in his turn of phrase, a "fictional shareholder" – and all shareholders are assumed to be interested only in "shareholder value" (i.e. the value of their shares). See Daniel J. H. Greenwood, "Fictional Shareholders: For Whom Are Corporate Managers Trustees, Revisited," *Southern California Law Review* 69 (1996), 1021–1104. Thanks to Eric Guthey for this reference.

42. Ch. 67, 1811 N.Y. Laws 111.

43. Charter of first Bank of the United States, ch. 10, §7, 1 Stat. 191, 193 (1791).

44. Charter of Second Bank of the United States, ch. 44, §11, 3 Stat. 266, 271 (1816). The 1816 law also referred to the stockholder not as "he" but as "he, she, or they, respectively."

45. Alexander Hamilton, "National Bank. Communicated to the House of Representatives, Dec. 14, 1790," *American State Papers*, vol. 5, 1st Cong., 3rd sess., no. 18 (1790), 73 (emphasis added); on the Bank of North America Bray Hammond, *Banks and Politics in America* (Princeton: Princeton University Press, 1957), pp. 40–64. Whether both charters were still valid was an open question, Hamilton noted, and not one that he ventured to settle, but public opinion, he reported, considered the Bank of North America to have become a Pennsylvania bank.

46. For an introduction to this approach, see Dan S. Felsenthal and Moshé Machover, *The Measurement of Voting Power* (Cheltenham: Edward Elgar, 1998). I am indebted to Steven J. Brams for alerting me to this literature.

47. This is based on a database of corporate charters granted in the United States, Britain, France, and Germany between 1825 and 1865/70. Information from the charters has been augmented by provisions of generic laws if it is clear that they applied to individual companies (usually this was indicated in the charter itself). Construction of the database has required many hours of locating and combing through published laws and, of course, a massive amount of data-entry, which would have been impossible without generous funding from the Alfred P. Sloan

Foundation. Once this research is completed, I will make the database available for public use on the Internet.

48. *Taylor* v. *Griswold*, 14 N.J.L. 222, 223–224, 240 (N.J. sup. ct., 1834). It is not clear from the judges' opinions what prompted this departure from the company's long-standing practice. For the company's charter, see 89:5 1797 N.J.L. 201 SB An act to incorporate the stockholders of the bridges over the rivers Passaick and Hackinsack, ch. 653, 1797 N.J. Laws 201.

49. *Taylor* v. *Griswold*, 237–8 (original emphasis).

50. *Taylor* v. *Griswold*, 238–9, 241 (original emphasis). Judge Hornblower's colleague on the court, Justice Ford, essentially agreed: "This claim of having one vote for each share, neither rests on the common law of the land, nor any of its principles. It wholly depends on the *grant* of the legislature." Since the bridge company's charter did not grant one vote per share, the common law would not allow them to grant it to themselves via their bylaws. *Taylor* v. *Griswold*, 251 (Ford, J., concurring; original emphasis).

51. Although the Hornblower opinion did not cite previous cases and the subsequent antebellum case law is very thin, one vote per person was recognized as the common-law rule in cases and legal treatises through the remainder of the century (although from the 1880s it was generally regarded as outmoded or having been superceded – see below). See, for example, 63 A.L.R. 1106–7; William W. Cook, *A Treatise on the Law of Stock and Stockholders* (New York: Baker, Voorhis & Co., 1887), §608; Arthur W. Machen Jr., *A Treatise on the Modern Law of Corporations*, vol. 2 (Boston: Little, Brown, and Company, 1908), §1216.

52. §2, 1841 N.J. Acts 116, 117.

53. §11, 1846 N.J. Acts 64, 66; §11, 1849 N.J. Acts 300, 302–3.

54. mass. rev. stat. Tit. 13, ch. 36, §23, ch. 37, §5, ch. 38, §7, ch. 39, §50 (1836).

55. Ch. 63, §9, 1837 Conn. Pub. Acts 49, 50–51.

56. Seavoy, 191–3. The single limitation occurred in its general railroad law of 1850, which specified one vote per share explicitly for the election of directors. Under the understanding articulated by Justice Hornblower in 1834, this would have required railroad companies to adhere to the common-law default for all other decisions.

57. A. B. Johnson, "Advantages and Disadvantages of Private Corporations," *Hunt's Merchants' Magazine* 23 (December 1850), 630.

58. No. 100, §3, 1848 La. Acts 70, 71.

59. Ch. 128, 1849–50 Cal. Stat. 347; ch. 65, §5, 1853 Cal. Stat. 87, 88; ch. 72, §11, 1853 Cal. Stat. 99, 102; ch. 121, §7, 1853 Cal. Stat. 169, 170.

60. 1852 Ohio Acts 274.

61. Ch. 84, §5, 1836–37 Va. Acts 74, 76; ch. 118, §18, 1836–37 Va. Acts 101, 108.

62. *A Convention of the Stockholders of the Greenville and Columbia Rail Road, for the Purpose of Organization, Held at Carolina Hall, Columbia, Tuesday and Wednesday, May 11, 12, 1847* (Columbia, SC: South Carolinian Office, 1847). Eighty-one shareholders attended the meeting, holding 19,813 shares and 4,155 votes. For the charter, see no. 2953, 1845 S.C. Acts 324 or *An Act to Authorize the Formation of the Greenville and Columbia Railroad Company* (Columbia, SC: J. G. Summer, 1846). The company's voting-rights provision was identical to that of the South Carolina Canal and Railroad Company, which dated from 1828. The latter is reproduced in Dunlavy, "Corporate Governance," 20.

63. *Proceedings of the Stockholders of the Vermont Central Railroad, at a Special Meeting Holden at Northfield Vermont, May 4, 5, 1852* (Montpelier: E. P. Walton & Son, 1852).

The proceedings were printed on a motion by the dissident Mr. Benedict. Quincy maintained that he had acted within his rights. See Josiah Quincy, *Letter to the Shareholders of the Vermont Central Railroad: From Josiah Quincy, Jr., March, 1852* (Boston: Eastburn's Press, 1852). To complicate matters, the charter specified voting rights only for the *first* election of directors. The charter is included in W. P. Gregg and Benjamin Pond, *The Railroad Laws and Charters of the United States*, vol. 1 (Boston: Little and J. Brown, 1851), pp. 707.

64. Ch. 120, 12 Stat. 489 (1862); ch. 278, 14 Stat. 292 (1866); ch. 122, 16 Stat. 573 (1871). The 1862 charter of the Union Pacific Railroad initially limited ownership to 200 shares, but the limit was removed in an 1864 amendment. ch. 216, 12 Stat. 356 (1864).

65. U.S. Statutes (1863), ch. 58, §38; (1854), ch. 106, §11.

66. va. code Tit. 18, ch. 57, §10 (1860).

67. ch. 277, §4, 1870–71 va. Laws 367, 369; ch. 233, 1885–86 Va. Acts 246.

68. No. 288, §11, 1886 S.C. Acts 540, 543.

69. Ch. 112 §53, 1882 Mass. Pub. Stat. 598, 611.

70. Henry O. Taylor, *A Treatise on the Law of Private Corporations Having Capital Stock* (Philadelphia: Kay & Brother, 1884), §580.

71. William W. Cook, *A Treatise on the Law of Stock and Stockholders* (New York: Baker, Voorhis & Co., 1887), §608. See also Victor Morawetz, *A Treatise on the Law of Private Corporations*, 2nd ed., vol. 1 (Boston: Little, Brown, and Company, 1886), 450.

72. *Keowee Courier* (Walhalla, SC), May 11, 1882 (emphasis added). I am grateful to Lisa Tetrault and Stephen Kantrowitz for this reference.

73. Except as noted otherwise, the remainder of this section is based on Dunlavy, "Corporate Governance," 22–7, 29–33, and on the charters database (see note 47). Each of the countries poses unique problems of data collection. France is the least troublesome; a nearly complete list of charters to 1867 appears in Charles E. Freedeman, *Joint-Stock Enterprise in France, 1807–1867: From Privileged Company to Modern Corporation* (Chapel Hill: University of North Carolina Press, 1979), pp. 145–97, and the charters were published in the *Bulletin des lois*. For the German states, they appear in the published laws of the states. For Britain, I have been unable to locate published charters before 1844; for companies formed under general incorporation laws after 1844 (with limited liability for most lines of business from 1856), the largest collection of their articles of association is in the Public Record Office in London.

74. Viktor Ring, *Das Reichsgesetz betreffend die Kommanditgesellschaften auf Aktien und die Aktiengesellschaften vom 18. Juli 1884* (Berlin: Carl Heymanns Verlag, 1886), p. 293.

75. Richard Passow, *Die wirtschaftliche Bedeutung und Organisation der Aktiengesellschaft* (Jena: Gustav Fischer, 1907), p. 201; Robert Liefmann, *Die Unternehmungsformen* (Stuttgart: Ernst Heinrich Moritz, 1912), p. 71.

76. The sample encompasses fifty-five charters granted in 1845 (5), 1850 (2), 1855 (6), 1860 (10), and 1865 (32); since some 1,643 companies were incorporated in these years, this amounts to a 3.3 percent sample (it will be expanded to 5 percent).

77. Francis Beaufort Palmer, *Company Law: A Practical Handbook for Lawyers and Business Men*, 3rd. edn. (London: Stevens and Sons, 1901), p. 11. The 1844 act applied to England and Ireland; the 1856 and 1862 acts applied to Scotland as well (see sources in Table 2.2). The default voting rights first appeared in the Companies Clauses Consolidation Act, 1845 (8 & 9 Vict. c. 16), which encompassed provisions "usually inserted" in charters; in "Table B" of the 1856 act; and in "Table A" of the 1862 act. The tables spelled out extensive provisions for the management of companies that served as default articles of association for companies with limited liability.

78. Norman Pearson, "Manhood Suffrage on the Principle of Shareholding," *The Nineteenth Century* 82 (December 1883), 1083–4.

79. C. E. H. Chadwyck-Healey, Percy F. Wheeler, and Charles Burney, *A Treatise on the Law and Practice Relating to Joint Stock Companies Under the Acts of 1862–1890*, 3rd. enl. edn. (London: Sweet and Maxwell, 1894), p. 272; Palmer, 11.

80. T. Eustace Smith and Arthur Stiebel, *A Summary of the Law of Companies*, 9th edn. (London: Stevens and Haynes, 1907), p. 70.

81. Francis Beaufort Palmer, *Company Law: A Practical Handbook for Lawyers and Business Men*, 9th edn. (London: Stevens and Sons, 1911), pp. 171, 516.

82. "The Powers and Responsibilities of Directors," 58 *The Merchant's Magazine and Commercial Review* 58 (Jan.–June 1868), 435.

83. "Stockholders – Their Rights and Wrongs," *Hours at Home: A Popular Monthly of Instruction and Recreation*, J. M. Sherwood (ed.), 7 (May–Oct. 1868), 100.

84. Charles F. Adams Jr., "The Government and the Railroad Corporations," *North American Review* 112 (1871), 47.

3

The Utopian Corporation

Kenneth Lipartito

Recent works on the history of the modern economy have emphasized the socially constructed, historically contingent reasons behind the emergence of large-scale corporate enterprise. These works highlight the late nineteenth century as the key moment when the corporation gained ascendancy, while denying that this ascendancy represented the best, most efficient economic outcome. Some authors stress class conflict involving labor, business, and agrarians to explain the corporate construction of America. Others have looked at the discourses of law and politics, locating the corporate impulse in a larger debate about the nature of capitalism in the modern era. Still others emphasize state institutions.[1]

This chapter finds the raw materials of the corporate order in early nineteenth-century debates over social reform. Rather than crediting the rise of the corporation to impersonal changes in markets, technology, and economy, it instead reconnects the corporation to the social controversies that accompanied these changes. In dealing with the implications of an expanded and freer market in the early nineteenth century, a variety of social reformers created institutional mechanisms that would pave the way for the managerial corporation. In unforeseen ways, the architects of reform institutions – ranging from schools, to churches, to utopian communities – propagated the idea that social order lay in bureaucratic means of market control. The business corporation, a highly successful alternative to the atomistic free market, rolled forth on the foundations laid by these earlier debates.

These connections between ideas of social reform and forms of business enterprise were not direct. Rather, they were part of a process by which certain aspects of organization and organizational structure became institutionalized

I wish to thank the following colleagues for their helpful comments and insightful criticisms: Michael Allen, Angel Kwolek-Folland, Steven Mintz, Peter Onuf, Scott Sandage, Rosalind Williams, Mary Yeager, and the contributors to this volume. This work was funded in part by a grant from the National Science Foundation.

in America. What were once flexible, historically specific ideas about how society should be run grew so fixed and permanent that they transcended their origins and hardened into models for other types of organization. Certain formal structures in turn became imbued with deep-seated social values. This process of institutionalization contrasts with traditional, functionalist explanations for the rise of the business corporation. Functionalism points to the problems that institutions solve – large-scale production through administrative coordination. I note that institutions not only solve problems but produce and reproduce meanings.[2]

Institutionalization of bureaucratic forms began in America with debates over moral and religious questions, questions of society and justice and other matters far removed from business. Out of these debates grew a nineteenth-century language of social order keyed to words such as science, efficiency, and reason.[3] That language privileged notions of rational thought and action, in the Weberian sense of exhibiting a clear relationship between the means and ends of behavior. Emphasis on the rational turned social critics and reformers toward structures of social organization that made behavior "legible," or easily read and understood by those at the top of the social hierarchy. Confidence in the power of reason fed a broader faith in human ability to master change, to plan society and economy and reconceive older institutional arrangements and political structures from the ground up.[4] As forms of rational action and hierarchical organization, managerial corporations came to express this same yearning for order based on modernist notions of reason, control, and efficiency.

The cultural values that accompanied the appearance of the business corporation have largely been lost in history, where managerial enterprise is often treated as something new, alien, and thoroughly opposed to principles of social reform and reordering. In what follows, I will trace the intersecting histories of the managerial corporation and debates over social order before they became "disarticulated" at the end of the nineteenth century. Here, we will see how the corporation acquired meanings associated with a certain understanding of organization and the division and coordination of labor.[5] Over time, lines separating religious, political, moral, and economic notions of order became more distinct as the corporation emerged as a full, legitimate institution by the end of the nineteenth century. But, as I will argue, the corporation never completely lost its connections to older values, even those rooted in Romantic and utopian notions of the good society. These values support an important, though often implicit, logic that makes the corporation an enduring institution.

REFORM AND ORGANIZATION

America experienced an intense wave of social reform in the decades leading up to the Civil War. This wave broke in many directions: antislavery, temperance,

Christian revivals, new religious sects, communal living, socialism, Fourierism, San Simonism, feminism. With astonishing speed, reformers – who were largely native-born New England Protestants – built asylums, hospitals, prisons, and schools to incarcerate, classify, and reform wayward, incapacitated, or dependent populations. Others branched off into experiments with new types of communities. What is noticeable is the role that formal organizations played in all these efforts.

To understand the connections between reform, organization, and finally the corporation, we have to begin by noting certain features of this reform movement. Historians often interpret antebellum reform as a reply to the ills of modern life, even as anti-modern. There certainly is evidence for this position. Rooted in reactions to the emergence of a more fully free and open market, some reform efforts seemed backward-looking and nostalgic.[6] For example, American utopians created experimental communities that practiced farming without technology or that returned to supposedly biblical notions of the good life, as in the case of the Shakers, the Amish, and the Hutterites. But some reformers took a different approach, even as they reacted against the free market. They looked forward, and sought ways to reconcile market freedom with moral frameworks of order inherited from republicanism through "modern" methods, particularly methods of organization. Through organization, they did not reject the market, but rather sought to rationalize it.[7]

These modernist reformers, often called "consolidators," understood well the dangers and opportunities present in a growing market economy.[8] Observing England, the world's first capitalist society, they noted the poverty and corruption bred by marketplace competition and unchecked individualism, as vividly portrayed in the works of Dickens and other social critics.[9] One way to avoid these dangers, they believed, was through new institutions to contain self-interest and mold character in an industrial age. Following an idealistic bent with strong roots in evangelical Christianity, consolidators sought moral order in the organization of human behavior. Accordingly, they erected formal structures designed to produce self-controlled actors capable of participation in market society.

These reformers had what Weber would have called an "elective affinity" with rationalizing, systematizing, and, especially, bureaucratizing impulses. Antebellum Americans built a great variety of bureaucratic institutions, from schools, colleges, and churches, to hospitals and insane asylums. All were corporate bodies, granted charters by the state for public purposes. All were designed to check, channel, and redirect self-interest. The business corporation, too, was a chartered body. By the middle of the nineteenth century, it would emerge as the most powerful of the new character-shaping institutions, but it would follow in the wake of others created for much different functions.

Before we pursue this train of thought further, let me point out that control of individual behavior through organization is what defines the modern managerial corporation. More than legal entities, corporations are bureaucratic tools for planning under capitalism. As such, they redirect individual behavior toward some larger collective purpose. Here, it is crucial to distinguish between structures and effects. Although corporations may be able to reduce competition and exert power, as many nineteenth century Americans feared, corporations themselves are devices for controlling and directing self-interest. They operate by using a functional division of specialized labor and reward and incentive systems to orchestrate individual behavior.[10] Through the "visible hand" of management, markets for labor, materials, and final products are internally coordinated by administrative means. Reformers who created institutions with the purpose of containing selfishness and perfecting individualism fit this same managerial pattern. A fundamental idea – that a market controlled was a market made virtuous – forges an unlikely bond between antebellum builders of reform institutions and later corporate tycoons such as John D. Rockefeller.[11] Both were dedicated to rationalizing market behavior and inculcating new values of collective action.

The first attempts to control individualism in the competitive marketplace appeared in the 1820s, as manufacturing began to move inside factories. One of the most striking examples comes, not surprisingly, from New England, the seat of social reform and the birthplace of American industrial capitalism. There, a group of successful entrepreneurs, the Boston Associates, shifted their capital out of trade and international commerce and into the new textile industry of the region. At Lowell, Massachusetts, they built textile mills and created a new type of social institution – the vertically integrated, large-scale factory. They used planning and new methods of workforce control to produce textiles in large quantity. The entire landscape of Lowell was designed for this purpose, from the ground up. The Lowell system marked the beginnings of a new type of production process. But the meaning of this business innovation is more complicated than has been appreciated. In fact, it was as important for the social vision it contained as for the textiles it produced.

One clue to the social vision embedded in Lowell can be found in the Associates' motives. Successful merchants, they made their move out of international trade as much to stabilize as to increase their capital. These entrepreneurs were not seeking the thrill of swashbuckling competition, but rather respite from the bellicose world of international trade.[12] At home, they could use their capital to refashion the New England environment to account for most of the major business variables. Competition and possessive individualism were fine, they understood, but to create a good society (and a stable market), these brute forces had to be harnessed to larger social goals. The institutions of Lowell – most famously its provisions for female workers – were designed to deal with the depredations of industrialism directly, at the factory itself. In founding the industrial community of Lowell, the Boston Associates were seeking an ordered marketplace. In building the factory, they were creating a machine not only for profit, but also for shaping virtuous character.[13]

Recent research on the textile industry indicates that Lowell was actually the exception rather than the rule. In Philadelphia and in England, specialization, external economies, and networks, rather than internalization and bureaucratic hierarchies, produced profits for textile makers. Indeed, it now seems clear that Lowell was not necessary to generate efficiency in production. If this is so, then it begs the question – what mattered in Lowell? I would argue that the Lowell system did not rest on functional efficiency, but rather arose on a vision of social order expressed in planning and in a factory system of labor. Many other antebellum Americans would gravitate to these sorts of tools for rationalizing market behavior and for improving the marketplace, whether they were required to do so by economic imperatives or not.[14]

Perhaps the strongest examples can be found in institutions that at first glance seem as far from the marketplace and the workaday world of business as possible – utopian societies. Utopian societies have long been recognized as a major part of the reform culture and religious revivalism that marked nineteenth-century America. Generally, they have been seen as one of those redoubts of protest against the coming order of cities, industry, and soulless bureaucratic organization. The very adjective utopian suggests that they were attempts to construct idealized societies superior to the coarse new realities of competitive life. Some authors have likened them to the communes that appeared in America in the 1960s, rejections of mechanistic technology and alienated labor, refuges from markets and commerce.[15]

I have no doubt that utopias were pointed toward reform, but it is less clear that this reform yearned for some pre-modern, communal life. A closer look at structure and organization in utopian societies shows that they were not so far removed from the modern world as we (or their members) might think. Behind every utopian project, Marshall Berman has noted, lurks a Faustian impulse to reorder human relationships and a restless, projecting modern spirit.[16] Antebellum utopians drew on religious language, but they projected visions of human perfectibility and human malleability that embraced wholesale reorganization of society and its members.

For all their starry eyed optimism, utopian societies had very pragmatic and instrumental goals. Perfectionist brotherhoods aimed not at self-sufficiency, but rather at an ideal economy, a blueprint for the future.[17] While promoting love, harmony, and brotherhood, they worked at the more mundane tasks of improving productivity and increasing labor efficiency. The material base of this New Eden involved new methods of production, coordination, and planning. With these tools, mankind could surpass the seemingly chaotic relations of the market and competition. Properly organized, people would lose their petty jealousies and turn their self-interest toward the common good. The outcomes would be both an improved mankind and a more fruitful society. The methods were surprisingly similar to those of the modern managerial corporation.

Particularly important to the utopian aspiration were efforts to rein in destructive competitive impulses and naked individualism. This did not mean a backward glance at some earlier "organic" society, however. The communities wanted to perfect individuality, not eliminate it. To do so, they needed modern tools of organization. Many New World utopias organized themselves as joint stock companies.[18] In this fashion, they "incorporated" their members, who laid out funds or contributed labor as their down payment on membership.[19] Individual profit seeking and purely self-interested behavior had to be discouraged, as it is in modern corporations. But communities did not necessarily abolish profits. They shared them, and they channeled the energy of potentially destructive individualism to the common good. Because each member of the community partook of the rewards, it was possible to divide and coordinate labor without exploitation or coercion, in theory at least. Everyone was quite literally invested in the community. Emerson once expressed his contempt for market society by likening it to "mere joint stock company." Some reformers, however, were determined to give the joint stock company a transcendent meaning, in the spirit of John Quincy Adams' insight that they were "the truly republican institution."[20]

It is significant that utopian experiments often turned to the joint stock company form, as opposed to other options. When the communitarian movement was in full swing, America had already begun to pass easy general incorporation laws. Perfectionist communities generally did not incorporate, but instead relied on the older joint stock company provisions of common law.[21] The joint stock form offered many of the advantages of incorporation without any of the excess baggage. Corporations were artificial persons created by the state, often linked with public franchises and state monopolies. Stock companies, on the other hand, were purely private, voluntary contractual arrangements. The only advantage of incorporation, limited liability, was still not common in the early nineteenth century. In any case, common law was flexible enough to permit limited liability for joint stock companies as well. But in one key respect, corporations and stock companies were similar. Both collectivized ownership of capital, making the company and its designated managers the fiduciaries and decision-makers.[22]

Utopians thus chose an organizational form that removed the individual member from the levers of power. In this, they turned away from the far more common and traditional methods of carrying on business: partnerships and family firms. Unlike partnerships, stock companies possess agency authority, that is, the power to act in the name of the group. Like the full-fledged corporation, the joint stock company is a managerial device. In both the stock company and the corporation, one buys a stake in an enterprise, a claim that can be sold without affecting the capital, managerial structure, or existence of the organization.

Partnerships were at a disadvantage in this regard, unless they were limited partnerships, a close cousin to the corporation and the joint stock company. Because partners are "mutual" agents, able to take on debt and sign contracts that bind the other partners, they require a certain level of trust and familiarity. One does not admit new partners unless one is confident about their behavior. In corporations and joint stock companies, such concerns are eliminated. Only those delegated to act in the name of the collective have binding agency power. Decisions are made by a collective process (although not necessarily a democratic one) and individuals lose the power to act in the name of property they contribute.[23]

Ironically, then, the utopian "brotherhoods and communities" did not rely on partnerships of trust, but rather on organizational forms needed for management. As joint stock companies, they could issue shares and take on new members without worrying about character or background. They could bring in complete strangers and rest assured that they would not lose control of their society. It mattered little who joined, since in no case did individuals have the power to act in the name of the whole or use their ownership rights independently of the organization. Utopian societies found, in the joint stock company form, agency power to act as a collective and to restrict individual behavior to what the group as a whole decreed.

Important differences, of course, remained between utopian joint stock companies and managerial corporations. Utopian societies did not aim to become "merely" business enterprises, but rather were experimenting with forms of collective action that would later become part of the business world. As joint stock companies, they operated under a single name, but acted as trustees for their members, who continued to hold title to the property they no longer managed. In corporations, title was vested in the corporate body. In addition, in joint stock companies, ownership of property did not confer membership in the organization, as it did in true corporations. One could buy and transfer ownership, but ownership did not in and of itself bring membership to the group.

Even these differences, however, were more muted in the early nineteenth century, when corporations were small and closely held and voting was often done on the basis of one vote per member, rather than one vote per share of stock as now. And, although utopian joint stock companies generally sought familiarity and tight and lasting relations among members, in some cases they permitted members to withdraw by selling their shares. In other cases, communes admitted outsiders as "owners," with none of the rights and privileges of the communal brotherhood, or employed nonmembers as workers.

In choosing a medium that permitted collective action, utopian societies had found a means of reconciling individualism with the group. They had done so, however, though a legal and administrative structure. We see the same thing when we look inside the communes, at their organizational procedures. The most elaborate of these were established by John Humphrey Noyes in Oneida. Members of this New York experiment ceded their property to the group, although an account was kept and those who left received their investment back, without interest. Oneida's survival, Noyes understood, depended on making this investment pay.[24] The community began to prosper by innovation, producing a new type of high quality animal trap. By 1875 Oneida was manufacturing 300,000 traps per year.[25] Its products were successful because of low costs, high volume output, and good national marketing efforts. Despite radical commitments to social equality, Oneida soon had its labor hierarchies. They were generally based on religious criteria or the charismatic qualities of the leaders. But in seeking order and efficiency, Oneida, like other utopian societies, also turned increasingly to specialization and functional division of labor.[26]

Noyes established functional departments, forty-eight in all, appointed foremen of production, held weekly meetings, and instituted a series of committees to coordinate department policies. Heads of departments sent accounts to bookkeepers each month. A so-called "Business Board" planned strategy at weekly meetings. The meetings consisted of presentations from the community's twenty-one standing committees plus a number of special committees. Annually the Board held a long-term planning session, mapping out strategy for the coming year and reviewing estimates from the industrial departments for capital expenditures. Economically, this beloved community hummed like a well-oiled machine.[27]

As Krishan Kumar notes, "in reading accounts of [Oneida's] technical inventiveness, its business acumen and its social and scientific experimentation, it is sometimes difficult to remember that it was a religious community at all."[28] Still, Oneida remained dedicated to promoting Noyes' unique brand of Christian perfectionism. Its economy served this larger purpose. Other reformers, however, made issues of labor, market, and economy central to their concerns. They too, however, promoted economic reform through new organizational methods.

Robert Dale Owen and his American supporters, for example, sought to protect the weakest members of the working class through new methods of production and factory organization. Their goal was not to go back to a pre-capitalist world. Instead, they wanted to go forward into an even more productive, rational one that would culminate in a new harmony of class interests. At his New Harmony and other industrial communes, Owen tried to abolish the inefficiencies of the competitive economy. In its place he offered new sorts of rational enterprise based on large-scale production.[29]

To Owen, socialist utopia required high levels of planning and control. Believing humans to be products of their environment, he argued that greater social efficiency flowed, not just from the mechanics of production, but also from the organization of people. To these ends, he created an industrial village of mills and living quarters and strove for a more humane form of production. But the factory was also a system for improving human character. Workers were studied and mapped precisely to motivate higher levels of effort. Next to each hung a "silent monitor," a three-sided wood block that revealed by the face on display how well the worker was performing. The record of performance was written in a "book of character." Market society heightened the sense of seeing and being seen, as one's character depended on the opinion of others. Owen harnessed the power of surveillance to the cause of character building in a new institutional setting.[30] These invasive methods anticipated those used later by Frederick Taylor and Henry Ford.

Noyes and Owen were not alone in this fascination with the rational organization of people and their surroundings. It can be found even in "traditional" communities of antebellum America. Shakers planned their lives in the utmost detail, so that not a second of time or an ounce of human energy was wasted. They structured domestic space for maximum cleaning efficiency, and devised ingenious methods of storing and sorting articles in purpose-built bins, cupboards, cabinets, and pegs. Shaker agriculture operated as a "closed system" designed to waste no inputs. Efficiencies such as the "round barn" of radiating stalls allowed a single worker to feed cows with a minimum of motion – a sort of Panopticon for livestock.[31] The notable Shaker style of furniture anticipated the bare, stripped down functionalism of industrial design. Skill, function, and efficiency reigned supreme over ornament, fancy, and waste in this community.[32]

Perfectionist communities generally manifested a strong preference for human artifice over untamed nature. New settlements built on the edge of the frontier quickly marked the land with the strong hand of design. Noyes laid out Oneida in quadrangles. Fourierists planned elaborate, symmetrical "phalansteries." Owen designed the living quarters of his workers in parallelograms. Other societies used grids or hexagons. Shakers imposed a severe "right angle" discipline on members, requiring bread and meat to be cut into squares, and avoiding movement along diagonals. In the mind of the reformer, straightening the chaos of nature by geometric pattern was a sure sign of civilization.[33]

Should this commitment to rational planning and the organization of people be called socialist? Or was it corporatist? In fact, the distinction is hard to make. Socialists sought to improve on the market by limiting individualism and self-interest in favor of the commonwealth. Modern corporations likewise seek to improve on the market, although they favor internalizing market functions and coordinating them through administrative structures. Both the communal order and the corporation had to overcome destructive self-interest and harness individual talents to the needs of the whole if they were to survive. Both discovered means of social control to get around the "free rider" problem, or the shirking of communal labor.[34]

Although utopian communes did not embrace the full range and force of legal–rational structures of bureaucracy, their commitment to management, organization, and productive efficiency made them halfway houses in the movement toward modern managerial organization. Well before most institutions, they were creating organizational charts and strategies for action and sorting people by skill and function. Like Weber's Protestants, utopians used religion and reform to set the stage for a secular economic revolution.

INCORPORATING BODY AND BEHAVIOR

Utopian communities created structures and practices of rational management and bureaucracy, but the values and spirit that accompanied these structures also can be found elsewhere. Particularly in matters related to the body, antebellum Americans put forth an astounding variety of methods to bend human beings to the dictates of rationality, methods that proved popular with middle-class Americans who believed the way to success lay with self-denial and self-discipline.[35] Such values were bottom-up efforts to regulate behavior, complements to the top-down methods of surveillance imposed by the likes of Robert Owen or the organizational innovations of Noyes. In all cases, the goal was to construct subjects capable of handling the dangerous but exhilarating freedom of market society.

The most extreme programs of self-discipline were to be found in perfectionist notions of human sexuality. Seemingly opposite tendencies of sexual liberation and sexual repression existed side-by-side in nineteenth-century America. Yet the elimination of sexuality from human affairs advocated by the Shakers and the "free love" practices of John Humphrey Noyes at Oneida shared the common goal of controlling passion through an exercise of will. To this end, Noyes advocated the radical new institution of complex marriage. Just as the community offered a cooperative alternative to traditional notions of private property, so did complex marriage provide a collective alternative to possessive, individualistic sexuality. The true community, Noyes argued, could not survive the jealousies and conflicts of sexual cupidity. As with all else, individualism had to be turned to the good of the whole. Noyes' liberation of the individual from sexual greed and jealousy, however, required tremendous self-control. Partners met through intermediaries, and all relationships were recorded in an account book. Sex itself required the practice of "male continence," or suppressed orgasm. In the end, Oneida's economy of free love was no less demanding than Shaker celibacy.[36]

Noyes and the Shakers focused on the sexual organs as the root of jealous passion, but other reformers aimed a bit higher, at the stomach. Americans had been hard drinkers for some two centuries. Then, suddenly in the 1830s, drink became identified with a whole host of social ills. It lurked behind domestic violence, poverty, licentiousness, and bankruptcy, all of which could be eliminated, so it seemed, by temperance and sobriety. No one enslaved by drink could be self-controlled, making the suppression of alcohol a prerequisite to human freedom.[37]

Food and drink were joined in the revealing dietary ethic of Sylvester Graham. Graham seemed determined to enact the principles of bodily economy first laid down by Benjamin Franklin, who admonished those seeking success to "bring the appetite in subjection to reason." Graham took literally Franklin's advice: "eat for necessity not pleasure."[38] His austere diet of unbolted wheat flour was meant to counteract the digestive consequences of America's vast intake of salt pork, white bread, and corn liquor. But Graham did not stop there. While teaching Americans how to regulate their bowels, he tried to uproot the pleasure principle in just about every bodily habit, from adolescent masturbation to adult drunkenness.[39]

Self-control was not necessarily connected to economics, but it was not hard to make the link. Drinking wasted capital as well as corporeal resources. Graham, who saw the body as a closed system, likened management of bodily essences to saving and investment, so that poverty was a consequence of unrestrained passion.[40] Self-made men were self-controlled and self-possessed.

Their habits were temperate, abstemious, and well regulated. Their passions were under control. Other historians have posited a somewhat different connection between reform and the emergence of market society – labor discipline. According to this literature, temperance, abstinence, and religion were forms of social control aimed at getting the working class ready for factory life. Certainly, as Robert Owen shows, reform could mean social control. But bodily discipline and rationalized behavior were as much about self-control as social control. The Boston Associates in Lowell and Owen in New Harmony were merely applying the same habits to workers that they were applying with even greater vigor to themselves. Scientific methods of bodily self-control, evangelical religion, transcendental philosophies of the sensitive soul, and the cult of domesticity all were called upon to uplift and civilize, smooth and tame the rough individualism and dangerous passions that subverted rational behavior. The object was to create people capable of freely interacting and exchanging while acting predictably and morally – a free market that was still virtuous and ordered.

Most importantly, to reformers self-control meant not only an exercise of will, but the institutionalization of such practice in new structures. The connections between reformist values of temperance and self-control and bureaucratic methods become clear in the biography of several key antebellum figures. There is perhaps no better example than Lewis Tappan.[41] A fervent evangelical and abolitionist leader, Tappan was a reformer with a talent for organization.[42] To the cause of antislavery, for example, he lent his considerable skills in ordering, managing, and administering. Tappan also sought to reform the market, notably the market for capital. He did so by institutionalizing moral values in a new sort of bureaucratic business structure.[43]

In 1841 Tappan founded the Mercantile Agency, which lives on today as Dun & Bradstreet.[44] The Mercantile Agency was the original credit-reporting bureau. It gathered information about businesses and businesspeople from thousands of agents across the country, collected and collated it in New York, and created reports for bankers, wholesalers, and investors to use when lending money and extending credit. Through formal organization, the Agency took highly personalized and idiosyncratic dispatches (in essence gossip) from field agents and transformed them into seemingly objective information. In a market world where appearance was deceptive, control and coordination of information was designed to assure integrity.[45] The Agency embraced the notion that order and rationality meant "legibility." It made it possible for others to read the messages encoded in individual personality and behavior. Once read, this information served as the basis for "sercuritization," or the offering of capital on what before would have been insecure property. Of course, legibility recapitulated the content of nineteenth-century morality. But, by organizing the content of character in this readable form, Tappan harnessed Protestant rectitude to the extension of credit. By bureaucratic means Tappan connected character and capitalism. In "check[ing] knavery and purify[ing] the mercantile air," he used organization and surveillance to make individual traits the guideposts of a rationalized market.[46]

The remaking of society by bureaucratic means certainly did not enjoy universal acceptance in antebellum America. Consolidators like Tappan, after all, were promoting abstract systems that penetrated local communities and cut across the decentralized antebellum economy. The Mercantile Agency was a national organization, detached from geography and parochial concerns. So, too, in a different way were the utopian societies. Although they existed in place, they were as utopias "nowhere," and hence unlimited by traditional bounds of time and space. This same detachment from the landscape would mark national corporations and the systems of technology, transportation, and distribution they commanded.[47] Such systems forced localities to adhere to standards of behavior set by non-local actors.

The result was conflict. Communities resented intrusion of increasingly trans-local railroads. They resented the power wielded by New York financial institutions. In like manner, antebellum Southerners and anti-abolitionists resented the dissemination of alien ideas and controversial literature by outside agitators. Local schools disliked Horace Mann's centralization of the school curriculum. Still, whatever the conflicts, actors often converged in ways that supported private, voluntary, and bureaucratic solutions to what were regarded as the ills of market society.

FROM VOLUNTARY ASSOCIATION TO CORPORATION

We can see this unwitting convergence in one institution above all – the business corporation itself. As a legal entity, the corporation had a surprisingly early presence in the USA. Corporations existed in significant numbers in the late eighteenth and early nineteenth centuries, in contrast to France, Germany, and even England. Most were not business enterprises. One-half to two-thirds of early corporate charters went to start towns. Many others were issued for religious, charitable, or educational missions. Even those for business initially followed the traditional pattern of promoting public works such as bridges, roads, and canals.[48] Still, by 1800 there were 350 business corporations in the United States. The nation's securities markets had grown adept at handling corporate stock. Indeed, in the early nineteenth century America had a higher percentage of its financial assets in corporate stock than any other nation.[49]

This openness to the corporation was no simple legal quirk. As Pauline Maier notes, "the American corporation faithfully reflected the society that gave it form . . . "[50] Corporations came to be seen as little republics in the tradition of voluntary self-rule. This included private corporations of all types, from towns to businesses. By incorporating banks, mills, or other enterprises, businessmen were seen as creating private, voluntary associations for promoting the public good, in the same fashion as the town or benevolent society.[51] Perhaps most importantly, incorporation in America was by the early nineteenth century becoming an organizational matter. In the corporation, traditional hierarchies rooted in clan, family, or kinship were replaced with formal structures of authority based on law, expertise, and trusteeship for the common good.[52]

In the 1830s, this organizational bent took on greater significance. Incorporation had, in legal thought and by historical precedent, generally implied a monopoly of some sort. Those Americans who believed freedom and competition promoted the social good severely criticized corporations on these grounds. But critics were far less worried about the organizational qualities of corporate business. They generally accepted arguments for corporations based on the rights of individuals to form associations for collective management of their interests.[53] Their only stipulation was that everyone should have access to this opportunity. Out went special legislative grants to incorporate and in came easy general incorporation laws.[54] As the corporation was "democratized," however, it gained even stronger tools of organization. This was a crucial, if unforeseen, outcome.

As corporate status became easier to obtain, Jacksonian jurists began legitimizing the corporation as just another type of private enterprise. They created a body of doctrine that Herbert Hovenkamp has termed the "classical" conception of the corporation.[55] Unlike special purpose corporations intended to carry out state-mandated functions, classical corporations were mere shells for private contracts between citizens. Indeed, the veils were so thin that jurists began to look right through them to the stockholders they cloaked. The result was to invest corporations with the rights and privileges of those veiled persons, even while stripping corporations of vested rights and special privileges from the state. As in essence "persons," corporations now had certain rights of property that no state could abrogate. The law placed fewer and fewer restrictions on internal management. Corporations, as Colleen Dunlavy demonstrates in this volume, moved from relatively "democratic" governance of one vote per member to "plutocratic" structures in which owners' votes were based on the shares they owned.[56]

Ironically, the legal focus on individuals was helping to create the conditions for strong organizations for collective action. Judges accepted the corporation as merely a convenient arrangement by private parties. But if the corporation was the stockholder's fictional person, then it and not the stockholders had the power to act, to own property, to sue and be sued, and to defend constitutional rights.[57] Except in certain situations, stockholders lost the right to act independently of the corporation itself. In protecting and extending individual rights of property and association, antebellum Americans had created strong, independent, centralized management bodies.[58] Like the joint stock companies that preceded them, corporations in America became excellent devices for collective action.[59]

From the utopian societies to business corporations, voluntary associations began to assume bureaucratic form in antebellum America. They became managerial organizations capable of coordinating a specialized division of labor.

At this point, the development of the managerial ethos owed little if anything to the functional needs of large-scale systems or vertically integrated manufacturing. Rather, it remained rooted in traditions of individualism and equality. Utopian perfectionists, like their seeming opposites, free-market supporting judges, both believed that by endorsing voluntary association, they were creating the means for individual, democratic action. Yet to make individualism more perfect, these same Americans also ended up encouraging the emergence of rational administrative and bureaucratic structures. Just as reformers and perfectionists experimented with new, perhaps better, forms of social organization, so too were businesses allowed to experiment with new economic forms and structures. The assumption in both cases was that voluntaristic experiments in organization would foster the public good.[60]

UTOPIAN TRADITIONS AND MANAGERIAL CORPORATIONS

The modern managerial corporation took its familiar shape after the Civil War. Historians have traditionally seen this as part of a sharp break with the past, a wholesale, if perhaps unwholesome, change explicable only by revolutions in technology and markets.[61] As I have suggested, however, strong distinctions between antebellum and postbellum organizational cultures do not hold up when we consider the bureaucratic values and structures to be found in earlier reform movements. Rather than seeing the modern corporation as a vast alien force darkening a pristine landscape, I have suggested that its origins are to be found in the debates and conflicts over market society that existed a generation earlier.

By refusing to make a sharp break with the past, we catch the continued relevance of these earlier traditions of reform and utopia in business in the later nineteenth century and beyond. In the nooks and crannies of the corporate economy, moral and spiritual concerns about order, association, and community persisted. Many utopian societies, for example, survived the Civil War, and fresh ones were started in the Gilded Age.[62] Communities continued to experiment with various organizational schemes and structures. More adopted the joint stock company form. Many that had been founded as beloved communities became profit-making enterprises, producing goods ranging from silverware to refrigerators.

The case of Oneida again is revealing. Pierpont Burt Noyes, a child of John Humphrey born out of the community's eugenics experiments, headed the Oneida Community, Ltd. from 1894 through 1950. He mixed his father's religious reform spirit with a driving commitment to commercial success, leading H. G. Wells to characterize him as a business "romantic."[63] Under the second Noyes, Oneida flourished, more and more as a profit-making enterprise, but with some intriguing links to the past. Noyes' management team, many like him "stirpiculture," or eugenics children, emphasized cooperation and team-work, the watchwords of early twentieth-century business management. He inspired fervent loyalty among the company's many field agents by holding meetings that mixed business and pleasure, strategizing and socializing. For workers, Oneida instituted an early version of what would later be called "welfare capitalism" in its factories. It provided insurance and profit sharing, and organized social activities. In many ways, P. B. Noyes was the most modern of managers, engaging in practices that would not become common until after the First World War. Yet the source of his ideas went back to an utopian experiment in social reform.[64]

Connections between reform and business strategy joined the emerging class of corporate executives to their antebellum parents. In 1876 John Harvey Kellogg assumed management of the Western Health Reform Institute at Battle Creek, Michigan. Founded by Ellen White at an old stop on the Underground Railroad, the "San" propagated Sylvester Graham's ideas for sound bodies. Kellogg's parents, devout Seventh-Day Adventists, had been members. Under their son, the San grew into perhaps the most influential dietary institution in America. It also hatched a new industry, breakfast cereals. With his brother Will, John Harvey formed a company to market the Graham diet and its products, most famously Kellogg's Cornflakes. Their efforts were a resounding success. In 1906, they incorporated the Battle Creek Toasted Corn Flake Company, destined to become a major national food processor. John and Will Kellogg's parents had participated in every major antebellum crusade: revivalism, temperance, antislavery, hydrotherapy, vegetarianism, the Graham diet. Their children invested this reform zeal in the new business of breakfast cereals, products that made palpable (if not always palatable) the antebellum ideal of the balanced body.[65]

It was no coincidence too that these food reformers turned business executives sold brand name products. Producers in many industries were coming to see how branding provided an element of protection from the market. Commodities in bins and barrels were replaced with packages on store shelves at the end of the nineteenth century.[66] One important result was higher profits, to be sure. But such market power could be placed in the service of social reform. Successful marketing not only sold goods, it also helped to regulate and control consumption, pointing it to loftier aims. The brand name separated the genuine from the artificial, the healthful from the suspect. Kellogg marketed his products as part of the Battle Creek health system, advertised in San books and pamphlets and in church publications. The original agents were Seventh-Day Adventist colporteurs. Later, the Kellogg brothers added the family name to their cereals to distinguish the true stuff of the real Battle Creek sanitarium from the hundreds of imitators soon on the market.

It was a principle well understood by antebellum reformers. A moral market required human intervention; it could not survive on unchecked competition. By asserting control over the meaning and message of consumption, branding was one means of market regulation.[67] It was also part of the process whereby bureaucratic structures replaced, controlled, or contained the otherwise unfet-tered and unplanned workings of the free market.

The architects of the corporate economy were in blood as well as spirit the children of the antebellum reformers. Mobility studies have consistently shown that the upper and middle management, even the executives of nineteenth-century corporations, were not born wealthy. In discrediting rags to riches myths, historians have overlooked the modest origins and middling backgrounds of "robber barons." Although privileged by education, race, and ethnicity, they were neither stereotypical plutocrats nor a tiny, insular elite.[68] They were in fact the children of the white, northern Protestant establishment that had led abolition-ist crusades, built schools and asylums, carried on the word of God through national bible and tract societies, and fought a war against slavery.[69]

Peter Dobkin Hall has explored the biography of some of these individuals, such as banker Jay Cooke, business journalist Henry Varnum Poor, and entre-preneur Henry Noble Day. Like the consolidators of antebellum America, they were successful, native born, New England Protestants.[70] Typical of this group was the popular theologian of the Gilded Age, Henry Ward Beecher. Son of evangelical Protestant Lyman Beecher, Henry Beecher outlined a guiding philo-sophy of social organization that accorded with the organizational changes taking place in American business.

Beecher embraced the evolutionary notion that society advanced by moving up the ladder from simple associations of individuals to complex interdepend-encies.[71] This functional division of labor, Beecher argued, was a law of history. The only way individuals could find contentment was by accepting their best, most proper function. This was a neat justification for large-scale organization, which in its division of labor could be seen as embodying the hierarchy needed in a complex and interdependent society. It also provided a historical logic to support Beecher's belief that human beings could be recon-ciled to work within large formal structures.[72]

Beecher's ideas were deeply rooted in the traditions of social reform that had motivated organizational experimentation a generation earlier. Functionalism, or the assignment of individuals to their highest and most proper duties in the social division of labor, can be found in the writings of Whig political economist Henry Carey, Fourierist Albert Brisbane, and feminist Catherine Beecher.[73] Like Beecher, they too saw functionalism as a way of instituting voluntary authority, with individuals freely submitting themselves to organizational structures as the rational way to make full use of human potential. At Brook Farm, George Ripley believed he could "guarantee the highest mental freedom, by providing all with labor, adapted to their tastes and talents, and securing to them the fruits of their industry."[74] The result, he and other utopians hoped, would be an "organic" community. But like the postbellum corporate order, this community depended on a perceived rational division of labor.

The logic of functionalism also was the logic of the machine, and both ante-bellum and postbellum thinkers saw in technology a powerful model for social order. Rather than portending soulless conformity, the machine seemed a vision of frictionless social relations based on voluntary acceptance of nature's laws. Whigs favored technology for enhancing human capabilities and smoothing over rudeness into civilized life. "The sooner we have railroads and telegraphs spinning into the wilderness," declared William Seward, "the more certain it is that light, good manners and Christian refinement will become universally diffused."[75] Technology seemed to fit the perfectionist and reformer search for some self-regulating system that compelled order and virtue without coercion. As an artifact of the laws of nature, the machine was beyond human frailty.[76]

These traditions stressing systems of technology and a functional order would find their strongest postbellum expression in the work of Edward Bellamy. In his wildly popular novel, *Looking Backward*, Bellamy outlined a vision of order consistent with the shape and structure of management and division of labor being enacted in America's first industrial corporations.[77] In Bellamy's utopia, society's most pressing problems were solved, almost miraculously, by machines hardly visible to the population (or reader). Human innovations made the earth fruitful and abundant – so abundant, in fact, that social conflict ceased. It was a virtuoso performance.

It was not, however, the machine in and of itself that made Bellamy so sure of progress. He traced his vision back to Brook Farm and other communitarian societies, seeing in them the centralizing "spirit" he sought.[78] Like his contemporary Beecher, Bellamy believed that meticulous organization was crucial, organization that divided labor and recombined it in conflict-free, functional ways. Through new organization of people and society it was possible, Bellamy believed, to achieve a peaceful "inward freedom" that "reconciles us to outward constraint and tyranny."[79] Once again, organization would square individualism with community. Through large-scale operations and frictionless efficiency, "mechanical force" produced a "vast economy of labor resulting from the perfect interworking with the rest of every wheel and every hand."[80] In the machines and in the methods that controlled machines seemed to be the real, physical embodiment of the true community.

Like the antebellum utopias, Bellamy's functional economy fits neatly in neither the socialist nor the capitalist camp. It abolished truck and barter, the deceptions of the hard sell, and the anxiety of exchange. But it did not eliminate the market. Instead, it ordered and rationalized market exchange through devices that today look suspiciously corporate: credit cards, point-of-sale inventory systems, giant warehouses, and retail centers whose covered colonnades suggest shopping malls. The economy Bellamy imagined was completely "socialized" yet "so logical in its principles and direct and simple in its working, that it all but runs itself." Adam Smith's self-regulating market had been reborn as a self-administering bureaucracy.[81]

If this brave new world seems a bit frightening to us today it is only because Bellamy carried to logical conclusion the idea of order through the rational allocation of human beings to their most efficient uses. He left little room for either spontaneous human interaction or politics. Instead, Bellamy offered the image of public life as a well-structured system, a conceit to be found in utopian schemes ranging from Fourierist phalanxes of the 1840s to urban planning today. In Bellamy's imagined world, citizens coursed streets and promenades like water flowing through pipes or electricity traversing power lines. The population suffered neither conflict nor, for that matter, much passion in their daily dealings, in sharp contrast to the "festering mass of human wretchedness" that nauseated the book's protagonist, Julian West, when he returned to nineteenth-century Boston.[82] Like antebellum reformers, Bellamy saw basic humanity as inefficient and wasteful, and was happy to dispose of corporeal needs such as eating as cleanly and quickly as possible.

CONCLUSION

Utopian faith in plan and design as the way to reconcile freedom with order accompanied the rise of the corporation, and indeed antedated it. Reacting to (and against) the free market, reformers carried out the organizational experiments that eventually led both legally and administratively to the construction of the managerial corporation. By merging technological ingenuity with rational bureaucratic structure, the modern corporation positioned itself at the confluence of several very powerful streams of social imagination. Corporate managers seemed to be putting into practice long-held beliefs that society would operate best with functional structures and technological marvels, such as the systems of transportation and communications long favored by pro-development consolidators. The corporation also carried forward the impulse to sculpt ordered social relations from the raw freedom and individuality found in the creative, but distressingly competitive, market.

Within the microcosm of the corporation and the macrocosm of the corporate economy was the tamed capitalist marketplace reformers had so long sought.[83] In America in particular the tendency to turn to the large scale, private corporation reflects enthusiasm for voluntary institutions unencumbered by tradition that can impose human will on nature and check the potential for social anarchy. Such institutions were meant to find freedom and democracy in a hierarchical bureaucracy. They were to liberate by rationalizing and systematizing. It was a project that only true utopians could have imagined.[84]

NOTES

1. Gerald Berk in this volume. See also Philip Scranton, *Endless Novelty: Specialty Production and American Industrialization, 1865–1925* (Princeton, 1997); Michael J. Piore and Charles F. Sabel, *The Second Industrial Divide: Possibilities for Prosperity.* (New York, 1984); Charles F. Sabel and Jonathan Zeitlin (eds.), *World of Possibilities: Flexibility and Mass Production in Western Industrialization* (Cambridge, 1996).

For a critical view of corporate power, see William Roy, *Socializing Capital: The Rise of the Large Industrial Corporation in America* (Princeton, 1997); Martin J. Sklar, *The Corporate Reconstruction of American Capitalism, 1890–1916: The Market, the Law, and Politics* (Cambridge, 1988).

2. Mary Douglas, *How Institutions Think* (Syracuse, NY, 1986). Other important works are Anthony Giddiness, *The Constitution of Society: Outline of a Theory of Structuration* (Berkeley, 1984); Paul DiMaggio and Walter Powell, *The New Institutionalism in Organizational Analysis* (Chicago, 1991). See also Neil J. Smelser and Richard Swedberg (eds.), *The Handbook of Economic Sociology* (Princeton, 1994).

3. By corporation I refer not just to a legal form, but to all private business organizations, legally corporate or not, that separated ownership from management and used professionally trained managers, a functional division of labor, and bureaucratic systems of control predicated on rational, cost-benefit type analysis to internalize economic functions previously carried out in the marketplace.

4. Although such values suggest stultifying formal order, it is important to remember the nineteenth century's countervailing celebration of liberation and experimentation. Reason had its Romantic and even utopian side, expressed in a willingness to abandon the past, start afresh, rethink and reconfigure the world along clean, geometric lines, to plan rather than react, to liberate people from enslavement to tradition. Marshall Berman, *All that is Solid Melts into Air: The Experience of Modernity* (New York, 1982). See also James Scott, *Seeing Like a State: How Certain Schemes to Improve the Human Condition have Failed* (New Haven, 1998); T. J. Jackson Lears, *No Place of Grace: Antimodernism and the Transformation of American Culture, 1880–1920* (New York, 1991).

5. Rationality, in other words, varies by situation and context. Notions of the rational are constructed through discourse. Jonathan Zeitlin, "Productive Alternatives: Flexibility, Governance, and Strategic Choice in Industrial History," in Franco Amatori and Geoffrey Jones (eds.), *Business History Around the World* (Cambridge, 2002); Sharon Zukin and Paul DiMaggio, *Structures of Capital: The Social Organization of the Economy* (Cambridge, 1990), 24; Ronald Jepperson and John W. Meyer, "The Public Order and the Construction of Formal Organizations," in DiMaggio and Powell (eds.), *The New Institutionalism in Organizational Analysis*, 204–31.

6. Gordon S. Wood, *The Radicalism of the American Revolution*, (New York, 1992). James Kloppenberg, "The Virtues of Liberalism: Christianity, Republicanism, and Ethics in Early American Political Discourse," *Journal of American History* 74:1 (1987), 9–33. Major works on the market include Charles Sellers, *The Market Revolution: Jacksonian America, 1815–1846* (Oxford, 1991); Winifred Rothenberg, *From Market Place to Market Economy: The Transformation of Rural Massachusetts, 1750–1850* (Chicago, 1992); Christopher Clark, *The Roots of Rural Capitalism: Western Massachusetts, 1780–1860* (Ithaca, NY, 1990). On the market and politics, see Joyce Appleby, *Capitalism and a New Social Order: The Republican Vision of the 1790s* (New York, 1984); Wood, *Radicalism*, 305–end; Daniel Walker Howe, *The Political Culture of the American Whigs* (Chicago, 1979).

7. Weber's concept of rationalization must be treated as an ideal type. Max Weber, *The Theory of Social and Economic Organization*, trans. A. M. Henderson and Talcott Parsons (New York, 1947), 92. The sort of rationality exhibited by religiously inspired reformers encompasses Weber's *Wertrationalität* – orientation of means to the achievement of a single, overriding goal, at any cost (p. 115). But as I shall argue, they also embraced a more instrumental form of rationality as well. An important

synthesis that emphasizes the modernizing aspect of reform is Steven Mintz, *Moralists and Modernizers: America's Pre-Civil War Reformers* (Baltimore, 1995); an older, but still insightful work is Ronald Walters, *American Reformers, 1815–1860* (New York, 1997 [1978]).

8. John Higham, *From Boundlessness to Consolidation: The Transformation of American Culture, 1848–1860* (Ann Arbor, 1969); Wilfred McClay, *The Masterless: Self & Society in Modern America* (Chapel Hill, 1994).

9. See, for example, Edward Everett, "Fourth of July Address at Lowell, Massachusetts, 1830" in Daniel Walker Howe, *The American Whigs*, 23–31; John Kasson, *Civilizing the Machine: Technology and Republican Values, 1776–1900* (New York, 1976), 55–61. Other works that deal with the problem of virtue in the age of the market are Gordon S. Wood, *The Creation of the American Republic, 1776–1787* (Chapel Hill, NC, 1969); John Ashworth, *Slavery, Capitalism, and Politics in the Antebellum Republic* (New York, 1995); Thomas Haskell, "Capitalism and the Origins of the Humanitarian Sensibility," parts 1 & 2, in Thomas Bender (ed.), *The Antislavery Debate: Capitalism and Abolitionism as a Problem in Historical Interpretation.* (Berkeley, CA, 1992); Thomas Haskell and Richard Teichgraeber III (eds.), *The Culture of the Market* (Cambridge, 1993); Kloppenberg, "The Virtues of Liberalism," 16–17; Richard Teichgraeber III, *"Free Trade" and Moral philosophy: Rethinking the Sources of Adam Smith's Wealth of Nations* (Durham, NC, 1986).

10. The most important theoretical work on corporate structures is Oliver Williamson, *Markets and Hierarchies, Analysis and Antitrust Implications: A Study in the Economics of Internal Organization* (New York, 1975). See also William Lazonick, *Business Organization and the Myth of the Market Economy* (Cambridge, 1991); and Richard Langlois (ed.), *Economics as a Process: Essays in the New Institutional Economics* (New York, 1986).

11. It is this understanding of a rationalized market that allowed the most powerful corporate giants of the postbellum era to crush opponents and dominate industries while speaking glowingly of competition. On Rockefeller and others like him, see Edward Chase Kirkland, *Dream and Thought in the Business Community, 1860–1900* (Chicago, 1964), 157.

12. Robert Dalzell, *Enterprising Elite: The Boston Associates and the World they Made* (Cambridge, MA, 1987); David Brion Davis, "Quaker Ethic," in Bender (ed.), *The Antislavery Debate*, 59–62, 294.

13. Kasson, *Civilizing the Machine*, 31–106.

14. Jonathan Prude, *The Coming of Industrial Order: Town and Factory Life in Rural Massachusetts, 1810–1860* (Cambridge, 1983); Mary Rose, "Family Firm, Community and Business Culture," in Andrew Godley and Oliver M. Westall (eds.), *Business History and Business Culture* (Manchester, 1996).

15. The tradition has been to make a sharp distinction here and differentiate antebellum communities from modern organizations. For example, Rosabeth Moss Kanter, *Commitment and Community: Communes and Utopias in Sociological Perspective* (Cambridge, 1972).

16. Berman, *All that is Solid*, 83. On the link between modernism and utopia, see Krishan Kumar, *Utopia and Anti-Utopia in Modern Times* (New York, 1987). For a discussion of utopian ideas and the rationalization of society, see Rosalind Williams, "Cultural Origins and Environmental Implications of Large Technological Systems," *Science in Context* 6:2 (1993), 377–403. Even "anti-modernism" can be rife with modernist impulses to control, rationalize and order in formal systems. See Jackson Lears, *No Place of Grace.*

17. John Whitworth, *God's Blueprints: A Sociological Study of Three Utopian Sects* (London, 1975).

18. Joint stock companies arose in sixteenth century England for crown chartered ventures in overseas trade. A century later, they were used for purely private business endeavors. Modern managerial corporations are the outgrowth of all these previous traditions, not simply the legal lineage of the corporation proper.

19. The Fourierist communities were set up by investors and paid dividends. So did Hopedale, founded by Unitarian minister Adin Ballou. Other communities, such as Amana and Oneida, were "closely held," in that they distributed shares to members only, though over time those shares could be sold or traded.

20. McClay, *The Masterless*, 52, 150; Adams, quoted in Daniel Walker Howe, *The Political Culture of the American Whigs*, 105. See also Carl Guarneri, *The Utopian Alternative: Fourierism in Nineteenth-Century America* (Ithaca, NY, 1991), 138–40, 345.

21. Perhaps they did so because corporations were still more restricted than were joint stock companies, which could be arranged in many ways to suit their members' purposes. On the restrictions on corporations, see Gregory Mark, "The Personification of the Business Corporation in American Law," *University of Chicago Law Review* 54:4 (Fall 1987), 1444; Pauline Maier, "The Revolutionary Origins of the American Corporation," *William and Mary Quarterly, 3rd series* 50:1 (Jan. 1993), 51–84.

22. On joint stock companies, see Norman Lattin, *The Law of Corporations* (Mineola, NY, 1971), 51; Charles Elliott, *The Principles of the Law of Private Corporations* (Indianapolis, 1897), 4–6; William Clark and William Marshall, *A Treatise on the Law of Private Corporations* (St. Paul, MN, 1903), 40–8; Joseph Storey, *Commentaries on the Law of Partnerships* (Buffalo, NY, 1980 [1841]), 254–6; Robert Hessen, "The Modern Corporation and Private Property: A Reappraisal," *Journal of Law and Economics* 26:2 (June, 1983), 273–89.

23. As Naomi Lamoreaux notes in this volume, corporations (and therefore joint stock companies) also reduced the power of individuals by removing the threat of "hold up" or dissolution. When a partner leaves, the firm dissolves; not so in collective enterprise. With the threat of breakup gone, the individual loses a significant means of exercising his or her will in the firm.

24. Like many utopian communities, Oneida was highly innovative. On invention and utopia, see Dolores Hayden, *Seven American Utopias: The Architecture of Communitarian Socialism, 1790–1975* (Cambridge, MA, 1976), 24–5.

25. Charles Nordhoff, *The Communistic Societies of the United States* (New York, 1961 [1875]), 277–87.

26. In 1880, Oneida had about 200 employed workers and 280 full members. It was forced to hire outside labor to keep up trap production, despite original intentions to use only members as workers. Kanter, *Commitment and Community*, 152. Although in theory anyone could do any job at Oneida, and many tasks were rotated to prevent boredom, heads of the Oneida committees were appointed for at least a year, and foremen of the manufacturing plants rarely changed. Nordhoff, *The Communistic Societies of the United States*, 280. On the division of labor in Fourierist societies, Guarneri, *The Utopian Alternative*, 188–90.

27. Other communities also worked carefully to plan production and coordinate labor and capital with the demands for their products. See Kanter, *Commitment and Community*, 126; Hayden, *Seven American Utopias*, 158, 189, 228. On the use of planning and management in Amana, see Diane Bartel, *Amana: From Pietistic Sect to American Community* (Lincoln, 1984), 25.

28. Kumar, *Utopia and Anti-Utopia*, 90.

29. Guarneri, *The Utopian Alternative*, 106–7, 128–30. Efficiency, Owen believed, would alleviate periodic and seasonal unemployment, which was the single most important reason for worker poverty.

30. Donald Pitzer, "The New Moral World of Robert Owen and New Harmony," in Donald Pitzer (ed.), *America's Communal Utopias* (Chapel Hill, NC, 1997), 92–5. One of Owen's partners was Jeremy Bentham, inventor of the great device for discipline by surveillance, the Panopticon. The power of surveillance and the Panopticon are discussed in Michael Foucault, *Discipline and Punish: The Birth of the Prison* (New York, 1979). On sensitivity to observation in antebellum American thought, see Michael Gilmore, *American Romanticism and the Marketplace* (Chicago, 1985), 71–95.

31. On Shaker style and economy, see Dolores Hayden, *Seven American Utopias*, 76–92. Even the Hutterites acted as a "corporation" toward the market and outside world, while within practicing a communal form of life. Gertrude Huntington, "Living Ark: Four Centuries of Hutterite Faith and Community," in Pitzer (ed.), *America's Communal Utopias*, 319.

32. Consider as well the American and English Arts and Crafts Movement in this regard. Elizabeth Cummings and Wendy Kaplan, *The Arts and Crafts Movement* (New York, 1991).

33. Guarneri, *The Utopian Alternative*, 123–4, 185; Walters, *American Reformers*, 63, 68; Dolores Hayden, *Seven America Utopias*, 36–7, 69. On the connections between mapping and marking the landscape and modernism, see James Scott, *Seeing Like a State*, 108–16.

34. The reason for the indeterminacy lies with the basic modernist impulses that underlay both the corporate economy and the socialist one. As James Scott notes, modernism is "politically promiscuous." Scott, *Seeing Like a State*.

35. On who was attracted to these programs, see Stephen Nissenbaum, *Sex, Diet and Debility in Jacksonian America: Sylvester Graham and Health Reform* (Greenwood, CT, 1980).

36. At one point Noyes apparently considered imposing celibacy. Jayme Sokolow, *Eros and Modernization: Sylvester Graham, Health Reform and the Origins of Victorian Sexuality in America* (Rutherford, NJ, 1983), 138–40.

37. Howe, *The Political Culture of the American Whigs*, makes this important distinction between self- and social control. On self-control and freedom in reformer thought, see Walters, *American Reformers*, 46–7, 57–9; also Lawrence Kohl, *The Politics of Individualism: Parties and the American Character in the Jacksonian Era* (New York, 1989), 77–8. On drinking, see Mark Edward Lender and James Kirby Martin, *Drinking in America* (New York, 1987); and William J. Rorabaugh, *The Alcoholic Republic, An American Tradition* (New York, 1979).

38. Quoted in Hillel Schwartz, *Never Satisfied: A Cultural History of Diets, Fantasies and Fat* (New York, 1986), 44.

39. Sokolow, *Eros and Modernization*, 72–7, 113–24, 158. On diet and the taming of the frontier, see Gerald Carson, *Cornflake Crusade* (New York, 1957), 29–34; Anne Rose, *Voices of the Marketplace: American Thought and Culture, 1830–1860* (New York, 1995), 63, 73–6; Cathy Matson and Peter Onuf, "Toward a Republican Empire: Interest and Ideology in Revolutionary America," *American Quarterly* 37:4 (1985), 518, on the tools and symbols of middle class respectability and refinement such as forks, clocks, pianos; also John Kasson, *Rudeness & Civility: Manners in Nineteenth-century Urban America* (New York , 1990).

40. Sokolow, *Eros and Modernization*, 85. On self-control, manners, and the market, Gordon Wood, *Radicalism*, 349–56.

41. Another example would be Elizur Wright, the abolitionist turned insurance actuary. See Lawrence Goodheart, *Abolitionist, Actuary, Atheist: Elizur Wright and the Reform Impulse* (Kent, OH, 1990).

42. Bertram Wyatt-Brown, *Lewis Tappan and the Evangelical War Against Slavery* (Cleveland, 1969).

43. The keenest insights into Tappan and credit reporting are to be found in Scott Sandage, "Deadbeats, Drunkards and Dreamers: A Cultural History of Failure in America," Ph.D. dissertation, Rutgers University, 1995.

44. Bertram Wyatt-Brown, "God and Dun & Bradstreet, 1841–1851," *Business History Review* 40:4 (Winter 1967), 432–50.

45. For a sense of what the original field reports were like before they were 'processed,' one can see the transcripts recorded in the Mercantile Agency Credit Ledgers, Baker Library Special Collections, Harvard University, Graduate School of Business Administration. On appearance and deception, see Karen Hultunen, *Confidence Men and Painted Women: A Study of Middle-class Culture in America, 1830–1870* (New Haven, 1982).

46. Wyatt-Brown, *Lewis Tappan*, quoted on p. 232.

47. On the conflicts between systems and local communities, see John Laritz Larson, *Bonds of Enterprise: John Murray Forbes and Western Development in America's Railway Age* (Cambridge, 1984).

48. Pauline Maier, "The Revolutionary Origins of the American Corporation," *William and Mary Quarterly, 3rd series* 50:1 (Jan. 1993), 53; George Heberton Evans, Jr., *Business Incorporations in the United States, 1800–1943*, (New York, 1948), 10–30; Ronald Seavoy, *The Origins of the American Business Corporation, 1784–1855* (Westport, CT, 1982), 9–38.

49. The stock traded involved not industrial corporations, which came later, but banks and canal, turnpike, and other public improvements companies. Richard Sylla, "U.S. Securities Markets and the Banking System, 1790–1840," *Federal Reserve Bank of St. Louis Review* (May/June 1995), 90; Oscar Handlin and Mary F. Handlin, "Origins of the American Business Corporation," *Journal of Economic History* 5:1 (May 1945), 4.

50. Maier, "Revolutionary Origins," 52.

51. Between 1818 and 1862, the New England states created 2081 corporations in manufacturing and mining, versus 1683 in public utilities. William C. Kessler, "Incorporation in New England: A Statistical Study, 1800–1875," *Journal of Economic History* 8:1 (May 1948), 47–8.

52. Seavoy, *The Origins of the American Business Corporation*, 49–50.

53. Maier, "Revolutionary Origins," 76. Maier (p. 82) also calls corporations "the most significant form of collectivism to emerge from the revolution."

54. Kessler, "Incorporation in New England," 47. Between 1862 and 1875, 65 percent of corporations in New England were created under general incorporation laws; in the preceding period, 1844–1862, only 27 percent were.

55. Herbert Hovenkamp, *Enterprise and American Law, 1836–1937* (Cambridge, MA, 1991), 11–64. See also Gregory Mark, "The Personification of the Business Corporation in American Law," *University of Chicago Law Review* 54:4 (Fall 1987), 1450–2; David Millon, "Frontiers of Legal Thought I: Theories of the Corporation," *Duke Law Journal* (Apr. 1990) 201–62; James Willard Hurst, *The Legitimacy of the Business Corporation in the Law of the United States, 1780–1970* (Charlottesville, VA, 1970).

56. The personhood doctrine evolved slowly and unevenly, as Naomi Lamoreaux shows in this volume. But the general drift was from the corporation as state-created "artificial" person, to the corporation as the aggregation of individuals who owned it, to the corporation as a "natural" person by the late nineteenth century. Hovenkamp, *Enterprise and American Law*, 42–8; Morton J. Horowitz, "Santa Clara Revisited: The Development of Corporate Theory," *West Virginia Law Review* 88 (1985); Mark Hager, "Bodies Politic: The Progressive History of the 'Real Entity' Theory," *University of Pittsburgh Law Review* 50:2 (Winter 1985), 575–653; Mark, "Personification of the Business Corporation," 1471–5.

57. Limited liability, a protection that was later broadened and extended, had the same effect. If individual stockholders were not liable, then it was incumbent on creditors to consider closely the strategies and behavior of the managers – that is, those who actually had control.

58. The classic work is of course Adolf Berle and Gardiner Means, *The Modern Corporation and Private Property* (New York, 1932).

59. Here, I am de-emphasizing the corporation as a vehicle of capital mobilization, which may well have been its original attraction to businesspeople. My point is simply that, like the joint stock company in the hands of utopian communes, corporations were being readied to perform a managerial role, perhaps even before such as role was of paramount concern. Consciously or not, the tools of bureaucratic management were emerging in an America where large-scale bureaucracies were both uncommon and controversial.

60. Indeed, it was more through private experiments than from conscious legislative intent that the broad legal form of the corporation yielded innovations such as limited liability, receiverships, and new classes of stocks and bonds, each of which also contributed to the separation of ownership from control. Thomas Cochran, "The Business Revolution," *American Historical Review* 79:5 (1974), 1449–66.

61. On periodization, see Thomas Bender, *Community and Social Change in America* (New Brunswick, 1978); Alan Trachtenberg, *The Incorporation of America: Culture and Society in the Gilded Age* (New York, 1982). See also George Frederickson, *The Inner Civil War: Northern Intellectuals and the Crisis of the Union* (New York, 1965), 101–3, 150.

62. Robert Foggerty, *All Things New: American Communes and Utopian Movements, 1860–1914* (Chicago, 1990).

63. H. G. Wells, *The Future in America* (New York, 1974 [1906]).

64. On the Oneida Community, Ltd., see Maren Lockwood Carden, *Oneida: Utopian Community to Modern Corporation* (Baltimore, 1969), 113–64.

65. Not surprisingly, Kellogg's devotees included a large number of men of business. Among them were John D. Rockefeller, J. C. Penney, Montgomery Ward, the efficiency and conservation advocate Gifford Pinchot, and the economist Irving Fisher, himself a best selling author of books on good health and long life. As Kellogg was concerned about the well-tempered body, so his prominent patients were concerned about the throughput of the economy. Both were closed systems that had to be kept regular and flowing. The "modern" value of convenience should also not be overlooked here. Kellogg claimed to have come upon the idea of cold breakfast cereal while living in New York as a student lacking adequate kitchen facilities. Carson, *Cornflake Crusade*, 118. Note also that Kellogg's main competitor, C. W. Post of Post Cereals, spent time as a patient at the "San."

66. On branding and its place in business history, see Richard Tedlow, *New and Improved: The Story of Mass Marketing in America* (New York, 1990), 8–14.

67. In Oneida, P. B. Noyes recognized the appeal of advertising based more on product image than information. He made Oneida silverware nationally famous through celebrity endorsements that suggested taste and refinement came with every order. On the importance of control over consumption through corporate strategies, see T. J. Jackson Lears, *Fables of Abundance: A Cultural History of Advertising in America* (New York, 1994).

68. Peter Temin, "The Stability of the American Business Elite," *Industrial and Corporate Change* 8 (June 1999), 189–210. As Robert Wiebe pointed out, businessmen were active participants in Progressive Era reform. I am merely suggesting that this connection goes deeper and back further. Robert Wiebe, *Businessmen and Reform: A Study of the Progressive Movement* (Cambridge, MA, 1962).

69. Robert Abzug, *Cosmos Crumbling: American Reform and the Religious Imagination* (New York, 1994), insists on the deep religious sources of reform ideas, though one could just as easily look at reform as a process of secularization. Secularization does not mean the abandonment of religion, but rather the transference of religious ideals and fervor to non-religious causes and institutions. That fits exactly my sense of how the corporation picked up the legacy of religion and reform. On secularization, see Eldon Eisenach, *The Lost Promise of Progressivism* (Lawrence, KS, 1994).

70. Peter Dobkin Hall, "Religion and the Organizational Revolution in the United States," in N. J. Demerath III, *et al.* (eds.), *Sacred Companies: Organizational Aspects of Religion and Religious Aspects of Organizations* (New York, 1968), 100–2, 107–12, discusses the social origins of such consolidators.

71. William G. McGloughlin, *The Meaning of Henry Ward Beecher* (New York, 1970), 17, 47–9. On the shifting frameworks of social thought, see Higham, *From Boundlessness to Consolidation*. See also James Livingston, *Pragmatism and the Political Economy of Cultural Revolution 1850–1940* (Chapel Hill, NC, 1994), 58.

72. In his spare time, Beecher also wrote tracts on the virtues of life insurance. It is revealing that Beecher proclaimed insurance as a way to give everyone a "stake" in society and make them "stockholders of public morality." McGloughlin, *The Meaning of Henry Ward Beecher*, 40–1.

73. Whig political economist Henry Carey, for example, had lauded the "power of association," which increased "control of the forces of nature," as society succeeded to higher levels of complexity and interdependence. Quoted in Howe, *The Political Culture of the American Whigs*, 114–15. On Brisbane and Beecher, see Rose, *Voices of the Marketplace*, 76.

74. Quoted in Carl Guarneri, "Brook Farm and the Fourierist Phalanx: Immediatism, Gradualism in American Utopian Socialism," in Pitzer (ed.), *America's Communal Utopias*, 165.

75. Eric Foner, *Free Soil, Free Labor, Free Men* (New York, 1970), 39.

76. David Nye, *American Technological Sublime* (Cambridge, 1997); Michael Fellman, *The Unbounded Frame: Freedom and Community in Nineteenth Century American Utopianism* (Westport, CT, 1973), 9–10, 105.

77. McClay, *The Masterless*, 98–101; John L. Thomas, *Alternative America: Henry George, Edward Bellamy, Henry Demarest Lloyd and the Adversarial Tradition* (Cambridge, MA, 1983), 237–61. *Looking Backward* was second in popularity only to *Uncle Tom's Cabin* in the nineteenth century.

78. McClay, *The Masterless*, 314.

79. Quoted in Thomas, *Alternative America*, 247. On interdependence, see Thomas Haskell, *The Emergence of Professional Social Science* (Urbana, IL, 1977), 24–47.

80. Edward Bellamy, *Looking Backward* (New York, 1887), 197.

81. Bellamy, *Looking Backward*, 147.

82. Bellamy, *Looking Backward*, 266. On circulation metaphors and the enlightenment project, see Williams, "Cultural Origins and Environmental Implications of Large Technological Systems."

83. For examples in labor relations and technology, see Gerald Zahavi, *Workers, Managers and Welfare Capitalism: The Shoeworkers and Tanners of Endicott Johnson, 1890–1950* (Urbana, IL, 1988); Sanford Jacoby, *Modern Manors: Welfare Capitalism Since the New Deal* (Princeton, 1997); Thomas P. Hughes, *American Genesis: A Century of Invention and Technological Enthusiasm, 1870–1970* (New York, 1989). For different views on corporate liberalism, see Louis Galambos and Joseph Pratt, *The Rise of the Corporate Commonwealth: U.S. Business and Public Policy in the Twentieth Century* (New York, 1988); Colin Gordon, *New Deals: Business, Labor, and Politics in America, 1920–1935* (New York, 1994).

84. In many ways, though, the utopian hope that structure alone was the key to community continued. Critics of "old style" vertically integrated corporations as constraining and out of date still believe that new, "flatter" structures and decentralization will provide, once again, an organizational scheme which will liberate individuals while providing abundance and a rational scheme of social order. For a sharp critique of the utopian belief that structure alone can produce the good society, see Michael Allen, "Flexible Production in Ravensbrück Concentration Camp," *Past & Present* 165 (1999), 182–217.

Whose Hubris? Brandeis, Scientific Management, and the Railroads

Gerald Berk

In 1910 the Eastern and Western Freight Associations complained to the Interstate Commerce Commission (ICC): we need money. The cost of labor, capital, and equipment has increased, but revenues have stagnated. As a result, we cannot finance, track and rolling stock is deteriorating, and rail service is in disarray. Unless the commission grants an across-the-board rate increase, the value of railroad property will continue to deteriorate. The commissioners balked: our legal mandate is not to ensure railroad profitability, they told the carriers; it is only to ensure the railroads earn a fair return on the objective value of property. On this criterion, the evidence demonstrates ample revenues. The 1910 fight was the opening salvo in a bitter and protracted stalemate between the carriers and the commission. Over the next six years, they locked horns four more times, without resolution. Regulation was paralyzed.

At the opening hearing in 1910, the commissioners heard from counsel for the Shippers Association, Louis D. Brandeis. Among his many witnesses was the prominent efficiency expert, Harrington Emerson. Emerson diligently explained how he had reduced costs in the Atchison, Topeka, and Santa Fe repair shops through scientific management. Extrapolating from similar experiments on other carriers, Brandeis' experts estimated that scientific management could save the railroads a million dollars a day. The press loved Brandeis' hubris, and scientific management was suddenly thrust into the public sphere. Modernity's remedy or ruin, it no longer was the obscure subject of trade journals. Now popular magazines, public forums, even Congress took up the debate over scientific management.

Brandeis' turn to scientific management was far more than a publicity stunt. When the railroads returned to the ICC in 1912, the commission brought Brandeis on as its counsel for the case. The more "the people's lawyer" learned about the relationship between management and rate regulation, the more he concluded that commission and carriers shared economic assumptions and practices whose consequences were perverse. At the heart of the matter was faulty cost accounting. Compared to manufacturing, Brandeis charged, the carriers used outdated techniques that hampered efficiency gains. The railroads were not the only guilty parties. The ICC also had faulty accounting procedures. Developed to secure its own legal legitimacy, commission cost accounting did little to foster economic improvement. A million dollars a day was mere hubris. These charges were heresy. Lawyers, economists, and regulators had devoted a generation to developing a scientific theory of natural monopoly, based upon objective costs, from which they derived a disinterested architecture for rate making called "rate of return regulation." Economic and "liberal legal" science promised to legitimate the state's police power, ensure economic efficiency and effective public administration, and dampen the bitter social conflict that rocked America in the final decade of the nineteenth century.

The proof, however, was in the pudding, said Brandeis. In practice, rate-of-return regulation delegitimated state power, reduced incentives for economic improvement, and exacerbated social conflict. There was another way. Drawing upon scientific management, Brandeis showed the commission and the carriers different accounting techniques; and drawing upon his successful experiments in "sliding scale" regulation in Massachusetts natural gas, he also demonstrated another way to set rates. Brandeis' alternative has been unintelligible to scholars since the mid-twentieth century. After the Second World War, consensus historians and pluralist political scientists agreed that, after a disorderly transition, Americans had come to accept the modern corporation as an inevitable byproduct of industrial society. The economic ideas of those, like Brandeis, who had protested "the curse of bigness" were dubbed anachronistic or irrational. Although economists, political scientists, and historians have re-read Brandeis' economics more sympathetically in the last decade, they remain baffled by his affection for scientific management. How could the critic of corporate power and friend to labor and small enterprise embrace the essential doctrine of managerial hierarchy and control? Brandeis, they conclude, must have been confused, naive, or cunning.[1]

Recent scholarship in the social construction of industry indicates that Brandeis' economic ideas merit another look. As the introduction to this volume shows, industrialization was far more diverse and socially determined than the naturalistic history of the modern corporation suggests. In one version of the new narrative, flexible and specialty production, industrial districts, and small-scale enterprise contributed as much to western industrialization as mass production organized in large-scale, national hierarchies.[2] In another, efforts to institutionalize diverse experiments in production resulted in broader political and cultural struggles, the outcomes of which determined discursive frameworks that shaped the most basic economic forms, from technology and markets to the measurement of costs. If the modern corporation emerged victorious, it was not because it was unambiguously the one best way. It was more likely because it found support in extra-economic arenas.[3]

From a social constructionist perspective, Brandeis' efforts to reform business regulation are better seen as part of a broader struggle over the nature of industrial order than an adaptive "response to industrialism." When Brandeis criticized railroad cost accounting, he was not merely asking about the appropriate political response to the modern corporation. He meant to raise social questions about what railroads could and should be in the first instance. As accounting scholar Peter Miller writes, "accounting is not a neutral device that merely documents of 'the facts' of economic activity." It is better understood as "a set of practices that affects the type of world we live in, the social reality we inhabit, the way in which we understand the choices open to business undertakings and individuals, the way in which we manage and organize activities and processes of diverse types, and the way in which we administer the lives of others and ourselves."[4]

This chapter shows how Brandeis found in scientific management's accounting techniques an alternative to the prevailing adaptive, or redistributive, model of regulation. I also render a brief in his favor. Brandeis did not develop a theoretical alternative to neoclassical economics or the prevailing deductive models of regulatory jurisprudence. To the contrary, his approach was decidedly anti-foundational. I hope to demonstrate, however, that Brandeis' critique of railroad cost accounting and rate-of-return regulation, as well as his alternative, were coherent. By coherent I mean, first, that the relationship between parts of his analysis are logical; and second, that there are plausible reasons to believe that Brandeis' proposals would have improved railroad efficiency, public administration, and social relations.

SCIENTIFIC FOUNDATIONS OF PUBLIC UTILITY REGULATION

Where did the theories of natural monopoly and rate-of-return regulation come from? In the 1870s, state legislatures in Illinois, Wisconsin, and Minnesota passed the "Granger Laws," which empowered state commissions to regulate grain elevator and railroad rates. These laws, complained the carriers, were unconstitutional intrusions into free contract. The Constitution, countered the defendants, left the states with a legitimate obligation to exercise police powers when the public interest was at stake. But what exactly constituted the public interest in rate regulation? In 1888, Supreme Court Justice Stephen J. Field posed the challenge in a way that would shape the controversy for some time. In *Munn* v. *Illinois*, the Court found for the state: all business "affected with the public interest," wrote Justice Bradley for the majority, were legitimately subject to state police power. The "affectation doctrine," Field complained in dissent, opened a Pandora's box. Since the Court made no effort to distinguish business affected with the public interest from any others, virtually any practices could fall into this category. Surely this could not be. Most businesses, Field pointed out, were "ordinary trades," best regulated by contract and competition. The liberal distinction between public and private enterprise, he concluded, was empirical, real, and objective. It was not to be decided by the interests of state legislators and their constituencies or the arbitrary whims of judges.[5]

What about railroads? Field conceded that this industry was devoted to "public use." Nonetheless, because railroad corporations relied on private investment capital, they were first and foremost private entities. Absent investment, neither public nor private interests would be served. The majority in *Munn*, Field charged, had erred in "converting private concerns with public duties into wholly public corporations." If railroads remained at the mercy of "hostile legislatures" investment would cease. The interests of state and corporation, consumers and property owners, Field concluded, were objectively opposed. The Court's duty was to "define the limits of the power of the state over its corporations . . . so that, on the one hand, the property interests of the stockholder would be protected from practical confiscation, and on the other hand, the people would be protected from arbitrary and extortionate charges."[6]

If the public–public distinction was empirical, this left the epistemological question wide open. How would you know a business with a public interest when you saw one? Perhaps no one stepped into the breach more completely than Henry Carter Adams. A founder of the American Economic Association, Adams was a pioneer in bringing the insights of the marginalist revolution in economics to bear on public utility regulation. Adams was an ambivalent reformer. Like many intellectuals of his generation, he was the son of a reformer: Adams' father was an abolitionist minister. In the 1870s, Adams joined other young American political economists in Germany, where they learned historical economics. Evolutionary in outlook, this school anticipated that cooperation and fraternity would naturally supersede individualism and competition in industrial society. Richard Ely, John Bates Clark, and Henry Carter Adams returned to the United States in the 1880s to find a society wracked by social conflict. Together, they formed the American Economic Association in 1885, with the express goal of fostering social reform. However, when they spoke out in support of labor unions and state intervention, their livelihoods were threatened. Ely was put on trial by the Board of Regents in Wisconsin; Adams lost his job at Cornell; and colleagues at Brown, Johns Hopkins, and the University of Michigan came under similar scrutiny. As a result, many economists adopted a posture of disinterested expertise. They divided scientific from moral inquiry and intervened in public controversy more and more as technical advisers.[7]

Adams is a good example. After 1885, he retreated from public controversy, secured tenure at the University of Michigan, and became chief statistician for the Interstate Commerce Commission. In 1887, he turned to science to solve Field's epistemological puzzle. The problem, as Adams now conceived it, was that nineteenth-century political economy had mistakenly formulated the public/private problem as only a political or moral issue. The marginalist revolution in economics furnished another way. On the continent and in Britain, Leon Walras, Carl Menger, and Stanley Jevons had reconceptualized political economy as an inquiry into nature. Physics, not ethics, was the appropriate model. The marginalists attempted to build a unified theory around a single foundational problem: the human allocation of resources under conditions of natural scarcity. How, they asked, given natural budget constraints, do economic agents best allocate resources between different uses?[8]

Drawing upon the mathematical formulations of the calculus and a utilitarian notion of subjective rationality, the economists demonstrated the "law of declining marginal utility." For each additional unit of savings an individual expends on a good or service, she receives a declining marginal increment of satisfaction or "utility." A unifying law, Jevons thought the principle of declining marginal utility was applicable not only to resource allocation, but also to production. He demonstrated that the relationship between industry inputs and outputs followed a similar pattern. Generalizing from earlier studies of agriculture, Jevons deduced that in manufacturing additional inputs of capital and labor made declining marginal contributions to output. From the "law of diminishing returns to scale," he concluded that most businesses would remain relatively small. In rare cases, the opposite occurred: each additional increment of capital and labor resulted in an increase in the marginal increment of output. The railroads were a paradigm case of the "law of increasing returns to scale."[9]

Paradoxically, a law of resource allocation rooted in subjectivity came to be understood as an objective law when applied to production. For Adams, the principle of diminishing returns to scale provided a deductive model that could be tested against reality to distinguish between ordinary trades and those affected with the public interest. "If there be any virtue in the scientific analysis of industrial relations," he wrote, "we should be able to determine, with some degree of accuracy, under what conditions the rule of private financiering [market competition], and under what conditions the rule of public financiering [government regulation] will best serve the rational ends of society."[10] Industries with decreasing and constant returns to scale, he went on, "call for no regulation by law." Firms remained sufficiently small so that competition would effectively regulate prices and ensure improvements in production. "*The struggling for superior success in these businesses is a struggle to depress the cost of rendering service rather than to raise the prices of services rendered.*" There was no need, then, for state action.[11]

By contrast, Adams wrote, "there are many other businesses, which conform to the principle of increasing returns, and for that reason come under the rule of centralized control." Railroads, for example, face such high fixed costs that each additional unit of labor and materials resulted in an increasing increment of output. "Such businesses are by their nature monopolies . . . It is for the interest of men to combine [and] no law can make them compete." Therefore, state control over prices was warranted. While laissez-faire ensured individual rights and cooperation in the first two cases, natural monopoly had unsettled the nation. Only public action, Adams concluded, would redress festering grievances and "restore social harmony" to the nation.[12]

Hovencamp has shown the legal profession was well aware of marginalist innovations in economics. With some time lag, lawyers internalized neoclassical science in legal doctrine.[13] In 1895, seven years after Adams had penned his analysis, the Supreme Court outlined a theory of public utility regulation appropriate to natural monopoly. Following on Field's dictum in Munn, the Court declared the railroad corporation was essentially a private entity. Writing for the majority in *Smyth* v. *Ames*, Justice Harlan said, "the railroad corporation is a person under the Constitution," thus, it was accorded rights appropriate to the private sphere. Any "statute or regulation which does not allow just compensation for railroad service deprives it of property without due process of law." Still, because railroads were not subject to competition, the public had a legitimate interest in fair rates. The problem was how to balance these competing interests. As the Court saw it, this was an objective, not a political, matter. Just as monopoly and competition were determined by the underlying cost structure of industry, so too were just rates. "The basis of all calculations as to the reasonableness of rates," Harlan went on, "must be the fair value of property being used . . . for the convenience of the public." Fair value was an empirical matter, to be determined scientifically by, among other criteria, the cost of construction and improvement, the market value of stocks and bonds, present costs, earning capacity, and operating costs.[14] Once the value of railroad property was determined, the state could set prices by comparing the rate of profit for similar sorts of investments. Thus, building on the theory of natural monopoly, *Smyth v. Ames* derived a scientific theory of rate making called "rate-of-return" regulation, which would shape the debate for some time to come.

BRANDEIS' PRAGMATISM

Though younger than Adams, Brandeis was also profoundly affected by the social unrest of the 1880s and 1890s. Unlike the economists, Haymarket and Homestead strengthened Brandeis' resolve for social reform. To be sure, by 1905, Brandeis had a lucrative legal practice, so his reform activities were less likely to threaten his livelihood. But it was not just Brandeis' affinity for practical politics that distinguished him from the economists. He understood the relationship between science, economy, and democracy quite differently. Brandeis was a pragmatist. As such, he shared with the philosophers a desire to shake off the metaphysical dualities that undergirded liberalism and a good deal of scientific thought. Like Dewey, Brandeis thought the sharp distinctions between objectivity and interests, truth and opinion, appearance and reality not only indefensible. They stalled the growth of democracy in everyday life. Where Adams and the economists hoped to distinguish scientific objectivity from political interests, Brandeis thought scientific practice was inescapably dependent upon human ends. Truth, for pragmatists, was an elusive goal. In Brandeis' view, marginalist theory did not provide a more accurate picture of real costs. The arbiter of competing perspectives on cost was utility: did they improve production, distribution, or regulation? Though critical of foundational epistemologies, Brandeis was enormously sanguine about science's potential to improve economic and democratic life. Like Dewey, he saw in scientific method not inviolable foundations to resolve political disputes, but methods of experimentation, collective inquiry, deliberation, and incremental improvement that accorded well with his vision of democracy.[15]

Consider Brandeis' critique of the scientific distinction between competition and monopoly and its corollary, the public–private distinction. Brandeis agreed with the economists that monopoly was more than a moral or political category, it was empirical. But he mistrusted reductionist theories. It might be, Brandeis said, that industries had different cost structures, but this alone did not determine whether they were competitive or monopolistic. Regardless of costs, the flux of market processes ensured winners and losers at any point in time. Experience had demonstrated, however, that those with temporary advantages were always tempted to turn them into unassailable privileges through predatory rivalry or political power. The consequences of competition were ambiguous. Though it provided incentives to improvement, left alone economic rivalry could just as easily undermine itself. Brandeis thought that the state had two legitimate roles in competition policy. First, it should help channel business rivalry from predation to improvement in products and production processes. Second, government should provide a forum for experimentation, information sharing, and deliberation over concrete standards of effective competition. In short, exogenous costs were an unreliable guide to policy, and action in the private sphere (the market) raised inescapably public questions.[16]

The converse was true for monopoly. It might be, Brandeis conceded, that some industries had technological economies to scale sufficiently large relative to market size that a single firm could produce more cheaply than many (though he also thought his contemporaries had vastly overestimated the effects of scale economies on firm size).[17] But exogenous costs were an unreliable foundation for rate making. In practice, Brandeis thought that the challenge of regulated monopoly was similar to competition policy. For, regulated or not, Brandeis said, "monopoly has a deadening effect." Economic "progress flows only from struggle," and "when you create a monopoly you remove the stimulus, the incentive, to all business." So "however well intentioned and however well regulated," Brandeis concluded that monopolies "inevitably become, in course of time, oppressive, arbitrary, unprogressive, and inefficient."[18] If price regulation was warranted, as it was in municipal utilities, the state's first obligation was to provide nonmarket incentives to improvement. Only then should government address the distributive question. Finally, Brandeis thought the state had a legitimate role to play in providing regulated industries with information about how to improve, unavailable in the market or from within the firm. The role of such information was to disconcert economic custom by providing superior examples.

In short, if competition failed to provide incentives for improvement and information about how to improve, the state should step into the breach. Like competition policy, exogenous costs were an unreliable guide to monopoly policy. And, whereas competition raised inescapably public questions about individual behavior, monopoly raised inescapably private questions about incentives to economic improvement. In practice, the public/private distinction collapsed.[19]

BOSTON GAS

Brandeis entered the debate over public utility regulation in a 1905 fight over natural gas in Boston. Massachusetts had been an early innovator in regulation. In 1869 the legislature created one of the nation's first railroad commissions. Sixteen years later, Boston followed suit. The Public Utility Commission was empowered to regulate natural gas and electricity rates according to a fair rate of return on capital. Critics, however, judged Boston's experiment a failure. The utilities had eluded regulation by "stockwatering," that is, by issuing more and more stock without new assets. The higher the "rate base," they realized, the higher the rates; and the higher the rates, the higher the dividends.

In 1894 the Massachusetts legislature passed an anti-stock watering bill, to ensure that the value of securities was related to plant and equipment devoted to public use. Utility financiers, however, were notoriously resourceful in outfoxing this law as well. In 1902, Boston streetcar magnate Henry M. Whitney and Kidder-Peabody partner James L. Richards proposed to merge eight natural gas companies in Boston and nearby Brookline. The combined capitalization of Boston Consolidated Gas would be nearly a third higher than the separate companies. No sooner had the state legislature passed the Special Consolidation Act of 1903 than reformers protested. The new corporation violated the 1894 law, charged the Massachusetts Franchise League.

As a prominent League member, Brandeis was roused to battle. But, to the dismay of his colleagues, the peoples' lawyer attempted to broker a compromise. Situating himself between reformers and financiers, Brandeis proposed to reduce Boston Consolidated's capitalization, but to allow the corporation to pay dividends on both stock and "surplus." While he agreed with the League that the corporate "surplus" account was built upon ill-gotten profits from overcapitaliztion, Brandeis counseled that "there is such a thing as vested wrongs as well as vested rights." Though the community had an equitable interest in the surplus, it no right to confiscate it altogether.[20]

Brandeis used the opening afforded by his distributive compromise to leverage a more substantial reform. The trouble with rate-of-return regulation, he told industry and reformers alike, was that it provided all the wrong incentives. Instead of working to improve service and lower costs, utilities had every reason to find political means to increase capitalization. Inevitably, the public responded in kind. The record was clear. Utilities and reformers locked horns in Massachusetts, while service deteriorated. So intent were both parties upon realizing the adversarial interests conferred upon them by law, that their shared interests in economic improvement went unheeded.

There was an alternative. "Fair price and fair value," Brandeis said, "were . . . but single facets of a much larger problem."[21] The public should abandon its obsession with the rate-of-return earned by regulated corporations. "The amount of dividend to be permitted at any time was a matter which should be determined only indirectly, namely, in fixing the price of gas."[22] "The proper aim of the public must not be to limit dividends, but to secure gas of good quality at low prices . . . a limitation on dividends was desirable only when it conduced to that end; and . . . under the proper conditions a reasonable assurance of the undisturbed enjoyment of large dividends might be the best method of attaining cheap gas."[23] Instead of rate-of-return regulation, Brandeis advocated a profit sharing system devised in London. In "sliding scale" regulation "the amount the company" received in dividends depended "upon what was given to the community." If, for example, it produced 75 cent gas, the utility ought to "be allowed to receive more in dividend than if they gave $1 gas."[24]

Brandeis' proposal garnered hostility from both sides. Utility officials initially criticized it for failing to protect shareholders more explicitly from property confiscation. A minority faction within the Franchise League and several members of the Boston Gas Commission – Brandeis called them the "fanatics" – thought the sliding scale idea admitted defeat. After all, it gave up state control over monopoly rents. But Brandeis found support from Massachusetts Governor Guild, other League members, and, in time, from Boston Consolidated's president, James L. Richards. Publicly, Brandeis argued that sliding scale regulation offered a way out of the endless political conflict that roused a growing movement for municipal ownership (which he opposed for the same reasons he opposed monopoly).

In 1906 Governor Guild signed the Boston Sliding Scale Act into law. It set 90 cents per thousand as the "standard price" of gas and 7 percent as the "standard dividend" for the company. The company was licensed to increase its dividends at a rate of 1 percent for every 5 cents reduction in the price of gas. New stock issues were to be regulated by the commission. Provisions were made for publishing in detail the cost of manufacturing and distributing gas. Finally, the commission was empowered, upon petition, to hold public hearings, where it would hear proposals to alter the ratio of rates to dividends in response to changing economic conditions.

At the end of one year, Massachusetts gas sales had increased 16.6 percent, Consolidated's dividends grew 1 percent, and the price of gas dropped to the Franchise League's initially proposed figure of 85 cents. In addition to providing the company with effective incentives to improve, standard prices and dividends provided a benchmark against which improvements could be compared. Brandeis noted that in 1907 stockholders gained an additional $151,240 and consumers about $400,000 more than what they would have received under the League's proposal. Moreover, Boston compared well with other cities. In New York, Brandeis pointed out, the state legislature had imposed a 20-cent reduction by fiat. The utility balked, contesting the law as unconstitutional. In the end, the state Supreme Court issued an injunction; the consumer continued to pay the old rate; and the company's stock lost half its value. The only cities with cheaper gas prices than Boston, Brandeis crowed, were those located in the richest natural gas and coal regions of the country.

This was clear evidence of economic improvement. But unlike the economists, Brandeis refused to separate political from economic ends. The 1906 Act effectively removed Boston Gas from the vice of manipulating its rate base through politics, he said. Instead, the company now accomplished public ends. "If this corporation is able to conduct its business without the necessity of a political department, there is good reason to believe that others of our public service corporations will follow the lead," Brandeis said. For "the principal evil that has been done by our public service corporations is not excessive charges, but the corruption of our municipal and state governments."[25]

In sum, where Adams thought science could separate economy from politics, Brandeis – like his republican predecessors – could not imagine such a distinction. The trick of statecraft, from his perspective, was not to locate the real boundary between public and private or confiscation and extortion. It was to design institutions that could redirect self-interest toward public ends. This was not just a problem of practical politics. Brandeis' democratic experimentalism was more coherent. In blurring the distinction between public and private, he attempted to show how it was possible to craft an institutional structure that made experimentation, deliberation, and collective learning possible. To be sure, conflict would not vanish – this is why there was ample opportunity for deliberation over the ratio between dividends and rates. On the other hand, unlike rate-of-return regulation, Brandeis' regulatory architecture also provided ground for cooperation and improvement.

THE PREDICAMENT OF RAILROAD REGULATION

Nowhere was the predicament of regulated monopoly more vexing than in railroad regulation. The more *Smyth* v. *Ames* and Adams' objectivist methodology shaped regulation, the more paralyzed it became. By the time Brandeis joined the struggle in 1911, the ICC had locked horns with the carriers in a decade-long stalemate over rate levels. Although Brandeis entered the contest a partisan (counsel for the shippers), he attempted to reframe the problem of regulation here as well. This section sketches the predicament of Progressive Era railroad regulation and Brandeis' part in it. Its purpose is to further flesh out the pragmatist critique of foundationalist theories of regulation and to describe Brandeis' alternative. Though Brandeis built upon his Massachusetts experience, his approach to railroad regulation became far more sophisticated and elaborate in its difference with the objectivist program. It would be in the arcane details of cost accounting that Brandeis made his greatest progress in overcoming the predicament of rate-of-return regulation.

The ICC was born in 1887, with a mandate to solve two problems: rate discrimination and extortionate rate levels. The former involved relative rates. The commission was to ensure that ratepayers paid roughly the same for like services. In particular, the Interstate Commerce Act outlawed the long-standing practice of charging more for short than long hauls along the same line. The ICC's second problem was like the one faced by the Massachusetts Utility Commission, namely, how to set rate levels to ensure a fair distribution between ratepayers and shareholders. As in Massachusetts, both issues were initially framed through a liberal scientific or neoclassical lens.

During its first decade, the ICC riveted its attention on discrimination. In 1887, the commission's first chair, Thomas McIntyre Cooley, enlisted Henry Carter Adams to chair the commission's department of statistics. Drawing upon the marginalist approach to cost/price relations, Adams thought the discrimination problem irresolvable. Efforts to arbitrate disputes over discrimination by reference to the cost of service, he wrote, were largely self-defeating. Following the pathbreaking work of neoclassical economist Frank Taussig, Adams argued that it was impossible to segregate the costs of many railroad services, because they made joint use of common capital equipment. As Taussig put it, long and short haul, car-load and less-than-car-load, bulk and specialty freight, even passenger and freight traffic made simultaneous use of railroad track and rolling stock. Most rail services, as Taussig put it, incurred "joint costs." Coupled with high fixed costs, joint costs meant that railroads could add freight and passengers with very little additional cost. The result was a counterintuitive, but efficient, rate structure. On competitive (typically long-haul) traffic, railroads tended to set prices just above variable costs. Any revenues mobilized to pay off the railroads' enormous capital costs were deemed useful. The trouble was that fixed costs had to be made up elsewhere and the burden fell upon noncompetitive – often local, specialized – freight. Despite its apparent inequities, this rate structure maximized total tonnage and gross revenues. As such, it resulted in sufficient scale economies to reduce *all* rates. In short, Adams said, drawing on Taussig, it made more sense to compare rates according to their "value of service" (or what the traffic would bear) than their costs. Indeed, though Adams actively lobbied Congress to increase the ICC's powers to collect statistics, following the joint cost principle, in 1894 he ordered his department to abandon even the simplest form of overhead cost segregation, namely, between freight and passenger traffic.[26]

By century's turn the Supreme Court handed down two rulings that made the discrimination problem a moot point. In *Alabama Midland* (1895), the Court echoed Taussig's message when it declared that the existence of competition was good reason to depart from the long-haul/short-haul clause of the Interstate Commerce Act.[27] Three years later, the Court codified Justice Field's balancing dictum in *Smyth* v. *Ames*. Recall that Justice Harlan declared the regulated railroad corporation a person under the Constitution, who could not be deprived of property without just compensation. The ICC, Harlan insisted, must ensure a reasonable rate-of-return on the "fair value" of property devoted to public use. Fair value was an objective empirical matter, subject to judicial scrutiny.

Adams agreed. "No tribunal upon which the duty [to set fair rates] may be imposed, whether legislative, administrative or judicial, can pass a satisfactory judgement upon the reasonableness of railway rates without taking into account the value of railway property."[28] The ICC's warrant, however, was inadequate for the task. The statistics department had always used "commercial value" (the value of stocks and bonds) to estimate railroad cost. After *Smyth* v. *Ames*, Adams began to doubt that "the par value of securities measures in any way the real value of railway property."[29] Debt, especially, did not represent the "real" value of property. If instead, Adams wrote, the physical value of railroad property was determined, then the courts and the commission might have something solid to work on. For nearly a decade, Adams officially requested from Congress authority and resources to compile a physical survey of American railroad costs. Until a coalition of progressive Republicans and Democrats took control of Congress in 1910 and passed the Mann–Elkins Act, his requests fell on deaf ears.

Those who thought that once the ICC had the proper administrative tools to regulate monopoly in 1910, the long and bitter struggle over railroads would come to an end, were sorely disappointed. From 1911 to 1920 railroad regulation was paralyzed by stalemate.[30] No sooner was the ICC empowered to set maximum rates in 1910, than the carriers joined together in regional rate associations to request across-the-board rate increases. While labor and material cost had steadily advanced over the previous decade, they complained, rates had stagnated. As a result, shareholders and bankers watched railroad operating ratios (the annual ratios of operating expenses to operating revenues) deteriorate and it became harder and harder to finance improvements.

The ICC balked. Did the carriers think that every time their costs increased the commission would compensate with an equal rate increase? Such a policy surely violated the balancing dictum outlined in *Smyth* v. *Ames*. It would ensure, for example, that the carriers took all the gain from new investment and the public none. Or, as Brandeis said, "it would be a most serious danger to the country to establish the principle that if, according to present conditions, they need more money they raise rates instead of doing what in every competitive business it is necessary to do, namely, to consider whether you can not make more money by reducing your cost . . . If we are to travel in the vicious circle of meeting higher costs by ever higher costs, if the burden of increased rates and other burdens are to come upon the community, then where is the limit?"[31]

Neither, the ICC added, did the operating ratio provide the sort of information necessary to judge rate levels. A fair rate-of-return could only be adjudicated on the basis of an objective account of investment. And Congress had authorized a full physical valuation of the railroads only once the full implications of the 1910 advance rate case became clear. It would be years, the commission said, before it completed the task. Until then the ICC would continue to use commercial value, and on this basis an across-the-board rate increase was unwarranted.

The railroads countered that they had invested vast sums in improvements in recent years only to watch their net revenues shrink. The more they invested, the worse their profitability became. "Need," the ICC said, does not in and of itself justify a rate increase. But if that was so, the carriers complained, then the commission was saying that all improvements must be funded from private capital (savings). The railroads were not allowed to accumulate a surplus from which to fund improvements and assure steady dividends necessary to raise new money at favorable rates. Surely this could not be the ICC's theory of regulation. If so, then ratepayers enjoy all the benefits of improvements and investors have no reason to invest. The logic is painfully circular.

In a single play in four acts, commission and carriers locked horns in a seemingly intractable conflict. So paralyzed did railroad regulation become that on the eve of the First World War, President Wilson nationalized the railroads for the duration of the conflict. In 1920, the carriers returned to private hands under the supervision of an ICC with new obligations and powers. Among other provisions, the Transportation Act of 1920 guaranteed the railroads a $5\frac{1}{2}$ percent return on capital. In the same year, legal realist Gerard Henderson looked back on the ICC's experience with rate-of-return regulation with the skeptical eye of a seasoned pragmatist. The positivist search for an objective rate base, he wrote, proved far more elusive than the Court and the economists thought. Henderson blamed the paralysis of regulation on *Smyth* v. *Ames*. Though the Court thought it had articulated a clear and determinate rule, its logic was circular. The search for an objective rate base was a chimera. Any way the commission and the carriers looked at it, the value of property depended not only on original investment; it also had to include some measure of earning capacity. Earning capacity was best measured by net earnings and net earnings, in turn, depended upon rates. "But," Henderson protested, "it was precisely the level of rates which the regulating commission was trying to fix. Whenever it reduces rates it reduces earnings and whenever it reduces earnings it reduces value. We cannot tell what rates the company is to charge until we know what its value is, and we cannot tell what its value is till we know what rates it may charge."

"The relation between the public utility and the community," Henderson charged,

cannot be expressed in terms of a simple, quantitatively ascertainable fact, for the relation involves numerous and complex factors which depend on compromise and practical adjustment rather than deductive logic. The whole doctrine of Smyth v. Ames rests upon a gigantic illusion. The fact, which for twenty years the court has been vainly trying to find does not exist. "Fair value" must be shelved among the great juristic myths of history, with the Law of Nature and the Social Contract. As a practical concept, form which practical conclusions can be drawn, it is valueless.[32]

To be sure, Henderson acknowledged, "a practical decision must be reached, however intellectually distasteful the task may be." But this should be an administrative, not a judicial, task. And "if a commission is appointed to investigate the relevant facts, to negotiate with the railroad interests, and to fix a fair and workable measure of competition, and if it appears that the commission has examined the evidence honestly and impartially, and has given all parties a fair hearing, . . . then the Supreme Court should give a very wide latitude to the discretion of the commission," Henderson wrote. "The constitutional function of the courts should be merely to guard against a rule of compensation so outrageous as to shock the common sense of justice."[33] But, it was precisely this sort of appeal to "interests" that Field and Adams were attempting to bypass, because it seemed such a relativist notion of justice. What was "common sense," after all, than the restatement of interests? And it was precisely the seemingly intractable clash of interests that led Adams to peg his hopes on science to restore social harmony in the first place. Moreover, in retrospect, twentieth-century studies of agencies that took Henderson's advice often found them captured by the very industries they were intended to regulate. It appears, then, there was no way out of the predicament of regulated monopoly.[34]

A PRAGMATIST ALTERNATIVE

Brandeis was a partisan to the advance rate controversy. He served first as counsel to the shippers; later the ICC hired him to help assess the legality of the carriers' claims. From the outset, however, Brandeis searched for a way out of the objectivist cul-de-sac. In calling Harrington Emerson to the stand in 1911, he began to lay the foundations for an alternative to regulatory paralysis. Though, in theory, scientific management was just as objectivist as neoclassical economics, Brandeis found in its engineering sensibility a means to solve the twin problems of standard setting and political conflict.[35] Where scientific economics made false promises to reveal the "real" costs of economic activity, scientific management provided a method to construct and compare costs through experience and deliberation. Unlike liberal legal science's elusive guarantee to balance the ineradicable conflict between extortion and confiscation, in engineering Brandeis found a method to serve the mutual interests of consumers and property owners by encouraging economic improvement. And unlike Adams' promise to protect liberty and democracy by locating a bright line between public and private, Brandeis found techniques in scientific management to focus deliberation on precisely what standards would be used to evaluate the railroads. Brandeis thought one need not capitulate to the false promises of objectivity or to Henderson's relativism. For in scientific management, he thought he had found a way to reconceptualize the two issues that plagued rate-of-return regulation: the problem of cost determination and the problem of standard setting.

Consider first the problem of cost. For Brandeis, a lawyer, to parade scientific managers before railroad managers seems the height of hubris. After all, as business historian Alfred Chandler has shown, the railroads were the leaders in managerial capitalism – the first to perfect economies of scale through high volume throughput, to create extensive managerial hierarchies, and to introduce modern cost accounting techniques. And yet it was precisely railroad accounting and efficiency that Brandeis found wanting. The carriers, he charged, had locked themselves into accounting techniques that led them to emphasize scale economies at a cost to all other improvements. By comparing railroad practices to the cost accounting techniques developed by scientific managers in manufacturing, Brandeis revealed the limits and perverse consequences of the high fixed cost paradigm shared by economists and managers alike. In so doing, he laid the groundwork not only for a critique of railroad management, but also for an alternative to physical valuation.

In 1914, Brandeis told the carriers and the commission that there was a "most surprising difference" between the cost accounting techniques used by railroads and manufacturers. While "leading American manufacturers know accurately . . . the cost of every one of the numerous items made and sold by them," the railroads, who "make and sell a most varied transportation service, do not know the cost of any of the services . . . they furnish." Only a few even "undertake to separate . . . the cost of freight and passenger service in the aggregate," and among them, there is virtually no consensus on the "proper basis for such a separation." Contrast the vanguard of American manufacturing. Here, accurate assessment of product costs was found necessary not only to ensure "high operating efficiency," but also to distinguish profitable from unprofitable products. The railroads could never conserve their "legitimate revenues," Brandeis charged, until they had "a reasonably accurate knowledge of whether a particular service [was] rendered at a profit or at a loss." Worse still, "in the absence of such knowledge, the traffic manager's success or failure is tested by the tonnage moved instead of the profit earned."[36] The carriers' overemphasis on scale economies was an artifact of poor accounting, not nature.

Brandeis' critique did not end with the railroads. If he was correct, it seemed that the economists and the regulators had reified bad accounting techniques as though they were accurate measures of nature. Recall how in Taussig's model railroads took on tonnage at a loss in order to cover fixed costs. Given the high ratio of fixed to variable costs inherent in railroad technology, such behavior was rational, because it maximized gross revenues and scale economies. Brandeis, the pragmatist, refused to accept the realist premises of the marginalist's model. The method by which railroads measured costs, he said, shaped their traffic market strategies (not the other way around). There was good reason to believe, moreover, that those market strategies failed to serve the carriers themselves, never mind the public at large. Thus, cost was not so much an objective measure, as it was a human construct, shaped inescapably by human ends.

If the carriers were wanting for cash, Brandeis charged, it was more likely due to the "disastrous financial results" of their cost accounting practices than it was to the ICC's failure to raise rates. As counsel for the shippers and the ICC, Brandeis pressed this point with the railroads. Do you evaluate service and production according to the spread between cost and rates, Brandeis asked the managers? Do you break transportation processes down into their component parts and compare performance over time? Do you measure the cost and profitability of the wide variety of services you offer, so you can make improvements and concentrate on cultivating your most profitable services? When Brandeis asked Baltimore and Ohio President Daniel Willard the cost of locomotive repair on his road, he responded with the average annual cost per locomotive mile. "Just see how uncertain that factor is," Brandeis charged. "You are taking the average. [But] the only way you tell whether the work on any one of those cars was efficiently done, is it not, would be for you to know the particular thing that was done on that particular car?" But management, like marginalists, saw little sense in disaggregating the costs of production and service. In an industry where they perceived most costs to be joint, it made sense to add service if it brought any additional revenue to service debt.[37]

Was Brandeis correct? After all, management, economists, and even many regulators, agreed that railroads had high fixed and joint costs. There is compelling evidence, however, to support Brandeis. Henry Carter Adams' successor on the ICC, Otto Lorenz, conducted a series of studies from 1907 to 1916, which showed that the high-fixed-cost model held only at lower levels of traffic density. Once railroads achieved the density typical of twentieth-century carriers in the East and the Midwest, average costs remained constant regardless of traffic density, and almost 100 percent of operating expenses were variable. While these conditions did not hold for lines with lower density in the South and the West, Lorenz concluded that even in those regions most costs were variable. In a recent article on the subject, Gregory Thompson reports that "if fixed costs are limited to interest on debt and leases of other railroads, they amounted to only 10 to 20 percent of total expenses in the early 1870s, on the eve of the first world war, and in the 1920s and 1930s. They constituted a higher percentage of total costs in the 1880s during extensive new construction in a period of high interest rates, but still only 25 to 35 percent. In 1916 . . . [fixed costs accounted for] 19 percent of costs." Moreover, a survey of the leading twentieth-century studies of railroad costs reveals "a relationship between fixed and variable railroad costs that is precisely the opposite of the conventional wisdom." Like Brandeis, Thompson concludes "the ability of a railroad to reduce operating expenses and adjust supposedly fixed plant in the face of traffic reduction is far greater than commonly thought . . . The popular notion of a railroad line having unlimited capacity once it is put down is entirely inaccurate."[38] There is also evidence to indicate there was another way. Recognizing that most costs were variable, management for the regional Chicago Great Western Railroad organized operations to optimize the complex mix of local and less-than-carload with through and car-load freight. By doing so, it outperformed many of its larger scale, interregional competitors, who were the subject of Brandeis' critique.[39] Despite this compelling evidence, my purpose here is not to conclude the historical debate over railroad costs. It is merely to demonstrate there were good empirical reasons for Brandeis' contemporaries to consider his critique and alternative seriously.

From Brandeis' perspective scientific management could rectify three perverse consequences of the high fixed cost paradigm: an overemphasis on long-haul heavy tonnage, an underemphasis on reducing overhead costs, and the widespread provision of unprofitable services. Improved cost accounting involved two techniques. In contrast to the joint cost model, the first involved what today's accountants call "product costing."[40] As Brandeis' witnesses conceived it, product costing involved three steps. The first was to disaggregate diverse rail services, such as passenger and freight, long haul and short haul, car-load and less-than-car-load. The second step was, where possible, to measure the distribution of overhead costs to each service. The third was to develop more refined measures of variable cost – labor, fuels, and so on – for each category of service. With these sorts of measures, Brandeis' witnesses said, it was possible to discriminate between profitable and unprofitable services and to make decisions accordingly. Brandeis, for one, suspected that product costing would reveal that railroads relying on cruder measures systematically overemphasized the big tonnage over less-than-car-load, the long haul over the short, and freight over passengers.

The second agenda Brandeis and his witnesses drew from scientific management was standard setting through disciplined comparison. This involved two techniques: intrafirm standard costing and interfirm benchmarking. In standard costing, accountants drew upon historical measures to predetermine costs before they were actually incurred. In many cases, this involved calculating a running average for some production cost category. Printers, for example, had long calculated cost standards for many categories of material, labor, and the distribution of overheads to different departments and products. This allowed them to make useful judgements during the production process and, where possible, to make adjustments in real time.[41] By contrast, charged Harrington Emerson, "no railroad has ever determined any cost standards either for maintenance or operation of equipment, maintenance of right of way, or consumption of fuel, yet there is not a railroad in the country on which each one of these cost standards could not be determined in a very short time and with very close accuracy, at a cost equal to the saving effected in a single month."[42] The Atchison, Topeka, and Santa Fe, Emerson claimed, succeeded in reducing overall repair costs by as much as 35 percent by predetermining detailed standard costs.[43]

While comparison to standard costs was critical to Brandeis' case against the carriers, his proposal for interfirm benchmarking is more important to the argument here, because it provided an alternative – pragmatist – framework for state action. As we shall see, Brandeis rejected rate-of-return regulation for railroads as well as natural gas. In doing so, he also rejected its corollary accounting task: physical valuation. Instead, he thought the ICC should facilitate disciplined comparisons of detailed cost performance between firms. Unlike objectivist efforts to discover bedrock standards upon which rates could be calculated, the pragmatist approach was to construct comparative standards of best practice by encouraging railroads to adopt a common cost accounting language. Brandeis put it this way.

We have had combinations to increase prices, of which the proposed rate increase is an instance. What we need to reduce the cost of living is a combination to reduce the costs of production. As a first step to accomplishing this it is necessary (1) that unit costs be determined; (2) that these unit costs of all the railroad be published though the Interstate Commerce Commission so as to be available to each road. In this way we hope, as a first step toward scientific management and increased efficiency, to learn the lowest cost at which each operation is produced by any road so that each company may reach the lowest then existing record in that department. After such unit costs are ascertained, there may then be an advance in the science by elimination of waste and by improvement of method, to secure a still lower cost.[44]

To this end, Brandeis advocated the establishment of the government Bureau of Railroad Costs, empowered to set cost accounting standards, calculate useful comparisons, and disseminate the results to railroads and shippers alike. The Bureau would ensure that the "unit costs of each operation in every department of every railroad . . . be ascertained." In this way, cost calculations would be "properly supervised, analyzed, classified, and compared, so that each railroad should have the benefit of knowing the lowest unit cost of each operation attained by any American railroad, and how it was attained."[45]

Brandeis suggested the ICC employ Emerson's colleague, F. Lincoln Hutchins, to head the Bureau. Hutchins' design for interfirm benchmarking, Brandeis added, could be found in a series of articles in *The Engineering Magazine* published in 1912. Like Brandeis, Hutchins criticized rate-of-return regulation. Restrictions on return removed incentives to improve. More to the point, he found Adams' neoclassical approach to railroad statistics at best incoherent, at worst counterproductive. "The present attempt to fix return to capital invested in railroads, by means of physical valuation of the property," Hutchins wrote, "has no scientific foundation and will lead to no satisfactory result to the railroad capitalist, or to the community." Like Henderson, he thought physical valuation indeterminate. What basis, Hutchins asked, could be used to set the rates of several roads running between the same points, when there are large differences in physical property and capitalization? What should one do with a carrier expensively located initially, whose costs have gone up over time? Should rates be set to permit the least advantageously situated road to realize an average return? If so, how should the ICC restrict the better situated from earning more? If, on the other hand, rates are set so the most favorably situated earns only an average return, what happens to those who cannot live up to that rate? Similarly, how would a regulator adjust rates between classes of passenger and merchandise traffic on a rate-of-return logic? "Just rates," Hutchins concluded, cannot be determined according to neoclassical logic. The "community" has no interest in whether a railroad secures a "very high or a very low" rate, per se. Instead, the community's interest lies in ever better service at lower rates.[46]

The ICC, Hutchins went on, cannot achieve this end as currently constituted. Instead of saddling the public with a costly bill for physical value of railroads, the commission ought to devise a uniform system of cost accounting for the carriers, so that detailed efficiency comparisons could be conducted. Given the vast diversity of conditions, "the problem is to obtain a unit in which each kind of service is equated to the same value; like the engineer's 'benchmark,' it must serve as the base from which to measure the variation from any standard selected. This unit must be such as to measure the cost of service and efficiency, not only as to one road at different periods [i.e. "standard costs"], but as to various roads one with the other."[47] Under Adams, the ICC's Statistics Department had "done little toward investigating the operating conditions of the roads," charged Hutchins. Its annual reports "gave no figures by which to judge the performance of individual roads." They provided no record of the "amount of service given by the roads." Nor did they reckon a "satisfactory unit from which intelligent comparisons can be made." Having internalized the theory of joint costs, the ICC's figures did not "permit the determination of direct costs with overhead burden connected therewith so that intelligent comparisons may be made as to efficiency."[48]

Hutchins demonstrated how to design a benchmarking system. The first step was to construct a common unit of measure, so that diverse practices could be compared. Drawing upon ICC average rate data and aggregate passenger-miles and freight ton-miles, Hutchins constructed a single metric – the "service unit" – for comparison. He then chose a sample of twenty large railways from among the carriers whose claim was currently before the ICC. For each he calculated the unit costs – in "cents per service unit" – for six categories of expenditures: maintenance of way and structures, maintenance of equipment, traffic costs, general charges, labor, and material. (Hutchins pointed out that once a Cost Bureau was empowered to request additional information, comparisons could become more refined.) Using the railway with the lowest unit cost as the benchmark for each category, Hutchins formed a scale (the benchmark at 100 percent) and graphed costs trends in each category for ten years for all twenty carriers in his sample.

To be sure, benchmarking was the beginning, not the end, of collective inquiry. Instead of adjudicating questions in the abstract – 'does the current rate of return merit a rate increase?' – benchmarking revealed more refined empirical questions. Is comparatively high maintenance cost, Hutchins asked, the result of more complex equipment, poor investment, or a failure to attend to repair shop efficiency? Do irregularities in units costs over time reveal changing conditions or the fact that the carriers have "no settled policy, no fixed standards" of improvement? With more refined benchmarking categories, Hutchins thought an "efficiency bureau" could provide information, which would lead individual railroads and the state to "investigate methods by which to bring all roads up to the best practice found on any."[49]

For Brandeis, then, Hutchins' benchmarking system provided a pragmatist alternative to Adam's scientific naturalism. Properly measured, Adams wrote, railroad accounts are "true records of administration, and he who controls accounts, can in large measure control the policy of management." Subject to "strict supervision" by the Statistics Bureau, railroad management could be monitored to "test compliance . . . with the rules of the Commission." Physical valuation promised administrative bedrock, a measure to test the probity of railroad accounts and to provide a regulatory lever to adjudicate an otherwise intractable conflict. Scientific measurement, in other words, provided a foundation for moral judgement.[50] Benchmarking, by contrast, promised a common language through which individual firms could compare across diverse experiences. As Brandeis and Hutchins imagined it, a Railroad Cost Bureau would provide information unavailable in the market or within the firm by which management could see how they compared with the best and worst performers in the industry. In this sense, the goal of regulatory measurement was to coordinate comparison, not to monitor compliance.

In Brandeis' view, benchmarking was not merely a better technical solution to the challenges of economic improvement and public administration. It also provided a moving standard by which individuals could evaluate personal development and their contribution to the social good. In the midst of the railroad controversy, Brandeis testified before a Senate committee investigating scientific management in the workplace. Asked whether the goal of scientific management was to strip craft workers of individual creativity in work, he said if that were its necessary consequence, he would surely oppose it. "After all, our business is not to make goods, but to make men, in my view of it . . . One of the first things that ought to be done to develop a man is to make him realize the possibilities of accomplishment, the joys of accomplishment, and the possibility of development in the work which he is doing. He has got to conclude . . . that is it something which he does . . . better or may do better than he did before, or perhaps better than others do. He ought to realize all the time that he has not gotten to the end." One of the great challenges of contemporary work, Brandeis added, is that men have no "standard by which their accomplishment can be measured as compared with somebody else, [no] tests as to the excellence of their work." A man wants to "play a game of ball," to compete and to win. But most of all he "delights in his particular performance" compared to his own past or to the performance of others. None of this can be accomplished without a standard, a benchmark for measurement; and scientific management, Brandeis told the senators, provided just such a technique.[51]

Benchmarking was not the only means by which the ICC could coordinate standard setting and economic learning. In addition to a Bureau of Railroad Costs, Brandeis also proposed the ICC establish a series of experiment stations.

Modeled on those run by the Department of Agriculture, the commission would "develop valuable inventions and discoveries" of its own. Perhaps of greater service, it would test inventions and methods devised by others and disseminate its findings. "There are undoubtedly in existence today hundreds of inventions . . . which, if adopted, would enhance the efficiency of railroads operation . . . , but which are not known to the operating men because no adequate means exist for bringing them to their notice." Such demonstration projects, Brandeis concluded, were a "proper function of government," since they helped "raise the standards" of railroad safety and efficiency.[52]

If a cost bureau and experiment stations provided railroads with information about how to improve, the problem of ensuring incentives to improve remained. Here, Brandeis drew upon his experience with sliding scales in Massachusetts natural gas. He thought that rate-of-return regulation gave railroads, no less than local utilities, perverse incentives to raise costs. Any rule fixing a maximum return on capital inevitably reduced efficiency by "placing a limit on achievement," he said. "The public interest, as well as justice [for the carriers], demands, therefore, the due appreciation of greater efficiency in management; and some method must be found of determining the degree of efficiency attained and providing adequate rewards."[53] Sliding scales, Brandeis thought, were up to the task.

When private capital is engaged in a "quasi-public business," he told the Hadley Railroad Securities Commission, it should receive compensation on a "sliding scale, so that the greater the service to the public, the greater the profit to those furnishing that service." Massachusetts successfully reduced the selling price and raised the stock dividends of natural gas by pegging one against the other. To be sure, implementing sliding scales in railroad regulation was more complex. Rates and service were more diverse and coordination between inter- and intrastate regulation presented a number of challenges. Nonetheless, Brandeis thought the principle of profit sharing sound and its technical details tractable.[54]

Brandeis found, in scientific management, an alternative to the positivist standard setting process advocated by Field and Adams. Instead of the elusive promise to discover nature's line between public and private, Brandeis reconceived standard setting as a process in which decentralized practices (experiments) were subject to disciplined comparison through uniform measurement. The scientific challenge of regulation was not to discover a measure beyond politics to arbitrate distributive disputes. It was to provide the carriers with ongoing incentives to improve and to provide them with information unavailable from the market or from within the firm about how to improve. Technically sophisticated as this framework was, Brandeis never lost sight of the political ends of regulation. The pragmatist alternative offered "individual and social development . . . worth infinitely more than . . . financial gain," he told the ICC in 1911. The Massachusetts experience demonstrated that a cooperative alternative to regulatory paralysis was possible. Instead of "standing always with shield and with sword to protect themselves against popular clamor and criticism, [railroad managers] could be looked upon as James L. Richards, of Boston, is looked upon to-day": a model "public servant," who raised Consolidated Natural Gas from a "state of inefficiency and scandal" to one of steady improvement in rates, service, and profits. "The possibility lies before the railroads to-day. They may become in fact, as they are legally, public servants. They may secure the admiration and gratitude of the public as well as of the stockholders." Or they could sustain the paralyzing discord that marked railroad regulation so far. Scientific management and sliding scales offered a technical means to moral development and cooperation, should government, the railroads, and the public muster the collective will to make them a reality.[55]

WHOSE HUBRIS?

America's first experiment in national economic regulation failed. In the story recounted here it was not because of Brandeis' confusion, utopianism, cunning, or hubris. It was due, instead, to what political scientist James Scott has recently called the hubris of "high modernism."[56] From Prussian forestry to Brasilia, modern states, Scott writes, have failed miserably when they have pursued utopian programs of enlightenment rationalism. To be sure, the greatest disasters, like Soviet collective agriculture, have occurred in the absence of organized opposition in civil society. This was not the case with American railroad regulation. As paralyzed as it became in the Progressive Era, the Transportation Act of 1920 forged a fragile bargain between the ICC, shippers, and the railroads. Still, railroad regulation never became anything more than a jumbled compromise between economic objectivity and Henderson's procedural pluralism. It continued to be plagued by conflicts of jurisdiction, confusion over goals, and contradictions in policy.[57]

Faced with the modern state's many failures, Scott argues that we should reject high modernist pretensions for an older notion of practical reason he associates with the Greek idea of "metis." More than simply craft or folk knowledge, metis "represents a wide array of practical skills and acquired intelligence in responding to a constantly changing natural and human environment."[58] Of course, advocates of self-regulating markets have long levied similar criticisms against the pretensions of the twentieth-century government. Hayek, especially, argued that decentralized, self-regulating markets were superior precisely because they ensured practical reason in the face of uncertainty and the limits of human rationality.[59] But self-regulating markets were unsustainable in railroads (if, as economic sociologists remind us, they ever existed at all). Left alone, well over one half of the railroad mileage in the United States collapsed and fell into court ordered receivership between the 1870s and the 1890s. Railroads also generated rate structures so inequitable that in an open democracy it was likely that groups would demand public redress. Practical reason, it seems, foundered with the self-regulating market.

Brandeis' pragmatism represented an alternative to practical reason and high modern rationalism. This case illustrates how modernism was not of a single piece. Science was syncretic, decomposable, that is, into component parts that could be combined with existing and novel ideas or institutions in surprising ways. Brandeis and his adversaries drew upon science in very different ways. Where liberal scientific jurists and neoclassical economists thought science could ensure a clear separation of public and private, Brandeis thought it could be used to bring private criteria into the public sphere. Where Adams thought science could ensure objectivity in the face of particular interests, Brandeis thought it could harness private interests to the public good. The trouble with practical reason alone, pragmatists like Brandeis thought, is that it could become locked into unreflective custom (witness, for example, railroad accounting practices). Through benchmarking and democratic deliberation over the proper ratio between rates and dividends, Brandeis thought railroads, ratepayers, and the state might disconcert old assumptions and generate new hypotheses. In the course of doing so, he hoped they would learn to improve the way they ran railroads, regulated industry, and communicated with one another.

Of course, we shall never know for sure whether Brandeis' proposals would have worked better than Adams' version of rate-of-return regulation or Henderson's procedural pluralism. Nonetheless, Brandeis' design was coherent, and two pieces of evidence – the high ratio of variable to fixed costs in railroads and the success of sliding scale regulation in Massachusetts natural gas – indicates it was promising. More confidently, we can conclude that Brandeis' attraction to scientific management should no longer appear puzzling.

NOTES

1. Prior to 1950, political scientist Alpheus Mason wrote cogently and sympathetically about Brandeis' efforts in economic reform. See, for example, Alpheus T. Mason, *Brandeis: A Free Man's Life* (New York: Viking, 1946). After 1950, scholars tended to criticize Brandeis for his atavistic approach to economics. See, for example, Richard Hofstadter, "What Happened to the Antitrust Movement? Notes on an American Creed," in Earl Cheit (ed.), *The Business Establishment* (New York: John Wiley, 1964), pp. 113–51; Richard Hofstadter, *The Age of Reform: From Bryan to F.D.R.* (New York: Vintage, 1955), pp. 244–56; Louis Hartz, *The Liberal Tradition in America: An Interpretation of American Political Thought Since the Revolution* (New York: Harcourt, 1955), pp. 219–25, 237–48. The publication of Alfred D. Chandler's *The Visible Hand* in 1977 seemed to lay the final blow to Brandeis's economics. See especially Thomas K. McCraw, *Prophets of Regulation* (Cambridge, MA: Harvard University Press, 1984), pp. 80–142. On Brandeis' purported confusions and cunning in railroad regulation see Albro Martin, *Enterprise Denied: Origins of the Decline of American Railroads, 1897–1917* (New York: Columbia University Press, 1971), pp. 206–19; and S. Skowronek, *Building a New American State* (Cambridge: Cambridge University Press, 1982),

pp. 269–70. For more sympathetic recent readings, which, nonetheless, see scientific management as a contradiction in Brandeis' thought, see R. P. Adelstein, "Islands of Conscious Power: Louis D. Brandeis and the Modern Corporation," *Business History Review* 63: 3 (Autumn 1989), 614–56; Philippa Strum, *Brandeis: Beyond Progressivism* (Lawrence: University of Kansas Press, 1993), pp. 43–5; P. Strum, *Louis D. Brandeis: Justice for the People* (Cambridge, MA: Harvard University Press, 1984), pp. 163–7; Louis J. Paper, *Brandeis* (Englewood Cliffs, NJ: Prentice Hall, 1983), pp. 151–4; and C. Spillenger, "Elusive Advocate: Reconsidering Brandeis as People's Lawyer," *Yale Law Journal* 105 (April 1996), 1511–7.

2. Phillip Scranton, *Endless Novelty: Specialty Production and American Industrialization, 1865–1925* (Princeton: Princeton University Press, 1997); Gary Herrigel, *Industrial Constructions: The Sources of German Industrial Power* (Cambridge: Cambridge University Press, 1996); John K. Brown, *The Baldwin Locomotive Works, 1831–1915* (Baltimore: Johns Hopkins University Press, 1995); Regina C. Blaszczyk, *Imagining Consumers: Design and Innovation from Wedgewood to Corning* (Baltimore: Johns Hopkins University Press, 2000).

3. Charles F. Sabel and Jonathan Zeitlin, "Historical Alternatives to Mass Production: Politics, Markets and Technology in Nineteenth-Century Industrialization," *Past and Present* 108 (August 1985), 133–74; Charles F. Sabel and Jonathan Zeitlin (eds.), *World of Possibilities: Flexibility and Mass Production in Western Industrialization* (Cambridge: Cambridge University Press, 1996); Gerald Berk, *Alternative Tracks: The Constitution of American Industrial Order, 1865–1914* (Baltimore: Johns Hopkins University Press, 1994); Margaret R. Somers, "Narrativity, Narrative Identity, and Social Action: Rethinking English Class Formation," *Social Science History* 16 (Winter 1992), 591–630; Gary Herrigel, "Identity and Institutions: The Social Construction of Trade Unions in Nineteenth-Century Germany and the United States," *Studies in American Political Development* 7: 2 (Fall, 1993), 371–94; Jacob A. Vander Meulen, *The Politics of Aircraft: Building an American Military Industry* (Lawrence: University of Kansas Press, 1991).

4. Peter Miller, "Accounting as Social and Institutional Practice: An Introduction," in Anthony G. Hopwood and Peter Miller (eds.), *Accounting as Social and Institutional Practice* (Cambridge: Cambridge University Press, 1994). There has been a good deal of excellent scholarship on the social studies of accounting in recent years. In addition to the articles in Hopwood and Miller, see Theodore M. Porter, *Trust in Numbers: The Pursuit of Objectivity in Science and Public Life* (Princeton: Princeton University Press, 1995); and Mary Poovey, *A History of the Modern Fact: Problems of Knowledge in the Sciences of Wealth and Society* (Chicago: University of Chicago Press, 1998).

5. Berk, *Alternative Tracks*, 80–3.

6. Ibid.

7. Dorothy Ross, *Origins of American Social Science* (Cambridge: Cambridge University Press, 1991), 98–116; Dorothy Ross, "Socialism and American Liberalism: Academic Social Thought in the 1880s," *Perspectives in American History* 11 (1977–78); Mary O. Furner, *Advocacy and Objectivity: A Crisis in the Professionalization of American Social Science, 1865–1905* (Lexington: University Press of Kentucky, 1975).

8. On the marginalist revolution in economics, see Ernesto Screpanti and Stefano Zamagni, *An Outline of the History of Economic Thought* (Oxford: Oxford University Press, 1993), pp. 147–9, 169; Craufurd D. W. Goodwin, "Marginalism Moves to the New World," in R. D. C. Black, A. W. Coats, and C. D. W. Goodwin (eds.), *The Marginal Revolution in Economics* (Durham: Duke University Press, 1973), pp. 285–304;

Joseph Dorfman, *The Economic Mind in American Civilization*, 1865–1918, vol. 3 (New York: Viking, 1959), pp. 188–204; James Livingston, "The Social Analysis of Economic History and Theory: Conjectures on Late-Nineteenth Century American Development," *American Historical Review* 92 (1987), 69–95.

9. Screpanti and Zamagni, *An Outline of the History of Economic Thought*, 155–8.

10. H. C. Adams, "Relation of the State to Industrial Action," *Publications of the American Economic Association* 1 (1887), 54.

11. Adams, "Relation of State to Industrial Action," 55–9.

12. Adams, "Relation of State to Industrial Action," 64.

13. Herbert Hovencamp, *Enterprise and American Law*, 1836–1937 (Cambridge, MA: Harvard University Press, 1991).

14. *Smyth* v. *Ames*, 169 U.S. 466, 546 (1898). See also Berk, *Alternative Tracks*, 156–7.

15. Philippa Strum, *Louis D. Brandeis: Justice for the People* (Cambridge, MA: Harvard University Press, 1984), 95–6; Philippa Strum, *Brandeis: Beyond Progressivism* (Lawrence: University Press of Kansas, 1993); Alpheus T. Mason, *Brandeis: Lawyer and Judge in the Modern State*, 18–19. On Brandeis' pragmatism, see Daniel A. Farber, "Reinventing Brandeis: Legal Pragmatism for the Twenty-First Century," *University of Illinois Law Review* 1995 (Winter 1995), 163–90. On pragmatism and progressivism more generally, see James T. Kloppenberg, *Uncertain Victory: Social Democracy and Progressivism in European and American Thought*, 1870–1920 (New York: Oxford University Press, 1986); Richard Rorty, *Philosophy and Social Hope* (London: Penguin, 1999); Robert Hollinger and David Depew (eds.), *Pragmatism: From Progressivism to Postmodernism* (Westport, CT: Praeger, 1995). On Dewey's thinking about the relationship between science and democracy, see Robert B. Westbrook, *John Dewey and American Democracy* (Ithaca: Cornell University Press, 1991), 140–7. In the 1930s, a debate emerged among philosophers over the differences between pragmatist and positivist approaches to science, which parallels the debate recounted in this essay. See Daniel J. Wilson, "Fertile Ground: Pragmatism, Science, and Logical Positivism," in Hollinger and Depew (eds.), *Pragmatism*, 122–41.

16. Louis D. Brandeis (ed.), "The Competition that Kills," in *Business – A Profession* (Boston: Small & Maynard, 1914); Gerald Berk, "Neither Competition nor Administration: Brandeis and the Antitrust Reforms of 1914," *Studies in American Political Development* (Spring 1994), 24–59. On Brandeis's critique of the public/private distinction more generally, see Morton J. Horwitz, *The Transformation of American Law*, 1870–1960 (New York: Oxford University Press, 1992), 204–5.

17. On Brandeis' understanding of scale economies, see Berk, "Neither Competition nor Administration," 33–7.

18. *Boston American*, June 18, 1907, excepted in Lief, *The Brandeis Guide*, 179.

19. Legal historians have noted the influence of pragmatism and Brandeis on the development of "legal realism" in the interwar years. Like Brandeis, the realists criticized the public/private distinction. See, for example, W. W. Fisher III, M. J. Horwitz, and T. A. Reed (eds.), *American Legal Realism* (New York: Oxford, 1993), pp. 98–129. On Brandeis's influence on the realists, see Horwitz, *The Transformation of American Law*, 169–71, 184–90.

20. Mason, *Brandeis*, 130–1.

21. Mason, *Brandeis*, 128.

22. Mason, *Brandeis*, 133.

23. Brandeis, *Business – A Profession*, 108.

24. Mason, *Brandeis*, 133.

25. Mason, *Brandeis*, 137.

26. F. W. Taussig, "A Contribution to the Theory of Railway Rates," *Quarterly Journal of Economics* 5 (July 1891), 438–65; Hovencamp, *Enterprise and American Law*, 155–6; P. J. Miranti, "The Mind's Eye of Reform: The ICC's Bureau of Statistics and Accounts and a Vision of Regulation, 1887–1940," *Business History Review* 63 (Autumn 1989), 469–509; H. C. Adams, "A Bureau of Railway Statistics and Accounts," *The Independent*, 44 (October 1892), 1384–5.

27. *Interstate Commerce Commission* v. *Alabama Midland Railway Co.*, 168 U.S. 172.

28. Interstate Commerce Commission, *Annual Report*, 1901 (Washington, 1901), pp. 26–7.

29. Interstate Commerce Commission, *Report of the Statistics of Railways in the United States*, 1888 (Washington, 1889), pp. 5–6.

30. This account of the advance rate cases comes from Berk, *Alternative Tracks*, 153–178.

31. Quoted in Mason, *Brandeis*, 325.

32. G. Henderson, "Railway Valuation and the Courts," *Harvard Law Review* 33 (1920); 902–28, 1031–57. The quotations are from 1031–2, 1035, 1051. For more on Henderson's place in "legal realism" and his critique of *Smyth* v. *Ames*, see Horwitz, *The Transformation of American Law*, 104–5, 162–3.

33. Henderson, "Railway Valuation," 1054–6.

34. See McCurdy, "Justice Field." On twentieth-century "capture" and for a cogent critique of Henderson's "procedural pluralism," see Theodore Lowi, *The End of Liberalism: The Second Republic of the United States* (New York: Norton, 1969).

35. Like the economists, the father of scientific management, Frederick Taylor, also made claims to objectivity. But Brandeis thought scientific management was decomposable. To accept some of Taylorism was not to accept it all. This was as true for labor relations as it was for railroad regulation. For example, Brandeis thought that shop floor scientific management could never be effective without unions. This was not only because workers without power would resist rationalization. More importantly, he thought accurate measurements of productivity impossible unless labor controlled formation of accounting categories and the processes of measurement. See Brandeis' testimony before the *Senate Commission on Industrial Relations*, *Vol. XIX*, 64th Cong, 1914, pp. 996–7, 1006, where he says that scientific management ought not only give unions a voice in decision-making, but more importantly "in ascertaining the facts."

36. "Five Percent Rate Case, brief of Louis Brandeis," April 27, 1914, 31 ICC 103–5, quoted in G. L. Thompson, "Misused Product Costing in the American Railroad Industry: Southern Pacific Passenger Service between the Wars," *Business History Review* 63 (Autumn 1989), 520.

37. *Evidence in Matter of Proposed Advances in Freight Rates* (1910–11), 61st Cong., 3rd Sess., Sen. Doc. No. 725, Vol. 4, 2400–1. Hereafter cited as *Advance Rate Case*. Brandeis' complaints were not new. In fact, a similar critique of railroad costing practices underlay the long-standing charge of rate discrimination. Among the most articulate critics of the overemphasis upon long-haul, high volume traffic was the Chicago Great Western Railroad's president, Alpheus Beede Stickney. See Berk, *Alternative Tracks*, 91–100, 116–49.

38. Thompson, "Misused Product Costing," 522–32.

39. See Berk, *Alternative Tracks*, 116–49.

40. On the decline of product costing, or "management accounting," in Brandeis' era and its re-emergence in our own, see H. T. Johnson and R. S. Kaplan, *Relevance Lost: The Rise and Fall of Management Accounting* (Boston: Harvard Business School Press, 1991).

41. Gerald Berk, "Discursive Cartels: Uniform Cost Accounting among American Manufacturers before the New Deal," *Business and Economic History* 26: 1 (Fall 1997); 229–51.

42. Louis D. Brandeis, *Scientific Management and Railroads (Being Part of a Brief Submitted to the Interstate Commerce Commission)* (New York: The Engineering Magazine, 1912), pp. 67–8. On contemporary product costing, see Johnson and Kaplan, *Relevance Lost.*

43. *Advance Rate Case*, 2400–2.

44. *Boston Evening Transcript*, November 21, 1910, quoted in Mason, *Brandeis*, 327. See also *Scientific Management*, 75, where Brandeis says that the ICC should require "each company [to] ascertain and report to it the simple ultimate unit costs of each operation in every department of the road. The further fact that the railroad business is largely noncompetitive makes it proper to publish these costs, and to give to each railroad the benefit of knowing the lowest elementary unit cost of each operation attained by any railroad, and how it was attained. The ascertainment of the ultimate unit cost is necessary before an instructive basis of comparison can be had . . . What is needed as a basis for comparison are the ultimate unit costs; the cost of turning a wheel, the cost of laying a tie or rail under particular conditions, and even that relatively simple operation must again be analyzed and separated into its ultimate simple elements."

45. "The Best Solution is a Government Bureau" (Statement before the Hadley Railroad Securities Commission, published in *Engineering Magazine*, vol. 42, October 1911) in O. K. Fraenkel (ed.), The *Curse of Bigness: Miscellaneous Papers of Louis D. Brandeis* (New York: Viking, 1934), pp. 192–4.

46. Mason, *Brandeis*, 335; F. Lincoln Hutchins, "The Railroad Problem: Rates, Unit Costs, and Efficiency," *The Engineering Magazine* 42 (January 1912), 489–90; F. Lincoln Hutchins, "The Railroad Problem: Capitalization and Regulation," *The Engineering Magazine* 42 (February, 1912), 711.

47. F. Lincoln Hutchins, "Rates, Unit Costs, and Efficiency," 490–1.

48. Hutchins, "Capitalization," 713.

49. Ibid.

50. Adams to ICC Commissioner Wheelock G. Veazey (1893) quoted in Miranti, "The Mind's Eye of Reform," 478–9.

51. See Brandeis testimony before the *Senate Commission on Industrial Relations, Vol. XIX, 64th Cong*, 1914, 1003–4.

52. L. D. Brandeis, "The Best Solution is a Government Bureau" in Fraenkel (ed.), *The Curse of Bigness*, 193.

53. Brandeis, "The Best Solution is a Government Bureau," 193.

54. Ibid.

55. The 61st Cong, 3d sess. Sen Doc 725, *Evidence in the Matter of Proposed Advances in Freight Rates*, vol. 8 (Wash, GPO, 1911) , 5277–8.

56. James C. Scott, *Seeing Like A State: How Certain Schemes to Improve the Human Condition have Failed* (New Haven: Yale University Press, 1998).

57. Skowronek, *Building a New American State*; Samuel P. Huntington, "The Marasmus of the ICC: The Commission, the Railroads, and the Public Interest," *Yale Law Journal* 51 (April 1952), 467–509.

58. Scott, *Seeing Like a State*, 313.

59. For a fascinating comparison of Scott and Hayek, see J. Bradford DeLong's review of Scott's *Seeing Like a State*, "Forests, Trees, and Intellectual Roots . . . ," www.j-bradford-delong.net/Econ_Articles/Reviews/seeing_like_a_state_html.

II

CORPORATE–STATE INTERDEPENDENCIES

5

The Monopoly Enigma, the Reagan Administration's Antitrust Experiment, and the Global Economy

Louis Galambos

The U.S. government instituted the antitrust policy during an era of rapid economic, political, social, and cultural transformation. Indeed, from the perspective of the late 1990s, the United States was changing more rapidly and in more ways between 1880 and 1920 than it had since the establishment of the Constitution. The transitions of the forty years following 1880 were also more decisive than the change in any subsequent era of American history until the 1980s and 1990s. Then, in our era – from 1980 to the present – another restructuring began and continues today, with momentous implications for the nation's economy, polity, social relations, and culture.

Historians are just beginning to examine this most recent transformation, and one of the goals of this chapter is to suggest an interpretive context for their study of some of the significant changes that have taken place since 1980. One of the other goals is to encourage business and economic historians to give more emphasis than they have in recent years to the shifting boundaries between public and private policies and institutions. My specific subject is monopoly and the manner in which Americans tried to understand and cope with it through their national government and through market-oriented activities. In 1981, the first administration of President Ronald Reagan launched a bold experiment in public policy – an experiment that lasted until 1998 – by turning its back on seventy years of antitrust experience with monopoly. The experiment succeeded. As did a U.S. business system that had been struggling for some years to cope with intense global competition. While the new public policy was only one of the many factors that contributed to America's business recovery, it was an important aspect of the nation's economic turnaround and deserves our attention and understanding. For the latter purpose, it is necessary to return to the 1890s and the origins of America's antimonopoly policy.

MONOPOLY AND THE SHERMAN ACT

In 1890, Congress passed and Republican President Benjamin Harrison (1889–93) signed into law the Sherman Antitrust Act. While it remains uncertain whether the legislators who drafted and passed the bill or the President who signed it intended the Sherman Act to alter decisively the course of America's business development, it is obvious that it did not achieve that objective.[1] Certainly not in the first two decades of the federal antitrust policy.

During the years 1894 through about 1907, industrialists, bankers, and their legal advisors guided the economy out of the age of the entrepreneurial firm[2] and into the age of the modern industrial corporation.[3] The corporate merger movement of those years changed the market structure of most of the leading industries of a nation that had recently become the world's leading industrial power.[4] Perhaps the most dramatic symbol of the new institutions was U.S. Steel, the country's first billion-dollar corporation and a combine that absorbed the giant steel mills of Andrew Carnegie, among others. Seeing the conciliatory Judge Gary (J.P. Morgan's man) supplant the arch-competitor Carnegie as the leader of the nation's top steel-maker, one could hardly fail to note that something decisive had changed in the American economy.[5]

The measure Congress had fashioned in 1890 as a response to the combination movement in industry was solidly based on a complex foundation of legal and statutory precedents, most of which were preindustrial. Thus, Adam Smith would have had no difficulty understanding and approving Section 1 of the Sherman Act: "Every contract, combination in the form of a trust or otherwise, or conspiracy, in restraint of trade or commerce among the several States, or with foreign nations, is hereby declared to be illegal."[6] In 1776, Smith had alerted the readers of *The Wealth of Nations* to the ubiquity and dangers of restraints of trade. "People of the same trade seldom meet together," he wrote, "even for merriment and diversion, but the conversation ends in a conspiracy against the public, or in some contrivance to raise prices."[7] Price fixing, pooling, and other similar restraints were well understood in both law and business: in the former profession because they had been so universally condemned by American courts; in the latter because they were so universally appealing as a means of muffling price competition and shoring up one's position in the market.

Price-fixing was almost always the first line of resistance to intense competition (often called "cut-throat competition" by those suffering its effects) in the nineteenth-century U.S. economy.[8] It was a simple response to economic situations that were usually quite complex. It appears, however, to have been only a temporary measure in most cases because such agreements could not be enforced at law in the United States. Consequently, the temptation to violate the agreements was overwhelming and American businessmen of that day were routinely overwhelmed. During a downturn of the business cycle, the restraints usually collapsed, were renewed, and collapsed again as a result of overproduction and price-cutting.

Although the Sherman Act was clear and unambiguous in its prohibition of such restraints of trade, neither manufacturers nor their legal advisers were certain for many years that the new law applied to what they were doing. That was why announcements of price-fixing agreements regularly appeared in the business press between 1890 and 1911.[9] But the Supreme Court decisions against Standard Oil and American Tobacco in 1911 struck fear in the ranks of industry. No longer were the price-fixing meetings announced. Businessmen continued to strike the illegal agreements, of course, giving the courts frequent opportunities to condemn them, as they have done with vigor from that day to the present. Section 1 of the Sherman Act thus created problems for business, but not for the judges and lawyers who were enforcing or interpreting the law.[10]

INDUSTRIAL MONOPOLY AND THE LAW

Section 2 of the Sherman Act – my sole concern in this chapter – was another matter entirely. According to the law, "Every person who shall monopolize, or attempt to monopolize, or combine or conspire with any other person or persons, to monopolize any part of the trade or commerce among the several States, or with foreign nations, shall be deemed guilty of a misdemeanor . . ."[11] Monopoly was outlawed, but what was monopoly? For the man or woman on the street or farm in the 1890s, the definition of monopoly presented no problems. The railroads were monopolies, Standard Oil was a monopoly. Almost every combine created in the great merger movement, including U.S. Steel, was organized in search of monopoly and most, from their perspective, had achieved that antisocial goal.[12]

Unfortunately, the Justice Department and the Federal Trade Commission (after 1914),[13] the courts, and many generations of attorneys found the enigma of monopoly more difficult to solve. The problem stemmed in part from the fact that they had to apply a preindustrial concept to a rapidly changing business system that was poorly understood, even by many business leaders. Monopolies in previous centuries had been granted by governments and were, thus, easy to identify and to resent. But that was no longer the case in turn-of-the-century America.[14] Thus, it was 1911 before the matter seemed to be clarified in the Standard Oil and American Tobacco cases, and by that time the combination movement had already transformed the industrial sector. Most of the successful large corporations were by 1911 already rounding out their businesses through vertical integration, a process that seemed at the time to be totally different from monopolization.[15] This pattern of slamming the barn door shut after the horse was gone would be repeated again and again.

Nevertheless, the 1911 decisions put large corporations and their legal advisers on an antitrust alert. The barn door was slammed and they knew it. The 1911 decisions left no doubt that the antitrust policy applied to large industrial enterprises, all of which would now have to take the law into consideration.

Among the largest firms, mergers and acquisitions would have to be cleared by the corporation's attorneys and might involve substantial risk. At the level of the individual company, the law now had an impact on corporate strategy and frequently on structure as well. At the industry level of analysis, the new legal setting appears to have slowed the rate of concentration slightly, without reversing the effects of the great merger movement at the turn of the century. At the aggregate or national level of analysis, the nation's industrial system was already highly concentrated and would remain so following the 1911 decisions.

The Standard Oil and American Tobacco decisions were supposed to have clarified Section 2 of the Sherman Act by establishing "the rule of reason." But that still left to the Justice Department, the FTC, the courts, and the corporate lawyers the job of discerning what was an unreasonable level of concentration. The enigma of monopoly persisted. During the First World War (1917–18, for the United States), no level of concentration seems to have been unreasonable; antitrust enforcement was relaxed on the assumption that large enterprises, even those that were near-monopolies, were efficient and should be encouraged, not attacked.[16] This was a curious position for the government to take given the widespread contentions that big business was so inefficient it had to be protected by high tariff walls. Nevertheless, antitrust was temporarily put on the shelf and even the largest businesses were encouraged to cooperate under the loose control of a government agency headed by Wall Street tycoon Bernard Baruch.[17]

In the immediate aftermath of the war, the Supreme Court decided the antitrust suit against U.S. Steel in the company's favor. This set a rough standard for concentration. It now appeared that controlling 50 percent of one of the nation's major industries and temporarily engaging in price-fixing to boot was not unreasonable under the Sherman Act. Oligopoly was affirmed. The Court duly observed that one of U.S. Steel's major acquisitions (the Tennessee Coal and Iron Company) had been given the blessing of President Theodore Roosevelt and that the steel interests had stopped holding the so-called Gary Dinners, the price-fixing meetings.[18] At the level of the firm, even the largest ones, oligopoly appeared to be sanctioned and relatively secure from attack under the antitrust policy. So long as one of the major firms in an oligopoly did not attempt to merge with one of the other major producers in the same industry or engage in predatory behavior toward its smaller competitors, an antitrust suit was unlikely. The legal standing of oligopoly under Section 2 of the Sherman Act was thus stabilized and would remain relatively stable for the next sixty years.

This ruling, the lenient enforcement of the Sherman Act in the 1920s, and the booming stock market encouraged another round of mergers and acquisitions. While not of proportions comparable to the merger movement at the turn of the century, the 1920s developments had a significant impact on the structure of important industries like chemicals and pharmaceuticals. Apparently impervious to these changes in structure and policy, the already highly concentrated industrial economy experienced a surge of rapid growth driven by new products and productivity increases. A paradox was in the making. Productivity – the most basic aggregate measure of economic efficiency – was increasing hand-in-hand with the growth of large enterprises operating in oligopolistic industries.[19]

Meanwhile, the emergence of a new style of corporation, the multidivisional (or M-form) company, was dramatically increasing the ability of a few firms to manage national and international operations and to provide with efficiency diversified products and services. The M-form corporation – a major innovation in business organization – pushed back the boundary at which a company would become dysfunctional, opening the way for further expansion just as the political environment in the United States was about to become hostile once again to big business.[20] As the contrast between public policy in the 1920s and 1930s suggests, the government's interest in pursuing monopoly was sensitive to the general performance of the economy.

A NEW DEAL ON MONOPOLY?

The Great Depression of the 1930s prompted the New Deal administrations of Franklin D. Roosevelt to reinvigorate the antitrust policy. This followed a two-year experiment with government-supervised cartelization under the National Recovery Administration. When that effort failed, the administration unleashed Assistant Attorney General Thurman W. Arnold to attack *The Bottlenecks of Business*, that is, "bigness wherever bigness is blocking the channels of trade." Arnold made it clear that bigness per se was not the problem. "Size in itself is not an evil, but it does give power to those who control it. That power must be constantly watched by an adequate enforcement organization to see that it does not destroy a free market." Under the Sherman Act, Arnold said, the government should prosecute "simultaneously all of the restraints which hamper the production and distribution of a product . . ." and, thus, deal with "the evils of monopoly."[21] True to this antimonopoly ideology, Arnold presided over a series of suits against major American companies, including those manufacturing aluminum, tires, and tobacco.

In addition to Arnold and his Antitrust Division, the government set Professor Walton Hamilton of Yale and a large contingent of economists the task of launching in 1938 a "thorough study of the concentration of economic power" in America.[22] Like most "thorough" academic studies, this one was not completed for several years. "In the beginning," historian Ellis Hawley concludes, "the agency [the Temporary National Economic Committee or TNEC] had hopes of finding some magic formula that would cure the nation's ills to the satisfaction of everyone. . . . When it came time to write the final report, however, the mountain of facts had failed to produce any magic formula. . . . The result was a report as timid as it was unoriginal." Even if the agency had found its "magic formula," it would not have been used because by that time mobilization for war was once again trumping antitrust as a national policy.[23]

The climax of this brief, dramatic expansion of antitrust enforcement was the decision against Alcoa, the Aluminum Company of America.[24] Using a narrow definition of the market for aluminum and finding that Alcoa had thwarted potential competitors by anticipating demand, the court employed the sale of the government's wartime aluminum capacity to transform a monopoly into an oligopoly – now manifestly the sanctioned form of industrial organization.[25] At the level of the firm and the industry, the Alcoa decision inevitably fostered caution about mergers and acquisitions on the part of corporate executives and their legal advisors. Even circumspect, innovative companies could expect antitrust scrutiny if their market share exceeded 60–64 percent.[26] By bringing Reynolds Metals and Kaiser Aluminum into the business, the court changed the aluminum industry's markets decisively and encouraged some to believe that the federal government would at last embark on a vigorous campaign to restructure the American business system.[27]

MONOPOLY IN THE AMERICAN CENTURY

To the contrary, between 1945 and 1981, the antimonopoly policy rumbled along its well-beaten track without further efforts to discover a "magic formula." The Celler–Kefauver Act (1950) brought the FTC and Department of Justice into the business of blocking mergers, and the Hart–Rodino Act (1976) instituted a waiting period when mergers were being organized.[28] Both laws, in particular the 1950 measure, had a negative impact on the market for corporate control. Insofar as very large corporations, like DuPont, had used acquisitions as a major element in their growth strategy, they had to look to internal sources of innovation.[29] The Celler–Kefauver Act thus had the impact of stabilizing an existing, oligopolistic industrial setting at a time when the American business system was enjoying tremendous success and seemed in little need of restructuring.

Neither of these statutes changed the government's fundamental position on oligopoly as set forth in the Alcoa decision, and during the first two postwar decades, there was little economic incentive either to clarify the law on monopoly or to step up its enforcement significantly.[30] The so-called "American Century" – dubbed by Henry Luce – was a prosperous era in which U.S. businesses using the M-form of organization became increasingly multinational and diversified.[31] They grew to enormous proportions and many of them began to experiment with conglomeration as a means of ensuring long-term growth. Vertically integrated, internally financed, multinational, and technologically driven, these "center firms" enabled the United States to maintain a position of overwhelming strength in the global economy.[32]

Despite the expansion of these center firms, the U.S. economy did not experience a higher degree of concentration.[33] One reason was the growth of the economy, a process that was spawning many small start-ups and medium-sized enterprises. Another reason was the expansion of the service economy, a sector in which small, not large, firms were for some years predominant. Although the service sector had been expanding its role in the economy since the nineteenth century, it was not until the post-Second World War era that services became substantially more important than manufacturing.[34]

Not all of the service firms were small, and indeed the largest private corporation in the world at that time, AT&T, was in this sector. Over the years, various other companies solved the problems of providing services through national and international organizations, sometimes through franchising, sometimes through merely decentralizing, and sometimes through hybrid structures tailored to particular markets.[35] But, initially, the expansion of services reduced the aggregate level of concentration in the post-Second World War economy.

GLOBAL COMPETITION AND THE GREAT ANTITRUST EXPERIMENT

Americans were cheated out of a large part of the century Henry Luce had led some of them to believe was theirs. Instead of a full century of economic and political dominance, the United States suddenly found its hegemony cut short by global competition. The first wave of competition began to cripple U.S. firms as early as the late 1960s, and following the first oil shock in 1973 very few of the nation's major firms were left unscathed. Productivity increases were declining and inflation mounting in the 1970s (Table 5.1). More efficient, innovative firms in Japan and Germany began methodically to take market share away from American oligopolies like the ones that had long existed in tires, steel, and automobiles.[36]

In the midst of this economic struggle and America's tragic war in Vietnam, the U.S. Justice Department launched two antitrust suits that seemed to indicate that the government would once again attempt to spur recovery by attacking *The Bottlenecks of Business*. The suit against IBM took on one of the world's most successful and powerful companies. It was followed by an equally ambitious assault on AT&T, the nation's highly regulated telecommunications monopoly.[37]

Neither case was completed, however, before the Reagan Administration moved into the White House and opted for a new approach to antitrust policy. In 1981 and 1982, the government launched a bold experiment that would last until the Department of Justice filed a suit against Microsoft in 1998. Four presidential administrations – from Ronald Reagan's first administration through the first four years under President Clinton – conducted this experiment by abandoning efforts to change highly concentrated industries with the law's prohibition of monopoly, that is, Section 2 of the Sherman Act. After almost a century of combating the evils of monopoly, the federal government suddenly

Table 5.1. *Productivity and Inflation in the 1970s*

Date	CPI, % change	Annual % change in output per hour in private business
1970	5.7	−0.8
1971	4.4	
1972	3.2	
1973	6.2	6.6
1974	11.0	−1.9
1975	9.1	−1.9
1976	5.8	6.3
1977	6.5	
1978	7.6	4.7
1979	11.3	2.8
1980	13.5	−0.8

Source: U.S. Department of Commerce, *Statistical Abstract of the United States* (1981).

and with no fanfare stopped enforcing that part of the law. This raises two important questions: Why did it happen? And what were the consequences of this shift in federal policy?[38]

To answer the first question, we can look to events transpiring in early January 1982, when CEO Charles Brown of AT&T and Assistant Attorney General William Baxter agreed to settle the government's antitrust suit against the Bell System. Everyone involved knew from the start that this was a historic occasion, maybe even a "defining moment," in U.S. political economy.[39] A Republican Administration was breaking up a monopoly, in this case, the largest private corporation in the world. Ma Bell was such a fixture in American life that her passing at first elicited shock and then a flood of sentimentality.

Despite its vigorous and successful action against the Bell System, however, President Reagan and his Administration were extremely friendly to American corporate enterprise. They favored the sort of deregulation that was already well underway in the United States, and they looked as well to privatization as a means of reducing government intrusion and improving the efficiency of the public and private sectors. At that time, as we noted above, many of America's largest firms were beset by fierce competition from abroad. Mergers and acquisitions were two of the many ways American companies were attempting to get up to speed in this new environment, and the Reagan Administration did everything it could to ease them through that transition. To the deep concern of some commentators, the United States was developing the world's most lively market for corporate control and such financial innovations as the "junk bond" were energizing that market in the 1980s. In that setting many companies were able to spin off conglomerate or even diversified activities (sometimes using leveraged and managerial buy-outs) so they could concentrate on their core activities.

Baxter, who was directing antitrust policy, was convinced that the only monopolies that warranted attack were the rare ones (like the Bell System) whose markets were closed off to competitors by the government. Baxter was devoted to Chicago-School economics with the same intensity that others worship a deity. One of the central concepts of the Chicago School was the idea that, without government intervention, markets would drive sluggish monopolies out of business or into the arms of more aggressive competitors – as it had Western Union, the largest monopoly in the United States in the nineteenth century.[40] Efficient, innovative monopolies would give consumers all of the advantages of competition, so there was no reason to invoke the antitrust laws against them. With that in mind, in 1981 Baxter had abruptly terminated the government's antitrust suit against IBM at the same time that he had energized the attack on AT&T.

Once he had the Bell System's scalp on his belt, Baxter was happy to preside over the first phase of a quiet experiment in public policy. He simply ignored the numerous opportunities the government had to attack large-scale mergers and strategic alliances among competing firms. Microsoft was safe under this antitrust regime, as were Intel and other large U.S. companies. DuPont now could develop a strategic alliance with pharmaceutical giant Merck & Co., Inc., an arrangement that would have been impossible to consider before 1981. The antitrust experiment continued after Baxter left government, and George Bush's administration found no reason to revive the antimonopoly policy. Indeed, the policy of ignoring mergers and alliances that would in an earlier day surely have been considered attempts "to monopolize" continued through the first Clinton administration, although both the Department of Justice and the Federal Trade Commission began to growl at some mergers and to rev up their investigation teams.

While Section 2 of the antitrust policy was on the shelf, important intellectual developments further eroded its theoretical and empirical underpinnings. These developments took place in a fertile academic triangle between economics, business studies, and business history. Transactions cost analysis focused attention on the positive aspects of vertical integration and threw some analytical sand into the gears of the neoclassical model of the market. Meanwhile, leading analysts in business schools were developing important studies of the conditions that made for long-term success or failure among firms engaged in oligopolistic competition. Business history – sometimes leading and sometimes following close behind these frontiers of inquiry – was during the same years providing an alternative narrative of business development, one that located in the evolving capabilities of the large firm and its managers the main source of economic progress in capitalist economies.[41]

Although these various academic subdisciplines were all leaning against the rationale for structural antitrust as embodied in Section 2 of the Sherman Act, in 1998 the Department of Justice filed its now famous antitrust suit against

Microsoft and decisively ended the experiment that had begun in 1981.[42] By that time merger and acquisition activity was at an all-time high in the United States, and many foreign firms were creating liaisons of various types with American corporations.[43] In telecommunications, for example, the so-called Baby Bells (children of the antitrust settlement) were recombining, AT&T was looking to cable as a means of regaining a foothold in local service, and wireless was entering a consolidation phase. Overseas, deregulation and privatization had opened markets for American firms and presented many new opportunities for multinational alliances. In this industry and others, one can see the outlines of a future in which global oligopolies will be the norm.

Seen in that context, neither the Microsoft antitrust suit (now settled without a structural change) nor the Clinton Administration's efforts to block mergers were likely to change the trend toward global consolidation. They could handicap U.S. firms attempting to achieve strong positions in the new global oligopolies, but they were unlikely to prevent further globalization. Like the Standard Oil and American Tobacco decisions of 1911, federal actions against Microsoft and other companies asserted the power of the federal government to shape a business system that had already been transformed by economic and technological changes beyond the control of any single government.[44]

Since the great antitrust experiment has ended – if only temporarily – we should ask what impact it had on the United States.[45] Were the results as bad as those Thurman Arnold might have predicted? What happened to the American economy during those years? Were we hurt or helped by relaxing the scrutiny of monopoly under Section 2 of the venerable Sherman Act? During the first decade of the experiment, many Americans certainly suffered through a painful era of transition. Millions were forced into early retirement, obligated to change jobs, or driven out of the labor market entirely. The shock waves of what economist Joseph Schumpeter called "creative destruction" were felt in every American city and every large company.[46]

During those years, the U.S. business system experienced the most formidable transformation in its history – one that dwarfed even the 1890s, when the giant corporation was becoming the dominant form of enterprise in the U.S. industrial economy. In the years before the First World War, business and federal policy had both been adjusting to the demands of an economy that was primarily national in scope. Back then, most of America's business was at home. But during the 1980s and 1990s, the U.S. economy was adjusting to a vast global system in which goods, services, and currencies were trading on a real-time basis and American-based companies were being forced to meet international competition or go out of business entirely – as many did.[47] Reengineering, restructuring, spinning off, deconglomerating, combining, getting back to the core and close to the customer – U.S. companies were trying frantically to meet global standards of efficiency and innovation.[48] In this setting, a national antitrust policy directed against monopolies (under Section 2 of the Sherman Act) was no longer relevant to the most important changes taking place. What mattered was having plenty of effective companies that could meet and best their international competitors.[49]

For the corporate leaders who were trying to guide their firms through this transition, it was a great relief not to worry about antitrust suits while they were attempting to rebuild their organizations and reorient their workforces. One of the main reasons AT&T's Charles Brown had agreed to break up the Bell System was so that he and his fellow executives could concentrate on running a telephone company instead of tending to law suits. During the 1980s and early 1990s, managers as well as their employees in most American companies had every reason to focus all of their energies on weathering this era of intense global competition.

By the mid-1990s, it was apparent that the fruits of the transition were worth the pain. Creative destruction had worked. America had weeded out many of the weak competitors in its ranks, improved its ability to innovate, and once again taken a leading position in the world economy.[50] The U.S. rate of unemployment was one of the lowest of the world's advanced economies.[51] While the change in antitrust policy had been only one of the several factors favoring this transformation, it had clearly had a positive impact. Mergers and acquisitions had helped, as had strategic alliances that enabled U.S. companies to broaden the front across which they were introducing new products and services (see Table 5.2).[52] Compare these figures with those in Table 5.1.

The transformation of U.S. business between 1981 and 1998 enabled American corporations to acquire strong positions relative to two of the major changes taking place in the world economy: the development of a system of global oligopolies; and the emergence of three large economic blocks – in Europe, in the Western Hemisphere, and to a lesser extent in Asia. Companies that do not have secure footholds in these blocks in future years are likely to face a very uncertain future.[53] Companies that are not up to scale to compete in the global oligopolies are also likely to encounter severe difficulties.[54] If leading American corporations

Table 5.2. *Productivity and Inflation, 1970–1994*

Date	Output per hour, business sector (1992 = 100)	Output per hour, U.S.	CPI, % change
1970	70.4		5.7
1980	84.3	71.9	12.5
1985	92.0	87.7	3.6
1990	96.1	97.7	5.4
1992	100		3.0
1993	100.2	101.6	3.0
1994	100.7	105.8	2.6

Source: U.S. Department of Commerce, *Statistical Abstract of the United States*, 1997.

continue to make their way successfully through this transition, they should do so with a bow toward the several factors that helped pave their way to success – including the Reagan Administration's bold policy experiment.

CONCLUSION

What conclusions can one draw from this quick trip through more than a century of antimonopoly policy and economic and business developments? I see four generalizations suggested by this historical experience, and I believe they provide us with some useful policy lessons for the present. First, it should be apparent that monopoly was ill-defined in 1890 and, for that matter, still not very well understood a century later. Given the fact that the government was developing a policy that could have had a powerful impact on what became the very heart of the industrial economy – a major source of investment, economic growth, jobs, and opportunities for advancement for the entire nation – it would have been preferable to advance a less ambitious policy until the economic situation was clarified, unless, of course, the original objective was to mount a policy that was largely symbolic in intent and in economic results. That was what happened during the first two decades under the new policy while the great merger movement was restructuring the most advanced sectors of the American economy.[55] The policy lagged so far behind a rapidly changing business system that the government could never hope to catch up. For one thing, the American administrative state lacked the capabilities required for that task, a fact that was readily apparent during the mobilization for the First World War. Given that the government lacked these capabilities, it was, perhaps, suitable that it did not acquire a substantial measure of authority until 1911, when the Department of Justice at last used Section 2 of the Sherman Act to curb the power of two carefully selected companies.

The decisions against Standard Oil and American Tobacco transformed the antimonopoly policy from a symbolic to a real constraint on the largest American companies if they were seeking to enhance their market shares or block entry to their already highly concentrated industries. These decisions raised the risks of mergers or acquisitions in these particular circumstances without, however, defining with clarity what a Section 2 illegal monopoly was. Nine years later, the U.S. Steel decision established that oligopoly could be distinguished from monopoly and was, barring predatory behavior, an acceptable form of industrial organization.

The second lesson the history of antitrust provides is that by trusting markets more than those reformers who wanted a substantial restructuring of the business system, the United States prospered. So long as the business system was primarily oriented to the domestic market, and firm strategies and structures could evolve slowly, national oligopolies and this version of antimonopoly were compatible. Neither public policy nor the high level of concentration in the economy prevented the United States from achieving satisfactory rates of growth over the long term and maintaining its position as the world's leading industrial power.

The third lesson I see in this experience is that the conditions that might have justified an antimonopoly stance in 1900 or 1911 no longer exist today. We no longer need to convince anyone that our federal government can, if it chooses, curb the power of private enterprise. Nor are our markets overwhelmingly national, as they were at the turn of the century. We are players in a global economy that demands global responses in both the private and public sectors. We are also in a global economy in which the unique advantages the United States once possessed – incredible natural resources and a relatively young and fast-growing population, for instance – either no longer exist or are no longer as important as they were. Our willingness to accept rapid, painful changes, what Europeans call "The American Solution," is now especially important, and that process of transformation needs to play a more important role in our public and nonprofit sectors if we are going to hold the leading economic position we held by the end of the twentieth century. The global transformation is far from complete.

Fourth, and finally, I believe the historical experience with an antimonopoly policy demonstrates why our democratic polity has, with some exceptions, continued to be successful over the long term. We have two ways to send signals to our leaders and institutions, signals that call for change. One is through markets. The other is through politics. Most of our difficulties have arisen when these signals gave us conflicting messages. When that happens, mediation of the conflict, frequently by the courts, becomes all-important. In the field of antimonopoly, the courts and the public have long tolerated a policy that called for relatively minor changes in the business system. There were other alternatives, and occasionally the United States came close to adopting some of them. But the nation always backed away and preserved a system that involved a skewed distribution of power, wealth, and income because it generated unique economic opportunities and the continued growth Americans sought. It is that sort of compromise that carried us through the difficult era from 1880 to 1920. It is that sort of compromise that will help us through the critical transformations the United States is now experiencing in a rapidly changing global economy. One can only hope that these compromises and transformations will receive more careful, balanced scrutiny from business and economic historians than they have to date received in our newspapers, magazines, and television coverage.

NOTES

1. Hans B. Thorelli exhaustively researched and analyzed the setting in which the Sherman Act was passed; to my knowledge, no subsequent author has either duplicated his research or changed Thorelli's conclusions in any decisive way. *The*

Federal Antitrust Policy: Origination of an American Tradition (Baltimore, 1955). See also William Letwin, *Law and Economic Policy in America: The Evolution of the Sherman Antitrust Act* (New York, 1965).

2. Louis Galambos and Joseph Pratt, *The Rise of the Corporate Commonwealth: U.S. Business and Public Policy in the Twentieth Century* (New York, 1988), provides a brief discussion of the nineteenth-century entrepreneurial firm.

3. Ralph L. Nelson, *Merger Movements in American Business, 1895–1956* (Princeton, 1959).

4. There is a substantial bibliography on "The Great Merger Movement." For guides to the primary and secondary sources, see the following: Alfred D. Chandler, Jr., *The Visible Hand* (Cambridge, MA, 1977); Naomi R. Lamoreaux, *The Great Merger Movement in American Business, 1895–1904* (Cambridge, 1985).

5. On public perceptions of the mergers see Louis Galambos, *The Public Image of Big Business in America* (Baltimore, 1975).

6. *United States Statutes At Large*, 26, ch. 647 ("An act to protect trade and commerce against unlawful restraints and monopolies"), 209.

7. Adam Smith, *An Inquiry into the Nature and Causes of The Wealth of Nations* (New York, 1937 edn), 128.

8. In addition to the sources and examples cited by Chandler and Lamoreaux see: William Z. Ripley (ed.), *Trusts, Pools and Corporations* (Boston, 1916); William H.S. Stevens, "A Classification of Pools and Associations Based on American Experience," *American Economic Review*, III 3 (1913), 558–9; Ralph W. and Muriel H. Hidy, *Pioneering in Big Business, 1882–1911* (New York, 1955), 10; Julius Grodinsky, *The Iowa Pool: A Study in Railroad Competition, 1870–84* (Chicago, 1950).

9. See, for instance, *Commercial and Financial Chronicle*, LXII, 1618 (June 27, 1896), 1186; and LXIII, 1641 (Dec. 5, 1896), 994.

10. Executives have continued, however, to yield to temptation. See, for instance, *Wall Street Journal*, May 21, June 11, and Sept. 15, 1999, on the price-fixing conspiracy among vitamin manufacturers.

11. See note 6, above.

12. Louis Galambos, *The Public Image of Big Business in America, 1880–1940* (Baltimore, 1975), especially pp. 79–221.

13. *United States Statutes At Large*, 38, ch. 323, 730–40.

14. President Woodrow Wilson and other liberal reformers attempted to link the Trusts to government protection under the tariff; the reasoning was that the combines were inherently inefficient and could only survive if protected from foreign competition by the federal government. That turned out not to be the case, of course, and the nation's largest businesses thrived, with or without protection.

15. The best treatment of vertical integration during these years is Chandler, *The Visible Hand*.

16. The most useful study of events before and during the War Industries Board's tenure is still Robert Cuff, *The War Industries Board* (Baltimore, 1973).

17. Prior to the war, price control along these lines would clearly have been condemned as illegal collusion under Section 1 of the Sherman Act.

18. Gabriel Kolko, *The Triumph of Conservatism* (New York, 1963), discusses T. R.'s deal with J. P. Morgan.

19. See the late Robert Gallman's masterful essay on "The Pace and Pattern of American Economic Growth," in Lance E. Davis *et al.* (ed.), *American Economic Growth: An Economist's History of the United States* (New York, 1972), 15–60; John W. Kendrick,

Productivity Trends in the United States (Princeton, 1961); and the same author's *Postwar Productivity Trends in the United States, 1948–1969* (New York, 1973). See also Kendrick's study with Elliot S. Grossman, *Productivity in the United States: Trends and Cycles* (Baltimore, 1980).

20. The pioneering work on the multidivisional corporation is Alfred D. Chandler, Jr., *Strategy and Structure: Chapters in the History of the Industrial Enterprise* (Cambridge, MA, 1962).

21. Thurman W. Arnold, *The Bottlenecks of Business* (New York, 1940), 4, 20, 191, 125.

22. Ellis W. Hawley, *The New Deal and the Problem of Monopoly: A Study in Economic Ambivalence* (Princeton, 1966) provides an excellent study of Thurman Arnold's career and of the origins and activities of the Temporary National Economic Committee. After the National Recovery Administration had collapsed and Arnold had begun his work, Congress passed the Robinson–Patman Act, which was apparently designed to protect small retailers from the competition of the large national chains that were driving them out of business. An obscure law at best, Robinson–Patman spoke to America's small-firm past and could do little to slow the trend toward large retail organizations.

23. Hawley, *New Deal and the Problem of Monopoly*, 464–5.

24. This case began in 1937 and was finally resolved by a three-member panel of circuit court judges in 1945. George David Smith, *From Monopoly to Competition: The Transformations of Alcoa, 1888–1986* (New York, 1988) describes the case and the industry context.

25. Anticipation of demand, which is usually achieved by having a thorough and up-to-date knowledge of the markets for a company's goods or services, would seem to be the essence of an innovative performance. But the court was concerned about power, not entrepreneurship.

26. Judge Learned Hand commented that controlling 90 percent of a market " 'is enough to constitute a monopoly; it is doubtful whether sixty or sixty-four percent would be enough; and certainly thirty-three percent is not.' " F. M. Scherer and David Ross, *Industrial Market Structure and Economic Performance* (Boston, 1990), 455.

27. There is an excellent discussion of the decision and its aftermath in Scherer and Ross, *Industrial Market Structure and Economic Performance*, 453–8. By excluding competing metals such as steel and copper from consideration as part of Alcoa's market, the court made it far more likely that the company would be identified as a monopoly. Even then, it was necessary to use the most restrictive of three definitions of the market to support its conclusion.

28. Neil Fligstein, *The Transformation of Corporate Control* (Cambridge, 1990) gives more emphasis than I do to the changes introduced by the Celler–Kefauver Amendments.

29. David A. Hounshell and John Kenly Smith, Jr., *Science and Corporate Strategy: DuPont R&D, 1902–1980* (New York, 1988), especially pp. 332, 346–50, 510–15, 519–20, 597.

30. T. Kovaleff, *Business and Government During the Eisenhower Administration: A Study of the Antitrust Division of the Justice Department* (Athens, 1980).

31. Chandler, *Strategy and Structure*, especially pp. 374–82; Galambos and Pratt, *The Rise of the Corporate Commonwealth*, especially pp. 127–200.

32. Robert Averitt, *The Dual Economy* (New York, 1968) describes the "center firms."

33. Scherer and Ross, *Industrial Market Structure and Economic Performance*, 79–85, discuss the concentration ratios.

34. Dorothy I. Riddle, *Service-Led Growth: The Role of the Service Sector in World Development* (New York, 1986); Victor S. Fuchs, *The Service Economy* (New York, 1968); *Economic Report of the President* (Washington, Feb. 1998), 334–5.

35. Eric Abrahamson, "Managing the Heart: Labor and Systematization in the Birth of the Modern U.S. Service Economy" (manuscript). I have also discussed the service sector in Louis Galambos, "The U.S. Corporate Economy in the Twentieth Century," in Stanley L. Engerman and Robert E. Gallman (eds.), *The Cambridge Economic History of the United States*, vol. 3, 927–67. See also, Louis Galambos, "Myth and Reality in the Study of America's Consumer Culture," in Karen R. Merrill (ed.), *The Modern World's of Business and Industry: Cultures, Technology, Labor* (Turnhout, 1998), 183–203.

36. For different perspectives on the problems that developed see David Teece (ed.), *The Competitive Challenge: Strategies for Industrial Innovation and Renewal* (Cambridge, 1987); Thomas McCraw (ed.), *America Versus Japan* (Boston, 1986); Paul R. Lawrence and Davis Dyer, *Renewing American Industry: Organizing for Efficiency and Innovation* (New York, 1983); Michael J. Piore and Charles F. Sabel, *The Second Industrial Divide: Possibilities for Prosperity* (New York, 1984); Donald N. Sull, Richard S. Tedlow, and Richard S. Rosenbloom, "Managerial commitments and technological change in the U.S. tire industry," *Industrial and Corporate Change* 6:2 (1997), 461–501. The average annual percentage change in output per hour in manufacturing for the United States was 3.4 for 1970–75; and 1.6 for 1975–80. In Germany the comparable figures were 5.4 and 4.2, and in Japan, 6.7 and 7.9. Even the United Kingdom had better figures for the second half of the decade (1.9) than the United States. U.S. Department of Commerce, *Statistical Abstract, 1981*. See also John W. Kendrick (ed.), *International Comparisons of Productivity and Causes of the Slowdown* (Cambridge, 1984).

37. Peter Temin and Louis Galambos, *The Fall of the Bell System: A Study in Prices and Politics* (New York, 1987); Richard H. K. Vietor, *Contrived Competition: Regulation and Deregulation in America* (Cambridge, 1994), 167–233.

38. I have also discussed this subject in "When Antitrust Helped, And Why It Doesn't Now," *Washington Post*, June 13, 1999.

39. For the final word on "defining moments" see G. Pascal Zachary, "Junk History: It's Bigger Than Big; It's More Than News; It's a Defining Moment," in the *Wall Street Journal*, Sept. 19, 1997.

40. David Dale Martin, "Industrial Organization and Reorganization," in Warren J. Samuels (ed.), *The Chicago School of Political Economy* (East Lansing, 1976), 295–310. See also the slashing review of Theodore P. Kovaleff (ed.), *The Antitrust Impulse: An Economic, Historical, and Legal Analysis* (Armonk, 1994), I and II, by Lester G. Telser (University of Chicago) in the *Journal of Economic Literature* 34:1 (1996), 167–70.

41. In economics, the work of Oliver Williamson is of central importance: *Markets and Hierarchies: Analysis and Antitrust Implications* (New York, 1975); *The Economic Institutions of Capitalism: Firms, Markets, Regional Contracting* (New York, 1985); and "Hierarchies, Markets and Power in the Economy: An Economic Perspective," *Industrial and Corporate Change* 4:1 (1995), 21–49. See also Richard Nelson, "Capitalism as an Engine of Progress," *Research Policy* 19 (1990), 193:214; and as editor, *National Innovation Systems: A Comparative Analysis* (New York, 1993). Nelson's paradigm guides Maureen D. McKelvey, *Evolutionary Innovations: The Business of Biotechnology* (Oxford, 1996). Examples of business studies include Richard S. Rosenbloom and Clayton M. Christensen, "Technological Discontinuities,

Organizational Capabilities, and Strategic Commitments," *Industrial and Corporate Change* 3:3 (1994), 655–8; Donald N. Sull, Richard S. Tedlow, and Richard S. Rosenbloom, "Managerial Commitments and Technological Change in the U.S. Tire Industry," *Industrial and Corporate Change* 6:2 (1997), 461–501; Rebecca M. Henderson, "Architectural Innovation: The Reconfiguration of Existing Product Technologies and the Failure of Established Firms," *Administration Science Quarterly* 35:1 (1990), 9–30; and Mary Tripsas, "Surviving Radical Technological Change through Dynamic Capability: Evidence from the Typesetter Industry," *Industrial and Corporate Change* 6:2 (1997), 341–77. I have discussed the development of business history elsewhere, but the interested reader might want to start by exploring Chandler, *The Visible Hand* (Cambridge, 1977); and *Scale and Scope* (Cambridge, 1990). In a review essay on "The Dynamics of Industrial Capitalism: Perspectives on Alfred Chandler's Scale and Scope," *Journal of Economic Literature* 31 (Mar. 1993), economist David Teece said: "The implication of this tour de force is that much of what is in the textbooks in mainstream microeconomics, industrial organization, and possibly growth and development ought to be revised, in some cases relegated to the appendices, if economic analysis is to come to grips with the essence of productivity improvement and wealth generation in advanced industrial economies." See also W. Bernard Carlson, *Innovation as a Social Process: Elihu Thomson and the Rise of General Electric, 1870–1900* (New York, 1991); David A. Hounshell and John Kenly Smith, Jr., *Science and Corporate Strategy: DuPont R&D, 1902–1980* (New York, 1988); and Louis Galambos, with Jane Eliot Sewell, *Networks of Innovation: Vaccine Development at Merck, Sharp & Dohme, and Mulford, 1895–1995* (New York, 1995).

42. This shift in policy did not take place suddenly; one could date the beginnings of the transition in 1994 and 1995, when the DOJ and the FTC began to scrutinize mergers and acquisitions more carefully and to demand more concessions from the firms involved. Stephen Labaton, "At Justice, the taming of a whirlwind," *New York Times*, Oct. 22, 1995. The appointment of Joel Klein as DOJ's antitrust chief was important. In an interview, Klein harkened back to Thurman Arnold, saying: "he especially wants to take on cases that can clarify antitrust law in a fast-changing and increasingly global economy. Particularly in new technology-intensive industries, 'we need to think very hard and carefully about the use of antitrust law, to make sure that these rapidly developing markets don't get *bottlenecked . . .'* " *Wall Street Journal*, Mar. 3, 1997. Italics mine. Stephen Paul Mahinka and Kathleen M. Sanzo, who examine this initial stage in the policy shift for one industry in "Pharmaceutical Industry Restructuring and New Marketing Approaches: Enforcement Responses," *Food and Drug Law Journal* 50:2 (1995), 313–25. Another line of research involved the hypothesis (questioned by Chicago School economists) that there was a relationship between levels of concentration and prices. See Leonard W. Weiss, (ed.), *Concentration and Price* (Cambridge, MA, 1989); although the editor clearly leaned toward the traditional industrial organization assumption, he concluded on p. 283 that "monopoly is not our most serious economic problem." See Richard J. Gilbert and Michael L. Katz, "An Economist's Guide to *U.S.* v. *Microsoft*," *Journal of Economic Perspectives* 15:2 (2001), 25–44.

43. See Steven Lipin, "How Long Can Merger Boom Continue," *Wall Street Journal*, July 11, 1996; and the same author's article on "Gorillas in Our Midst," *Wall Street Journal*, Jan. 2, 1997; and Paul M. Sherer, "The Lesson from Chrysler, Citicorp and Mobil: No Companies Nowadays Are Too Big to Merge," *Wall Street Journal*, Jan. 4, 1999.

44. The European Community was adopting a Section 2 approach to antitrust while the United States was abandoning it. In the aftermath of the Second World War, the United States had used the Marshall Plan as a lever in an effort to change certain well-established European public policies and institutions. One of them was the tolerant European policy toward combinations and cartels. Michael J. Hogan, *The Marshall Plan: America, Britain, and the reconstruction of Western Europe, 1947–1952* (New York, 1987), especially pp. 22–3, 53–60, 89–101, 327–8, 364–79, 427–45. See Simon J. Evenett, Alexander Lehmann, and Benn Steil (eds.), *Antitrust Goes Global: What Future for Transatlantic Cooperation?* (Washington, DC, 2000) for discussion of some leading cases and the recent development of formal and informal interaction on antitrust policies between the United States and the European Union. See the *Wall Street Journal*, July 3, 2001, 1, "Competing Views," for a suggestion that the current administration of U.S. President George W. Bush is returning to the Reagan policy and breaking with Europe, in this case over the proposed GE-Honeywell merger. See also *Wall Street Journal*, July 5, 2001, A3 and A4.

45. See *ibid.*, and *Wall Street Journal*, June 29, B1, and July 16, 2001, for developments in the Microsoft case that already pointed toward a settlement that did not involve breaking up Microsoft. The outcome of this case indicated the current U.S. administration has adopted the Reagan approach to Section 2 of the Sherman Act.

46. Joseph A. Schumpeter, *Capitalism, Socialism and Democracy* (New York, 1942).

47. See the "Symposium on Globalization in Perspective," *Journal of Economic Perspectives* 12:4 (1998), 3–50. See also David Held, Anthony McGrew, David Goldblatt, and Jonathan Perraton, *Global Transformations* (Stanford, 1999) for an excellent survey of the literature and historical development of the global economy.

48. See, for instance, Michael Hammer and James Champy, *Reengineering the Corporation: A Manifesto for Business Revolution* (New York, 1993); Joseph G. Morone, *Winning in High-Tech Markets: The Role of General Management* (Boston, 1993).

49. See, for example, Joseph Morone, *Winning in High-Tech Markets: The Role of General Management* (Boston, 1993); Richard R. Nelson (ed.), *National Innovation Systems: A Comparative Analysis* (New York, 1993); and Michael Hammer and James Champy, *Reengineering the Corporation: A Manifesto for Business Revolution* (New York, 1993).

50. It is difficult to measure international competitiveness, but see IMD, *The World Competitiveness Yearbook, 1997* (Lausanne, 1997), for the most serious attempt with which I am familiar. See also Leslie Hannah, "Survival and Size Mobility Among the World's Largest 100 Industrial Corporations, 1912–1995," *American Economic Review* 88:2 (1998), 62–5. Hannah concludes that "Europe has been the home of Chandlerian stable oligopolies; America has more obviously been the creative (and destructive) dynamo of the Schumpeterian paradigm."

51. One report in 1998 indicated that high-technology companies added about 200,000 jobs in 1997 alone; about two-thirds of these jobs were in software and computer-related activities. *Wall Street Journal*, May 19, 1998.

52. On the market that facilitated mergers and acquisitions see Michael C. Jensen, "The Market for Corporate Control," in Peter Newman *et al.* (eds.), *The New Palgrave Dictionary of Money and Finance*, II (London, 1992), 657–66.

53. Jeffrey A. Frankel, *Regional Trading Blocs in the World Economic System* (Washington, 1997); and Yoichi Funabashi, *Asia Pacific Fusion: Japan's Role in APEC* (Washington, 1995).

54. Note, for example, what has recently happened in the aluminum industry, where Canada's Alcan Aluminium Ltd., France's Pechiney SA, and Switzerland's Alusuisse Lonza Group AG have explored consolidation, and Alcoa made a successful bid for Reynolds Metals Co. *Wall Street Journal*, Aug. 11, 12, 16, 17, and 20, 1999. Similar changes are taken place across national borders in telecommunications and pharmaceuticals. On telecommunications see Mark A. Jamison, "Emerging Patterns in Global Telecommunications Alliances and Mergers," *Industrial and Corporate Change* 7:4 (1998), 695–713.

55. For a similar conclusion see William E. Kovacic, "Failed Expectations: The Troubled Past and Uncertain Future of the Sherman Act as a Tool for Deconcentration," in *Iowa Law Review* 74:5 (1989), 1105–50; this issue included several papers presented as part of a "Symposium: The Sherman Act's First Century: A Historical Perspective." See especially Peter C. Carstensen, "How to Assess the Impact of Antitrust on the American Economy: Examining History or Theorizing?" 1175–1217. For a different approach to America's experience with the Sherman Act see David M. Hart, "Antitrust and technological innovation in the U.S.: ideas, institutions, decisions, and impacts, 1890–2000," *Research Policy* 1286 (2001), 1–14. Hart stresses a cyclical process, with major swings toward or away from concentration every few decades.

6

Corporate Technological Capabilities and the State: A Dynamic Historical Interaction

David M. Hart

INTRODUCTION: BRINGING THE STATE IN FROM THE MARGINS OF BUSINESS HISTORY

Business historians are ambivalent about the state. On the one hand, political forces are often simply too important to be ignored. Alfred D. Chandler, Jr., for instance, acknowledges that differences across nations lead to differences among businesses, a conclusion that helps to organize his volume *Scale and Scope*. On the other hand, any causal significance assigned to things political diminishes the creative agency accorded to managers, whose stories constitute the central threads of most business history narratives. *Scale and Scope* is primarily about the managerial exploitation of technological and market opportunities; it is not called *National Varieties of Capitalist Enterprise*.[1]

The tendency of business historians to downplay the influence of the state (and, indeed, a range of other social and cultural factors that shape business) has been noticed widely. Richard John's twenty-year retrospective on *The Visible Hand*, for example, points out that some of Chandler's most vigorous champions as well as some of his most vehement critics have sought to incorporate politics into the master narrative. Chandler's champions argue that the state interferes with management and that this interference helps to account for differences among otherwise similar businesses. The critics assert a more constitutive role for the state (and, more generally, the polity), shaping markets and even managerial mind-sets, and thereby shaping business organization.[2]

Helpful comments were provided by Colleen Dunlavy, Peter Dobkin Hall, Carl Kaysen, and the editors of this volume.

Mainstream business historians may be ambivalent about the state, but they are positively paradoxical in their treatment of technology. Technological opportunities are the prime movers of the Chandlerian narrative, placing fundamental constraints on corporate strategy and structure. The sources of these opportunities lie outside the narrative, despite their importance in explaining differences across industries. At the same time, managerial agency is the essential force that converts technological opportunities into business realities. By integrating backward into knowledge production and by investing in the capacity to manage new knowledge, successful firms demolish rivals, transform business processes, and open new markets. Technology is simultaneously a rigid constraint on businesses and a flexible tool for them.[3]

This paradox, too, has been widely noticed. A growing body of literature seeks to address it by softening the conceptual boundaries that constrict the mainstream account. This work locates the sources of technological innovation, whether radical or incremental, in inter-organizational "systems" or "networks" of innovation that encompass but go beyond corporate R&D labs and production facilities. Several types of innovation systems – regional, industrial, and global – can be delineated, but the *national* innovation system is particularly important for my purposes. State agencies are important participants in the national innovation system. More importantly, public policies profoundly shape the relationships among all the actors in the system, including those that link firms to one another. Technological innovations made by firms can be seen, in this framework, to owe as much to nonmarket exchanges and non-market incentives as to internal R&D and market-mediated transactions.[4]

If one adopts the innovation systems approach and if one continues to hold, with Chandler, that technological innovation is a key element in the evolution of business organization, then one must accept the following conclusion: The state is a critical area for business history research, because the state has a central place in the national system of innovation. A quick glance at several of the key growth industries of the late twentieth century lends empirical support to this conclusion. In pharmaceuticals, electronics, and aircraft, government organizations, government-funded university laboratories, government procurement, government regulations, and publicly provided infrastructure have been essential to technological change and to the organizational development of firms. But the argument is not confined to recent times. During the late nineteenth and early twentieth centuries, the period that most occupies Chandler's attention, and even before, national innovation systems profoundly shaped business history.

Louis Galambos and Jane Eliot Sewell's *Networks of Innovation: Vaccine Development at Merck, Sharp & Dohme, and Mulford, 1895–1995*, which won the Newcomen Prize in 1997, demonstrates that the innovation systems approach has begun to have some influence on business history. As the title suggests, Galambos and Sewell attend to the traffic in knowledge across organizational boundaries that dates back to the origins of Merck. Constrained by the "corporate biography" genre, however, the book remains essentially a Chandlerian story of managerial and scientific opportunity-seeking, enriched at the margins by reference to actors and forces outside the firm, including public hospitals and research organizations, regulations, patent laws, and the like.[5]

This chapter goes beyond Galambos and Sewell's pioneering effort to identify ways to bring the state further in from the margins of business history. My claim is that the state shapes corporate technological capabilities fundamentally. The agency of managers is not eliminated in this approach, but they must share the spotlight with other actors. A deeper understanding of the linkages between firms and the rest of the innovation system will strengthen the explanatory power of business history. Equally important, business historians can add substantial value to the ongoing interdisciplinary dialogue about innovation systems. As Richard R. Nelson, a major figure in this dialogue, puts it, firms comprise "the heart" of innovation systems. Most of us are general practitioners when it comes to diagnosing the system, and we could use a few more cardiologists.[6]

CORPORATE TECHNOLOGICAL CAPABILITIES

Corporate capabilities distinguish firms as organized entities from mere bundles of resources. Entrepreneurs and managers assemble resources, including other people, facilities and equipment, money, and some forms of knowledge (such as licensed intellectual property); they attempt to add value to this assemblage by linking these resources together in specific ways. These linkages lead over time to the development of commitments, routines, practices, and firm-specific knowledge, which comprise the capabilities that allow the firm to execute its strategy.[7]

Technological capabilities are a subset of corporate capabilities. They allow the firm to discover, develop, assimilate, deploy, and extend new ways of doing things. Whereas Chandler conceives of the essential function of "organized human capabilities" as the "exploit[ation of] the potential of technological processes," the definition advanced here emphasizes the firm's creativity. This creativity is embedded in people, including R&D personnel and production workers as well as the managers who devise strategies and allocate resources. It may be enhanced by certain routines and practices and perhaps even by the layout of equipment and facilities (including the architecture of information systems).[8]

Corporate technological capabilities have consequences of great importance to business historians. As Chandler (among many others) shows, creative firms grow rapidly, and they evolve in form and function. They produce goods and services valued by large segments of society. They create jobs and contribute substantially to the overall growth of the economy. They may also produce negative externalities, including new forms of environmental degradation and displacement of older forms of economic life. Firms that have developed significant technological capabilities are, as Joseph A. Schumpeter famously put it, the main agents of "creative destruction."[9]

Although managers assemble the resources to build technological capabilities, they could not do so in the absence of an institutional infrastructure in which the state figures significantly. For example, technological capabilities depend heavily on public goods, such as a highly educated population. Firms are unlikely to invest in the education of people who can take their human capital out the door at the end of their contracts, but contracts with terms long enough to reap the benefits of such investments would look suspiciously like slavery. Government subsidies provide one way around this impasse. Similarly, firms are unlikely to create technological knowledge unless they have some protection against the threat of imitation by competitors. Without this protection, all firms have an incentive to free ride on knowledge created by others. In the extreme, these incentives create a prisoner's dilemma in which no firm will create knowledge. Intellectual property rights, enforced by public institutions, provide one solution to this conundrum; public spending on R&D provides another.

These public policies – and the institutions that comprise innovation systems more generally – can be characterized as responses to market failures that derive from the properties of knowledge itself. Knowledge simply cannot be exchanged in the same way that material goods can.[10] This understanding of innovation systems poses a challenge to the Chandlerian paradigm, but it is only a beginning. Political popularity, military effectiveness, and a host of other motivations that go far beyond the desire to perfect the market, influence the development of these systems. Corporate technological capabilities emerge not merely from market processes nor from deliberate attempts to solve market failures, but from a range of societal endeavors, including those of the state.

NATIONAL SYSTEMS OF INNOVATION: BIG STRUCTURES, HUGE COMPARISONS

The evidence linking national innovation systems to corporate technological capabilities is just beginning to be amassed. In this section, I simply want to establish a prima facie case that such a linkage exists, to set the stage for a more detailed discussion of the mechanisms through which it works. The prima facie case turns on (as Charles Tilly would have it) "huge comparisons" that illuminate these "big structures."[11] One set of comparisons is between premodern and modern societies. Lacking states, premodern societies were technologically stagnant and organizationally sluggish. The second set of comparisons ranges across modern states. Differences among states coincide with differences in patterns of technological innovation. These patterns also coincide with variations in forms of economic organization, several of which confusingly share the same label, "capitalist." These two huge comparisons suggest that modern states and business enterprises (including corporations from the mid-nineteenth century on) evolved together and together gave birth to industrial technology.

Martin van Creveld writes that "the rise of the state is inseparable from that of modern technology." Before there were modern states (which he defines as abstract, self-authorizing, and territorially exclusive organizations), the pace of technological innovation was relatively slow, even in empires that could concentrate vast resources on their intellectuals and craftspeople. China, for instance, which was far and away the world's most technologically advanced society during Europe's Middle Ages, did not generate an industrial revolution, despite the possession of nearly all the requisite physical components. In the absence of a state that provided incentives for private risk-taking and accumulation of wealth, Chinese technology stagnated when the imperial court turned conservative.[12]

Early European states did not have the luxury of such stagnation. Their constant conflicts stimulated them to seek new ways to fight wars and to pay for them. These efforts, in turn, helped to transform social and economic institutions. In Western Europe (and North America) in particular, as Nathan Rosenberg and L. E. Birdzell argue, states secured legitimacy in part by withdrawing from major spheres of economic activity, although they continued to guarantee property and contracts and to provide other essential services. The complex bargains that produced this withdrawal, ironically, enabled the state to extract more resources from society than ever before, because they accelerated the pace of innovation and, thus, wealth creation. The new legal regime made possible "economic experiments," not merely with new technologies, but with new organizational forms for making and selling them as well.[13]

The corporate organizational form that emerged from these experiments proved especially well-suited to technological innovation. It spread risk more widely and allowed larger long-term investments than earlier forms of enterprise. These properties made possible the backward integration of corporations into scientific research in the late nineteenth and early twentieth centuries. Science in the service of industry, from which it had previously been isolated, produced extraordinary entrepreneurial opportunities. The development of corporate technological capabilities also made it possible for firms to take advantage of science produced outside the firm, leading to the emergence of knowledge networks that spanned private, public, and academic boundaries.[14]

Where "economic experiments" were restricted, as they were in much of southern and eastern Europe through most of the modern era, innovations made elsewhere might be adopted and even imitated, but little more. The twentieth century socialist experiments of the Soviet Union and Mao-era China demonstrate the point even more vividly. These states made impressive strides in catching up to their western rivals, but only when they focused enormous resources on doing so, for instance, in strategic weaponry. Otherwise, the citizenry made do with shoddy copies of western goods, if that. Both states and corporations were necessary to produce the most technologically innovative societies of the twentieth century.[15]

Although the differences between capitalist and communist political economies in innovative capacities were most dramatic, capitalist nations differed (and continue to differ) from one another in this regard as well. Such distinctions among "varieties of capitalism" (as a growing literature in political science labels them) have been obscured for most of the twentieth century by the Cold War dichotomy, even as the varieties multiplied with the economic success of Japan, Korea, and other newly industrialized countries. Early work in this vein focused on differences in capitalist states' macroeconomic and planning capabilities; a second generation of work concentrated on labor relations and financial systems. Henry Ergas pioneered the incorporation of innovation systems into the typology of capitalisms in the mid-1980s, and his example has now been widely followed.[16]

Ergas argued that some capitalist countries tend to "shift" from one technological trajectory to the next, while others "deepen" their capabilities within an existing trajectory. Japan, he claimed, does both. These differences in technological style across national systems of innovation cannot be fully accounted for by state-monopolized activities, such as military R&D spending; private decisions shaped by public policies are critical. Even multinational corporations seem to innovate differently in different countries. Parimal Patel and Keith Pavitt, for instance, have used a patent database to show that "revealed technological advantage" varies systematically across countries in the OECD. If one looks at other sorts of indicators, especially those that track the interactions between corporations and other institutions, such as trade associations and universities, the cross-national differences are even more stark.[17]

The most recent work in this genre labors to give these indicators a microeconomic underpinning by showing that systematic differences among the varieties of capitalism produce systematic differences in the innovation strategies of the firms that are governed by them. Richard Whitley, for instance, offers six types of capitalism, characterized by thirteen features, which he maps onto five types of corporate innovation strategies. Peter Hall and David Soskice offer a more parsimonious typology of two capitalisms, five arenas of firm endeavor, and two corporate innovation strategies. Although this stream of work is still in its infancy, both conceptually and empirically, it suggests that there is a correlation between each variety of capitalism and the technological capabilities of firms that reside within it.[18]

Why differences among varieties of capitalism should emerge and endure are complex and challenging questions, and it is not my intention to answer them here. By most accounts, the institutional arrangements that differentiate them and their constituent national systems of innovation are path-dependent; in other words, barriers to alternative paths of development (including convergence to a single, global variety of capitalism) have been erected by societal investments in existing structures.[19] Or, to put it crassly, these social scientists have concluded that history really matters. Business historians, plainly, have much to add to this discussion, particularly if they redirect their attention to research sites where the state's influence on corporate technological capabilities can be traced.[20]

FROM NATIONAL SYSTEMS TO CORPORATE CAPABILITIES: FOUR MECHANISMS OF INFLUENCE

The literature on the varieties of capitalism seeks to find a one-to-one correspondence between each national innovation system and the dominant strategy of its domestic firms. The desire for law-like causal statements, which drives this effort, forces this school's proponents into overly broad generalizations that transcend industries, technological systems, and historical eras. By attempting to explain too much with too little, they open themselves to a devastating empirical critique. They also wash out many of the details that motivate historical research, details that – given the presumption of path-dependency – are necessary to build a convincing causal story.

On the other hand, mainstream business historians, to the extent that they consider the state at all, err in the opposite direction. A contract here, a tax break there, and a lawsuit over there sometimes add up to a set of incentives that drives the scientific and technological investment of a firm in a new direction. In telling the story of a firm, a corporate biographer of course ought to attend to such instances. Yet, this approach tends to push too much into the background the long-term and pervasive policies and institutional processes that shape the firm's underlying technological capacities. The interactions between public and private are more intricate and subtle than can be captured by following the headlines.

An alternative to both of these approaches arises from new thinking about the nature of the state. Political scientists, who have debated the issues intensely over the past couple of decades, disagree about whether the state stands (to use a crude metaphor) within, outside, above, or beneath the rest of society. Historians need not choose among these factions. Rather, they may simply observe that each approach identifies a mechanism by which the state may influence the corporation and that the importance of each mechanism undoubtedly varies over time, among countries, and across economic sectors. This debate, then, supplies a checklist of potentially promising research questions that can be used to explore particular historical cases. The checklist that I work through below encompasses four ways of looking at the state – as organization, fisc, system of rules, and normative order.[21] Each of these "states" may shape corporate technological capabilities, and sometimes all do so simultaneously. This approach navigates between the one-size-fits-all approach of the "varieties of capitalism" literature and the custom tailoring of the corporate biographers.

THE STATE AS ORGANIZATION

One way to see the state is as an organization (or collection of organizations) that participates in markets just like firms. Though the state has a different revenue source and authority structure than the firm, these distinctive features are more or less irrelevant in interactions mediated by the market. Corporate technological capabilities are shaped by this state in much the same way that they are shaped by other firms: as customer, insurer, supplier, and competitor.

The state as customer is the most familiar and most important of these relationships. Public tasks have often proven to be the "killer app" that launched important technological innovations as commercial products. Jet aircraft, nuclear power plants, and electronic computers, for instance, were supplied to military organizations before they found civilian uses. Thomas Watson, Sr., the founder of IBM, famously stated that the market for computers was limited to a few big government customers. The Atomic Energy Commission was a particularly important customer for early computers; the U.S. Air Force and Navy also bought them and much other high-technology hardware. Security provided by government customers allows firms to invest in people, equipment, and knowledge that become crucial assets in the long-run battle for civilian markets. Public customers, in turn, sometimes serve as "lead users" that provide knowledge essential for making incremental improvements in products and processes. Second World War-era relationships among procurement officers and aircraft manufacturers illustrate this sort of relationship, in which the customer's influence extended deep into the innovation and production processes and provided producers with feedback essential for making improvements in design and manufacturing.[22]

The influence of the state as customer may be so pervasive that it affects the organizational structure and strategic decisions of the firm. Some firms, for example, establish divisions specifically to serve government organizations, while others eschew this segment of the market for fear that relationships with these customers will undermine their ability to compete in other markets. These organizational decisions may have important consequences for corporate technological capabilities. Whether new technologies can be "spun off" from government to nongovernment uses, for instance, may depend on whether networks within the firm span internal boundaries created in response to government customers.[23]

Government organizations exert a somewhat weaker gravitational pull on corporate technological capabilities as insurers than they do as customers. The insurer may encourage investments in such capabilities by sharing the risk taken by consumers of new products, or it may refuse to do so and have the opposite effect. U.S. government health insurance plans, for instance, generally have been unwilling to cover experimental medical treatments. Pharmaceutical and medical device companies that bring these treatments to market must find knowledge and legitimacy elsewhere. (The reader should bear in mind, though, that these treatments often are subsidized by the government in other ways, such as through direct and indirect support of R&D.) On the other hand, government insurance has typically paid high prices for such treatments once they are proven, setting the pattern for private insurers as well.[24] The latter effect seems to have been the stronger one, helping U.S. firms to become among the world's most innovative (and profitable) in these industries. While health coverage is the biggest element of the American state's insurance portfolio, crop insurance, mortgage insurance, and disaster assistance might also be cited as potential influences on corporate technological capabilities.[25]

Government organizations, in the U.S. context at least, are more often customers or insurers of private firms than they are competitors. One exception to this generalization was the Tennessee Valley Authority (TVA) of the 1930s, which was intended to serve as a "yardstick" for private power producers and to spur technological innovation among electric appliance manufacturers and fertilizer makers. The TVA's "business model" of high-volume, low-cost electricity and electricity-using devices changed the practices of its private competitors, a response which ultimately forced the TVA itself out of these markets. (A few decades later, the TVA served as a lead user of privately produced nuclear power plants, an effort also intended to serve as an example to private utilities.)[26]

Government organizations may supply technological ideas as well as products and services to businesses through the market. Indeed, ideas produced by government organizations increasingly have been offered to the private sector on commercial terms over the final third of the twentieth century. Cooperative research and development agreements (CRADAs) between governments and firms have put price tags on the know-how of public organizations, like the laboratories of the Department of Energy and the National Institutes of Health. CRADAs are intended to nudge the technological capabilities of their corporate participants in directions that meet public goals, such as environmental protection. They also aim to extend the time horizon of private R&D, encouraging firms to engage in long-term projects that private capital markets will not support. Twenty-first century firms may produce more environmentally friendly vehicles and devise the next generation of lithography technology more quickly as a result of CRADAs. The shift to CRADAs and other market mechanisms for mediating the transfer of knowledge across the public–private boundary surely is a subject that will attract future historians.[27]

States, then, influence the technological capabilities of firms within their jurisdictions, because they are comprised of organizations with the capacity to participate in markets. Organs of the state can buy and sell goods, services, and ideas, and they can provide insurance. In doing so, states may shift the incentives of the firms that they deal with in ways that lead those firms to employ different sorts of people, invest in different sorts of projects, and adopt different sorts of practices. Treating the state in this fashion is but a modest extension of existing practices in business history. Studies of industries, business groups, and supply chains have already moved down this path. The way that states as organizations influence firm technological capabilities is similar to the way that firms influence one another. Other mechanisms of state influence, however, are more distinctive.

THE STATE AS FISC

Although the state may at times appear to be just another participant in the market, appearances are deceptive. The state has at least two crucial monopolies. One is its monopoly on legitimate force, which, among other things, allows it to impose taxes. The other is its monopoly on the means of exchange; unlike firms, the state can print money and spend it. The state's power to tax and spend has important consequences for the technological capabilities of firms within its jurisdiction. The fiscal state can create markets for innovations where none would have existed otherwise, subsidize or penalize specific firms, groups of firms, or organizations involved in science and technology, and regulate the availability of funds that might be used to make investments in technological capabilities.

Excessive taxation, of course, can crush all forms of business activity, including innovative activity. For my purposes, however, the scale of taxation is less interesting than the taxing authority's ability to privilege some business activities over others. The increasing thickness of the Federal tax code illustrates the U.S. government's burgeoning capacity to deploy such incentives. Especially in periods in which resistance to direct spending has been high, tax breaks have spurred firms to augment the resources devoted to technological capabilities. The U.S. research and experimentation tax credit, for instance, subsidizes spending on research personnel. The pharmaceutical industry has taken advantage of this credit more fully than any other industry. This industry also has used other provisions of the tax code, like the possessions and "orphan drugs" tax credits, to reduce the cost of drug development and manufacturing. Although the scale of these incentives has been too modest to shape noticeably the capacities of the largest pharmaceutical firms, start-up firms have grown up in the lee of their shelter. Genzyme, for instance, took advantage of orphan drug protection to bring a key early product, Ceradase (for the treatment of Gaucher's disease) to market.[28]

Direct government subsidies (including "soft" loans and the like) are a more precise tool for fostering the development of specific technologies than tax breaks, and such policies are sometimes enacted even when the state is not the main customer for the end product. The Airbus consortium, which has benefited from generous government "launch aid," for instance, brought contemporary Europe into the large civilian aircraft industry in the 1980s. Airbus accelerated the pace of innovation in the industry by introducing, among other things, "fly-by-wire" technology. Withdrawal of U.S. government subsidies for Boeing's supersonic transport (SST) in 1970, by contrast, ended the SST development effort (probably to Boeing's benefit if one considers the experience of the Concorde). Advocates of such subsidy programs usually claim that they will be temporary and that the firms that they benefit ultimately will be subject to market discipline. Nonetheless, firms receiving even temporary support evolve differently than they would in the absence of such subsidies. The development and production processes of Airbus, for instance, have historically been distributed according to the political weight of its national sponsors, and the firm also is seen as having a special responsibility to keep jobs and contracts in Europe.[29]

The state also subsidizes universities and other non-corporate scientific and technological organizations, with important consequences for the technological capabilities of firms. Public and tax-privileged charitable contributions have accelerated the growth of important new scientific and engineering disciplines, for instance. Molecular biology grew largely because of the support of the Rockefeller Foundation and the National Institutes of Health (NIH). Computer science thrived at the hands of the Advanced Research Projects Agency (ARPA) of the Department of Defense (DOD) and the National Science Foundation (NSF). These new fields of knowledge, in turn, generated inventions with important industrial applications, which in some cases eroded the value of investments made by Chandlerian firms. The packaged software industry, for instance, put the existence of IBM, once the dominant player in the computer industry, in doubt in the early 1990s. Today, university connected biotechnology start-ups threaten pharmaceutical giants, while e-commerce spin-offs put "bricks and mortar" retailers at risk. Chandlerian firms must adapt under such circumstances by, among other things, hiring outsiders (as Galambos and Sewell show that Merck did) or acquiring newer firms.[30]

Finally, the state's role as macroeconomic stabilizer has important consequences for corporate technological capabilities. By manipulating the public budget, interest rates, and exchange rates, Keynesian policies stabilized the growth of aggregate demand, assuring firms that their investments would not go unrewarded. Investments in technological innovation (or, as the economist Seymour Harris put it, "optimum expenditure in science") were among those that Keynesians had in mind. These hopes have largely been realized, even though the business cycle has not been eliminated entirely. The mind-set of those who fund R&D in firms – the technology community's business confidence, if you will – is in part a product of the fiscal state.[31]

THE STATE AS A SYSTEM OF RULES

The organizational state participates in high-technology markets, and the fiscal state funds R&D and related activities. A third mechanism by which the state may shape corporate technological capabilities is by establishing and enforcing the rules under which market participants engage one another. This arrangement, in which a player is also the umpire, may not seem entirely fair, and sometimes it is not. Like excessive taxation, collusion between privileged enterprises and legal authorities may destroy private incentives for innovation. Yet, the lack of a system of rules may be even more stifling. In between the extremes, where the most technologically advanced states operate, the details of the rules and the nature of compliance with them are critical to the determination of corporate technological capabilities.

One fundamental set of rules distinguishes between domestic and international trade. By expanding the scope of the market, Adam Smith tells us, states extend the division of labor. The exceptionally large U.S. domestic market, within which interstate commerce was constitutionally protected from interference, gave American manufacturing firms a technological leg up on their foreign counterparts in the nineteenth and early twentieth centuries. Before the dramatic expansion of the Federal government in the New Deal and the Second World War, this "customs union" was probably the most important way in which the American state shaped corporate technological capabilities. The post-Second World War closing of the gap by some European and Asian firms, in turn, owed much to the free trade policies of the *pax americana*, which leveled the playing field to a great extent. Under some conditions, trade restrictions may cultivate firms' technological capabilities more effectively than openness. Tariffs that limited foreign competitors' access to the U.S. market were an important complement to the customs union. A similar combination of domestic trade protection and aggressive exporting were essential ingredients in Japanese manufacturers' rise to global leadership more recently.[32]

Another fundamental set of rules establishes property rights, including intellectual property rights (IPR). As with trade restrictions, the state must strike a balance in this area if it is to foster the technological capabilities of its subject firms. Too loose an IPR regime will deter private investment in researchers and knowledge out of fear that competitors will free ride; too strict a regime will raise the ratio of lawyers to engineers to stifling levels. In their high-tech heydays, General Electric (1920s and 1930s), IBM (1960s and 1970s), and Microsoft (1990s and 2000s) all faced bitter complaints that their imitative capabilities, made possible by loose IPR regimes, suppressed otherwise competitive entrepreneurs who were unable to protect their innovations from these giants. On the other hand, aviation, automobiles, and radio were all plagued in their early years by patent deadlocks that hamstrung the innovation process in these industries. Survey research has shown that the pharmaceutical industry relies most heavily of all industries upon IPR. Not surprisingly, changes in the U.S. IPR regime around 1980, such as the Bayh–Dole Act (which expanded the scope of universities' IPR) and the *Chakrabarty* decision (which authorized patents on genetically engineered life forms), contributed significantly to a restructuring of the innovation process in this industry, including the strengthening of academic–industry relationships, the emergence of new firms, and the reorganization of old ones.[33]

Financial regulations comprise a third item on this list of essential rules. By regulating the mechanisms with which firms raise capital, the state structures their capacity for taking risks, including technological risks. The U.S. venture capital sector boomed, for example, only when banking and securities regulations were altered in 1979 to permit a very high-risk component in pension fund portfolios. The venture capital industry has facilitated the creation of many new technology-based firms, not just in new sectors of the economy but in older industries as well. Indeed, entire regional economies, particularly those of Silicon Valley and the greater Boston area, have been energized by venture investments.[34]

A state is not really a state without trade, property, and financial rules. But the regulatory state typically extends far beyond these minima. Codes of conduct or, in the American lexicon, fair trade practices, for example, may place limits on cooperation among competitors and on mergers and acquisitions and other means of corporate reorganization. These limits may significantly affect firms' technological capabilities. The merger wave at the turn of the twentieth century in the United States was provoked in part by an antitrust policy that outlawed market sharing agreements. This movement set the stage for the establishment of central corporate research laboratories by dominant high-technology firms in the ensuing decades. The tightening of antitrust enforcement in the 1930s and 1940s and the imposition of compulsory patent licensing as a remedy for violations of antitrust law helped strengthen the technological capabilities of smaller and weaker firms in the post-Second World War era.[35]

Many other forms of regulation also have influenced firms' technological capabilities. Price regulation in the U.S. aviation industry between the 1930s and the 1970s created incentives for rapid technological change, particularly in luxury features, since these became the primary basis for airline competition. In the telephone industry over roughly the same period, a regulatory regime of price controls combined with monopoly to limit the pace of change in switching and transmission technology, even as it fostered basic research at Bell Labs. The rules governing labor relations affected the pace and direction of technological innovation, too, as when firms sought to substitute capital for labor to ward off unions that threatened their control and cost structure. More recently, environmental, safety, and health regulations have changed the innovation investment calculus. In some cases, these regulations have forced the development and diffusion of new technologies; in others, they have frozen the "best available control technology" (as many U.S. environmental laws put it) in place.[36]

The regulatory state infiltrates the mind-set of actual and would-be innovators more profoundly than does the fiscal state. In a well-functioning regulatory state, the threat of enforcement, rather than enforcement itself, deters smuggling, infringement of property rights, and noncompliance with other regulations. Indeed, compliance may come to seem natural, even in areas in which the initial intervention by the regulatory state provoked shock. The threat of enforcement may be reinforced as well by the moral sentiment of citizens both inside and outside of business. The process of deploying new technologies on the shop floor, for instance, involves consultation with and adaptation to the workforce in some settings for legal, business, *and* normative reasons, while in other settings all three of these motivations may be absent. The regulatory state, thus, helps to erect and maintain a set of norms that influences the process of technological change.[37]

THE STATE AS NORMATIVE ORDER

The norms that attach to the regulatory state illustrate the fourth mechanism by which the state influences corporate technological capabilities. The shared beliefs and experiences of citizens who serve corporations as scientists, engineers, managers, and workers shape the way that they carry out that service. Nationalism, liberalism, socialism, and plenty of other -isms, not to mention a bundle of less well-articulated elements of political culture, motivate and channel their energy and attention.

The most powerful of these norms has been nationalism. Even the academic scientific community, which maintains a powerful counter-norm of internationalism, has been riven regularly by nationalist sentiment. The fervor with which professors served their nations' militaries in the First World War, for instance, stunned the community's idealists. Close collaboration between the national security apparatus and high-technology companies has been even more common than military–academic collaboration. To be sure, money changes hands in these relationships, preferably from state to business and not the other way around. But they are sealed by shared beliefs. IBM engineers who worked with the U.S. National Security Agency undoubtedly wanted to safeguard national secrets and break Soviet codes as well as get paid and stay at the cutting edge of technology.

Patriotic sentiments need not be harnessed to national security to have an effect on industrial innovation. For instance, the project of nation-building through the development of energy, transportation, and communication systems may mobilize the efforts of the corporate technical community. Companies such as Bombardier and Nortel, which are centers of excellence in the Canadian national system of innovation, have their roots in such a project. One would expect to find this pattern in developing countries when technological innovation in the private sector is perceived to be a necessary element of any growth strategy. Technical elites in these countries, whether in the public or private sector, are quite likely to be ardent nation-builders.[38]

The conception of the state as normative order also embraces economic and political values other than nationalism. Individualism, for example, permeates the U.S. system of innovation, in which entrepreneurial spin-offs from large companies are a critical component. Fairchild, itself a spin-off from Bell Labs, was the spawning ground for some of Silicon Valley's most innovative new firms in the 1950s and 1960s. American culture's acceptance of risk-taking and failure enables entrepreneurs in the United States to start up new firms more easily than those in other countries. Such risk-taking occasionally finds expression even in larger firms. In societies in which risks are more fully socialized, bet-the-company efforts like the IBM 650 or the Boeing 747 would be even more difficult to carry off than they were in the United States.[39]

Economic individualism is not incompatible with the civic republicanism that has been prominent at times in U.S. history. The provision of new goods and services to all the people can be conceived of as a fulfillment of one's duty in this schema, and industrial innovation, therefore, as a means of national service. Richard John finds traces of this ideological commitment in Theodore Vail's universal service strategy for AT&T. In the twentieth century, rights-based liberalism has overshadowed civic republicanism, and it too has had an influence on industrial innovation. The gay rights movement's deep involvement with AIDS drug development is one powerful example.[40]

The state as a normative order is not monolithic. States usually encompass regional or ethnic variations as well as dissenting individuals. The degree and extent of cultural variety may have implications for corporate technological capabilities. Minority groups such as Jews and overseas Chinese, for example, have been disproportionately represented in the annals of industrial science and technology. Immigrants may bring new ideas and perspectives with them; contemporary Silicon Valley thrives as much on these newcomers as on good old American know-how, although it should be noted that many of these immigrants have been trained in the United States.[41]

THE END OF BUSINESS HISTORY?

The state shapes the technological capabilities of firms through a variety of mechanisms. It is a participant in markets, a channeler of financial flows, a maker of rules, and a creator of beliefs and attitudes. Cumulatively, these influences are so profound that the combined technological capabilities of all the firms in each nation differ substantially from one another. National innovation systems are marked by variations in institutional pattern, innovative output, and technological style. Firms account for much of this variation in large part because they are shaped by states.

One might conclude, if one accepts these claims, that institutional history, narrowly construed, should be scrapped once and for all. Their boundaries blurred, corporations and government agencies no longer serve as satisfactory units of analysis to explain larger social outcomes. We must think more comprehensively, it might be argued, about industrial networks, say, or policy communities. I think this extreme conclusion is unwarranted. The existence of an organizational hierarchy (or an array of such hierarchies) has important and often decisive consequences for the mobilization of capital, skills, and attention. It shapes communication patterns and structures conflict and cooperation.

Historians of business, government, and technology ignore formal organization at their peril. We should continue to welcome excellent studies of corporate R&D laboratories and highly innovative companies. However, such work will be less welcome if their authors strap on the organizational blinders too tightly. Corporate biographies should be of the "life and times" variety, setting their subjects in a social, political, and cultural context. Galambos and Sewell point the way.

The recognition that the state is an intimate partner of the corporation is not the end of business history, but rather a new beginning. This way of thinking expands the range of potentially fruitful loci for research, providing, as I suggested earlier, a checklist of opportunities. We might want to take a closer look, for instance, at corporate functions (and the people who perform them) that span organizational boundaries, particularly between government and industry. Legal, financial, public relations, and government relations offices whose work bears on science and technology come to mind. Consultants might also be interesting subjects.

Moving further away from the organizational approach, business historians might indeed take networks and communities as subjects more often. Studies could be built around perceived problems and the people in a variety of organizations who aim to solve them. They might center on regions or on educational cohorts. Such research would illuminate organizational questions by indicating the constraints and opportunities that organizational boundaries create, but it would move beyond these questions by incorporating social, political, and cultural influences on corporate science and technology.[42]

There may also be industries, times, and places in which state–corporate interactions that usually lie in the background come to the fore. Moments of contention and transition bring to the surface norms, rules, patterns of allocation, and inter-organizational relationships that are otherwise taken for granted. Historians working in this mode are likely to focus on the emergence of new industries and periods of depression, social conflict, and war. Similarly, studies of technologically lagging countries, including relationships between these countries and the leading countries, seem more promising than those of the leaders themselves in this regard.

We may come to see the Chandlerian firm as a special case of the innovation process that was the product of particular historical conditions. It is ironic that a schema that aimed to make sense of a late nineteenth and early twentieth century phenomenon continues to hold sway in business history at the beginning of the twenty-first century. The era of big government stands between us and Chandler's era, and it may not be over yet, despite the rhetoric issuing from Washington in recent years. I suspect that when historians of economic, scientific, and technological institutions look back fifty years from now, they will be students of some kind of inter-organizational synthesis, which retains the best of contemporary business history but enriches, enlivens, and complicates it.[43]

NOTES

1. Alfred D. Chandler; Jr., *Scale and Scope: The Dynamics of Industrial Capitalism* (Cambridge, MA: Belknap Press, 1990).

2. Richard R. John, "Elaborations, Revisions, Dissents: Alfred D. Chandler, Jr., *The Visible Hand* After Twenty Years," *Business History Review* 71 (1997), 151–200; Peter Dobkin Hall, "The Managerial Revolution, the Institutional Infrastructure, and the Problem of Human Capital," *Voluntas* 7:(1) (1996), 3–16. This volume takes a similar approach.

3. Michael J. Piore and Charles F. Sabel, *The Second Industrial Divide: Possibilities for Prosperity* (New York: Basic, 1984), 25–6.

4. For an introduction, see Bengt-Ake Lundvall, "Introduction," in Lundvall (ed.), *National Systems of Innovation: Toward a Theory of Innovation and Interactive Learning* (London: Pinter, 1992), 1–19.

5. Louis Galambos with Jane Eliot Sewell, *Networks of Innovation: Vaccine Development at Merck, Sharp & Dohme, and Mulford, 1895–1995* (New York: Cambridge University Press, 1995).

6. Richard R. Nelson, "Preface to Part V," in Giovanni Dosi *et al.*, *Technical Change and Economic Theory* (London: Pinter, 1988), 309.

7. This "resource-based" view of the firm is typically contrasted with the "nexus of contracts" perspective. See Nicolai J. Foss (ed.), *Resources, Firms, and Strategies* (New York: Oxford University Press, 1997); and Naomi R. Lamoreaux, Daniel M. G. Raff, and Peter Temin (eds.), *Learning By Doing in Markets, Firms, and Countries* (Chicago: University of Chicago Press, 1999). There are, of course, forms of business enterprise other than corporations, and my arguments may not apply to all of them. The vast bulk of technological innovation in the contemporary private sector, however, occurs within corporations.

8. This section draws on the articles included in Foss, 1997, and on Mary O'Sullivan, "The Innovative Enterprise and Corporate Governance," *Cambridge Journal of Economics* 24 (2000), 393–416. Quote from Chandler, 1990, 24.

9. Joseph A. Schumpeter, in Harper Colophon, (ed.), *Capitalism, Socialism, and Democracy* (New York: Harper and Row, 1950), 81.

10. Richard R. Nelson, "The Simple Economics of Basic Scientific Research," *Journal of Political Economy* 67 (1959), 297–306; Kenneth J. Arrow, "Economic Welfare and the Allocation of Resources for Invention," in *The Rate and Direction of Inventive Activity* (Princeton: Princeton University Press, 1962); Paul M. Romer, "Endogenous Technical Change," *Journal of Political Economy* 98 (1990), S71–S102.

11. Charles Tilly, *Big Structures, Large Processes, Huge Comparisons* (New York: Russell Sage, 1984).

12. Martin van Creveld, *The Rise and Decline of the State* (New York: Cambridge University Press, 1999), quote from 377; Joel Mokyr, *The Lever of Riches* (New York: Oxford University Press, 1990), 209–38.

13. Van Creveld, 1999; Nathan Rosenberg and L. E. Birdzell, *How the West Grew Rich* (New York: Basic, 1986), 117–23; Nathan Rosenberg, "Economic Experiments," in *Exploring the Black Box* (New York: Cambridge University Press, 1994), 87–108. See also Charles Tilly, *Capital, Coercion, and European States*, rev. edn. (Cambridge: Blackwell, 1992).

14. Rosenberg and Birdzell, 186–268.
15. Rosenberg, 1994; Manuel Castells, *End of Millennium*, 2nd edn. (Oxford: Blackwell, 2000), 4–46.
16. Andrew Shonfield, *Modern Capitalism* (New York: Oxford University Press, 1965); William Lazonick, *Business Organization and the Myth of the Market* (New York: Cambridge University Press, 1991); John Zysman, *Governments, Markets, and Growth* (Ithaca: Cornell University Press, 1983); Peter J. Katzenstein, *Small States in World Markets: Industrial Policy in Europe* (Ithaca: Cornell University Press, 1985); Henry Ergas, "Does Technology Policy Matter?," in Bruce R. Guile and Harvey Brooks (eds.), *Technology and Global Industry* (Washington, DC: National Academy Press, 1987), 191–245.
17. Ergas, 1987; Parimal Patel and Keith Pavitt, "National Innovation Systems: Why They Are Important, and How They Might Be Measured and Compared," *Economic Innovation and New Technology* 3 (1994), 77–95; Richard R. Nelson and Nathan Rosenberg (eds.), *National Innovation Systems* (New York: Oxford University Press, 1993).
18. Richard Whitley, "The Institutional Structuring of Innovation Strategies: Business Systems, Firm Types, and Patterns of Technical Change in Different Market Economies," *Organization Studies* 21:5 (2000), 855–86; Peter A. Hall and David Soskice, "An Introduction to Varieties of Capitalism" in Soskice and Hall (eds.), *Varieties of Capitalism: The Institutional Foundations of Comparative Advantage* (Oxford: Oxford University Press, 2001).
19. Paul Pierson, "Increasing Returns, Path Dependence and the Study of Politics," *American Political Science Review* 94 (2000), 251–68.
20. One demonstration of the promise of this approach is Johann Peter Murmann, "Knowledge and Competitive Advantage in the Synthetic Dye Industry, 1850–1914: The Coevolution of Firms, Technology, and National Institutions in Great Britain, Germany, and the U.S.," *Enterprise and Society* 1:4 (2000), 699–704, which won a dissertation prize from the Business History Conference.
21. This typology draws on Stephen D. Krasner, "Approaches to the State: Alternative Conceptions and Historical Dynamics," *Comparative Politics* 16 (1984), 223–46.
22. Kenneth Flamm, *Targeting the Computer: Government Support and International Competition* (Washington, DC: Brookings, 1987); Allen Kaufman, "In the Procurement Officer We Trust: Constitutional Norms, Air Force Procurement, and Industrial Organization, 1938–1947," manuscript, 1997; Jonathan Zeitlin, "Flexibility and Mass Production at War: Aircraft Manufacture in Britain, the United States, and Germany, 1939–1945," *Technology and Culture* 36 (1995), 46–79. In many cases, of course, the public customer also subsidized, protected, or otherwise helped its supplier firms. These activities fall elsewhere in my typology; their coincidence in some, but not all, cases emphasizes the point that these approaches to the state are complementary, not exclusive.
23. John A. Alic *et al.*, *Beyond Spinoff: Military and Commercial Technologies in a Changing World* (Boston: Harvard Business School Press, 1992); Ergas, 1987.
24. Richard A. Rettig, "Medical Innovation Duels Cost Containment," *Health Affairs* (Summer 1994), 7–27.
25. Rebecca Henderson, Luigi Orsenigo, and Gary P. Pisano, "The Pharmaceutical Industry and the Revolution in Molecular Biology: Interactions Among Scientific, Institutional, and Organizational Change," in David C. Mowery and Richard R. Nelson (eds.), *Sources of Industrial Leadership* (New York: Cambridge University Press, 1999), 267–311; David A. Moss, *When All Else Fails: The Government as the Ultimate Risk Manager* (Cambridge, MA: Harvard University Press, 2002).

26. David M. Hart, *Forged Consensus: Science, Technology, and Economic Policy in the United States, 1921–1953* (Princeton: Princeton University Press, 1998), 68–71; Gregory B. Field, " 'Electricity for All': The Electric Home and Farm Authority and the Politics of Mass Consumption," *Business History Review* 64 (1990), 32–60; Ronald C. Tobey, *Technology as Freedom: The New Deal and the Electrical Modernization of the American Home* (Berkeley: University of California Press, 1996).

27. Christopher T. Hill and J. David Roessner, "New Directions in Federal Laboratory Partnerships with Industry," *Science and Public Policy* 25 (1998), 297–304; David H. Guston, *Between Politics and Science: Assuring the Integrity and Productivity of Research* (New York: Cambridge University Press, 2000), 113–37.

28. United States Congress, Office of Technology Assessment, *Pharmaceutical R&D: Risks, Costs, and Rewards* (Washington, DC: GPO, 1993).

29. Laura D'Andrea Tyson, *Who's Bashing Whom: Trade Conflict in High-Technology Industries* (Washington, DC: International Institute of Economics, 1992); Mel Horwitch, *Clipped Wings: The American SST Conflict* (Cambridge, MA: MIT Press, 1982); Linda R. Cohen and Roger G. Noll, *The Technology Pork Barrel* (Washington, DC: Brookings, 1991).

30. Henderson, Orsenigo, and Pisano (1999); Flamm (1987); Galambos and Sewell (1995).

31. Hart (1998), 145–74, quote from 157.

32. Richard R. Nelson and Gavin Wright, "The Rise and Fall of American Technological Leadership: The Postwar Era in Historical Perspective," *Journal of Economic Literature* 30 (1992), 1931–64; David Hounshell, *From the American System to Mass Production, 1800–1932: The Development of Manufacturing Technology in the United States* (Baltimore: Johns Hopkins University Press, 1984); Chalmers Johnson, *MITI and the Japanese Miracle: The Growth of Industrial Policy, 1925–1975* (Palo Alto: Stanford University Press, 1982).

33. Richard C. Levin *et al.*, "Appropriating the Returns from Industrial R&D," *Brookings Papers on Economic Activity* 1987, no. 3, 783–820; Henderson *et al.*, 1999.

34. Samuel Kortum and Josh Lerner, "Assessing the Contribution of Venture Capital to Innovation," *Rand Journal of Economics* 31 (2000), 674–92; Martin Kenney (ed.), *Understanding Silicon Valley: The Anatomy of an Entrepreneurial Region* (Stanford: Stanford University Press, 2000).

35. David C. Mowery, "The U.S. National Innovation System: Origins and Prospects for Change," *Research Policy* 21 (1992), 125–44; Hart (1998), 84–96.

36. Richard H. K. Vietor, *Contrived Competition: Regulation and Deregulation in America* (Cambridge, MA: Belknap, 1994); Kenneth Flamm, "Technological Advances and Costs: Computers vs. Communications," in Flamm and Robert W. Crandall (eds.), *Changing the Rules* (Washington, DC: Brookings, 1989), 13–61.

37. Jeffrey Keefe, "Do Unions Hinder Technological Change?," in Lawrence Mishel and Paul B. Voos (eds.), *Unions and Economic Competitiveness* (Armonk, NY: M. E. Sharpe, 1992), 109–41; Kathleen Thelen, *Union of Parts* (Ithaca: Cornell University Press, 1991).

38. Mark Elam, "National Imagination and Systems of Innovation," in Charles Edquist (ed.), *Systems of Innovation* (London: Pinter, 1997), 157–73; Jorge Niosi, "Canada's National System of Innovation," *Science and Public Policy* 18 (1991), 83–92.

39. Gordon Moore (with Kevin Davis), "Learning the Silicon Valley Way," paper presented at Stanford University, Jul. 28, 2000.

40. Richard R. John, "Vail and Universal Service," paper presented at the Business History Conference, Chapel Hill, NC, Mar. 7, 1999; Steven Epstein, *Impure*

Science: AIDS, Activism, and the Politics of Knowledge (Berkeley: University of California Press, 1996).

41. Annalee Saxenian, "Silicon Valley's Immigrant Entrepreneurs," Public Policy Institute of California, June 1999.

42. Some recent examples include Ann Markusen *et al.*, *The Rise of the Gunbelt: The Military Remapping of Industrial America* (New York: Oxford University Press, 1991); Robert Kargon, Stuart W. Leslie, and Erica Schoenberger, "Far Beyond Big Science: Science Regions and the Organization of Research and Development," in Bruce Hevly and Peter Galison (eds.), *Big Science* (Palo Alto: Stanford University Press, 1992), 334–54; Saxenian, 1999; Philip Scranton, "Manufacturing Diversity: Production Systems, Markets, and American Consumer Society, 1870–1930," *Technology and Culture* 35 (1994), 476–505.

43. Much of what I say here echoes Louis Galambos, "Technology, Political Economy, and Professionalization: Central Themes of the Organizational Synthesis," *Business History Review* 57 (1983), 471–93.

The Corporation Under Siege: Social Movements, Regulation, Public Relations, and Tort Law since the Second World War

David B. Sicilia

The history of the United States in the second half of the twentieth century has received selective attention from historians. There are sizeable literatures on family life in the 1950s, on the civil rights and counter-culture movements, on environmentalism, and on political and diplomatic history. But few scholars of business and economy in general or of the corporation in particular have undertaken works of broad interpretation or synthesis.[1] Although the turn of the millennium inspired several historians to reflect upon the broad contours of the twentieth century, no one has yet offered a period-specific synthesis for the postwar era akin to what Robert Wiebe (in *The Search for Order, 1977–1920*) put forward a generation ago for the "age of organization."[2] Many seem content to assume that the postwar decades were defined by trends and structural relationships defined before and during the war by – as the editors of this volume note in the Afterword – "the forward projection of the *fin de siècle* paradigm."

This approach missed much of what is unique about the postwar era. In 1986, Alan Brinkley argued in an influential essay that several existing interpretative frameworks for analyzing late nineteenth and early twentieth-century history – in particular, the organizational synthesis and the consensus school – work poorly when applied to the postwar period. Brinkley did not go forward to suggest one or more frameworks that might work better, however.[3]

In this chapter, I propose a framework for understanding the history of corporate America and U.S. political economy in the postwar period by exploring, first, how three large industries – chemical manufacturing, nuclear power, and tobacco – came under intense political, legal, and rhetorical attack by a variety of public and private individuals and institutions after the Second World War;

and, second, how those industries formulated and executed strategies to counter the attacks. While unique in many regards, these three industries also shared some striking similarities. Each came to be regarded as a major menace to public health and safety. Each was plagued with at least one major accident or "scare." Each became a prime target for private consumer and citizen action groups. Each came under increasing scrutiny and control by local and state ordnances and federal regulatory agencies. Each inspired journalists to produce scores of popular books, and Hollywood movie producers to produce major motion pictures alleging industry conspiracy and cover-up. And leading firms in each industry increasingly found themselves in court as defendants in high-stakes tort litigation.

More broadly, the three industries moved – at varying times and with a few notable exceptions – through five distinct stages: success and optimism imme-diately following the war; sustained challenges by social movements; increasing regulatory control by the "new social" regulatory state of the early 1970s; new accommodationist public relations strategies and tactics; and involvement in large-scale tort litigation.

How representative were the experiences of these three industries under siege? My focus on three of the least popular, most politicized industries in the American economy is an attempt to locate the shifting boundaries of social–state–business relations in the postwar era. What happened at the bound-aries reveals much about the limits of what was, or became, possible through social action, government regulation, corporate voluntarism, and litigation. Moreover, narratives at the margins tend to powerfully define ideologies and beliefs at the center. Middle class beliefs about whether "corporate America" was acting responsibly, or destroying the environment, or harming consumers were shaped by highly publicized struggles and episodes like the ones dis-cussed in this chapter. More than that, industries that intentionally or unwit-tingly test the limits of what is socially, politically, and legally acceptable often foreshadow a fundamental redefinition of political economy to come.

POSTWAR OPTIMISM AND STATE–BUSINESS PARTNERSHIP

For two of America's oldest and most well-established industries – chemicals and tobacco – the period immediately following the Second World War brought robust growth and product innovation. They were joined by a new industry – nuclear power – that also innovated, expanded rapidly, and enjoyed enormous popularity.[4] The chemical industry entered the postwar period with consider-able momentum. After lagging far behind Europeans, particularly Germans, in chemical production generally and organic chemicals in particular, American producers in the early 1900s finally began to make significant gains in advanced fields such as fine chemicals, dyestuffs, and pharmaceuticals. During the First

World War, widely regarded as "the chemist's war," U.S. producers – with considerable support from the federal government in the form of protective tariffs – tripled their capital investment and made great strides in ammonia fixation and the synthesis of potash, nitric acid, and coal tar for munitions. In the 1920s, the burgeoning automobile industry gave rise to strong demand for protective coatings, thermoplastics, and petroleum products, and a series of mergers created two new giants, Allied Chemical and Dye and Union Carbide and Carbon, that joined Du Pont and American Cyanamid to form a dominant oligopoly. In the 1930s, chemicals proved to be one of the few "Depression proof" industries, thanks to strong sales of pesticides, fertilizers, cellophane, and rayon. March 1930 alone saw the introduction of what would become two enormously successful products, neoprene (synthetic rubber) and polyester. Such new products flowed from the chemical industry's aggressive investment in Research and Development, making it the most intensively science-based industry in the economy. The interwar period saw the establishment of some 1200 new chemical R&D laboratories, and the number of researchers employed by the industry grew tenfold, to 27,700. The Second World War gave another boost to the industry, in large measure because of business–government cooperation in government-owned, company operated (GOCO) munitions plants; in a dramatically successful program to develop synthetic rubber; and in the sharing of confiscated German chemical technological know-how.[5]

After the war, the industry did not rest on its laurels. Exploiting German polymerization techniques and abundant domestic supplies of oil and natural gas, several American companies mass produced hydrocarbon-based "miracle" plastics – polyethylene, polypropylene, polyester, and polyvinylchloride (PVC) – as they rushed to join the emerging "petrochemicals revolution."[6] This, in turn, supported a synthetic fibers "revolution," so that by the late 1960s Americans would consume more synthetic than natural fibers.[7] The chemical industry also participated in heavy Cold War investment in aerospace, as several leading producers entered or expanded their investments in rocket and missile propulsion systems or even (in the case of Du Pont) atomic development.[8] The industry achieved yet another so-called technological revolution – the "green revolution" – by synthesizing an array of highly effective new agricultural chemicals (pesticides, insecticides, fungicides, and herbicides) that helped make postwar American agriculture one of the most productive sectors in the economy. Dichlorodiphenyltrichloroethane (DDT) had paved the way. Discovered by the Swiss, tested by the U.S. Office of Scientific Research and Development, and – with the OSRD's strong encouragement – mass produced by several U.S. chemical companies during the Second World War, DDT prevented massive G.I. casualties from insect-born diseases such as typhus, dengue fever, and, especially, malaria. After the war, DDT was embraced by American farmers as a highly potent and effective "broad spectrum" pesticide. It was, as one of DDT's biographers put it – aptly, in this context – "the atomic bomb of insecticides."[9]

With all of this, the chemical industry in the 1950s and 1960s enjoyed a reputation as a wellspring of new producer and consumer products that were greatly improving the quality of American life. This was reflected in new company advertising and public relations slogans, as exemplified by Du Pont's slogan: "Better Things for Better Living . . . Through Chemistry."[10] Chemistry and chemical engineering were well-regarded college majors for men (though unwelcoming fields for women), yet the industry struggled to find enough college trained researchers to staff its burgeoning laboratories. Between 1950 and 1970, the chemical industry employed roughly 70 percent of the nation's chemists.[11] Chemistry sets for children were commonplace in postwar American households. In 1957, the chemical industry, measured by capitalization, was the fifth largest manufacturing industry in the nation, with 10 percent of total manufacturing capital.[12]

Like the chemical industry, the tobacco industry had a long and successful history. Taking root in early British North America, tobacco became the cash crop of the Jamestown settlement. Tobacco farms grew up to meet heavy European demand. Spreading north to the Chesapeake, then into North Carolina by the end of the seventeenth century, tobacco growing increasingly was concentrated into large plantations worked by slaves. The manufacturing (versus cultivation and sale) of tobacco products began in 1760, when French Huguenot immigrant Pierre Lorillard erected a snuff mill in lower Manhattan.[13]

The modern U.S. tobacco industry emerged in the 1880s, when the American Tobacco Company, then headed by the indefatigable James Buchanan Duke, spearheaded a fundamental shift from handmade snuff, chewing tobacco, pipe tobacco, and cigars to predominantly mass-produced cigarettes. Duke was the first to purchase a cigarette-making machine patented in 1881 by James Bonsack that was capable of churning out more than 70,000 cigarettes in a ten-hour shift – twenty-four times more than the most skilled hand-roller could produce in the same period and at a fraction of the per unit cost. Duke leveraged the vast economies of scale of his Bonsack machines (for which he controlled exclusive rights for several years) to take over some 250 competitors around the world, and in the process built one of the most powerful monopolies in American business history. In 1911, the U.S. Supreme Court found Duke's "tobacco trust" in violation of the Sherman Antitrust Act, and it subsequently was broken up into four entities: American Tobacco Company, R. J. Reynolds Tobacco Company, P. Lorillard Company, and Liggett & Meyers Tobacco Company.[14]

During this period, the cigarette industry sustained a serious assault from social reformers, led by Lucy Page Gaston of Illinois. Tobacco use always had attracted critics (as illustrated by King James I's famous *Counterblaste to Tobacco*), but before Gaston they made limited headway. During the reformist antebellum decades, attacks rested mainly on moral grounds, but were far overshadowed by antislavery and temperance movements, and were countered by growing legions of smokers who heralded the weed for aiding digestion, mental acuity, and the like. After Gaston formed the Chicago Anti-Cigarette League in 1899 (she considered other kinds of tobacco use a hopeless cause), other cities followed, then a national organization in 1901. By that time eleven states had banned the sale and use of tobacco. Although the East was the slowest region to join the cause, in 1908 New York City passed the Sullivan Ordinance, which banned women from smoking in public, starting a municipal trend. Gaston's reformers also pressed several railroads and other companies into banning smoking (a strategy that would be repeated by antismoking forces a century later). But the coming of world war boosted smoking, and Gaston's movement began to unravel. The National Anti-Cigarette League disbanded in 1917, and soon thereafter the states began to repeal their anti-tobacco laws, completing the process by 1927.[15]

Three years before the American Tobacco breakup, U.S. production of cigarettes had edged past cigar output.[16] But cigarette sales soon surged dramatically because of two developments. First, in 1913, Reynolds introduced a revolutionary new product – an inexpensive Burley blend cigarette named Camel. Packaged to look and taste much like premium Turkish cigarettes, Camel captured a third of the U.S. cigarette market within four years. By that time the United States had entered the First World War, and cigarettes – convenient to light and puff – joined coffee and doughnuts as welcomed respites from boredom and battle. U.S. cigarette production rose from 18 billion in 1914 to 54 billion in 1919. Reynolds' competitors were forced to respond in kind, by bringing out inexpensive Burley blend cigarettes and advertising them heavily. Overwhelmingly, the tobacco business became a battle among a few leading cigarette brands, and has remained so ever since.[17]

During the Great Depression, the tobacco industry received significant support from the New Deal's Agricultural Adjustment Acts (AAA), which provided acreage controls and price supports for cooperating growers. Whereas non-tobacco farmers reached 70 percent parity of 1920–9 prices between 1934 and 1937 under AAA programs, tobacco growers garnered 97 percent. Federal allotment and price support systems continued, with occasional interruptions, until the 1980s.[18] The federal government continued to privilege tobacco in the Second World War. President Roosevelt declared it an essential crop, tobacco growers were granted draft deferments, and free cigarettes were included in G.I. field rations. Amid the wartime economic disruptions in Europe, cigarettes became a more accepted medium of exchange than currency, to the great benefit of U.S. soldiers who purchased them at a discount on military bases. G.I.s so revered their smokes that when the war in Europe ended they dubbed transit camps in France "Camp Lucky Strike," "Camp Chesterfield," "Camp Philip Morris," and "Camp Pall Mall."[19]

Cigarette smoking was firmly embedded in American culture by the early 1950s. Before and during the war, Hollywood stars like Humphrey Bogart and Lauren Bacall masterfully crafted their mannerisms around smoking to express all manner of emotions. The tradition continued after the war with a new generation of chain-smoking romantic anti-heroes such as James Dean, along with rock' n' rollers, crooners, television hosts, and movie goddesses. In real life – as on the silver screen and the flickering tube – most adult Americans smoked, with the rate among adult males approaching 75 percent. Per capita consumption of cigarettes stood at an all-time high at more than 2600. This demand was met by a six-firm oligopoly (the post-tobacco trust "Big Four" had been joined by Philip Morris and American Brands), which controlled 99.4 percent of the cigarette market.[20]

This was not a complacent oligopoly, however. Many industry experts believed that per capita consumption was approaching the saturation point. Competition among the "Big Six" was fierce. Cigarette companies were the heaviest buyers of print advertising in the economy, and among the biggest buyers of broadcast commercial time. To encourage smokers to shift brands, they brought out new king size, filtered, cork-tipped, mentholated, and boxed varieties, and quickly imitated the successes of competitors. Because some smokers complained of throat irritation, filtered and mentholated brands began to gain popularity. The stakes involved in hitting the right combination – or getting it wrong – would be demonstrated in subsequent decades by some dramatic successes and failures among the Big Six. Between 1949 and 1979, Reynolds and Lorillard made solid gains; Philip Morris and Brown and Williamson each roughly tripled its market share; while American Brands and Liggett & Meyers suffered staggering losses, the former falling from holding 31.3 percent of the cigarette market to 11.5, the latter from 20.2 to 2.7 percent.[21] All in all, however, the early 1950s were a heyday for the tobacco industry as a whole. Sales were soaring, profits were strong, and the key managerial challenge was battling for market share. As one historian of the industry put it, "There were no external problems for the industry to overcome in this period."[22]

Unlike chemicals and tobacco, nuclear power was a new industry in the early 1950s – or rather, a new hybrid. Electric utility companies date back to the 1880s. Before they used nuclear energy, they generated electricity by burning coal, oil, or natural gas, or running their generating plants with flowing water (hydropower). Burning fuel generated steam that turned turbines that spun the armatures of electric generators. The resulting electricity was carried over long lines at high voltages and then stepped down for local distribution. What changed with the coming of nuclear energy was the means of boiling water, which is achieved by using a controlled nuclear fission reaction to generate boiler heat. The first nuclear power plants, therefore, merged a well-established system for generating, transmitting, and distributing electricity with a brand-new and commercially untested technology for splitting atoms.[23]

At the moment of this merger in the United States, nuclear power enjoyed great confidence from utility and scientific experts. Virtually every American regarded electric utilities as one of the nation's great success stories. Utility interests had reached an accommodation with the state that gave them monopoly status in exchange for regulatory oversight of rates and service. This compromise retained private ownership; in stark contrast to Europe, some 90 percent of U.S. electricity has come from privately owned monopolies regulated by state commissions. The remaining 10 percent has been composed of local municipals and (beginning in the 1930s) the federal Tennessee Valley system.[24] One of the key ways private utility interests were able to fend off state ownership was by developing progressive marketing and public relations methods, most notably a "grow-and-build" strategy of constructing large generating plants to capture economies of scale, passing much of those savings on to customers in the form of lower rates, thereby expanding their customer base to justify another round of plant construction, and so on. This virtuous cycle caused both nominal and inflation-adjusted utility rates to decline steadily and dramatically throughout the first half of the twentieth century, and made U.S. electric utilities productively the highest of any sector in the economy.[25]

Not surprisingly, electric power companies enjoyed enormous popularity – or, more precisely, benign invisibility. Pleased with their declining electric bills, consumers took their power companies for granted, except on the rare occasions when the power went out. At those moments, power companies publicized their heroic efforts to restore service. Only the Great Northeastern Blackout of November 1965 raised serious questions about system reliability, but utility experts ultimately convinced the public and regulators that they had instituted a technological fix and no fundamental structural changes were imposed from outside the industry. Rather, as historian Richard Hirsh has documented, electric utility managers reached the "pinnacle" of their success in the 1960s as stewards of economic growth and material progress. They were not the most dynamic cohort of industry leaders, but they were reliable and had an impressive record of accomplishment.[26]

The coming of nuclear reactors promised to infuse the predictable utility industry with a new sense of technological novelty and prowess, and to move the nation toward a new age of almost limitless harnessed energy. For all of this, however, nuclear power probably would not have been launched in the United States without considerable intervention from the state. From an investment standpoint, even if long-term profit prospects were attractive, the new plants required immense capital investment in unproven systems. Under such conditions, the state could step in to reduce risk or increase incentives for private investors. Such was the case in the nineteenth century, when local, state, and federal governments offered railroad builders a variety of incentives, from the construction of terminals, to stock and bond underwriting, to rights of way and massive land grants. Government officials offered such assistance because they saw railroads as a key component of the nation's transportation infrastructure, whose expansion would yield enormous social and economic benefits (or positive externalities).

In the case of nuclear energy, some of the same thinking applied. No one doubted that cheap and abundant energy would have an enormous positive ripple effect on the economy. The Cold War clinched the case for federal intervention. A peaceful nuclear power program promised a steady source of fissionable plutonium for atomic weapons. In 1946, Congress passed the Atomic Energy Act, which created a civilian Atomic Energy Committee (AEC). For the first few years, military considerations dominated the Joint Committee for Atomic Energy (JCAE) and the AEC. But in December 1953, Eisenhower outlined his Atoms for Peace initiative to the United Nations. Since the Cold War was as much about technological and ideological posturing as it was about brute military strength – especially once the Soviet Union possessed the bomb – federal officials wanted to ensure that the United States did not become a technological laggard. Development of a strong domestic peacetime nuclear energy industry offered the federal government a way to bring the first generation of nuclear scientists, engineers, and professional managers into what Brian Balogh has called the "prominstrative state."[27]

A JCAE made up of nine senators and nine congressmen oversaw the AEC. As political scientist James Temples argues, the JCAE's members, its autonomy, its focus and determination, and its structural relationship to other government bodies made it arguably "the most powerful joint committee in Congressional history."[28] The Joint Committee wanted even greater private participation in nuclear energy development, and successfully pushed for a 1954 amendment to the Atomic Energy Act that buttressed its own power and gave much greater emphasis to commercial nuclear development. Now the AEC was authorized to encourage rather than prohibit private companies from building, owning, and operating atomic power plants. Still, a serious obstacle to private investment remained, dubbed "the insurance problem." In the event of a nuclear plant accident, liability could be massive: 43,000 injuries, 3,400 deaths, and $7 billion in damages, according to an AEC-commissioned study. Accordingly, the JCAE drafted and Congress passed the Price–Anderson Act, which essentially indemnified private utility corporations from liability from a nuclear accident.

The first U.S. nuclear power projects were launched soon thereafter; and the first three went on line in 1957. Meanwhile, the AEC continued to promote nuclear energy through, among other things, a Power Reactor Demonstration Program and an aggressive public relations campaign, all of which ultimately cost taxpayers about $9 billion. For its part, the nuclear power industry distributed educational materials, sponsored public service advertising, and lobbied through the Atomic Industrial Forum, the American Nuclear Energy Council, the American Nuclear Society, the Edison Electric Institute, and other industry organizations. There were few countervailing voices, as a nuclear consensus had emerged to reinforce the broader "grow-and-build" consensus enjoyed by the electric utility industry. But by the 1970s, the year of the first Earth Day, the consensus had begun to crack. By that time thirteen nuclear plants were operating with total capacity of 5.6 billion kW.[29]

For the chemical, tobacco, and nuclear industries, then, the 1950s were a time of growth, optimism, and accommodating business–government relations. Chemical companies, coming out of a strong partnership with government during the war, were bursting forth with new "miracle" products. Tobacco manufacturers were struggling to meet demand for cigarettes from a strong majority of the nation's adult smokers. And the young nuclear power industry, with the strong support of the federal government and the promise of a new energy future, was attracting billions of dollars of investment capital. While not all industries were in similarly good shape, the 1950s generally were a satisfying time for corporate America. As a leading public opinion expert reported in 1957, the reputation of big business had improved in recent decades, and "all important census categories report generally friendly feelings toward large companies."[30] Opinion polls a generation later would paint a very different picture, one of widespread public disillusionment and mistrust toward large institutions in general, and toward big business in particular. My task in the next section is to show how, why, and by whom the tobacco industry came under attack in the 1950s, the chemical industry in the 1960s, and the nuclear industry in the 1970s.

THREE INDUSTRIES UNDER SIEGE

For the tobacco industry, the first serious post-Second World War challenge to its legitimacy came from the public health and medical community. Several studies in the late 1940s and early 1950s pointed to a correlation between smoking and lung cancer in males, but the public was largely oblivious to such findings until the 1952 publication of "Cancer by the Carton" in *Reader's Digest*. Other widely read articles in *Time* and *Reader's Digest* followed, buttressed by new research findings, most notably the 1953 Sloan–Kettering Report in *Cancer Research*, which also linked cigarette smoking with lung cancer. Leading private health organizations soon joined the cause. In 1953 the American Cancer Society asserted that smokers had a higher death rate than non-smokers. The American Lung Association and the American Heart Association later came out with similarly troubling statements. The "cancer scare" of the early 1950s was underway. And, in response, millions of Americans reduced their smoking or quit, driving down cigarette sales nearly 6 percent in 1954 and 1955.[31] But the downturn was short-lived, in part because many smokers switched to filtered cigarettes rather than quitting.

The federal government entered the arena in the mid-1960s. In 1963, anticipation grew within the tobacco industry about the impending release of the findings of U.S. Surgeon General Luther L. Terry's special panel on smoking and health.[32] The worries were well-founded; the 1964 Surgeon General's Report, based on a review of 7000 articles on smoking and health, concluded that cigarette smoking was a cause of chronic bronchitis, laryngeal and lung cancer in men, and (probably) lung cancer in women, and called for "appropriate remedial action." Although this first of many Surgeon General's Reports to take increasingly strong positions against smoking appeared to have little impact on smokers' behavior, it opened the door for further federal intervention in the late 1960s. Now the Federal Communications Commission took the lead. In 1964, the Federal Trade Commission (FTC) passed an Advertising Code that required the following warning on all cigarette packages: "Caution: Cigarette smoking may be hazardous to your health." Congress, influenced by tobacco-growing states, passed the Cigarette Labeling and Advertising Act of 1965, which made the package warning requirement federal law but exempted advertisements and prohibited the FTC from acting on cigarette advertising for three years.[33] In an effort to leverage the FTC's power in a different way, in 1967 attorney John Banzhaf filed a fairness-doctrine complaint with the FTC calling for health hazard warnings by cigarette advertisers. The tactic worked; later that year the FTC declared cigarette advertising a controversial issue, and therefore subject to its Fairness Doctrine, which requires that broadcasters offer balanced coverage. For the next three years, the airwaves carried antismoking messages so effective that they drove down cigarette sales 5.7 percent. At the end of 1969, Congress (with the Public Health Cigarette Act) banned all television and radio cigarette advertising.[34]

Anti-cigarette advertising became one of the most controversial episodes in the battle against smoking. The Fairness Doctrine advertisements appeared to be working so well that some industry insiders welcomed the Congressional broadcast ban. But cigarette companies also counterattacked, developing new products (most notably higher filtration cigarettes), and by making health claims about them to woo customers away from competitors. Congress banned the health claims, but it also put an end to the antismoking ads. Smoking increased again. As an FTC regulator later it put it: "[D]issemination of negative product information in competitive markets is a remarkably robust process. Governmental efforts to regulate this kind of information can easily make the market worse, for the FTC seems mainly to have retarded rather than hastened market adjustment to new information on the health effects of smoking."[35]

In the 1970s and 1980s, federal regulation moved further in already established directions. In 1972, health warnings were required on all forms of cigarette advertising, and in 1984 the single health warning was replaced by a rotating system of warnings about specific health hazards (such as smoking during pregnancy). But more importantly, the U.S. Surgeon General's Report that year declared that cigarette smoke also posed risks for non-smokers, thereby legitimizing the "passive" or "second-hand smoke" issue. Other federal agencies moved to limit smoking on interstate buses (the Commerce Commission in 1971) and airlines (the Civil Aeronautics Board in 1973). The states were soon to follow. In 1973, Arizona banned smoking in public places; and two years later Minnesota enacted an Indoor Clean Air Act. California, taking a different approach to discourage smoking, passed a 1988 referendum that significantly boosted the state cigarette tax. Over the next dozen years, most states passed similar prohibitions and punitive taxes, as well as minimum age requirements and controls over free samples. The states were joined by hundreds of municipalities, which banned smoking in stores, restaurants, museums, hospitals, and virtually all other public venues.[36]

Along the way, federal and state agencies were joined in their antismoking efforts by government health officials from the Centers for Disease Control and the National Institutes for Health (NIH). In 1982, three NIH entities formed a Coalition on Smoking OR Health. The American Medical Association issued its own statements and guidelines for physicians. In addition, consumer and citizen action groups pitched in against the tobacco industry and smoking. These included Americans for Non-Smoker's Rights, Ralph Nader's Common Cause, and Action on Smoking and Health (ASH). Finally, corporations, wary lawsuits by non-smokers and aware that non-smokers took fewer sick days, layered on their own restrictions and bans.[37]

Thus, the public and private medical establishment, municipal, state, and federal government agencies and legislatures, consumer and citizens' groups, and private businesses were allied against cigarette smoking. Their collective efforts seemed to be working. After rising steeply (with a few interruptions) since the end of the Second World War, cigarette consumption declined sharply in the late 1980s. Although cigarette smoke loomed in the air wherever people had congregated in the 1950s, by the late 1980s the nonsmoker could avoid cigarette smoke with little or no effort. Indeed, there were reasons to believe that the attacks on smoking had done as much as they could. With nonsmokers effectively shielded from the habit, smoking seemed more and more a matter of individual choice, and hence not amenable to further regulation. This reasoning did not dissuade the most committed antismoking activists, however. They agreed with health officials that smoking was the nation's leading cause of preventable death, responsible for some 400,000 premature deaths each year, and were dedicated to eliminating the manufacture, sale, and distribution of tobacco products in the United States.

In the 1960s and 1970s, the chemical industry saw its reputation undergo a major reversal. Amid growing public concern about industrial damage to the environment and to human health, the chemical industry became, as one industry expert put it, "the *bête noire* of environmentalists."[38] The strength and rapidity with which social attitudes about the environment, in general, and the chemical industry, in particular, shifted astounded public opinion analysts, who were accustomed to seeing major attitudinal changes unfold over many years. But in this case, as a public opinion researcher exclaimed, "the unprecedented speed and urgency with which ecological issues have burst into American consciousness" is no less than "a miracle of public opinion."[39]

The initial wave of attacks against the chemical industry took three major forms. First was the publication of Rachel Carson's *Silent Spring*, which is often identified as the starting point of the postwar environmental movement. Carson's book – recently voted by a group of journalists as one of the most influential pieces of American journalism in the twentieth century – undoubtedly had tremendous impact.[40] Although Robert Rudd's *Pesticides in the Living Landscape* was regarded by pesticide experts as a more knowledgeable synthesis of scientific work, Carson's book truly was a great work of journalism. Elegant and filled with powerful prose, it brought widespread attention to an important contemporary issue. Worse for chemical firms, it appears that their response to *Silent Spring* served only to amplify Carson's message.

While chemical companies were wrestling with the new journalistic criticism, they also had to contend with a series of attacks from community based grass-roots movements. Most of these groups were temporary coalitions of local residents mobilized by a specific real or perceived threat to their community: a toxic waste dump, a chemical spill, concern about smokestack emissions or water pollution, and the like. Such coalitions typically were made up of core and peripheral members. The core was composed of a small number of activists who had been involved with other social movements and were more highly educated and ideologically motivated than other members of the coalition. Core members held leadership positions, published newsletters, negotiated with the industry and public officials, and devoted much more time to the cause than others. Peripheral members – the vast majority – were less engaged; they participated by paying dues, reading newsletters, attending some coalition meetings, and so on. Unlike the core members, who saw the local struggle as a manifestation of a much larger one, periphery members focused on removing or ameliorating the tangible threat to their neighborhood. For this reason, as environmental historian Samuel Hays has noted, most "environmental groups . . . organized locally to deal with community problems . . . disappeared almost as rapidly as they surfaced." For many social scientists who specialized in social movement theory, the experience of these kind of community based grass roots movements seemed to exemplify the "free rider" problem that Mancur Olsen argued was the main obstacle to sustained collective action; that is, the large majority on the periphery remained less engaged because they could ride for free on the efforts of the dedicated core.[41]

Chemical industry foes also organized on the state and national levels. State activists united by having to deal with a common state government agency. At the national level, old and well established groups from the late nineteenth century era of conservation such as the Audubon Society (1905) and the Sierra Club (1892) began to retool toward the new "ecology" movement. A host of new national organizations also appeared: Ralph Nader's Public Citizen, Inc. (1969), Friends of the Earth (1969), the Environmental Defense Fund (EDF) (1970), and others. Local grass roots coalitions shared information with state and national organizations through informal networks.

The fourth variety of early round attacks sustained by the chemical industry were citizen protests and demonstrations against specific companies. Dow Chemical of Midland, Michigan, bore the brunt of these assaults during a painful three-year period that began in October 1966. As historian David Vogel has observed, "Dow Chemical Corporation enjoys the distinction of being directly challenged by more people using a greater variety of tactics than any other firm in the postwar period."[42] Given the variety, intensity, and notoriety of these assaults, they deserve closer inspection.[43]

In 1965, Dow was known by 38 percent of Americans mostly as the manufacturer of Saran Wrap and Handi-Wrap. Four years later, 91 percent – the same percentage who could name the sitting president – knew of the company, but for very different reasons. What initially drew the attention of anti-Dow protesters and demonstrators was not its pollution of the environment, but rather its production of napalm used by the U.S. military in Vietnam. Because Dow was the leading producer of polystyrene, a key ingredient in napalm, it became one of several U.S. napalm producers in July 1965. Demonstrators first went after the largest napalm contractor, United Technology Center, and a smaller one, Witco, in the spring of 1966. Soon they found Dow, which conveniently operated offices at Rockefeller Center. Several groups of activists organized these efforts, including Citizens' Campaign Against Napalm and Women Strike for Peace. They distributed leaflets, organized boycotts of Saran Wrap, and chanted slogans such as: "Napalm burns babies, Dow makes money!"

The demonstrators then focused on Dow's recruitment operations on college campuses. Ultimately, Dow was the target of 221 major demonstrations on U.S. campuses. Antiwar protesters similarly had been targeting CIA and military recruitment offices. But whereas the government moved its office off campus to cool down the level of confrontation, Dow hunkered down. "We're not going to hide off-campus somewhere," proclaimed one Dow official. Rather, the company held a few summits with protesters, which produced no tangible results. The clashes escalated. In 1967 alone, Dow was involved in 133 campus recruiting incidents, with recruiters forced to flee their posts in a few cases. In an effort to keep its top managers informed of fast-breaking developments, Dow launched a newsletter for executives with the catchy name *Napalm News* (which ran from November 1967 through March 1969).

Dow held a troubled annual meeting in March 1967, but shareholders voted to continue making napalm. The company appealed to the military for support, arguing that the Defense Department should "as inventor, buyer, and user of the material, initiate its own vigorous defense of napalm rather than continuing to allow Dow to take the full brunt of the war protest focused on napalm." Defense Secretary Robert McNamara responded with a letter of support to Dow, but the government otherwise left Dow to fend for itself. As a next step, Dow sent a doctor to Vietnam, and consulted with other physicians there to make the case that napalm was not being used against Vietnam's civilian population. But the troubles escalated. On May 8, 1968, between 300 and 500 demonstrators carried out a "March on Midland," and scores of them, having purchased a single share each of Dow stock, temporarily disrupted the shareholders' meeting. The largest incident occurred that year in Wisconsin, when fourteen policemen and forty-seven demonstrators were injured, and seventy-one students were arrested.

The protests wound down rapidly over the next two years. Then a second wave of demonstrations hit the company when the news spread that Dow was a producer of Agent Orange (2,4,5-T and 2,4-D). Between 1962 and 1970, the U.S. military sprayed 3.5 million acres with the defoliant, and also used large quant-ities of Dow-produced "Agent White" to kill North Vietnamese food crops. The patterns repeated those of the napalm era, down to Dow's launching of an in-house newsletter, this one named *Dioxin Dialog*. In this case, Dow ultimately paid a $184 million settlement in a class-action suit involving 9000 Vietnam veterans and 1200 lawyers. After nine protestors ransacked the company's Washington offices in March 1969, the anti-Dow protests faded.

Dow, thus, brought together antiwar activists and environmental activists. Branded as the archetypal enemy of those causes, the company became more vulnerable to protests of other kinds as well. For example, when migrant farm worker activist Cesar Chavez launched his famous lettuce boycott, he targeted Dow. To be sure, Dow owned about $1 million of stock in the Antle Company, a major lettuce grower. But when Dow officials tried to explain to Chavez that their company, as a minority shareholder, had very little influence over the strategies and policies of Antle, Chavez reportedly replied that Dow was "an easy target."

Protests against the nuclear power industry shared a great deal in common with those against the chemical industry. Both were driven in large part by environmental concerns. Both were animated by industry ties to the military establishment – in this case to the AEC's efforts to control and exploit both peaceful and military uses of the atom for Cold War ends. Both began with grass roots efforts that later were complemented by the efforts of state and national organizations. The anti-nuclear movement relied on some of the same national organizations that had mobilized against chemical pollution, such as the Sierra Club, Friends of the Earth, and the Natural Resources Defense Council. Not surprisingly, Ralph Nader joined the fray, this time with his Washington, DC-based Critical Mass Project.

There were also important differences between the two protest movements, however. Whereas Rachel Carson had provided an accessible and compelling rationale for why chemical manufacturers had to be controlled, the technical and safety issues at stake in nuclear power seemed to be much less open to scrutiny by nonspecialists. Actually, the two problems were quite similar in this regard. Indeed, a central thrust of Carson's argument was that chemical poisoning of the natural environment was an *invisible* threat. As historian Ralph Lutts has pointed out, the chemical threat in *Silent Spring* resonated powerfully with Cold War fears about nuclear fallout.[44] Nevertheless, anti-nuclear groups moved much more quickly than anti-chemical environmentalists to marshal the support of technical experts. The first important group of this kind was the Greater St. Louis Committee for Nuclear Information, founded at Washington University by a group of scientists, (including biologist Barry Commoner), which began publishing *Nuclear Information* (later renamed *Science and the Citizen*) in 1964. This group was joined by the MIT-based Union of Concerned Scientists, the Scientists' Institute for Public Information, and the Committee for Nuclear Responsibility.[45]

The issues under dispute evolved rapidly. The original concern of anti-nuclear activists was thermal pollution, that is, the effect of reactor-warmed water on surrounding marine life. But that issue soon was joined by concerns about possible radioactive contamination of cooling water, about the human health effects of "normal" plant leakage, and, especially, about reactor safety. The latter issue gained salience as scientists and activists unearthed more and more information about previous nuclear "incidents," such as accidents at Idaho Falls (1961), the Fermi reactor near Detroit (1966), and Browns Ferry,

Alabama (1975). The growing weight of evidence suggested that government officials had understated or even concealed the public hazards of these events.[46]

Because the anti-nuclear power movement started later than the attacks on smoking and chemical pollution, its period of collective action was relatively foreshortened. Instead, the fate of nuclear protest was linked to a new regulatory movement. In the early 1970s, what became known as the "new social regulation" shifted the battleground for nuclear power, and for chemicals and tobacco as well.

INDIAN SUMMER FOR THE REGULATORY STATE

The new social regulation of the late 1960s and early 1970s was one of the nation's great state-building projects. This tidal wave of regulation, embodied in dozens of major pieces of legislation and a dozen new regulatory agencies, included the Consumer Product Safety Commission (CPSC), the Environmental Protection Agency (EPA), the Occupational Safety and Hazards Administration (OSHA), and the Clean Air Acts. These and other pieces of legislation put into place a new trans-industry regulatory regime designed to protect consumers, workers, and the environment. The new social regulation was the culmination of a corporate liberal impulse that had gained momentum throughout the prosperous postwar period, particularly in the 1960s. It was in many ways a product of the nation's "grand expectations" for creating a safe, healthy, and prosperous society.[47]

Much of the new social regulation was aimed at the corporation – specifically at increasing the accountability of big business in the marketing of its products, the treatment of its workers, and its pollution of the environment. But the new social regulation affected the controversial chemical, tobacco, and nuclear power industries in a remarkably uneven fashion. Chemical industry behavior was dramatically transformed by the new social regulation, nuclear power was somewhat effected, and tobacco effected the least, especially considering the federal government's potential regulatory powers over that industry in the early 1970s.

The chemical industry was affected enormously by the health, safety, and environmental regulations of the early 1970s, as well as by a number of new laws passed in the late 1970s and 1980s. Along with the pan-industry regulations that changed how all companies did business, such as those promulgated by OSHA, the chemical industry had to deal with a broad scope of new controls specifically governing the production, handling, and disposal of chemical, especially toxic products – as indicated by the partial list in Table 7.1.

The Toxic Substances Control Act (TSCA) (1976) and the Comprehensive Environmental Response, Compensation, and Liability Act (CERCLA) (1980) had the greatest influence on the industry. The latter established the so-called Superfund, which pays for cleaning up toxic land sites. It is funded by fines on

Table 7.1. *Key U.S. federal regulatory measures affecting chemical production, use, and disposal*

1960	Federal Hazardous Substances Labeling Act
1960	Color Additives Amendment
1970	Clean Air Act
1972	Clean Water Act
1972	Insecticide, Fungicide, and Rodenticide Act
1974	Safe Drinking Water Act
1976	Resource Conservation and Recovery Act (hazardous waste disposal)
1976	Toxic Substances Control Act (TSCA)
1980	Comprehensive Environmental Response, Compensation, and Liability Act (Superfund)
1984	Amendments to Resource Conservation and Recovery Act
1986	Superfund Amendments and Reauthorization Act
1990	Clean Air Act amendments

responsible polluters and a tax on the polluting industry. In its first fifteen years, 324 so-called Superfund sites were reclaimed at a cost of roughly $15 billion.[48] Compared with the tobacco and nuclear industries, however, the chemical industry was relatively responsive to national regulatory initiatives in order to participate in the process and ensure uniformity.[49]

Regulation of the nuclear power industry also underwent fundamental change in the early 1970s. The AEC and the JCAE were losing credibility, the former because of conflicts and tensions inherent in its dual promotional and regulatory missions, the latter because of its insularity from other significant stakeholders in the nuclear bargain. In 1974, the AEC was abolished, its regulatory functions assigned to the newly created Nuclear Regulatory Commission (NRC) and its R&D functions to a new Energy Research and Development Administration. Congress abolished the Joint Committee three years later, and distributed its authorization and oversight responsibilities among five House committees (Armed Services, Interior and Insular Affairs, Foreign Affairs, Commerce, and Science and Technology). Although nuclear regulation remained controversial, within a few years the NRC demonstrated a kind of independence and firmness not seen during the AEC days. For example, in 1979 the Commission disavowed the Rasmussen Report (named for MIT scientist Norman Rasmussen), which estimated the chance of *any* fatalities from a catastrophic nuclear accident to be one in one million. The Joint Committee had been quite comfortable supporting such wildly optimistic projections. As Kian Esteghamat has argued, the NRC's replacement of the AEC represented a shift from a "distributive" state regime to a "regulatory" one in the nuclear power industry. That is to say, during the industry's infancy, the state's chief role was to encourage development by dispensing special privileges to private actors, whereas later it took on a more truly supervisory and controlling role.[50]

As for the tobacco industry – the government actions against tobacco and smoking reviewed in the previous section seem impressive at first glance: the labeling requirements and advertising bans enacted by Congress and the FTC; the Surgeon General's antismoking reports; the smoking restrictions imposed by the Interstate Commerce Commission and the Federal Aviation Administration. Indeed, the FTC's interventions against cigarette advertising expanded its powers. Prior to the passage of the Trade Regulation Rule for the Prevention of Unfair or Deceptive Acts or Practices in the Sale of Cigarettes in 1964, the Commission had proceeded by adjudication. The 1964 rule was, according to law professor Dorsey D. Ellis, Jr., "the Commission's first significant effort to exercise a substantive rule-making power."[51]

Viewed from a broader perspective, however, the tobacco industry escaped many, perhaps even most, forms of appropriate federal control, including those fashioned as part of the new social regulation. Early in the twentieth century, the tobacco industry had been explicitly excluded from the what became known as the Food, Drug, and Cosmetics Act. Similarly, for reasons that have not been well researched, it never came under the purview of two key pieces of early 1970s legislation or their supervisory and enforcement agencies: the Consumer Product Safety Act and the Toxic Substances Control Act.[52] For its part, the EPA has played a cameo role in the tobacco wars since the early 1990s, when it published a report in 1991 stating that second hand smoke was responsible for 53,000 U.S. deaths a year, and in 1993 classified cigarette smoke as a "Class A" carcinogen.[53]

The only major federal agency that has moved to expand significantly its jurisdiction over tobacco in the postwar period is the Food and Drug Administration (FDA). In 1993, spurred on by continual prodding from anti-tobacco activists, FDA Commissioner David Kessler made smoking and health the key battle of his administration. Kessler's strategy – aided by industry defectors – was to establish that cigarette manufacturers were manipulating nicotine levels in order to keep smokers addicted, and – since nicotine is a drug – the companies were in the pharmaceutical business and thus subject to FDA regulation. After five years of intense lobbying by Kessler, the FDA gained a number of new powers to regulate warnings, advertising, and tobacco toxicology. But in 1998 the U.S. Court of Appeals unraveled these gains by rejecting FDA jurisdiction over tobacco.[54]

FROM REACTION TO ACCOMMODATION

The tobacco, chemical, and nuclear industries responded to the attacks they sustained in the postwar decades in a variety of ways, depending on the perceived nature and seriousness of the threat. But there was an overarching pattern to the corporate responses. In the short term, a few companies and industry associations stepped forward in an attempt to defend themselves and discredit their challengers. Some assumed a bunker mentality, hunkering down and reducing communication with potentially harmful outside interest groups. Overall, a sense of frustration and confusion reigned among business leaders in these three industries.

But, after a decade or so, the industries under attack devised ways of regaining a greater sense of control over their external political and social environments. They did this by making some concessions to their critics and by employing new, specialized forms of public relations. For both reasons, the industries under siege began to claim many of their former opponents' issues for themselves. By the 1990s, all three industries had moved decisively from a reactive to a much more proactive posture toward the social movement activists, regulators, and government agencies who had challenged them in earlier decades.

The immediate response of some chemical industry representatives to *Silent Spring* was shrill hyperbole. To accept Carson's ideas, proclaimed one of its outspoken critics, would lead to "the end of all human progress, reversion to a passive social state devoid of technology, scientific medicine, agriculture, sanitation. It means disease, epidemics, starvation, misery, and suffering."[55] A few ordinarily low-profile companies could not resist joining the fray. Monsanto, according to its corporate historian, "responded [to *Silent Spring*] in non-Monsanto style – with a rebuttal which burst upon the scene like a skyfull [sic] of skyrockets." The October following *Silent Spring's* publication, Monsanto published "The Desolate Year" in *Monsanto Magazine*, a story that speculated about a world without pesticides. Ironically, Monsanto then manufactured some selective weed-killers, but was not a leading producer of insecticides (except parathion) and had discontinued making DDT years earlier.[56]

Most chemical companies, however, quietly went about the business of adapting to the new regulations. Du Pont, the nation's largest chemical producer, had conducted toxicological research at its Haskell Laboratory since 1935, which now was expanded dramatically; its budget grew from $2.1 million in 1970 to $13.3 million in 1979. Hercules – whose agricultural pesticide toxaphene was indicted in *Silent Spring* as particularly destructive to fish – began monitoring legal developments in the area, set up an Environmental Health Committee with "pollution abatement coordinators" to liaison with plant operations, testified before House and Senate committees about toxaphene, and invested large sums in new toxicological testing and waste air and water treatment. Most other companies relied on technical solutions aimed at treating plant waste – the so-called "end-of-the-pipe" solutions.[57]

Over the course of a decade or so, however, this "compliance mentality" gave way to a more sophisticated, public relations-oriented approach.[58] A few firms and industry associations moved early in this direction. Midwest Agricultural Chemical Association was founded in 1958 to address public concern about agricultural pesticides. Foreshadowing the kind of industry approaches that would become commonplace, the MACA promoted a growth ideology by working to "control the language of public debate," by cooperating closely with presumably neutral institutions, such as land grant colleges, and by exerting influence over the local political process.[59]

In both practical and rhetorical ways, the U.S. chemical industry in the 1970s and 1980s started "going green." Some firms simply pursued business opportunities in environmentally related businesses such as the manufacture of water treatment chemicals and industrial catalytic converters. This was a rapidly growing global business, one with strong advantages for first-movers. Because the United States was lagging behind Europe in the environmental area, for example, American industry had to import 70 percent of its air pollution control equipment after the passage of the more stringent 1990 Clean Air Act.[60] A growing roster of U.S. chemical companies now saw opportunities to exploit niches in this field. On the other hand, a number of companies moved in the opposite direction by outsourcing their environmental functions. As one consultant observed, compliance is a "data-intensive" process that requires "a large bureaucracy" and can "lead to staff burnout, yield little or no competitive advantage, and have a high cost."[61]

On the rhetorical front, consultants became a growing force behind the chemical industry's new proactive approach. Some were recruited from the ranks of environmental activists.[62] Others, such as Burson–Marstellar, were retained to manage the aftermath of crises, in this case the Exxon Valdez oil leak and the devastating Union Carbide gas leak in Bhopal, India. They had learned their lessons from the adversarial 1960s and 1970s. In those days, according to an executive for Bechtel Environmental, Inc., public relations had been "defensive and reactive – and not very successful." But in the 1990s, he argued, to be effective public relations needed to be continuous and "truly two-way"; chemical companies should "furnish reliable information, apologize when necessary, open your doors."[63] Arguably, the leading environmental consultant to the chemical industry was E. Bruce Harrison, who literally wrote the book on this subject, with the revealing title *Going Green: How to Communicate Your Company's Environmental Commitment* (1993).[64] Harrison's approach was thoroughly accommodationist, as summarized in his "Three Steps to the Green":

(1) Commit to pollution prevention beyond what the current laws require of you;
(2) Team up with people outside your organization to solve general environmental problems, including those you do not cause; and
(3) Take the initiative in dialogue that ensures continuous environmental improvement.

Sounding much like a 1970s environmentalist's agenda, these principles worked to diffuse an immeasurable amount of anti-industry criticism. But many skeptical critics were only inflamed by the industry's "going green" campaign. They pointed to industry efforts designed to confuse and obfuscate, such as the 1990 fight over Proposition 128 in California, an environmental protection act also known as "Big Green." Working in cooperation with timber and utility interests, the chemical industry spent some $16 million to defeat the measure by a two-to-one margin. As part of its campaign, the industry introduced the Consumer Pesticide Enforcement Act, otherwise known as "Big Brown," which, according to environmental writer and consultant Jacqueline Switzer, "had the dual purpose of confusing voters because of [its name] and making it seem as if the state were being overcome with environmental legislation."[65]

Switzer was one of a growing cadre of journalists and academics who wrote about what they call "green backlash." The term applies mainly to political and corporate efforts to discredit environmentalists, and so should be distinguished from the accommodationist approach described here. For chemical industry opponents, the industry's green positions posed a more subtle challenge: how to separate the rhetoric from the reality.[66]

The tobacco industry's responses to its adversaries changed with the nature of the attacks it sustained. But cigarette producers came very late to the kind of accommodationist position exemplified by the chemical industry. The "health scare" of the 1950s evoked several responses. One was a market response: cigarette makers came out with scores of new brands, most with higher filtration, lower tar and nicotine yields, or both. The most illustrative case is Lorillard's Kent brand. In March 1952, Lorillard introduced its first filtered cigarette, named for its soon-to-retire president, Herbert A. Kent. Lorillard then supplied only about 5.5 percent of the U.S. cigarette market. But with the first "cancer scare" in 1953, Kents flew off the shelves. *Reader's Digest* gave the brand another big boost in 1957, when it identified Kent as the lowest tar and nicotine cigarette of the major brands. That year Lorillard announced with great fanfare a reformulated Kent with a space-age "micronite" filter. The filter was made of asbestos (although asbestos was not yet associated with respiratory disease). Between 1956 and 1958, Lorillard's profits grew sixfold. But in 1960, *Financial World* declared that "The boom in Kent sales [is] over." The larger cigarette producers had launched competing brands that squeezed out Kent, not only because of their marketing power, but because the competing brands were more "flavorful." Kent's filter worked too well; most smokers preferred a "full bodied" cigarette, and the industry had responded.[67] At the same time, the FTC stepped in to restrict health-related claims, thereby preventing smaller competitors such as Lorillard from competing on the basis of lower tar and nicotine yields.

The second tobacco industry response to the "health scare" came on the public relations front. In 1953, the industry retained Hill & Knowlton to formulate a strategy for coping with its increasingly hostile environment.[68] The following year, on the advice of Hill & Knowlton, the industry established the Tobacco Industry Research Committee (renamed the Council for Tobacco Research – U.S.A. a decade later) to conduct research into the health effects of cigarette smoke, although industry critics have characterized TIRC as purely a lobbying and public relations front. The TIRC took the position that scientific evidence indicating that smoking caused cancer and other illnesses was "inconclusive," which remained the industry's central stance on smoking and health for decades.

In response to the growing fervor about cigarette advertising, the tobacco industry also attempted voluntary self-regulation. On January 1, 1965, the major producers put into effect a self-imposed "Cigaret Advertising Code," which – because it included fines for non-compliance – was dubbed the first move of its kind in advertising history. The code was approved by the Justice Department, which agreed to exempt compliant companies from criminal (but not civil) prosecution. But like the FTC's new advertising rules, the "Cigaret Advertising Code" became moot with the passage of the Cigarette Labeling and Advertising Act of 1965.[69]

The industry's response to the threat of growing federal and state regulation was, generally, to make jurisdictional and broad constitutional arguments about federal agency powers and free speech. As suggested in the previous section, the tobacco makers fared well at the federal level, especially against the FTC, but lost considerable ground against the wave of tightening state laws and municipal codes to restrict or prohibit smoking. As for First Amendment issues, the tobacco industry continued to argue for the protection of advertising as free speech, and for the protection of smokers' civil rights. Following the early FTC and Congressional controls over advertising to minors, the industry never took an official position regarding the marketing of cigarettes to children, although critics continued to allege that the companies were not doing enough to discourage smoking by youths.

The cigarette industry's fifth and sixth strategic responses to the challenges of the 1950s and 1960s – by far the most important economically – were diversification and globalization. In 1955, each of the Big Six was solely in the tobacco business. Five years later, Philip Morris had moved into packaging products, industrial products, shaving products, and paper products, while Reynolds had begun making wrapping materials. By 1970, all six firms were solidly diversified, mostly in consumer household products and alcohol. (Lorillard had been acquired by Loew's, itself a diversified company.) Accordingly, the tobacco portion of the Big Six's total sales declined significantly. At the same time, five of the Big Six (again Lorillard, which sold its international operations to BAT, was the exception) moved aggressively to expand their cigarette exports. In 1950 they collectively exported roughly 15 billion cigarettes; by 1980, nearly 80 billion; and by 1995, the number topped 225 billion. To be sure, the 1960s and early 1970s were an age of conglomerates (unrelated diversified firms) and international expansion for American big business. But as corporate strategy analyst Robert Miles has shown, these two strategies for the tobacco companies were "domain creation" moves largely in reaction to the increasingly hostile political and social environment in which the companies found themselves.

The other four strategies were "domain defense" moves, and the industry sustained them with relatively little change for decades. When the CEOs of the nation's leading cigarette companies testified at the Congressional hearings on the regulation of tobacco in March 1994, their equivocation about whether smoking causes cancer and their uniform statements, "I believe nicotine is not addictive," harkened back to the companies' stance on smoking and health in the early 1950s.

All of this changed within a few short years. In the late 1990s and after, the tobacco companies – like the chemical and nuclear industries before them – agreed with most of the arguments of their critics. Philip Morris now not only acknowledges, but aggressively promotes positions on smoking and health that are almost indistinguishable from those of its staunchest critics of twenty or even ten years ago. Its corporate web site is not so much a resource for and about the company as it is a statement of the company's position on smoking, health, and advertising. There and elsewhere one finds the Philip Morris positions on long-disputed issues stated clearly and unequivocally: "cigarette smoking causes lung cancer, heart disease, emphysema and other serious diseases"; "smoking is addictive"; to reduce these health effects, the best thing to do is quit, not smoke fewer or lower-tar and nicotine cigarettes; lower-tar and nicotine brands are neither "safe" nor "safer" than other brands; the FDA should regulate cigarettes and "assess their toxicological effect"; the public should take the advice of public health officials regarding smoking; adults should not smoke around children.[70] Big Tobacco, too, arrived at the accommodationist position.

TO THE COURTS

Three major motion pictures released in 1998, 1999, and 2000 portrayed recent events in the troubled history of, respectively, the chemical, electric power, and tobacco industries. *A Civil Action* (1998), based on the 1995 best-selling book of the same name by Jonathan Karr, starred John Travolta as protagonist Jan Schlichtmann. A thirty-something Boston attorney with "lavish tastes," Schlichtmann is reluctantly but inexorably drawn into representing eight surviving families of leukemia victims in nearby Woburn, Massachusetts – whose drinking water, we quickly come to suspect, has been poisoned by toxic wastes. Schlichtmann loses his firm and, even worse, his Porsche in his legal battle against two giant chemical companies, W. R. Grace and Beatrice Foods. When ultimately we learn the illegal dumping was done by a local tanner probably without the knowledge of his corporate parent, it matters little. The morality tale about an egotistical lawyer turned social advocate against the "giant multinational corporations" is complete. In the 1999 film *The Insider*, Russell Crowe played Jeffrey Wigand, a scientist fired from Brown & Williamson Tobacco Company who ends up testifying on television and in a Mississippi court that his former employer knew nicotine is addictive. And in 2000, Julia Roberts won the Oscar for best actress for her starring role in *Erin Brockovich*, a story about a feisty, twice-divorced mother of three who uncovers illegal dumping of toxic chromium by the electric power company serving Hinkley, California.

Although the "little guys" are the heroes of these stories – the small-time attorney struggling with his conscience, the corporate whistle-blower struggling with his conscience, the working-class mom struggling with her clothing – it is high-powered law firms that ultimately deliver the goods, and on a massive scale. At the end of *Civil Action*, Schlichtmann wins a modest $8 million settlement, but the EPA later orders Grace to pay for a $69.4 million clean-up, the largest in New England history.[71] At the end of *The Insider*, it's clear that Wigand's purloined documents have opened the door for giant lawsuits against the tobacco companies. And at the end of *Erin Brockovich*, a major law firm pitches in to prosecute the utility, which ultimately is assessed $333 million, the largest settlement ever paid in a direct-action lawsuit in U.S. history. At the end of the twentieth century, the notion of attorneys as effective enforcers of corporate behavior was a normalized phenomenon.

It was normalized because the policing of the chemical, nuclear, and tobacco industries by civil litigation had been ongoing and widely publicized for at least two decades. Before reviewing the history of each industry's legal travails, however, it is important to consider two critically relevant postwar trends: the erosion of state regulatory power, particularly in the environmental area; and the evolution of post-second World War business tort law.

President Ronald Reagan's declaration that government was "the problem," not the "solution," and therefore should be reigned in, proved to be a very challenging goal. During the Reagan–Bush 1980s, spending for the military and for Social Security, Medicare, and Medicaid soared. But the two Republican Administrations, nevertheless, managed to reduce spending in the remaining small portion of the federal budget. One of the areas that suffered deep cuts was health, safety, and environmental regulation, that is to say, the new social regulatory state. Within the Reagan Administration, the prevailing mind-set among those assigned the task was that health, safety, and environmental regulation had become unnecessarily "burdensome" for American business. Overall, the reductions came in the first half of the decade, followed by some recovery and expansion in the late 1980s; and they came in the form of staff rather than agency budget cuts. In fact, overall federal obligations for health, safety, and environmental regulatory agencies grew from $3.3 billion dollars to $5.75 billion in the 1980s, while the number of full-time staff members fell from 51,182 to 45,775. Factoring in both the expansion of gross domestic product and inflation for the decade reduces the proportion of the budgetary growth rather significantly, and amplifies the importance of the staffing cuts. Moreover, the resource allocations fell quite unevenly on particular regulatory agencies. Both the budget and staff of the Consumer Product Safety Commission, for example, contracted dramatically, the latter by nearly half.[72]

The contraction of health, safety, and environmental regulation encouraged the simultaneous expansion of tort law, a phenomenon with roots in the early postwar period. Building on intellectual foundations laid by legal scholars

Fleming James and Friedrich Kessler, a new concept of "enterprise liability" took hold in the early 1960s, displacing the long-standing prior legal tradition of strict liability. Enterprise liability rested on the notion of asymmetrical information between buyer and seller; the new view was that because producers intrinsically know much more about the products they make than the buyers, they should assume a greater burden for harm resulting from the use of those products. The concept became law in two key cases: *Henningsen* v. *Bloomfield Motors, Inc.* (1960) and *Greenman* v. *Yuba Power Prods., Inc.* (1963). The year after *Greenman*, the American Law Institute extended liability to all sellers of dangerous or defective products, regardless of fault, in its second Restatement of Torts, Section 402A. By 1971, twenty-eight states had adopted Section 402A.[73] Why was the new law adopted so quickly nationwide? As Yale law professor George Priest explained in his landmark article on the history of modern tort law:

> By the 1960s, negligence and warranty law had a staid character. . . . Enterprise liability theory in contrast appointed the judge an agent of the modern state. Negligence and warranty law were by their terms addressed solely to the one specific incident of product use before the court. Enterprise liability theory, in contrast, charged the judge to internalize costs and distribute risks. [It] also allowed judges to join the effort to aid the poor. Indeed, the theory conceived of courts as possessing unique powers to achieve these ends in comparison to alternative branches of government.[74]

The problem with the new synthesis, according to Priest, was that "as courts are faced, case by case, with successively compelling complaints for relief, [judicial] reluctance is tested. The protests of a remaining difference become more earnest. But the distance between prevailing standards and a standard of absolute liability progressively narrows."[75]

Priest's concerns about the inherently expandable nature of enterprise liability tort law seem to be supported by the experiences of several industries in the late twentieth century, most notably tobacco. In this regard, the experience of the cigarette manufacturers diverged from that of nuclear power and chemical manufacturing. The nuclear power industry encountered only limited legal challenges. In the 1960s, public interest lawyers challenged AEC procedures, but they did not succeed.[76] In the early 1970s, members of the Environmental Defense Fund began using lawsuits to obtain crucial information about utility rate structures, which they then used to challenge requests for rate hikes and for new plant authorization. But the EDF's legal techniques were a means toward a different end: economic arguments that favored conservation over the traditional "grow and build" approach.[77]

In the chemical industry, the Superfund system has been the epicenter of litigation. The Superfund is structured around a unique liability system. The law allows for retroactive recovery from current and *previous* owners and users, plus those who create or transport materials to the site, even if their actions were legal at the time. It also allows for joint and several liability, so that a single party can be held liable for the actions of many (including former polluters). Some assessments have held liable banks that financed the businesses of polluters. Somewhere between 30 and 70 percent of Superfund costs have gone to legal and transaction costs. So while the Superfund system arguably has prevented an even larger wave of litigation over the enormously expensive job of toxic land cleanup, litigation has played a large and growing role in the relationship between the chemical industry and society. As Kian Esteghamat has aptly observed, "The combination of America's adversarial approach in formulating environmental regulation and its reliance on *civil law for implementing regulatory policy* has meant that lengthy and expensive court proceedings have become common in managing hazardous wastes"[78] [emphasis added].

For the tobacco industry, the battlefield shifted decisively in the 1980s and 1990s from the public health establishment, government agencies and legislatures, consumer and citizens' groups, and private firms, to the courts. Two events signaled the shift. In 1983, a Morristown, Pennsylvania, attorney named Mark Edell sued three cigarette makers on behalf of fifty-seven-year-old Rose Cipollone, who was dying of cancer after decades of cigarette smoking. The following year, a Northeastern University Law Professor founded the Tobacco Products Liability Project, which would serve as a clearinghouse for tobacco litigation. The Cipollone case stretched on for years, sadly well beyond Rose's life, and ultimately reached the Supreme Court, which ruled that Rose Cipollone, because she continued to smoke in spite of Surgeons General warnings on packages and in advertisements, was responsible for her death, not the defendants. But this did not discourage Edell and other attorneys from continuing to take big tobacco to court. He and others drew inspiration from *Beshada* v. *Johns-Mansville*, a 1982 case that brought down a giant manufacturer of (in part) asbestos products even though it was not fully aware of the health risks of its product – the same kind of argument long used by cigarette producers.

Finally, in the late 1990s, the plaintiffs started to win in what became known as the "third wave" of tobacco litigation. During the first two waves (*c.* 1954–73 and 1983–92), the tobacco companies won every case by relying essentially on their three long-standing arguments: that the biological mechanism by which cigarette smoke might cause cancer has not been demonstrated; that the industry had responsibly sponsored extensive health and smoking research; and that smokers choose to smoke of their own free will. The cracks in this legal strategy began to appear, for several reasons: the use of a new class of plaintiffs (states attorneys general, who teamed up to sue to recover smoking-related medical costs) who could not be blamed for smoking; new damaging evidence (garnered mostly from industry insiders); class action suits that marshaled much greater resources for plaintiffs. The contest of legal resources became more balanced as a number of well-heeled law firms for plaintiffs cooperated closely in sharing information and pooling resources.[79]

In this regard, the recent legal experiences of the tobacco industry – including a $28 billion verdict against Philip Morris in California – may suggest the most likely scenario for companies that are found to cause widespread harm.

The national network of law firms dedicated to bringing such suits against such industries used approaches developed against one industry to pursue others.[80] And they use the proceeds from awards and settlements against one industry to bring suits against new ones.[80] The firm of Peter Angelos, for instance, earned gigantic fees from asbestos litigation, moved on to represent the State of Maryland in the attorneys general suits against tobacco, then took on the lead paint industry, and recently filed a set of class action suits against four manufacturers of cellular telephones.[81] In California, several major class-action suits have been filed against fast food companies for failing properly to warn consumers about the health effects of a junk food diet. Bill Lerach of San Diego-based Milberg Weiss Bershad Mynes & Lerach began to specialize in shareholder class-action suits soon after the Supreme Court's 1966 class action rule change. Lerach saw the new rule as "an opportunity for a young firm to make a mark," and his firm is now responsible for most of the shareholder class-actions in the United States. Demand for Lerach's services has grown alongside the diminishing effectiveness of the U.S. Securities and Exchange Commission.[82] These anti-corporate super-lawyers, lionized in numerous popular books as great "civil warriors," are gaining celebrity status.[83] Meanwhile, Republicans in Washington are actively pursuing tort litigation reform. They want to cap the size of settlements, rather than address the more fundamental issue: that civil litigation has largely replaced regulation, and thus the focus has shifted from prevention to retribution.

CONCLUSION

It is important to keep in mind that the corporate challenges and responses described above unfolded against a backdrop of dramatic economic, techno-logical, and cultural change for the nuclear, chemical, and tobacco industries. Firms in these industries suffered sharp competitive setbacks. The nuclear industry ran up against limits to its economies of scale for the first time in the 1970s, and was crippled by spiraling plant construction and waste disposal costs. The chemical industry overexpanded in petrochemicals and other com-modities, with devastating economic results, and faced increasingly fierce global competition. The tobacco industry became hemmed in by rising leaf and production costs, skyrocketing excise taxes, and plummeting demand for cigarettes.

There were clear linkages between these economic changes and the growing public suspicion, government regulation, and legal travails that the industries confronted. For example, antismoking forces lobbied hard for higher excise taxes in order to discourage smoking; and electric utility customers increas-ingly mistrusted their power suppliers, and thus opposed nuclear plant pro-jects, in part because their rates climbed in real dollars for the first time. These industries also suffered negative spillover effects from developments outside their economic and political domains, as when concerns about nuclear weapons rebounded on the nuclear power industry.

While it is difficult to separate the structural problems from the political and social challenges, it seems clear that social movements, regulation, and tort law profoundly shaped the experiences of the three industries under consideration. The chemical industry was first confronted in the mid-1960s by protestors and demonstrators who mainly objected to the industry's toxic contamination of the environment and its support of the Vietnam War. Although some anti-industry activists worked through national organizations, most were mobilized by specific local problems (such as spills and waste dumps), and disbanded when those problems seemed to be addressed. In the 1970s, the chemical industry was affected enormously by a panoply of new health, safety, and environmental regulations. Later analysis revealed that average environmental spending in the chemical industry (as a percentage of total operational investment) rose from 3 percent in the 1940s; to 6 percent in the 1960s; to 20 percent in the 1990s (versus 1.6 percent of GDP for all U.S. industry in 1990). Meanwhile, between 1970 and 1993, chemical production in the United States doubled while emissions of major pollutants decreased by one quarter.[84] This record, applauded even by some former critics, suggests that the new social regulation had a powerful effect on industry behavior. Compared with regulation, litigation, most related to Superfund liability, has been muted. Finally, in the 1980s and 1990s, the chemical industry took a new accommodationist stance through new forms of public relations that often involved "going green."

The nuclear power industry sustained challenges to its legitimacy later, in the 1970s. As with the environmental movement, many of these were motivated by broader concerns about the environment and took the form of incident–, company–, and site-specific protests. In some cases, protests delayed nuclear construction projects long enough to allow climbing costs to overwhelm the financial viability of projects. In its relationship with the state, the nuclear industry – like the chemical industry – shifted from a distributive to a regulatory policy regime, in this case with the transition from the AEC to the Nuclear Regulatory Commission in the early 1970s. The industry entered a holding pattern a few years later, when new reactor orders halted completely.

The tobacco industry was first challenged by the medical community in the 1950s, then by the Federal Trade Commission in the 1960s. It responded in several ways – new product innovation; new research, public relations, and lobbying initiatives; attempts at self-regulation; and, most importantly, massive diversification into non-tobacco lines and cigarette exporting. Over the next two decades (the 1970s and 1980s), the attacks against the industry evolved and broadened to include private health organizations, consumers' and citizens' groups, state and city governments, and businesses, all working either to bring to light more information about smoking and health or to limit where smokers could smoke. Then, beginning in the 1980s, anti-tobacco activism shifted decisively toward the courts, eventually winning some major settlements by exploiting changes in tort law that originated in the early 1960s. Conspicuously lacking from the army of tobacco industry opponents was a strong federal hand, in spite of the dramatic expansion of relevant regulatory powers in the early 1970s. This vacuum may largely explain why the tobacco industry adopted an accommodationist stance much later than the other two industries under siege.

These cases, thus, highlight the importance of four key cross-cutting developments in postwar political economy – social movements, new social regulation, accommodationist public relations, and enterprise liability tort law. Each made an important difference – whether through its presence or its absence – and unfolded in the same sequence, although at different times and at different rates – as each of these industries came under siege, and then responded. Federal regulation and tort law appear to have worked symbiotically, the latter expanding as the former contracted. In view of the "long" twentieth century, the change suggests an unraveling of the project begun long ago by the Progressives, who worked to formalize, regularize, and professionalize corporate oversight by removing it from the hands of the courts.

NOTES

1. In business, economics, and political economy, a few pioneering works have pointed the way toward the rich possibilities for interpreting postwar American institutional life in its own right. In *Rise of the Corporate Commonwealth*, Louis Galambos and Joseph Pratt survey business–government relations throughout the twentieth century, portraying the postwar period as a time of growing influence and rigidity in the 1950s and 1960s that laid the groundwork for profound weaknesses in the face of international competition in the 1970s and 1980s. Galambos and Pratt show how the state grew to become a major stakeholder with which the corporation had to contend as it worked to control risk, innovate, and maximize efficiency. Kim McQuaid (*Uneasy Partners: Big Business in American Politics, 1945–1990*) emphasizes even more than Galambos and Pratt the intricate web of interdependencies between business and the state after the Second World War. Whereas Galambos and Pratt see the corporation as the engine of growth, to be hindered or facilitated by the state, McQuaid adds institutional and political flesh and bones to the many works by economists who emphasize the "mixed economy" character of the postwar period. Robert Collins (*More: The Politics of Economic Growth in Postwar America*) chronicles how economic policymakers embraced an ideology of sustained growth in the postwar period as aggressively as their counterparts in diplomacy embraced the ideology of containment. Meanwhile, the eminent business historian Alfred D. Chandler has shifted his attention to the postwar period, where he projects forward the model of late nineteenth century industrial success that he formulated so persuasively in *The Visible Hand: The Managerial Revolution in American Business* and other works. Louis Galambos and Joseph Pratt, *The Rise of the Corporate Commonwealth: United States Business and Public Policy in the Twentieth Century* (New York: Basic Books, 1988); Kim McQuaid, *Uneasy Partners: Big Business in American Politics, 1945–1990* (Baltimore: Johns Hopkins

University Press, 1995); Robert M. Collins, *More: The Politics of Economic Growth in Postwar America* (New York: Oxford University Press, 2000); Alfred D. Chandler, Jr., "The Enduring Logic of Industrial Success," *Harvard Business Review* 68 (Mar.–Apr. 1990); and *Inventing the Electronic Century: The Epic Story of the Consumer Electronics and Computer Industries* (New York: Free Press, 2001).

2. Robert H. Wiebe, *The Search for Order, 1877–1920* (New York, 1967).

3. Alan Brinkley, "Writing the History of Contemporary America: Dilemmas and Challenges," *Daedalus* 113 (Summer 1986), 121–41.

4. Harold G. Vatter, *The U.S. Economy in the 1950's: An Economic History* (Chicago: University of Chicago Press, 1963); Robert Sobel, *The Age of Giant Corporations: A Microeconomic History of American Business, 1914–1992* (Westport, CT: Greenwood Press, 1993).

5. Ashish Arora and Nathan Rosenberg, "Chemicals: A U.S. Success Story," in Arora, Ashish, Ralph Landau, and Nathan Rosenberg (eds.), *Chemicals and Long-Term Economic Growth: Insights from the Chemical Industry* (New York: John Wiley & Sons, Inc., 1988), 71–102; Haynes, Williams, *American Chemical Industry*, 6 vols. (New York: Van Nostrand, 1945–1954); Davis Dyer and David B. Sicilia, *Labors of a Modern Hercules: The Evolution of a Chemical Company* (Boston: Harvard Business School Press, 1990); Daniel J. Kevles, *The Physicists: The History of a Scientific Community in America* (New York: Vintage, 1971), 137. For a concise overview, see David B. Sicilia, "Chemical Industry," in Paul Boyer (ed.), *Oxford Companion to United States History*, (New York: Oxford University Press, 2001), 113.

6. Peter H. Spitz, *Petrochemicals: The Rise of an Industry* (New York: Wiley, 1988).

7. David A. Hounshell and John K. Smith, *Science and Corporate Strategy: R&D at Du Pont, 1902–1980* (New York: Cambridge University Press, 1988), 385.

8. Dyer and Sicilia, *Labors of a Modern Hercules*, 316–23.

9. The literature on DDT is voluminous. An accessible piece that highlights the enthusiasm that initially greeted the new chemical is Darwin H. Stapleton, "The Short-Lived Miracle of DDT," *American Heritage of Invention and Technology* (Winter 2000), 34–41. See also Thomas R. Dunlap, *DDT: Scientists, Citizens, and Public Policy* (Princeton: Princeton University Press, 1981); "atomic bomb" quotation is from Dunlap, *DDT*, p. 3.

10. The advertising agency Batten, Barton, Durstine & Osborn created this slogan after it was hired by Du Pont in 1935 to remake the company's image from primarily an explosives maker. http://heritage.dupont.com.

11. Arnold Thackray, Jeffrey L. Sturchio, Thomas L. Carroll, and Robert, Bud, *Chemistry in America, 1876–1976: Historical Indicators* (Dordrecht: Reidel, 1985), 107–10.

12. U.S. Bureau of the Census, *Historical Statistics of the United States*, II, 685.

13. Lorillard's firm still produces tobacco products today as a subsidiary of the Loew's Corporation. P. Lorillard & Company, *Lorillard and Tobacco: 200th Anniversary, 1760–1960* (New York: P. Lorillard & Company, 1960).

14. Richard B. Tennant, *The American Cigarette Industry: A Study in Economic Analysis and Public Policy* (New Haven: Yale University Press, 1950), 15–66; Richard B. Tennant, "The Cigarette Industry," in Walter Adams (ed.), *The Structure of American Industry: Some Case Studies* (New York: Macmillan, 1950), 231–40. See also Chandler, *The Visible Hand*, 249.

15. Robert Sobel, *They Satisfy: The Cigarette in American Life* (New York: Anchor/Doubleday, 1978), 52–62; Raymond M. Jones, *Strategic Management in a Hostile Environment: Lessons from the Tobacco Industry* (Westport, CT: Quorum Books,

1997), 10. See also Maurice Corina, *Trust in Tobacco: The Anglo-American Struggle for Power* (London: Michael Joseph, 1975).

16. In 1908, 6.8 billion cigarettes were produced in the U.S. versus 6.5 billion cigars. Between 1880 and 1950, annual cigarette output grew nearly *24,500 times* (to 392 billion), whereas cigar production was less than 5 times greater than in 1880, and pipe and snuff tobacco less than 2.5 times greater. U.S. Department of Commerce, *Historical Statistics of the United States, 1776 to 1970* (Washington, DC: U.S. Government Printing Office, 1975), II, 690.

17. Ibid.; Tennant, "The Cigarette Industry," 240–2; Sobel, *They Satisfy*, 77, 83–5.

18. Anthony J. Badger, *Prosperity Road: The New Deal, Tobacco, and North Carolina* (Chapel Hill: University of North Carolina Press, 1980).

19. Sobel, *They Satisfy*, 131, 133, 142–6; Iain Gately, *Tobacco: The Story of How Tobacco Seduced the World* (New York: Grove Press, 2001), 265.

20. Gately, *Tobacco*, 267–71; Sobel, *They Satisfy*, 149; Jones, *Strategic Management in a Hostile Environment*, 8.

21. Paul R. Johnson, *The Economics of the Tobacco Industry* (New York: Praeger, 1984), 23.

22. Sobel, *They Satisfy*, 148.

23. Harold C. Passer, *The Electrical Manufacturers, 1875–1900: A Study in Competition, Entrepreneurship, Technical Change, and Economic Growth* (Cambridge, MA: Harvard University Press, 1953); Thomas P. Hughes, "The Electrification of America: The System Builders," *Technology and Culture* 20 (Jan. 1979), 124–61; Amy Friedlander, *Power and Light: Electricity in the U.S. Energy Infrastructure, 1870–1940* (Reston, VA: Corporation for National Research Initiatives, 1996).

24. Morton Keller, *Regulating a New Economy: Public Policy and Economic Change in America, 1900–1933* (Cambridge, MA: Harvard University Press, 1990).

25. Thomas P. Hughes, *Networks of Power: Electrification in Western Society, 1880–1930* (Baltimore: Johns Hopkins University Press, 1983), 201–26; David B. Sicilia, "Selling Power: Marketing and Monopoly at Boston Edison, 1886–1929," *Business and Economic History* 20 (Fall 1991), 27–31; Richard F. Hirsh, *Technology and Transformation in the American Electric Utility Industry* (Cambridge: Cambridge University Press, 1989), 1–80; Jacob M. Gould, *Output and Productivity in the Electric and Gas Utilities, 1899–1942* (New York: National Bureau of Economic Research, 1946), 22.

26. Hirsh, *Technology and Transformation*, 81–6.

27. Michael Smith, "Advertising the Atom," in Michael Lacey (ed.), *Government and Environmental Politics: Essays on Historical Developments since World War Two* (Washington, DC: Woodrow Wilson Center Press, 1991), 234–8; Brian Balogh, *Chain Reaction: Expert Debate and Public Participation in American Commercial Nuclear Power, 1945–1975* (New York: Cambridge University Press, 1991), quotation from p. 12.

28. James R. Temples, "The Politics of Nuclear Power: A Subgovernment in Transition," *Political Science Quarterly* 95 (Summer 1980), 242.

29. Temples, "The Politics of Nuclear Power," 239–60.

30. Robert O. Carlson, "The Use of Public Relations Research by Large Corporations," *Public Opinion Quarterly* (June 1957), 348.

31. Jones, *Strategic Management in a Hostile Environment*, 10–11.

32. "Smoke still swirls around cigarettes," *Business Week*, June 29, 1963; "Cigarette smokers still puffing away," *Business Week*, Dec. 14, 1963.

33. Public Law 89–92, 15 U.S.C. 1331–9. See also M. J. Garrison, "Should All Cigarette Advertising Be Banned? A First Amendment and Public Policy Issue." *American Business Law* 25 (Summer 1987), 169–205.

34. R. L. Dunbar and N. Wasilewski, "Regulating External Threats in the Cigarette Industry." *Administrative Science Quarterly* 30 (Dec. 1985), 547, 552.

35. John E. Calfee, "Cigarette Advertising, Health Information and Regulation before 1970," Federal Trade Commission, Bureau of Economics, Working Paper 134 (Washington, DC, Dec. 1985).

36. Robert A. Kagan and William P. Nelson, "The Politics of Tobacco Regulation in the United States," in Robert L. Robin and Stephen D. Sugarman (eds.), *Regulating Tobacco* (New York: Oxford University Press, 2001), 15–25.

37. Richard Kluger, *Ashes to Ashes: America's Hundred-Year Cigarette War, the Public Health, and the Unabashed Triumph of Philip Morris* (New York: Vintage Books, 1997), *passim.*

38. Steve Tombs, "The Chemical Industry and Environmental Issues," in Denis Smith (ed.), *Business and the Environment: Implications of the New Environmentalism* (New York: St. Martin's Press, 1993), 132.

39. Hazel Erskine, "Pollution and Its Costs," *Public Opinion Quarterly* 36 (Spring 1972), 120.

40. Stapleton, "The Short-Lived Miracle of DDT," 34.

41. Samuel P. Hays, *Beauty, Health, and Permanence: Environmental Politics in the United States, 1955–1985* (Cambridge: Cambridge University Press, 1987), 62; Mancur Olson, *The Logic of Collective Action: Public Good and the Theory of Groups* (Cambridge, MA: Harvard University Press, 1971).

42. Vogel, David, *Lobbying the Corporation: Citizen Challenges to Business Authority* (New York: Basic Books, 1978), 43.

43. This account of Dow's travails is based largely on E. N. Brandt, *Growth Company: Dow Chemical's First Century* (East Lansing: Michigan State University Press, 1997), 351–72. Brandt is both a company historian and a former public relations executive for the company involved directly in the events described.

44. Ralph H. Lutts, "Chemical Fallout: Rachel Carson's *Silent Spring*, Radioactive Fallout, and the Environmental Movement," *Environmental Review* 9:(3) 1985, 210–5.

45. Hays, *Beauty, Health, and Permanence*, 174–9.

46. Temples, "The Politics of Nuclear Power," 247; Richard F. Hirsh, *Power Loss: The Origins of Deregulation and Restructuring in the American Electric Utility System* (Cambridge, MA: MIT Press, 1999), 63–8.

47. David Vogel, "The 'New' Social Regulation in Historical and Comparative Perspective," in Thomas K. McCraw (ed.) *Regulation in Perspective: Historical Essays* (Cambridge, MA.: 1981), 155–85; James T. Patterson, *Grand Expectations: The United States, 1945–1974* (New York: Oxford University Press, 1996).

48. Kian Esteghamat, "Structure and Performance of the Chemical Industry under Regulation," in Arora, Ashish, Ralph Landau, and Nathan Rosenberg (eds.), *Chemicals and Long-Term Economic Growth: Insights from the Chemical Industry* (New York: John Wiley & Sons, Inc., 1988), 349, 365.

49. Anthony McGrew, "The Political Dynamics of the 'New' Environmentalism," in Smith (ed.), *Business and the Environment*, 15.

50. Esteghamat, "Structure and Performance of the Chemical Industry under Regulation," 342–3, 348–9.

51. Dorsey D. Ellis, Jr., "Legislative Powers: FTC Rule Making," in Kenneth W. Clarkson and Timothy J. Muris, *The Federal Trade Commission since 1970: Economic Regulation and Bureaucratic Behavior* (Cambridge, England: Cambridge University Press, 1981), 62.

52. V. Kasturi Rangan, "The Smoke Wars," in N. Craig Smith and John A. Quelch (eds.), *Ethics in Marketing* (Homewood, IL: Irwin, 1993), 92–3.
53. Jones, *Strategic Management in a Hostile Environment*, 16.
54. Kagan and Nelson, "The Politics of Tobacco Regulation in the United States," 30–1. For Kessler's view see David A. Kessler, *A Question of Intent: A Great American Battle with a Deadly Industry* (New York: Public Affairs, 2001).
55. Dunlop, *DDT*, 88.
56. Dan J. Forrestal, *Faith, Hope and $5,000: The Story of Monsanto* (New York: Simon and Schuster, 1977), 193–202.
57. Hunnshell and Smith, *Science and Corporate Strategy*, 569–72; Dyer and Sicilia, *Labors of a Modern Hercules*, 373–84; Robert D. Shelton, "The Greening of American Industry" in Michael D. Rogers (ed.), *Business and the Environment* (New York: St. Martin's Press, 1995).
58. An excellent study of chemical and oil industry adaptation to environmentalism is Andrew J. Hoffman, *From Heresy to Dogma: An Institutional History of Corporate Environmentalism* (San Francisco, New Lexington Press, 1997).
59. Jerry Harrington, "The Midwest Agricultural Chemical Association: A Regional Study of an Industry on the Defensive," *Agricultural History* 70 (1996), 415–38.
60. Esteghamat, "Structure and Performance of the Chemical Industry under Regulation," 360.
61. Shelton, "The Greening of American Industry," 13.
62. Sacha Millstone and Ferris Baker Watts, "Effect of the Green Movement on Business in the 1990s," in Thomas F. P. Sullivan (ed.), *The Greening of American Business: Making Bottom-Line Sense of Environmental Responsibility* (Rockville, MD: Government Institutes, Inc., 1992), 4–5.
63. Roger Strelow, "Corporate Public Relations in the Green Era," in Sullivan (ed.), *The Greening of American Business*, 165.
64. E. Bruce Harrison, *Going Green: How to Communicate Your Company's Environmental Commitment* (Homewood, IL: Business One Irwin, 1993).
65. Switzer, Jacqueline Vaughn, *Green Backlash: The History and Politics of Environmental Opposition in the U.S.* (Boulder, CO: Lynne Rienner Publishers, 1997), 134.
66. Esteghamat, "Structure and Performance of the Chemical Industry under Regulation," 372.
67. "Lorillard Paying More," *Financial World*, Mar. 21, 1962.
68. Stanton A. Glantz *et al.*, *The Cigarette Papers* (Berkeley: University of California Press, 1996), 33.
69. "Cigaret Ad Code Goes into Effect Jan. 1: Meyner," *Advertising Age*, Dec. 21, 1964; "Tobacco Code Seen Breaking New Legal Ground on Industry Self Rule," *Advertising Age*, June 29, 1964. For a full text of the code see "Cigaret Advertising Code," *Advertising Age*, May 4, 1964.
70. From a glossy, full-color, seventeen-page insert, recapitulating statements from www.philipmorrisusa.com, *New York Times* Sunday edn. Nov. 17, 2002.
71. Jonathan Karr, *A Civil Action* (New York: Vintage Book, 1995), 251, 291.
72. W. Kip Viscusi, "Health and Safety Regulation," in Martin Feldstein (ed.), *American Economic Policy in the 1980s* (Chicago: University of Chicago Press, 1994), 453–504.
73. George L. Priest," The Invention of Enterprise Liability: A Critical History of the Intellectual Foundations of Modern Tort Law," *Journal of Legal Studies* 14 (Dec. 1985), 461–527.

74. Priest, "The Invention of Enterprise Liability," 519.

75. *Ibid.*

76. Temples, "The Politics of Nuclear Power," 246.

77. Hirsh, *Power Loss*, 63–8.

78. Esteghamat, "Structure and Performance of the Chemical Industry under Regulation," 349, 365.

79. Kagan and Nelson, "The Politics of Tobacco Regulation in the United States," 179–98.

80. See, for example, Pam Belluck, "Lead Paint Suits Echo Approach to Tobacco," *New York Times*, Sept. 21, 2002, A12.

81. Following the Maryland tobacco settlement, Angelos claimed the state owned him $1 billion, but the state disagreed. Angelos sued and eventually settled for $150 million, calling his client-cum-adversaries a bunch of "tin-horned politicians." Donna M. Owens, "A Conversation with Peter Angelos," *Baltimore Sun*, Nov. 18, 2002.

82. Jeffrey Toobin, "The Man Chasing Enron: Why America's C.E.O.s hate Bill Lerach," *The New Yorker*, Sept. 9, 2002. 86+.

83. Examples are: *Civil Warriors: The Legal Siege on the Tobacco Industry* (New York: Delacorte Press, 2000); John A. Jenkins, *The Litigators: Inside the Powerful World of America's High-Stakes Trial Lawyers* (New York: Doubleday, 1989); and Michael Orey, *Assuming the Risk: The Mavericks, the Lawyers, and the Whistle-Blowers Who Beat Big Tobacco* (Boston: Little, Brown, 1999).

84. Esteghamat, "Structure and Performance of the Chemical Industry under Regulation," 353.

III

THE BUSINESS OF IDENTITY

8

The Business of Jews

Charles Dellheim

"Which is the merchant here, and which the Jew?" So asked Portia, herself disguised in male dress, when she came upon Shylock and Antonio in the famous trial scene of *The Merchant of Venice*.

Portia's question does more than remind us of the oft-forgotten fact that Shylock is not the eponymous merchant of the title. It also dramatizes the fundamental opposition drawn between the "merchant" and the "Jew." The Christian characters take Antonio to be an honorable merchant, a loving man who charges no interest on the loan he grants his friend Bassanio. And they take Shylock to be a devilish Jew, a cruel, vindictive, and avaricious usurer who will stop at nothing to exact his pound of flesh from the hapless merchant. The Shylock–Antonio antithesis epitomizes the damning economic stereotypes of Jews fashioned by the Christian West.[1] Scapegoating the Jew as the evil merchant helped legitimize non-Jewish capitalist enterprise.

For centuries, Shylock's shadow has trailed the Jews – an unwelcome emblem of alleged Jewish moral corruption manifest in economic practice. Though critiques of commerce and finance abound in various cultures, ancient and modern, representations of Jews in business indict the Jew as well as the merchant. Whereas the failings of non-Jewish businessmen may be individual flaws common to those who buy low and sell high, the behavior of their Jewish counterparts is ascribed to collective evil. The prevailing assumption is that the business of Jews is not only different from that of non-Jews but also morally worse.

No minority group has achieved greater business prominence or paid more deeply for it than the Jews. There is no gainsaying Jewish entrepreneurial triumphs in fields ranging from merchant banking to art dealing, publishing to chemicals, and clothing to real estate. Jews made their way in a hostile world by

My special thanks to Kenneth Lipartito, David Sicilia, Ezra Mendelsohn, and Jonathan Karp for their careful readings of previous drafts of this chapter. I would also like to thank the participants in the Sloan Conference at the Kennedy School, particularly Louis Galambos, for their helpful comments. Finally, I am grateful to the Lucius Littauer Foundation for its financial support.

building economic power, but thereby, exposed themselves to further anti-Semitic assaults. Business success was nothing if not a double edged sword because it exacerbated the ire and envy of those who blamed Jews for their own failures.

Convinced that the Jews had turned Wall Street into yet another "Judengasse," Henry Adams hoped that the mob would rise up to loot this "financial Ghetto" and "bombard New York."[2] His diatribes against Jewish power and corruption were elements of a broader anti-modern reaction, a Brahmin protest against the philistinism, greed, and vulgarity of industrial, democratic civilization. Yet his idealism, such as it was, did not make him indifferent to worldly goods. In the financial crash of 1893, Adams (and his brother Brooks) lost a good deal of money. Another man might have cursed fortune or faulted his own judgment. But Henry Adams responded as if wily Jews had forced him to invest in the stock market in an effort to ruin him. Drawing a lesson in political economy from the experience, he concluded: "After all, the Jew question is really the most serious of our problems. It is Capitalistic Methods run to their logical result." And, he added chillingly: "Let's hope to pull their teeth."[3]

When it came time for financial advice, though, Adams unabashedly sought out a Jew, Herman Scmidt. Adams claimed to admire him "for his splendid contempt and hatred for mankind."[4] Such ethical agility allowed Adams to excoriate Jewish greed while gaining from supposed Jewish acumen. To be sure, this was an old deceit. For who could give better monetary counsel than a Jew and who was more entitled to such profits than an Adams?

Anti-Semitic economic mythology is better known than the economic practices of Jewish entrepreneurs. This chapter contributes to understanding corporate boundaries in twentieth-century America by looking at the business of Jews. What follows is an interpretive synthesis focusing on the causes, components, and consequences of Jewish economic culture, by which I mean the social, political, economic, and cultural matrix in which business takes place. The first part of the chapter surveys the historical and sociological literature on Jews and capitalism. In addition to outlining prevailing approaches, it suggests why more attention has not been devoted to this subject in recent years. The second part offers a preliminary model of modern Jewish economic culture with particular reference to the United States. Given the diversity of economic activities in which Jews participate, this overview necessarily cannot encompass all sectors. Hence, the final part of this chapter looks at one industry more deeply in an effort to draw out larger trends. It offers a case study of Jews' entry into, and impact on, a business that has not received much attention from historians – book publishing.

Analyzing the economic culture of Jews raises methodological problems with moral implications. The most obvious and insidious problem is the risk of falling into the essentialist trap: confusing socially constructed behavior with intrinsic "racial" traits. Counting Jews involved in specific occupations is a dangerous business because it may feed into the implicit assumption that their numbers should be in keeping with their proportion of the general population.

The notion that Jews constituted a "disproportionate" number of players in a particular industry may be colored, consciously or not, by an informal quota system. Yet "disproportionality" is a conventional, useful sociological concept that dates back at least to Emile Durkheim's *Suicide*. It would be foolish to ignore clusters of Jews in, say, the garment trade, or symphony orchestras, or theoretical physics. But it would be equally foolish to regard such social facts as anything more than a starting-point for historical analysis. What complicates matters still further is the vexed question of who is a Jew. Do we define Jewishness in terms of matrilineal descent, religious affiliation, ethnic ties, or personal identity? Do we include mavericks and converts in our histories? The challenge is to determine how, if at all, Jewish origins or affiliation affected specific economic choices and practices. That is the approach adopted in this chapter.

The principal argument is that the Jewish experience in American business underlines the role of social marginality as an important source of innovation in the American business system. Ethnic origins, identity, and aspirations are powerful factors that shape the means and ends of entrepreneurial activity as well as patterns of consumption. Finally, and perhaps most importantly, the Jewish experience suggests that the corporate American anatomized by Alfred D. Chandler, Jr. was only one part a much broader and richer economic landscape.

The relationship between cultural values and economic performance is a classic theme of historical and sociological literature. Studies ranging from Max Weber's *The Protestant Ethic and the Spirit of Capitalism* and Werner Sombart's *The Jews and Modern Capitalism* to Benjamin Nelson's *The Idea of Usury: From Tribal Brotherhood to Universal Otherhood* and Peter Berger's *The Capitalist Revolution* analyze the complex interaction between religious beliefs, cultural values, and economic behavior.[5] Who is responsible for the genesis of capitalism? Are there "elective affinities" between religious affiliation and economic performance? Why are certain ethnic or religious groups notably more successful than others? Given the West's long economic hegemony, it is no wonder that historians and social scientists have paid considerably more attention to, say, Quakerism than Buddhism. Even so, scholarly inquiry on the traffic between religion and capitalism has not been confined to European or American societies. A mixture of admiration and anxiety brought about by the (short-lived) economic ascendancy of Japan in the 1970s and 1980s provoked a rash of studies on the impact of the Confucian ethic on capitalism.

Few subjects of scholarly investigation have aroused the degree of ideological controversy as the debates over religion and capitalism. Though Max Weber did not provide an extensive analysis of the relationship between the Jewish ethic and the spirit of capitalism, he touched on this subject in *Ancient Judaism*.[6] Weber views Judaism as a highly rational religion that accorded well with capitalist profit-seeking.[7] He regards Diaspora Jewry as a "guest" or "pariah" people, "who felt at home in the very forms of state- and booty-capitalism along with pure money usury and trade, precisely what Puritanism abhorred."[8] Weber contends that if Judaism regarded riches as the "wages of piety," it also imposed definite boundaries on economic activity. The animus against wealth, suspicion of the "fat people," was particularly strong in Hebrew prophetic tradition, as was the obligation to protect the poor and the sick, widows and workers. [9]

Finally, Weber stresses the significance of a dualistic Jewish morality that established one standard for brothers and another for strangers. (And while Judaism stipulated certain protections for the "ger," the sojourner who dwelt among the Hebrews, most commandments applied only to brethren.) This was most striking in the weighty Deuteronomic injunction that prohibited taking interest on loans to fellow Jews but imposed no such injunction on loans to others. By contrast, Weber calls attention to seventeenth- and eighteenth-century Protestant sects, especially Baptists and Quakers, who "pointed with pride to the fact that precisely in economic intercourse with the godless they had substituted legality, honesty, and fairness for falseness, overreaching, and unreliability."[10] But the supposed Jewish–Protestant antithesis is extremely misleading because it screens out the enormous difference in how Christians treated each other and how they treated Jews.

Writing contra Weber but in a Weberian vein, Werner Sombart both blamed and credited Jews for the genesis of capitalism. In *The Jews and Modern Capitalism*, Sombart argues that the role Weber ascribed to Puritanism properly belongs to Judaism. Contrasting traditional Christian and Jewish economic outlook, he comments: "the Jew rises before us unmistakably as more of a business-man than his neighbour; he follows business for his own sake; he recognizes, in the true capitalist spirit, the supremacy of gain over all other aims."[11]

Although Sombart shows how historical circumstances influenced Jewish economic behavior, his usual explanatory mode is essentialism rather than social construction. In his hyperbolic account Sombart maintains that the "Jewish religion has the same leading ideas as capitalism." Thus, he emphasizes the "businesslike" relation between God and Israel and accountability in Heaven.[12] And he virtually ignores the variety of biblical and talmudic limitations placed on economic activity.

Sombart's abstract, teleological Jew represents the "quintessence of capitalism." The Jew is well-equipped to play the role of entrepreneur "because of his strength of will and his habit of making for some goal or other," Sombart observes.[13] "His intellectual mobility is accountable for his readiness to discover new methods of production and new possibilities of marketing . . . And since in the world of capitalism there is nothing organic or natural but only what is mechanical or artificial, the Jew's lack of understanding of the former is of no consequence."[14] Sombart's binary oppositions between the "organic" German spirit versus the "mechanical" Jewish spirit, "hand" labor versus "head" labor, manufacturing versus finance, are all staples of anti-modernist, anti-Semitic German volkish philosophy.[15] They depend on a dubious ideological view of what is and what is not "productive."

Sombart's treatise is replete with unpleasant anti-Semitic undertones as well as more outright condemnations. Admitting that Jews had little or no place in big trusts or major corporations, he still contends that "America in all its borders is a land of Jews": and it is "filled to the brim with the Jewish spirit."[16] And Sombart goes out of his way to highlight "dishonest dealing" by Jews.

Although there has been considerable sociological speculation on the Jews and capitalism, there is no historical synthesis of Jewish economic practice or culture. Ideology has contributed to minimizing the role of economics in modern Jewish history and the role of Jews in modern economic life. The uneven occupational distribution of Jews, their heavy concentration in business, especially money lending and petty commerce, figure prominently in eighteenth-century debates on legal emancipation. Even those like Christian Döhm, who advocated political rights for Jews, exhorted them to abandon usurious practices and limit commercial activities that were allegedly harmful to Jews and Christians alike. The proposed dispersion of Jews away from banking and trade became a test of Jews' fitness for citizenship.[17]

The uneasy identification of Jews with capitalism was also fundamental to certain varieties of Zionism. Business was especially suspect to labor Zionists who contrasted productive and parasitic labor. Zionist leaders such as A. D. Gordon called for the "normalization" of Jewish economic life – which meant that the "new Jew" would turn away from capitalist profit-making and cultivate the soil rather than frequent the Bourse.

The dominant school of nineteenth-century German–Jewish historiography, *Wissenschaft des Judentums*, did not pay much attention to economics any more than did most historical scholarship of that time. But such issues loomed very large indeed in Jewish historiography of the 1920s and 1930s, most fruitfully in Poland, but also in the Soviet Union. Writing in Yiddish during the interwar era, a cadre of professional historians painted a very different picture of Jewish economic activity than that put forth by Sombart.

The central figure was Ignacy Schipper, who was born in 1884 and studied law and economics in Vienna. Affiliated at one time with Poale Zion, a political party dedicated to creating a Jewish socialist community in Palestine, Schipper's work was shaped by a mixture of Marxist materialism and Jewish nationalism. His premise was that the economic history of the Jews held the key to understanding the rich and varied character of Jewish life, the folk culture of Jews, their relationship to the surrounding milieu, and the nature of anti-Semitism. In his four-volume *Jewish Economic History* of the late-1920s and his *History of Jewish Commerce in Poland* in the 1930s, Schipper revised and enriched conventional views of Jewish economic history. His investigations underscored the important contributions of Jews to the material development of Europe, especially Eastern Europe. Thus, Schipper countered Sombart's representation of the Jew as an exploiter and parasite.[18]

The economic focus of interwar Yiddish historiography died with the destruction of its proponents during the Shoah. The Nazi war against the Jews nearly wiped out a generation of scholars. It also made investigations of Jewish economic activity suspect. And not without reason: the idea of an international Jewish financial conspiracy, after all, was a staple of Nazi propaganda. Fear of Shylock's shadow has taken its toll on postwar historiography. The anxiety that damning economic myths might be partly true, or, at least, that they are hard to disprove, has made certain Jews eager to insist that the business of Jews is no different than that of non-Jews; to downplay talk of disproportionate economic power; and to deny that some Jews (like certain other capitalists) exploited their workers, suppliers, and customers. When it comes to business, and indeed much else, it is prudent to claim with Heinrich Heine that "Jews are like everyone else only more so." But there is little reason to believe that refusing to acknowledge the existence of anti-Semitic economic myths will dispel hateful stereotypes and prejudices.

Economic issues have not been at the center of post-Second World War Jewish historiography. Historians have preferred to focus on religious, intellectual, and political life. In recent years, they have turned increasingly to social history and then to cultural studies. Intellectual fashions aside, the liberal or socialist orientation of certain Jewish scholars has contributed to downplaying the importance of capitalism. Irving Howe's *World of Our Fathers*, for example, says far more about Jewish labor than Jewish capitalists – a strange omission given its immense importance to immigrants' social mobility.[19]

Nonetheless, there are still numerous examples of Jewish historiography that deal with aspects of economic activity. Salo Baron and Arcadius Kahn's *Economic History of the Jews* is a valuable survey of Jewish involvement in trades and industries ranging from silk trading to cattle dealing. Nobel-Prize laureate economist Simon Kutznet's article, "Economic Structure and Life of the Jews," is still by far the best analysis of Jewish economic patterns. Meir Tamari's *With All your Possessions: Jewish Ethics and Economic life* analyzes Jewish religious and ethical teachings about the means and ends of business, but fails to examine their impact on economic practice. Derek Penslar's *Shylock's Children* examines economic ideology and thought with particular reference to their impact on Jewish identity. And Jonathan Karp's dissertation, *The Politics of Jewish Commerce,* examines the role of Christian attitudes towards Jewish economic activity in the debates over Jewish emancipation.[20]

If there is no major synthetic work on Jewish economic culture and practice, there are many specialist studies. Among them are examinations of individual societies such as Werner Mosse's *Jews in the German Economy* and Harold Pollins's *The Economic History of Jews in England*; of industries such as Leon Harris's *The Merchant Princes* and Neil Gabler's *An Empire of Their Own*; of families such as Ron Chernow's *The Warburgs*; of social circles such as Stephen Birmingham's *Our Crowd*; and of stereotypes such as John Gross's *Shylock* and David Goodman and Masanori Miyazawa's *Jews in the Japanese Mind.*[21]

In addition, sociologists have included Jews in comparative analyses of "middlemen minorities." For example, Roger Waldinger's *In the Eye of the Needle*, discerns no fundamental differences between the successive waves of immigrants in the New York garment industry.[22]

But such issues have received little attention from historians of business. Perhaps they have reacted partly against Sombart's overstated, overheated assertion of the centrality of the Jews in the genesis of capitalism. More to the point, however, is that the Chandlerian school of business history has been more concerned with the study of managerial corporations, especially with the rise of "big business," than with entrepreneurial firms. The relative neglect of Jews' economic activity is partly a function of inattention to small business. What makes this lacuna difficult to remedy, however, is a paucity of source materials.

Although Jews were significant players in heavy industry in Central Europe, few Jews were allowed into major American corporate enterprises. Such discrimination is well-known, but it has not been much analyzed. In any case, Jews barely figure in magisterial works such as *The Visible Hand* or *Scale and Scope*, and when they do, their origins are not considered relevant. And yet there is no doubt that ethnicity had an effect on determining who did, and did not, penetrate Anglo-Saxon Protestant corporate America.

Finally, it is only in recent years that business history, a field often plagued by excessively rationalistic assumptions and concerns, has begun to move away from the study of industrial organization to broader cultural and ideological issues. The current volume signifies the coming of age of a new wave of business history that draws on intellectual sources ranging from organizational behavior to ethnographical analysis and cultural studies.

Before turning to the patterns of Jewish economic culture, let me offer a necessarily brief sketch of Jewish economic activities in the United States. The modest beginnings of Jews in the New World predated the birth of the nation. During the colonial era, Jews, mainly of Sephardic origin, played a major commercial role in Atlantic trade in the new world. They settled in port cities such as New York, Philadelphia, Newport, and Charleston. Among them was Aaron Lopez, an eighteenth-century merchant prince in Newport who would have stood little chance of joining a club there during the "gilded age." In the mid-nineteenth century, German Jews such as the Seligmanns and Loebs made their marks as merchant bankers. As America industrialized, Jewish entrepreneurs set up businesses further to the west, settling in Cincinnati, St. Louis, and New Orleans. For example, Jewish merchants led by Jacob Cohen sent Daniel Boone on his mission to Kentucky.

The economic opportunities and egalitarian ethic promised by the frontier took Jews to Santa Fe, Denver, and, above all, to San Francisco. Usually starting out as peddlers, with luck they opened stores "where the horse stopped" (some horses proving smarter than others). Among the many department stores that Jews founded or took over were Goldsmiths in Memphis, Riches in Atlanta, Meiers and Franks in Portland, I. Magnin in San Francisco, Neiman Marcus in Dallas, as well as Macy's and Bloomingdale's in New York. The Jewish presence on the frontier, however, was screened out in the Westerns produced by Hollywood Jews such as Louis B. Mayer, Adolph Zuckor, and Carl Laemmle.

American Jews threw themselves into diverse activities in the nineteenth and twentieth centuries. The Jewish roots of the founders of companies such as Levi Strauss are well known though not much publicized. Those of other firms' founders, including Hertz and Polaroid, are obscure. And how many aficionados of Ralph Lauren (né Lipschitz) realize that a stickball bat would have been a more authentic logo for his clothing than a polo mallet? Jews were particularly prominent in the production of other consumer goods such as the cosmetics industry which boasted firms such as Helena Rubenstein, Revlon, Max Factor, and Estée Lauder. Other Jews went into the toy business: F. A. O. Schwarz, Mattel, Hasbro, and Ideal.

Still other Jews turned to cultural media and services. Arthur Hays Sulzberger ran the *New York Times* (and Eugene Meyer the *Washington Post*), but was reticent to "put a Jew in the showcase" – a fear that his son "Punch" did not share to the same degree. David Sarnoff, a Russian immigrant who started selling newspapers on the Lower East Side at age nine, went on to mastermind the creation of RCA. From the world of entertainment – vaudeville, theater, movies, and popular music – Jews branched out into professional sports, buying football, basketball, and baseball franchises. And Jews made reputations in the cultural arena in publishing firms such as Knopf, Random House, Praeger, Viking, Simon and Schuster, and Farrar, Straus & Giroux. In the art world, Julien Levy became the major dealer for the Surrealists; Sidney Janis for the Abstract Expressionists; and Leo Castelli for the "new American painters."[23]

Apart from the famous names who made fortunes in merchant banking, retail, clothing, real estate, and mass media, most Jews earned their livings in small, unglamorous businesses. These included candy stores, hardware stores, and taxicabs. And this is to say nothing of the Jewish underworld, the criminal empire organized – and it was organized – by Meyer Lansky, Bugsy Siegel, and Co.

Are there distinctive patterns in Jews' economic culture and practice or were they just like any other immigrant group? It is true that Jewish entrepreneurs responded to changing economic opportunities as did any sensible manufacturer, banker, or merchant. And no single factor shaped Jews' economic behavior. Yet anti-Semitic discrimination shaped Jews' historic skills and strategies by limiting the occupations open to them as well as by influencing the business sectors they entered and the organizational structures they favored.

The conventional sociological wisdom emphasizes the impact of social marginality on Jewish achievement, both commercial and cultural. In Thorstein Veblen's famous essay, "The Intellectual Pre-Eminence of Jews," he explains the high proportion of Jews in various realms of thought by underlining their position as outsiders as well as their native intellectual gifts.[24] The relative social marginality of Jews not only fueled a drive to succeed in diverse endeavors, but also may have fostered a different outlook that helped certain Jews spot new opportunities, invent or apply new methods, and enter new areas. Those who occupied the center inevitably had a greater investment in the existing order than those who were confined to the periphery. In this sense, then, Jews took advantage of the distance that separated them from what Sigmund Freud called "the compact majority" in a celebrated speech to B'nai Brith in 1926 in Vienna.

Even so, it is easy to overemphasize the role of social marginality as a casual explanation for Jewish economic or cultural prominence. Arguing that Jews succeeded by virtue of their marginality ignores the fact that most marginalized groups remain just that. I would suggest that it was the combination of marginality and mobility that accounted for modern Jewry's peculiar social position. For Jews were, in James Clifford's phrase, a "traveling culture," moving between, and living in, different social worlds, however uneasily at times.[25] Those Jews who set their sights and hopes on prospering in the gentile world made it their business to know more about non-Jews than they knew about them. Knowledge was a vulnerable minority's best defense.

Let me outline a few characteristic features of the business of Jews. First of all, family firms were fundamental to the structure of Jewish economic culture. Throughout the nineteenth century, "personal capitalism" was the predominant form of business organization in the United States, as in Europe. And Jews were not alone in trying to keep ownership and capital in the same hands: their own. But discrimination made it especially important for Jews to establish and sustain family firms that provided employment for themselves and their fellows. Striving for economic independence was not unique to Jews, but for Jews, as for other middlemen minorities such as Quakers, it was an attempt to evade religious discrimination and to sustain communal solidarity. A long radius of distrust separated Jew and non-Jew both in terms of work and sociability. No wonder, then, that Jews stood a far better chance of obtaining employment and finding favor with a "landsman" than with a non-Jew. That was especially true for those who needed to adjust their working lives so that they could observe the Sabbath and Jewish holidays.

The strength of kinship ties provided Jewish firms with a substantial competitive advantage, but the combination of blood and money was sometimes combustible. On one occasion, Harry Warner chased brother Jack around their Hollywood studio with a lead pipe, yelling that he was going to kill him. When Albert Einstein visited the lot, Jack told him: "You know, I have a theory about relatives, too – don't hire them."[26] Nevertheless, the brothers trusted the rest of the world far less than their own family, and stayed in business together.

Jewish family enterprises functioned as part of ethnic networks that often operated internationally. The quest for economic autonomy did not preclude close kinship ties or collective solidarity. On the contrary, freedom from the other meant dependence on the brother. Blocked from the citadels of power, Jews had to accumulate what James Coleman called "social capital," the ability to work together in groups for common purposes. The success of Jews in specific endeavors may be understood as what physicists call a "collective phenomenon." (No single molecule will make the water boil, but a team of heated molecules may do precisely that.)[27] That does not mean cooperation between Jewish firms precluded intense competition – far from it – or that their links stemmed more from emotional attachments than economic interests. But the existence of clusters of Jews within the same economic sector provided a "demonstration effect" of the possibility of success. And competition may have spurred superior performance.

Ordinarily, it was safer, or more comfortable, for individual Jews as well as Jewish-owned firms to work together than to try to break into non-Jewish circles where they were customarily unwanted. Hence, they kept the profits in the family or, at least, the community. The establishment of far-flung networks in the Diaspora provided competitive advantages in a variety of inter-national trades such as grain dealing. Family bonds and ethnic ties also proved indispens-able in merchant banking where information was power, trust was essential, and secrecy paramount. Nevertheless, the links between the Rothschilds, Warburgs, and Seligmanns – strained or cool as their relations sometimes were – fired anti-Semitic paranoia of an international Jewish conspiracy.

The garment industry exemplifies the mixture of cooperation and competition that obtained in Jewish commercial networks. In the late-nineteenth and early-twentieth centuries, clothing manufacturing was the scene of bitter conflict between capitalist and capitalist as well as between owner and worker. And Jews battled not only with non-Jews but also with each other. Nevertheless, there were practical benefits for Jewish affiliation. East European Jewish immigrants stood a better chance of gaining a hearing, and getting an order, by visiting German– Jewish manufacturers in their Broadway showrooms than they would have had from German or Irish firms. Ethnic bonds also put Jews in good stead when it came to recruiting workers. Massive immigration and persistent discrimination provided a steady, reliable source of labor. "Waiting for the boat to come in" was true in more ways than one for the owners of firms who went down to the docks to recruit arriving East European Jewish immigrants, "Columbus tailors." One reason they preferred working for Jewish firms was that they spoke Yiddish.[28]

International trading was also at the heart of Jewish economic culture; for good reason given the competitive advantages afforded by linguistic skill, cross-cultural knowledge, and ethnic networks. Among the first European art dealers who opened galleries in New York were the Duveens, Gimpels, Wildensteins, and Knoedlers.

Duveen Brothers was founded by Joel Duveen, a Dutch traveling salesman who had emigrated to England. Initially, Joel relied on merchandise supplied by Dutch relatives who sold antiques (as well as scrap metal). Fired by interna-tional ambitions, he sent his youngest brother, Henry, to New York in 1877 to establish a shop there. "There is surely a good business to be carried on here in articles," Henry quickly recognized. Gobelin tapestries, chairs, sideboards, and Friesian cupboards were all in demand. "Nice pieces sell at a good prices . . . but you have to push and chat a lot."[29]

Even American *arrivistes* with little liking for Jews did business with the Duveens and indeed other Jewish art dealers. When Joel Duveen's formidable son Joe hung a Van Dyck at the Frick mansion in New York, Mrs. Frick declared that "she could not bear to have those Jewish noses constantly before her eyes." In fact, these protruding organs belonged to those well-known Hebrew traders, the brothers Stewart, nephews of Charles, King of England.[30] Given such pow-ers of discernment, perhaps Mrs. Frick had little clue about the Duveens' Jewish origins. But the fact that old masters were unique works rather than ordinary commodities, meant those who wanted to buy, say, Rembrandt's *Aristotle Contemplating a Bust*, had little choice but to do business with its proud possessors, Jew or non-Jew.

Dispersed as Jews were in different lands, they tended to concentrate heavily in certain trades. Discrimination shaped patterns of Jewish economic presence and absence. Virtually excluded from landholding and guilds in medieval Europe, Jews were relegated to occupations such as money lending and petty commerce that were deemed unworthy of ecclesiastics and nobles (who often pursued such profitable endeavors in actual practice). Whereas the persecution of African-Americans undermined their ability to acquire the habits and skills necessary to make their way in a capitalist society, the opposite proved true for Jews whose pariah status had a silver lining.

Like other middlemen minorities, Jews engaged in a narrower range of occupations than the population-at-large, as Simon Kuznets observed.[31] How could Jews survive, much less prevail? In the United States as in Europe, individual Jewish entrepreneurs did well, sometimes extraordinarily so, in a variety of economic endeavors. (But other Jews failed at whatever they tried.) The pattern of Jewish economic activity was shaped partly by the character of the societies they inhabited. Thus, Jewish entrepreneurs in Central Europe played major roles in heavy industries such as metals. In America, Jews such as the Guggenheims made fortunes in mining.

Generally, though, it was in merchant banking and finance, retailing and wholesaling, consumer goods, real estate, as well as mass media and cultural services that Jews clustered.

If business provided one road to social mobility, the professions provided another. Law and medicine were particularly attractive because they were learned professions that carried social prestige and offered economic autonomy. But aspiring Jewish professionals bumped up against discriminatory barriers that limited their entry to American colleges and universities as well as professional schools.[32] Those who hurdled these barriers often established law firms of their own and entered relatively open areas such as labor law, as did Louis D. Brandeis. Even in the early-1960s, and in some cases well beyond, there were few Jews in Anglo-Saxon corporate law firms.

For the most part, Jewish entrepreneurs made their mark in businesses that were new and expanding rapidly. This was partly a matter of escaping from social discrimination. New industries were less crowded than established occupations and less fettered by anti-Semitic bias. As a result, they offered the prospect of relatively open playing fields unavailable in more prestigious endeavors controlled by non-Jews. The choice of occupation also depended on historic skills that often stemmed from historical contingencies. The long involvement of Jews in the diamond business, for example, came about partly because Sephardic Jewish immigrants to seventeenth-century Amsterdam were not barred from that particular guild. The fact that so many doors were closed to Jews made it all the more incumbent upon them to identify, and seize, economic opportunities where others saw dross. And so Jews often took chances in areas where the risks were higher than in tested pursuits, but so were prospective returns.

Equally alluring was the comparative ease of entry into emerging business sectors. Practically speaking, this meant that even modest capital investments were often enough to launch firms. Anyone who wanted to open a steel plant in the United States in 1900 needed a fortune in financing with bravura to match. That did not prevent Jews from founding Inland Steel. But it was much easier to scrape together the money needed to get started, say, in the nascent business of moving pictures which required more chutzpah than cash.

In business, as in much else, Jews often took the back door – the service entrance. Out of necessity, they found niches in relatively undesirable areas with little prestige. Much as Jews entered metals through scrap metal, they took the economic leftovers in the garment trade – as peddlers selling secondhand wares or as tailors of modest apparel.

The historic social position of Jews made mobile enterprises attractive. One reason for the alleged Jewish bias for trade over industry was that the former was movable and the latter fixed. As an embattled minority with a history of forced expulsions, sudden persecutions, and quick exits, Jews had good cause to seek businesses where "you can take it with you." In short, diamonds were a safer investment than coal; a pouch full of jewels was easier to move than a chemical plant. What made precious stones appealing was that they were readily transportable (and difficult to tax). Jewish agricultural middlemen – dealers in horses, cattle, and grain – in the Rhineland Palatinate, Alsace, and, to some extent, in the American Southwest – enjoyed a degree of mobility relative to other rural occupations.

But the mobility of Jewish economic endeavors is easily exaggerated. In Polish and Russian lands, for instance, Jews also played significant economic roles managing large estates and inns.

In American urban centers, Jews gravitated to real estate. As city people with more push than pull, Jews had opportunities to learn the ins-and-outs of the urban property world often as immigrants packed into tenement houses. What better way to avoid housing covenants or informal "gentlemen's agreements" that excluded Jews than to become urban property holders themselves? Unlike southern European peasants or artisans who hailed from agricultural societies in which land was sacred, Jews took a more instrumental attitude. Even so, real estate conveyed an urban equivalent of the status that accompanied land in aristocratic orders.[33] Owning land in the city proved that one had arrived and begun to belong. This was especially poignant for Holocaust survivors such as Laszlo Tauber who became a leading apartment and home builder in postwar Washington, DC.

What is perhaps most intriguing about Jewish economic culture was the role of Jews as arbiters of taste and the role of business in transforming identity and image. As Sir Isaiah Berlin noted, Jews became primary authorities on the natives, exceptionally acute detectives of trends and taste. Much as Jews had mediated between lord and peasant in traditional societies, they became cultural middlemen in modernity, intermediaries who translated and interpreted various cultural forms. Unlike other middlemen minorities in the United States, Jews gravitated to cultural services and mass media: book and newspaper publishing, art galleries, popular music, vaudeville, theater, movies, radio, and television. It is more accurate to regard such economic activities as means of acculturation rather than simply dismiss them as symptoms of assimilation – which is a considerably more ambiguous and uneven a process than many have assumed.

Where did Jews fit into corporate America? Admittedly, a small number of individual Jews penetrated "big business."[34] Nevertheless, it is necessary to distinguish between firms and enterprises that were "Jewish" in terms of their historical character or in the proportion of Jews who became prominent in them. In other words, though certain Jews entered steel manufacturing, this industry remained a Protestant stronghold in a way that, clothing production did not.

Despite the rise of managerial capitalism in the early-twentieth century, Jews continued to flock to family firms. The vast majority of Jewish-owned enterprises were comparatively small and had scant need for professional managers, managerial hierarchies, or functional divisions. The major exception was Germany where men such as Albert Ballin came to the fore in the shipping business – with disastrous consequences. Excoriated as a symbol of Jewish economic domination, Ballin, "the uncrowned King of Hamburg," committed suicide in 1900.[35]

Steering clear of corporate bureaucracies was necessary because "big business" discriminated openly and persistently against Jews. Henry Ford was the most notorious and open Jew-hater of American corporate leaders, but he was not alone. Ford, and indeed other automobile companies, were notoriously averse to hiring Jews. (Even so, Ford sometimes did business with Jews. He regularly bought antiques from Israel Sacks, the Boston dealer who became the leading authority on American colonial furniture.)

In the clubby world of insurance, automobiles, telecommunications, and corporate law firms, and in most smokestack industries, Jews were subject to persistent and systematic discrimination. This was a question of not getting in the door, much less getting to the top.

Bell Telephone, for instance, did not knowingly employ Jewish managers or workers until after 1945 (and continued to discriminate against African-Americans until after it was sanctioned by the U.S. Government in late 1960). The network of Anglo-Saxon Protestant managers who ran the company kept Jews at long distance, except, of course, as paying customers.

In 1925, Warner Brothers was in the midst of bitter negotiations with Bell over the rights to sound equipment for movies when its president invited Harry Warner in to iron out their grievances together. As Warner walked into the office, he said immediately: "Mr. Gray, this can be a very short meeting. I will give you all right to our patents. I will withdraw all our suits . . . I'll do it immediately and at no cost to you, if you'll do one thing. If you'll give me the name of one Jew who works for your company." When the startled executive could not "realistically" do so, Warner told him: "It's a policy of your company not to employ Jews. It's a policy of my company not to do business with you." And he left. As it turned out, Gray ordered his lawyers to work out a settlement, but did nothing to hire Jews.[36]

On occasion, Jews found their way into Protestant-dominated corporate America anyway, but this was largely a matter of individual success stories. The question of Jewish identity in mainstream corporate America is difficult to study, in large part because so few Jews were able to gain entry to major corporations. The attitudes of those who did ranged from anxiety about anti-Semitism to almost complete submergence of Jewish identity.

The rise of Gerard Swope was exceptional: He served as President of General Electric from 1922 to 1940, surely a long run. This was not simply a matter of Swope's considerable talents and personal determination. He concealed his Jewish background and married a Gentile. What Swope felt about his Jewish origins is a matter of speculation. But it is interesting to note that Swope bequeathed the bulk of his nearly eight million dollar estate to Israel's leading technical institution, the Technion in Haifa.[37]

Even Julius Rosenwald, who himself made no bones about being a Jew, was hard pressed to deal with Jewish issues. An extraordinarily munificent philanthropist and communal leader, Rosenwald turned Sears into an American icon as well as its top retailer. He did not shy away from hiring other Jews to major executive positions at the Chicago-based giant. But the same could not be said of the man who Rosenwald brought in to manage the firm in the 1920s, General Robert C. Wood. Gradually, Wood began closing out Jews at the firm, excluding them as buyers and executives. And Rosenwald did not stop him. Was he aware of the General's anti-Semitic policies? "It was obvious" noted Rosenwald's son Lessing. "During Wood's administration every Jew in an important position was relieved and not one was hired. My father really believed that if you hired a man to do the job you should let him do it and not interfere and to some extent he may have unconsciously hidden behind that."[38] As anti-Semitism roared through America in the 1930s, Rosenwald looked the other way.

For the most part, Jews entered the world of big business thanks to professional expertise, as "knowledge-workers" of one sort or another – in science, law, accountancy, and, more recently, computers. Though major corporations tended to do business with non-Jewish financiers, Sidney Weinberg of Goldman Sachs, a Brooklyn Jew from a humble background and with high ambitions, became the merchant banker of choice for many a corporate titan, including Henry Ford II. And it was Edward Bernays, Freud's nephew, who masterminded the development of public relations in the United States. Hence, he became an influential consultant to a wide range of firms from General Motors to General Foods.[39]

In recent decades, certain Jews came to occupy important positions in big business without having to cover their origins and identities. Perhaps the most striking and often-cited story is the rise of Irving Shapiro. The son of a Lithuanian pants-presser, he became the head of the Du Pont Corporation in 1973 and, three years later, of the prestigious Business Roundtable, a top organization of leading American chief executives. His achievement was all the more remarkable because Du Pont was notoriously anti-Semitic, as befitted a company that regarded Delaware as its rightful fiefdom. "I could understand a Jew becoming President of the United States," the American ambassador to Great Britain said after learning of Shapiro's appointment, "but not the chief executive officer of Du Pont."[40]

Unlike Gerard Swope, Shapiro never disguised his Jewishness. "I am what I am, and I can never change," he said.[41] That was more than talk. When his professors at the University of Minnesota law school advised him to change his last name, he demurred. Shapiro became prominent in Wilmington's local Jewish community, chairing the local United Jewish Appeal campaign and sitting on the board of a Jewish old-age home. The newly appointed chief executive even turned down an invitation to join a Wilmington Country Club in which he and his wife would have been the first Jewish members. "I told them that it just would not be comfortable for my wife and me to socialize there," Shapiro said.[42] Yet he did not underrate the significance of his appointment as a symbol of corporate America's growing openness to Jews.

"Big business" generally closed its doors to Jews, but that did not stop Jewish entrepreneurs from competing with Anglo-Saxon dominated firms or adopting corporate structures for their own purposes in diverse industries.

The story of certain Jews' entry into, and impact on, book publishing illustrates larger patterns. One did not, of course, have to be Jewish to become a major twentieth-century American publisher, but such was the case for the founders of preeminent publishing houses and book clubs, among them Bennett Cerf, Donald Klopfer, Ben Huebsch, Harold Guinzberg, Richard Simon, M. Lincoln Schuster, and Roger W. Straus, Jr.[43]

What makes this sudden explosion of talent all the more striking is the fact that when Alfred Knopf set up shop in 1915, book publishing was virtually closed to Jews. The industry was then dominated by establishment firms such as Houghton Mifflin, Harper & Row, and Little, Brown, gentile and gentlemanly defenders of the "genteel tradition" in literature.[44] Nothing of the sort was said of the upstart Jews who challenged these estimable houses.

Anti-Semitic discrimination kept Jews out of the established seats of cultural power and propelled them to build publishing houses of their own. Though the new houses soon became corporations, they did not develop complex managerial hierarchies. Generally, the firms were controlled by partners. Such was the case at Random House where Bennett Cerf and Donald Klopfer worked in tandem. They shared editorial duties, but Cerf took charge of publicity and advertising; and Klopfer was responsible for manufacturing.[45]

The New York Jewish publishers were friendly rivals who built a network that served as a counter-establishment to the clubby world of the old houses. Ambition rather than altruism inspired their firms. Even so, they provided opportunities for other Jews who stood about as much chance of getting hired by, much less rising in, a Boston house as they did of presiding over the membership committee of an exclusive Brahmin club. Shut out from the Publishers Lunch Club, Alfred Knopf gathered Jews and non-Jews alike at the Book Table where the food and wine were better anyway thanks to his gourmet taste.

The Jewish counter-establishment was based on shared economic interests and on ethnic bonds that united Jews who were eager to break away from tradition but not each other. The New York Jewish publishers saw themselves as rebels against an exclusive literary establishment that had snubbed them. Max Schuster figured the conflict in terms of a "gentlemanly, aristocratic, pseudo-snobbish culturally-closed society" versus an open society intent on democratizing publishing.[46]

Common educational and work experience strengthened the New York Jewish publishers' network. Cerf, Simon, and Schuster were students at Columbia around the same time, and Knopf too was a Columbia graduate. The founders of Viking, Guinzberg, and Oppenheimer met at Harvard. Marshall Best (whose family owned the department store Best and Company) served his apprenticeship with Ben Huebsch and joined Viking when Guinzberg bought Huebsch's firm for its splendid backlist and savvy owner. Guinzberg himself was a minority partner in Simon and Schuster before setting up his own firm. And several future Jewish publishers met while working for Horace Liveright.[47] Despite the firm's speakeasy atmosphere, Liveright published great lists that included Sherwood Anderson, Eugene O'Neill, F. Scott Fitzgerald, and T. S. Eliot. When Simon was about to leave Liveright to start his own firm with Schuster, he recommended that Liveright hire Cerf to take his place. Soon after, Cerf and Klopfer bought the firm.

The fault lines between Jewish and non-Jewish publishers affected business alliances. When George P. Brett, Jr. of Macmillan finally deigned to ask Alfred Knopf to lunch (after knowing him for years), Knopf hung up on him as soon as he figured out that Brett wanted to buy his firm. Nothing of the sort happened, however, when Cerf and Klopfer, the Knopfs' longtime friends, raised the same possibility. In 1960, the Knopfs sold out to Random House but retained editorial control.[48]

Moreover, Jews involved in book publishing tended to come from commercial or financial families or obtained such experience before setting up their own publishing firms. Richard Simon's father was a successful milliner, Blanche Wolf Knopf's father was a well-to-do jeweler, Alfred Knopf's father was a wheeler dealer who had his ups-and-downs as an advertising agent, bank marketing manager, and real estate developer; and Donald Klopfer's stepfather was in the diamond manufacturing business. Several Jews who ended up in the world of books started out in the world of bonds – a good illustration of Pierre Bourdieu's concept of cultural bankers. Liveright, Cerf, and Simon all had successful stints on Wall Street and brought financial and commercial habits, skills, connections, and capital to publishing. Even so, such experience was not necessarily a recipe for commercial success, as Liveright proved. A handsome, extravagant man with infinite style and limited sense, he rarely saw a ledger that caught his eye and rarely saw a beautiful woman who did not. His literary flair and personal panache did not prevent Liveright from turning the best-selling *Gentlemen Prefer Blondes* into a money-loser because he failed to check manufacturing costs before setting the retail price.

Other Jews, notably Guinzberg, Schuster, and Huebsch, came to book publishing through journalism or printing, both of which provided a back door to the "classier" world of trade books.

Publishing appealed to Jews partly because it presented relatively low barriers to entry and required modest capital investment. Knopf founded his firm with $5000 which came from his father and his savings. Klopfer and Cerf purchased Liveright's Modern Library with funds provided by Klopfer's sale of his share in his stepfather's diamond business, Cerf's Wall Street profits, and his favorite uncle's benevolence. They paid $100,000 because the Modern Library was a going concern even though it was going downhill along with Liveright himself. Surely this was nothing to sneeze at, but it was relatively modest compared to what starting a capital intensive business would have required.

Unlike businesses such as merchant banking where Jews numbered among the first movers, in publishing they were relative latecomers and, therefore, had to seek competitive advantage elsewhere. In short, the people of the book could not succeed if they played by the book. They published for highbrow, lowbrow, and middlebrow taste and mixed the usual categories. E. Haldeman Julius, a socialist who had the sense to marry a banker's daughter who could afford her husband's convictions, addressed his "Little Blue Books" to the common, but no doubt noble, man. Nevertheless, there was nothing lowbrow about his editions of classics which marked out a popular road to high culture. Alfred Knopf believed that Random House, which was run by the "smartest boys in the business," was virtually schizophrenic, publishing masterpieces like *Ulysses* along with very bad books.[49] And the house of Knopf, whose prestigious list included the likes of Willa Cather, Thomas Mann, and Knut Hamsun, earned one of its greatest commercial triumphs with Kahil Gibran's *The Prophet*. This huge best seller was hardly a work of supreme aesthetic value, but it fulfilled the promise of its title in more ways than one.

How did New York Jewish publishers gain a foothold in the literary marketplace? First, they competed by expanding their customer base and cutting prices. Much to the chagrin of booksellers, Harold Guinzberg's Literary Guild undercut retail networks by discounting books and mailing directly to customers.

Second, New York Jewish publishers competed by innovative advertising – there were no Trappists among them. Simon & Schuster's weekly book column, "The Inner Sanctum," symbolized their aggressively democratic approach to culture. It offered personal initiation into literary mysteries and conjured up the aura of an exclusive, indeed sacred, club that the reader could join at any time. As Schuster put it, the columns "seemed to give the impression of being taken backstage, behind the scenes" rather than shutting out the common reader.[50] Cerf, himself the author of an endless stream of humor books published by S & S, delighted in publicizing Random House and himself. He frequented show business circles with the likes of Frank Sinatra, served on the Board of Directors of MGM, and appeared for years as a regular panelist on the quiz show, "What's My Line?" His lightweight persona and media mania angered his longtime friend and rival, Harold Guinzberg, who disliked such trivial preoccupations. Nevertheless, as Guinzberg's son Tom recognized, "What's My Line?" contributed to Random House's bottom line.[51] It also earned Cerf a better table at the Stork Club.

Third, New York Jews competed by marketing western classics and championing modernist literature. Surely it was no accident that Jews, who were themselves seeking admission to the inner sanctum of European and American culture, loomed so large in the fabrication and diffusion of the canon, the list of books educated persons should know. While Columbia, Chicago, and Harvard were developing core courses in the humanities and social studies, New York Jewish publishers issued accessibly priced editions of Western literature, philosophy, and history, and catered to the growing education market. The classics appealed to the new guard partly because they were out of copyright and needed no royalties or advances: Homer's *Odyssey* required no book tour. In any case, canonization paid: the Modern Library sold more than a million copies during the Depression.

Likewise, modernism appealed to Jews partly because it offered a business opening. Knopf, Random House, Viking, and, after the Second World War, Farrar, Straus & Giroux, became the preeminent publishers of European modernist literature. Cerf and Klopfer's Modern Library, therefore, included would-be modern classics such as Joyce and Proust. The Knopfs published Mann, Gide, Hamsun, and Kafka. Jews entered literary modernism on the proverbial ground floor. Style and ideology apart, Jews had more to gain from gambling on experimental, controversial works than did the old guard. In fact, gambling was a term these literary "spielers" often used to describe their ventures. Cerf and Klopfer's brilliant campaign to rescue *Ulysses* from the censors did precisely what they hoped: it immediately established Random House as a serious trade publisher.

The modernist penchant of New York Jewish publishers was related to another striking characteristic of the business of Jews: internationalism. They served as cultural intermediaries between Europe and America, a natural role for immigrants and their heirs. The name of Guinzberg's house, Viking, captured a spirit of adventure, claimed native grounds and foreign lands, and implied American roots that would that would put the DAR to shame. And Alfred Knopf, passionate publisher of American history and literature that he was, put together the strongest international list of any house until Farrar, Straus, & Giroux came on the scene.

Finally, New York Jewish publishers competed by design, working on the assumption that you can tell a book by its cover, and, for that matter, its typography and paper. "We made an effort to lend a certain cachet to our books," commented Alfred Knopf, "that would make us a little different from just another book publisher."[52] Taking design seriously helped the Knopfs embody their aesthetic aspirations and, by the way, throw off the taint of vulgar commercialism that anti-Semites would not let Jews forget.

Publishing became an arena for self-fashioning. In short, publishing enabled the people of the book to revise themselves while contributing to literary culture. While the issue of Jewish identity was predictably complicated, generally the publishers were secular Jews, more interested in making it in America than cleaving to Jewish tradition. Most had some religious training in childhood, but there is little evidence that any were more than nominally observant as adults. But it is worth pointing out that Ben Huebsch's father was the rabbi of Prague's largest synagogue before American Jews brought him to Manhattan to lead a congregation there. The rabbi's son did not keep the faith, but he attributed his reverence for learning to his Jewish background. Much the same applied to Max Schuster who came from a family of talmudic scholars "where the supreme values were books and scholarship and literature."[53]

Publishing enabled New York Jews to reshape their identities. Firstly, it enabled those who were immigrant or immigrants' children to establish themselves as masters of the written word and its publication. Secondly, it furnished Jews with a means to overcome their relative cultural exclusion by immersing themselves in European and American literary culture. Hence, they brought together the commercial acumen and traditional literacy that Jews had honed for centuries as merchants and scholars.

What were the principal paths of cultural entrée? One was the modernist route. Much as Parisian Jewish art dealers such as the brothers Rosenberg championed Picasso, New York Jewish publishers spread the work of literary modernists such as Proust, Kafka, and Joyce. The other path was the classic route: as architects and advocates of the Western literary canon. This was as much a matter of appropriation as assimilation. Publishing Western old masters afforded Jews a place, however fragile and belated, in a cultural tradition from which pride and prejudice had excluded them. And so, around the same time that Columbia was instituting its core courses in "Contemporary Civilization" (1927) and "Literary Humanities" (1937), Knopf, Cerf, Simon, and Schuster, all Columbia graduates, pursued much the same agenda as their alma mater: fostering ties between Europe and the United States under the rubric of "Western" civilization; promoting democracy, citizenship, and patriotism to natives and immigrants alike; and trying to domesticate eastern and southern Europeans among others.[54]

In publishing New York Jews found a cultural power unavailable to them in the anti-Semitic world of American academia where Anglo-Saxon Protestants held sway. Nowhere was this more true than in departments of English where the self-appointed guardians of culture did their best to keep Jews away from their sacred ground.

Finally, publishing offered Jews a commercial road to cultural legitimacy. Publishing was, as the cliché goes, "a profession for gentlemen." The new guard were not to the manner born and they sometimes competed by methods that the old guard regarded as ungentlemanly at best. Eventually, though, the New York Jews' business success helped them raise their social status and accumulate cultural capital. Assuming the role of high-minded aesthetes and idealists dedicated to literary experimentation or democratic enrichment, New York Jews tried to outrun Shylock's shadow.

By the 1930s, the New York Jewish publishers had become a force to be reckoned with in the literary world and so they remained through the 1970s. What undermined them, ultimately, was the rise of conglomerates, the advent of corporate capitalism in the publishing world, combined with their inability or unwillingness to pass on their firms to their children. Harold Guinzberg's son Tom succeeded him, but after Penguin bought Viking he was soon tossed out. Simon and Schuster eventually became a Viacom Company. RCA bought

Random House which, then, became part of S.I. Newhouse's empire. And Random House now belongs to Bertelsmann. Even Roger Straus III, a redoubtable publisher known for his opposition to conglomerates, sold his house to another German publisher, von Holtzbrinck.

This chapter has suggested that fears of anti-Semitic libels as well as historiographic fashions have contributed to the relative neglect of the role of Jews in modern capitalism and the impact of capitalism on Jewish life and culture.

What lessons does the Jewish experience offer the historian of economic culture? First, it suggests the creative force of social marginality as a source of economic innovation. Initially working outside of the world of "big business," Jewish entrepreneurs rose to challenge the dominant players in a variety of endeavors, especially in financial services, consumer goods, and cultural brokerage. The publishing houses and book clubs founded by Jewish entrepreneurs became significant corporations in their own right, as did the great Hollywood studios that relegated Thomas Edison and Co. to the sidelines of the movie business. Second, the Jewish experience underlines the importance of ethnic origins, affiliation, and ambitions in understanding the production and consumption of goods and services. As producers of movies, impresarios of music, dealers in art, and publishers of books and newspapers, Jews sought cultural legitimacy through the firms they founded. The business of culture enabled Jews not only to join the club, but also to change its rules; not only to become American, but also to redefine what being American meant.

Finally, the Jewish experience enlarges our understanding of the nature and boundaries of corporate America. It suggests that the methods and goals of "big business" were neither universal nor inevitable. Far from being the sole agent of modernity, rationality, and capitalism, the small, exclusive Protestant corporation constituted by the Du Ponts and their friends was only one possible cultural form. It was product of history rather than its goal. The corporate world was not simply driven by the rational calculation of profit or the invisible hand of the market. Its hierarchies also were shaped by social choices and ethnic biases no less than by economic needs. For Jews, as for other would-be Americans, business was an arena for self-fashioning, a means to redefine identity. If the business of America was business, the business of business was meaning as well as money.

NOTES

1. See James Shapiro, *Shakespeare and the Jews* (New York: Columbia University Press, 1995) for an illuminating discussion of representations of Jews in early modern England.
2. See Henry Adams to Brooks Adams, 3 Jan. 1896 and Henry Adams to Mary Leiter Curzon, 30 December 1895, in J. C. Levenson, Ernest Samuels, Charles Vandersee, and Viola Hopkins Winner (eds.), *Letters of Henry Adams, vol. I:1892–1899* (Cambridge, MA, and London: Belknap Press of Harvard UP, 1988), 353 and 357.

3. Henry Adams to John Hay, 4 Oct. 1895, ibid., 337.

4. Henry Adams to Elizabeth Cameron, 13 August 1895, ibid., 30.

5. Charles Dellheim, "The Creation of a Company Culture: Cadburys, 1861–1931," *American Historical Review* 92 (Feb. 1987), 13–44.

6. There is, of course, a considerable scholarly literature on Weber and Sombart. See especially Freddy Raphael, *Judaisme et Capitalisme: essai sur la controverse entre Max Weber et Werner Sombart* (Paris: Presses Universitaires de France, 1982).

7. Max Weber, *Ancient Judaism*, trans. and edited by Hans H. Gerth and Don Martindale (New York: Free Press, 1952), 3–4.

8. Ibid., 345.

9. Ibid., 67, 71, 130, 155, and 255.

10. Ibid., 344.

11. Werner Sombart, *The Jews and Modern Capitalism*, trans. M. Epstein, (New York: Burt Franklin, 1969), first published London 1913, 121.

12. Ibid., 205.

13. Ibid., 255, 262, and 268.

14. Ibid., 276. I have substituted "entrepreneur" for the translator's inaccurate "undertaker."

15. On German anti-modernism, see especially Fritz Stern, *The Politics of Cultural Despair: A Study in the Rise of the Germanic Ideology* (Berkeley: University of California Press, 1961).

16. Ibid., 38–9.

17. For the debates on Jewish emancipation, see Jacob Katz, *Out of the Ghetto: The Social Background of Jewish Emancipation, 1770–1870* (New York: Schocken Books, 1978); Derek J. Penslar, *Shylock's Children: Economics and Jewish Identity in Modern Europe* (Berkeley and Los Angeles: University of California Press, 2000); and Jonathan Karp, *The Politics of Jewish Commerce*, Columbia University Ph.D. dissertation, 2000.

18. On Jewish interwar historiography, see Jonathan Karp's unpublished paper, "Interwar Jewish Economic Historiography, in Eastern Europe." Ezra Mendelsohn also shared his knowledge of Yiddish historiography with me.

19. See Irving Howe, with the assistance of Kenneth Libo, *World of our Fathers* (New York: Harcourt, Brace & Jovanovich, 1976).

20. See Salo W. Baron and Arcadius Kahan, in Nachum Gross (ed.), *Economic History of the Jews* (New York: Schocken Books, 1975); Simon Kuznets, "Economic Structure and Life of the Jews," in Louis Finkelstein (ed.), *The Jews: Their History, Culture, and Religion*, vol. II (New York: Harper, 1949), ch. 39; Karp, *Politics of Jewish Commerce*; Penslar, *Shylock's Children*; and Meir Tamari, *With all your Possessions: Jewish ethics and economic life* (New York: Free Press, 1987).

21. See Werner Mosse, *The German-Jewish Economic Elite, 1820–1935: A Socio-Cultural Profile* (Oxford: Clarendon Press, 1989); Mosse, *Jews in the German Economy: The German-Jewish Economic Elite, 1820–1935* (Oxford: Clarendon Press, 1987); Harold Pollins, *Economic History of the Jews in England* (Rutherford, NJ: Fairleigh Dickinson University Press, 1982); Stephen Birmingham, *Our Crowd: The Great Jewish Families of New York* (Syracuse, NY: Syracuse University Press, 1996); John J. Gross, *Shylock: A Legend and its Legacy* (New York: Simon & Schuster, 1992); Leon Harris, *Merchant Princes: An Intimate History of Jewish Families Who Built Great Department Stores* (New York: Kodansha International, 1904); David Goodman and Masanori Miyazawa, *Jews in the Japanese Mind: The History and Uses of a Cultural Stereotype* (New York: Free Press, 1995); and Ron Chernow, *The Warburgs* (New York: Random House, 1995). There are also useful essays on Jews and other minorities in

Elise S. Brezis and Peter Temin (eds.), *Elites, Minorities, and Economic Growth* (Amsterdam: North Holland, 1999).

22. See Roger Waldinger, *Through the Eye of the Needle: Immigrants and Enterprise in New York's garment trades* (New York: New York University Press, 1986); and Walter P. Zenner, *Minorities in the Middle: A Cross-Cultural Analysis* (Albany: State University of New York Press, 1991).

23. There is much valuable material on Jewish economic activity in Henry Feingold (ed.), *The Jewish People in America* (Baltimore: Johns Hopkins University Press, 1992), 5 vols.

24. See Thorstein Veblen, "The Intellectual Pre-eminence of Jews."

25. See James Clifford, *Routes: Travel and Translation in the Late Twentieth Century* (Cambridge, MA: Harvard University Press, 1997), chs 1–3.

26. See Neal Gabler, *An Empire of their Own: How the Jews invented Hollywood* (New York: Crown Publishers, 1988).

27. My thanks to Ralph Amado for bringing to my attention a physicists' definition of collective phenomena.

28. On the clothing industry, see especially Nancy L. Green, *Ready-to-Wear and Ready-to-Work: A Century of Industry and Immigrants to Paris and New York* (Durham, NC: Duke University Press, 1997) as well as Andrew R. Heinze, *Adapting to Abundance: Jewish Immigrants, Mass Consumption, and the Search for American Identity* (New York: Columbia University Press, 1990).

29. See Colin Simpson, *Artful Partners: Bernard Berenson and Joseph Duveen* (New York: Macmillan, 1986), 17.

30. See René Gimpel, *Diary of an Art Dealer*, translated by John Rosenberg (New York: Farrar, Straus, and Giroux, 1966), 38.

31. See Kuznets, "Economic Structure," 1600–1.

32. On anti-Semitic discrimination in academia, see Susanne Klingenstein, *Jews in the American Academy, 1900–1940: The Dynamics of Intellectual Assimilation* (New Haven: Yale University Press, 1991); Peter Novick, *That Noble Dream: The "Objectivity question" and the American Historical Profession* (Cambridge and New York: Cambridge University Press, 1988); and Dan Oren, *Joining the Club: A History of Jews and Yale* (New Haven: Yale University Press, 1985).

33. See Nathan Glazer, *American Judaism* (Chicago: University of Chicago Press, 1957).

34. On Jews in corporate America, see especially Abraham Korman, *The Outsiders: Jews and Corporate America* (Lexington, MA: Lexington Books, 1988).

35. See Lamar Cecil, *Albert Ballin, business and politics in imperial Germany, 1888–1918.* (Princeton: Princeton University Press, 1967).

36. Gabler, *Empire of their Own.*

37. On Swope, see Stephen Whitfield, *American Space, Jewish Time* (Hamden, CT: Archon Books, 1988), 144.

38. Quoted in Harris, *Merchant Princes*, 320.

39. On Bernays, see Larry Tye, *The Father of Spin: Edward L. Bernays & the Birth of Public Relations* (New York: Crown Publishers, 1998).

40. See Edward P. Shapiro, *A Time for Healing: American Jewry since World War II* (Baltimore: Johns Hopkins University Press, 1992), 115; and Charles Silberman, *A Certain People: American Jews and their Lives Today* (New York: Summit Books, 1988), 84–5.

41. Silberman, Ibid., 85.

42. Quoted in Shapiro, *Time for Healing*, 116.

43. The following discussion of New York Jewish publishers is based on my research in archives at Columbia University, the University of Texas at Austin, and the New York Public Library. See Charles Dellheim, "A Fragment of a Heart in the Knopf Archives," *The Chronicle of Higher Education*, July 16, 1999, B4–5, and Dellheim, "Of the Book but not by the Book: New York Jews Publish High and Low," paper presented at the Association for Jewish Studies, 1998.

44. For the publishing scene before the entry of New York Jews, see especially John Tebbel, *Between Covers: The Rise and Transformation of Book Publishing in America* (New York: Oxford University Press, 1987); and Tebbel, *A History of Book Publishing in the United States* (New York: R. R. Bowker, 1972–81); vols 2–3. Other valuable works on publishing include the personal memoirs and reflections of two eminent editors: Michael Korda, *Another life: a Memoir of Other People* (New York: Random House, 1999); and Jason Epstein, *Book Business: Publishing Past, Present, and Future* (New York and London: W. W. Norton, 2001). Also see Jonathan Freedman, *The Temple of Culture: Assimilation and Anti-Semitism in literary Anglo-America* (New York: Oxford University Press, 2000).

45. See *Donald Klopfer*, unpublished typescript, Columbia University Oral History Library, 1976, 62. For a more general account see Bennett Cerf, *At Random: The Reminiscences of Bennett Cerf* (New York: Random House, 1977).

46. See *The Reminiscences of Max Schuster*, unpublished typescript, Columbia University Oral History Library, 10–16.

47. On Liveright, see Tom Dardis, *Firebrand: The Life of Horace Liveright* (New York: Random House, 1995).

48. See Alfred A. Knopf, *Autobiography* (unpublished draft), Columbia University Archives, 4.

49. Ibid., 269.

50. Schuster, *Reminiscences*, 3–9.

51. Thomas Guinzberrg, *The Reminiscences of Thomas H. Guinzburg*, unpublished typescript, Columbia University Oral History Library, 1981, 89, 146, 274, 299–300, 325, 582–5, 590, 584.

52. Knopf, *Autobiography*, 40.

53. Schuster, *Reminiscences*, 17–23.

54. See Lawrence Levine, *The Opening of the American Mind: Canons, Culture, and History* (Boston: Beacon Press, 1996).

9

White Corporate America: The New Arbiter of Race?

Juliet E. K. Walker

Despite the growing awareness among corporate leadership of the bottom-line value and economic imperative of including minorities and women in senior corporate management, progress has been disappointingly slow, and barriers persist which prevent able people from achieving their full employment potential.

Federal Glass Ceiling Commission Report, 1995

Welcome to the world of the black entrepreneur. For us, a recession is always just around the corner, and the success of our companies can never be taken for granted.

Earl G. Graves, Sr., CEO *Black Enterprise*

Economic Empowerment: The Next Civil Rights Frontier. It is not a slogan: it's a necessity.

Hugh B. Price, President, National Urban League

INTRODUCTION: WAVES OF RACIALIZED ECONOMIC INEQUITY

In 1900, some thirty-five years after the end of African-American slavery, William E. B. Du Bois, Harvard's first African-American Ph.D., said: "The problem of the twentieth century is the problem of the color line."[1] A century later, the color line persists, especially in the economic life of Black America. Even at the end of the twentieth century, glaring racial disparities in employment positions, salaries, and business profits indicate that Black America had yet to achieve economic parity with White America. In the last government assessment of black business in 1997 (information is compiled every five years), the receipts of black American business accounted for only 0.4 percent ($72.1 billion) of total American business receipts. Although Black Americans comprise 12.3 percent (34.7 million) of the nation's population, they own only 2 percent (832,000) of the nation's businesses. Only 10 percent of black businesses had revenues over $1 million. Also, in 2001, while the nation's leading business in White Corporate America, Wal-Mart, had revenues of $219 billion, the largest business in Black Corporate America, the Houston-based Camac Holdings, had receipts that year of $975 million.

This two-part chapter considers the late twentieth century impact of White Corporate America on African-American participation in the nation's economic life as both employees and business owners. It proposes that at least some of these dramatic racial inequalities in business and employment can be attributed to the decisions of white owned-and-managed enterprise, collectively termed "White Corporate America." Throughout U.S. history White Corporate America has been a principal arbiter of race in the nation's economic arena.[2] By contrast, black businesses largely have been forced to participate on the margins, where they remain even today.

To be sure, black business activities have changed substantially over the twentieth century. There have been four waves in the growth and expansion of black business in American history.[3] The emergence of Black Corporate America began with firms that catered to the segregated consumer markets of the early twentieth century. The black hair care product manufacturing companies established in the early twentieth century remained the bedrock industry of Black Corporate America until the 1990s. With few exceptions, these enterprises were individually owned as sole proprietorships. And, aside from the black financial industry, banks and insurance companies, and the few large black construction companies, most black enterprises were retail and service establishments. The second wave began in the 1930s and lasted until the early 1960s. Whereas leading black businesses in the first phase of the Rise of Black Corporate America, primarily the black hair care products manufacturers, *approached* millions of dollars earned in business receipts, in the second phase there were several black businesses with receipts in the millions of dollars by the 1950s. Still excluded from the mainstream consumer market, black enterprises in the second phase continued to provide goods and services to a black consumer market. These included black hotel, transportation, funeral, and construction industries, as well as segregated sports entities such as the Negro Baseball League. Blacks in publishing (magazines and newspapers) and hair products also ran profitable enterprises.

In many ways, then, black business activity changed very little throughout the first six decades of the twentieth century, particularly regarding the kinds of enterprises established, the consumer markets reached by these enterprises, and the form of business ownership. So while there was black business expansion, it was not until the Civil Rights Era – which marked the beginning of the Third Wave Rise of Black Corporate America – that black business activities were viewed as joining mainstream American business activity. The fourth wave began in the 1990s and led to an increase in the number of black businesses with receipts in the hundreds of millions of dollars. Whereas in the first two waves large black businesses were sole proprietorships, invariably 100 percent owned and controlled by blacks, with markets limited primarily to black consumers, the post-Civil Rights third and fourth waves in the Rise of Black Corporate America saw an upsurge in new forms of black business ownership and activities, distinguished by joint ventures, mergers, acquisitions, strategic alliances, and equity partnerships.

Changes in both technology and government policy have played significant roles in these patterns of evolution. In the third wave (late 1960s to the late 1980s), black-owned firms finally had a serious chance to compete for municipal, state, and federal government contracts, although often as subcontractors to white firms. The revolution in high technology starting in the 1970s, on the other hand, opened up new opportunities for start-up firms outside of the heavy industrial sectors such as steel and automobiles dominated by White Corporate America. The growth of services and media-based economic activity also provided opportunities for black performers and sports stars to amass personal fortunes and to launch their own business careers. But these changes, ironically, also heightened the economic disparity between the fortunate few black superstars and entrepreneurs and the great mass of African-Americans who have remained only employees of White Corporate America. Nor have recent black entrepreneurial successes erased the racial facts of life for black business. Black business receipts remain woefully small compared with both white American businesses and many other minority businesses.

The impact of federal government policies has also been mixed. It was the federal government, with its Civil Rights agendas, that made the difference for the entry of blacks as both employees in White Corporate America and as owners of enterprises that compete in the mainstream American economy. In the absence of these unprecedented race-based, federally mandated economic initiatives, the doors to the nation's mainstream American business community would have remained closed not only to black enterprise but also to other minority businesses, including those established by women. But the opening of Civil Rights also undermined many of those sole proprietorships that distinguished black business activity in the first three waves of the Rise of Black Corporate America. Such firms have found it increasingly difficult to survive in this new age of increasing transnationalization of global corporate enterprises.

In the new age of global capitalism, competitive incursions of multinationals have affected not only the profitability of black businesses in several industries, but also their survival as distinct race-based business entities.[4] On the other hand, the end of segregation has provided opportunities for black firms to form strategic alliances with White Corporate America, which has provided access to capital and markets. Yet, the fact that black business receipts overall are so abysmally low, compared not only with white American businesses but also with other minority businesses, raises questions about the persistence of race as it has shaped Black America at the end of the twentieth century. Race in the nation's economic life, moreover, has constrained not only black entrepreneurial opportunities but has also limited the advancement and salaries of blacks as employees in White Corporate America.

EMPLOYMENT RACISM IN WHITE CORPORATE AMERICA

Just as black business activity expanded in post Civil Rights America, black employment also expanded in White Corporate America beginning with Title VII of the 1964 Civil Rights Act. That Act (as amended) "prohibits employment discrimination on the basis of race, color, religion, sex, or national origin." In this respect, the federal government made a difference. Beginning in 1961, Executive Orders have also been important in promoting affirmative action race-based hiring in White Corporate America, including the following:

- *1961 Executive Order 10925*, issued by President John F. Kennedy, required all federal contractors to take "affirmative action to ensure that applicants are treated equally without regard to race, color, religion, sex, or national origin." It also created the Committee on Equal Employment Opportunity.
- *1965 Executive Order 11246*, issued by President Lyndon B. Johnson, required all government contractors and subcontractors to take affirmative action measures to eliminate discrimination in employment and expand job opportunities for minorities in their companies. The Office of Federal Contract Compliance (OFCC), now the Office of Federal Contract Compliance Program (OFCCP), was established in the Labor Department to administer the order.

Notwithstanding the increase in the numbers of blacks employed in White Corporate America, overall disparities in the percentages and salaries of blacks in upper management have persisted over the past thirty-six years. According to the March 2000 U.S. Census, there were 15,248,000 blacks over age sixteen in the labor force.[5] With the exception of some 718,000 blacks in the labor force employed in African-American-owned enterprises, the 1,631,000 employed in the Public Sector, federal, state, and local, and the 280,000 in the armed services, employed black Americans to work primarily in businesses owned and managed by whites.

Information on job patterns for minorities and women in private industry reveals continuing inequities, especially in management positions. (See Table 9.1, which provides information on the percentage of those employed as "Officals & Mangers" by race, ethnicity, and gender in 1999.) While 16.1 percent of white males are employed as managers, only 5.5 percent of black males hold those positions. The Equal Employment Oppurtunity (EEO) Report for the Year 2000 indicates that there was an increase in the percentages of all Americans employed in the occupational position as officials and managers in private industry, with the percentage of black men rising to 5.8 percent and of black women to 4.2 percent. Notwithstanding this increase, few hold executive positions. Data in the 1995 Federal Glass Ceiling Commission report (a survey of senior-level male managers in Fortune 500 companies and in the top 1,000 U.S. industrial firms) indicate that 97 percent of top executives were white males. In the overall distribution of managers in private industries for 1999, based on

Table 9.1. *Percentage of Occupational Employment Managers in Private Industry by Race/Ethnic Group/Sex, United States, 1999*

All industries (193,284 units)	
All employees	10.5
Male	13.3
Female	7.4
White	12.7
Male	16.1
Female	8.8
Minority	5.1
Black	4.7
Male	5.5
Female	3.9
Hispanic	4.6
Male	5.2
Female	3.7
Asian/Pacific islander	7.5
Male	9.5
Female	5.4
Amind/Alaskan native	7
Male	8.5
Female	5.3

Source: Extrapolated from U.S. Equal Employment Opportunity Commission, "Job Patterns for Minorities and Women in Private Industry," in the Equal Employment Opportunity Report 1 (EEO-1). Data obtained from the following: "public and private employers; private employers with 100 or more employees; federal contractors with 50 or more employees; and unions and labor organizations." The data collected were compiled from "nearly 40,000 employers with more than 51 million employees."

information from 193,284 business units, the figures were somewhat improved, although they are inclusive of managers at all levels.

It was not until 1987 – when Clifton R. Wharton, Jr., took the helm of Teachers Insurance and Annuity Association-College Retirement Equities Fund (TIAA-CREF), a position he held until 1992 – that an African-American became head of a Fortune 500 company.[6] As the decade progressed, three other blacks achieved the position of CEO at Fortune 500 companies: A. Barry Rand at Avis Group Holdings, Inc.; Franklin Raines at Fannie Mae; and Lloyd Ware at Maytag.[7] In April 1996, Ware joined Maytag as executive vice-president and president of Maytag Appliances. Moving rapidly up the corporate ladder, he was promoted to president and chief operating officer (COO) in February 1998 and was appointed Chairman and CEO in November 1999. Some fifteen months later, Ware resigned. As for A. Barry Rand, he was appointed Chairman and Chief Executive of Avis Rent A Car in November 1999, but almost fourteen months later, in January 2001, Rand resigned after the Cendant Corporation purchase of Avis. Despite his brief tenure as CEO, Rand reportedly received about $15.1 million in severance pay and other compensation in addition to the salary he was paid as he assumed a position as special adviser to Cendant's board and to its Chairman and CEO.[8]

Thus, of the four blacks who held CEO positions in White Corporate America in the 1990s, only one (Raines) still retained the position at the end of 2000. After two years of serving as director of the Office of Management Budget (OMB) at the White House, Raines assumed the position of CEO and chairman of Fannie Mae in January 1999, where he earlier had served as vice-chairman. It is ironic, then, that the one black "Fortune 500" CEO from the 1990s who survived his position into the year 2001 did so in a corporation defined by Congress as a "government-sponsored enterprise." Initially, Fannie Mae was the Federal National Mortgage Association. Consequently, Raines' advancement to the position of CEO, in contrast to the career trajectories of Rand and Ware, represents the rise of a high-level government employee in the federal bureaucracy.

In January 2001, Kenneth Chenault, Harvard JD and MBA, joined the ranks of African-American CEOs when he was appointed to the top office at American Express.[9] In the rarefied world of the Fortune 500, Chenault was joined by Richard Parsons, who in 2002 was appointed CEO of AOL-Time Warner. A member of the Time Warner Board of Directors since January 1991, Parsons was elected President of Time Warner Inc. on October 1, 1994. As Co-COO of AOL-Time Warner, Parsons was responsible for the company's film and music businesses, including Warner Brothers, Warner Music Group, and Time Warner Trade Publishing. Then, in 2002, Parsons was appointed CEO of AOL-Time Warner, Fortune's 37th ranked company, with 2001 revenues of more than $38 billion. An Albany School of Law graduate, Parsons in his early career worked as a lawyer and aide to New York governor and former Vice-President Nelson Rockefeller.[10] In April 1999, John W. Thompson was appointed President, CEO, and Chairman of Symantec, making him "the only African-American Silicon Valley CEO." Formerly, Thompson was IBM's highest-ranking executive.[11]

Stanley O' Neal broke the color bar on Wall Street when he was appointed President, COO, and Director of the U.S. Private Client Group at Merrill Lynch & Co., Inc., the nation's largest brokerage firm. He is scheduled to become the company's CEO in 2004.[12] A Harvard MBA, O'Neal (50) spent his early life in Georgia picking cotton and walking a mile to a one-room, log-burning schoolhouse before his family moved to Atlanta, where they lived in project housing until his father got a job at General Motors, where O'Neal also got his start.[13]

The end of the twentieth century, thus, marked the beginning of the rise of black senior-level managers in White Corporate America. At the beginning of the twenty-first century, there are an increasing number of blacks in other high-ranking positions, including CEOs, COO, CFOs, Presidents, and vice-presidents. According to the *Fortune* List of the "50 Most Powerful Black Executives," they hold high ranking positions in companies such as General Electric, General Mills, Oracle, Citigroup, Verizon, CNBC, Merck, Ford, Dell, IBM, and Xerox, and in leading private banking and asset management houses and insurance companies. Yet, as emphasized in the preface to the this list of high-ranking black executives, "This list of the 50 Most Powerful Black Executives in America can be seen as a celebration of what's been achieved by finally reaching the corner office – and an acknowledgment of how far there is still left to go."[14]

Black Americans make up 12.3 percent of the nation's population. One would expect, if all things were equal, to see at least fifty black CEOs in the Forbes 500 rather than the present three plus CEO designate McNeal. As emphasized in the 1995 Federal Glass Ceiling Commission report, "Despite the growing awareness among corporate leadership of the bottom-line value and economic imperative of including minorities and women in senior corporate management, progress has been disappointingly slow, and barriers persist that limit able people from achieving their full employment potential."[15]

Despite the growing percentage of blacks in senior-level management positions within White Corporate America, overall black economic life continues to lag behind that of whites. In 1997, 8.8 percent of black men and 1.7 percent of black women earned more than $50,000, compared with three decades earlier, when (in 1967) only 1.7 percent of black men and 0.6 percent of black women had comparable earnings (in inflation-adjusted dollars). Yet despite the rise in black earnings, in 1997 20.8 percent of white men and 6.7 percent of white women earned more than $50,000.[16] The racial earning disparities are also reflected in median household income, which for blacks was $25,351 in 1998, or only 60 percent of median white income. Overall, black household income has made comparatively little gain since the passage of the Brown decision in 1954, when it stood at 59 percent of white household income.

An even more glaring example of racial economic inequality is in wealth-holding. In 1995, the median black household had a net worth of $7,400, including home equity, some 12 percent of the $61,000 in median wealth for whites. Five years later, economist William Bradford projected that "It will take exactly 200 years for the median of black family wealth to reach half the median of white family wealth."[17] Still, the move to economic parity for black American workers was slowed by growing wealth disparities more broadly within American society at the close of the twentieth century, when the top 1 percent of American households held almost 40 percent of the nation's wealth, while the top 10 percent commanded two-thirds. Moreover, this group – the top 10 percent, which averaged $7.8 million in net worth per household – gained 62 percent of all wealth generated in the United States from 1992–98.[18] This group includes the leading black wealth-holders (see Table 9.5), including black executives in White Corporate America.

The advancement of blacks from managers in White Corporate America to business owners is neither new nor unique in the nation's business history. The second richest black in antebellum America was a former slave who purchased his freedom, described in the R. G. Dun Mercantile Credit Reports in 1857 as "king of the darkies, w. $100 m [thousand]." Smith was a lumber merchant who also owned railroad cars to transport his lumber and coal from Pennsylvania to several Atlantic states. He had earned the money to purchase his freedom by managing his slave owner's lumber yard. With the coming of the Civil War, Smith's wealth increased. By 1865, Dun records indicate that Smith was worth $500,000.[19] Even among the slave driver managers, a few held positions comparable to CEOs. Benjamin Montgomery, a slave, managed the large Mississippi plantations owned, ironically enough, by the family of the president of the Confederacy, Jefferson Davis and his brother Joseph, who refused to let the valuable slave purchase his freedom. The owner even began to train Montgomery's young son to manage the plantation. After the Civil War, Montgomery purchased two of the Davis plantations, which he co-managed with his wife, while a son and daughter, who was a bookkeeper, managed the business office of the plantations worth $300,000, according to the R. G. Dun Mercantile Credit Reporting Agency that described the family as "negroes, but negroes of unusual intelligence & extraordinary business qualifications."[20]

Nowhere is systemic racism more evident than in the increasing numbers of employment discrimination suits that escalated in the 1990s, a response not only to Title VII of the Civil Rights Act of 1964, but especially to the Civil Rights Act of 1991, which provides for monetary damages in cases of intentional discrimination and which clarifies provisions regarding disparate impact actions.[21] A review of Civil Rights Complaints in U.S. District Courts from 1990–8 showed that the number of cases pertaining to employment issues nearly tripled. As the report indicated, this growth was "largely due to the increase in employment cases between private parties."

In state courts, the number of civil rights complaints between private parties also more than doubled during the same period, from 16,310 to 38,835. Here, again, the increase was "due largely to the rise in employment cases between private parties which more than tripled from 6,936 in 1990 to 21,540 in 1998." A review of 311 civil trial cases in large counties in 1996 indicated that "The most common type of case was one in which an individual sued a corporation (62 percent) followed by those in which an individual sued a state or local government (22 percent)." The median award in state court for plaintiffs was $200,000, with 12 percent receiving $1 million or more.[22] Punitive damages were awarded in nearly one-third of the cases, another fact that underscores the extent to which racism has persisted in White Corporate America.

In 2000, Winn-Dixie Stores paid $33 million for racial discrimination; Shoney's paid $132.5 million; and Texaco, $176.1 million. The following year, Coca-Cola agreed to pay to end litigation brought in 1999 in a class-action suit by 2,200 current and past black employees, who worked in the company from April 22, 1995 to June 14, 2000. At $192.5 million, it was the largest monetary settlement in a race-based discrimination lawsuit in U.S. history. In the course of the litigation, plaintiffs provided numerous specific examples of race-based employment discrimination, and thereby hoped to prove that Coca-Cola tolerated a racially hostile workplace culture. Racial harassment and insults were pervasive, including disparaging remarks about the alleged inability of black employees to perform their jobs satisfactorily. The plaintiffs were given the worst assignments and only limited chances for promotion because of their race.[23] Several examples of the 127 specific race-based acts of discrimination African-Americans experienced at Coca-Cola and presented at the trial are listed in the Box. While specific to Coca-Cola, these charges are illustrative of race-based discrimination experience by blacks in White Corporate America in the post-Civil Rights Era of U.S. history.

Particularly egregious, according to the plaintiffs, was Coca-Cola's toleration of discrimination in promotions through such practices as not requiring the

---

Coca-Cola lawsuit: Employment race discrimination charges

32. "For example, in or about 1996 or 1997, one of the few African-American Assistant Vice Presidents attended a meeting in Atlanta with some representatives of the bottling companies. He was the only African-American at the meeting, but high-level Caucasian marketing executives from Coca-Cola were present. The head of marketing of the bottling company for the state of Alabama introduced himself as the "Grand Cyclops" of Alabama. Despite the obvious Ku Klux Klan reference, no Company employee responded to this outrageous comment at the Company meeting. This type of comment highlights the challenges facing African-American employees who are required to work with the bottlers on a regular basis, and who cannot penetrate the glass ceiling or overcome the glass walls because of the connections between these bottling companies and Coca-Cola."

35. "These discriminatory practices extend to Coca-Cola's relationships with ethnic marketing agencies. Upon information and belief, David Weldon, a Caucasian employee who was then the Vice-President of Advertising, told an African-American advertising agency in about 1997, words to the effect that '*I don't hire you to do good advertising, I hire you to do black advertising*' and '*it's not my fault you are black – it's yours.*'"

61. "Defendant even paid Orton less than Caucasian employees whom she supervised. Thus, Orton had to determine the salary increases for employees who already outpaced her in pay. In 1995, when Orton held a grade 12 position, she was making about $78,000 and one of the people she was supervising, Dave Williams, a Caucasian grade 11 employee, was making approximately $85,000. In 1996, she made $80,000 and Elizabeth Barry, a grade 12 Caucasian employee under her supervision, was making $86,000. Unlike Barry, Orton has a college degree. According to the 1996 salary guidelines, Orton's pay of $80,000 put her near the bottom of her pay grade."

87. "The five Caucasian managers Abdallah supports have made inappropriate demands. They have asked her and the other African-American administrative assistant to run personal errands and do personal chores. *They made Abdallah feel like their 'black maid.' Abdallah complained to her principal manager, who told her that he could not change grown people and their attitudes about race.*"

109. "When Ingram was placed on her new work team in 1995, she was the only African-American on the team. Her Caucasian manager, Elaine Arnold, refused to give her adequate work space for several months. *Ingram had a cubicle and no phone, while the Caucasian employees on the team had their own offices.*"

110. "In 1996, Arnold yelled at Ingram during a team meeting with every team member present, and also stated, upon information and belief, '*this is why you people don't get anywhere.*' Ingram initiated an EEO investigation and Arnold was terminated, apparently because of sexual harassment charges and other complaints and not because of Ingram's complaint. After Arnold was fired, other co-workers then revealed to Ingram that Arnold had referred to Ingram by racist and derogatory terms such as 'black bitch' behind her back."

Source: *Abdallah* et al. v. *The Coca-Cola Company*, Filed on: April 22, 1999, *U.S. District Court, Northern District of Georgia, Motisola Malikha Abdallah, Gregory Allen Clark, Linda Ingram, and Kimberly Gray Orton Individually and as Class Representatives, Plaintiffs*, v. *The Coca-Cola Company, Defendant.* Civil Action No. 1-98-CV-3679 (RWS) complaint – Class Action Amended Complaint at www.essentialaction.org/spotlight/coke/complaint.html.

posting of all positions and relying on "management nomination" in addition to subjective panel interviews, where evaluation scores were manipulated, often in favor of a preselected candidate for the announced position. The plaintiffs claimed that, as a result of these illegal practices, "African-Americans [were] denied the opportunity to advance to the same level and at the same rate as equally qualified Caucasian employees." They further asserted that these kinds of race-based disparities in employment practices affected the terms and conditions of their employment in several ways, including racial disparities in performance evaluations and in compensation, as evidenced by Coca-Cola's job grading system, which allowed for significant pay disparities. As a result of this discriminatory system, blacks faced both a "Glass Ceiling" (see Table 9.2) in salaries and promotions and "Glass Walls" (see Table 9.3) that "virtually segregate[ed] the Company into divisions where African-American leadership is acceptable, and divisions where it is not" (See also Table 9.4.)

In substantiating these charges, the plaintiffs presented evidence that showed that African-Americans in senior positions were concentrated primarily in the "less powerful and non-revenue-generating areas" of the company, primarily in Human Resources and Corporate Affairs. Indeed, more than 50 percent of Coca-Cola's African-American senior management staff in the corporate headquarters held various positions in Human Resources, whereas "high-level positions of significant influence in divisions such as Global Marketing, Finance, Information Systems and Technical Operations (purchasing

Table 9.2. *The "Glass Ceiling" at Coca-Cola – Percentage of African-Americans and Caucasians in selected pay grades*

	Caucasian (%)	African-American (%)
Corporate Office Total	77.4	15.7
Pay Grade 5	58	36.5
Administrative		
Pay Grade 11	85	7.8
Professional/managerial		
Pay Grade 14	87	4.4
Director level		
Pay Grade 15	95	1.5
Vice-President level		

Source: Abdallah et al. v. *The Coca-Cola Company,* Filed on: April 22, 1999, *United States District Court, Northern District of Georgia, Motisola Malikha Abdallah, Gregory Allen Clark, Linda Ingram, and Kimberly Gray Orton Individually and as Class Representatives, Plaintiffs,* v. *The Coca-Cola Company, Defendant.* Civil Action No. 1-98-CV-3679 (RWS) Complaint – Class Action Amended Complaint at www.essentialaction.org/spotlight/coke/exhibitB1.html.

and production-related activities) have virtually all Caucasian employees." See Tables 9.2 and 9.3.

The evidence presented by the plaintiffs in the Coca-Cola employment race discrimination suit underscores the extent to which blacks continued to suffer discrimination based on race in White Corporate America.[24] Ultimately, the plaintiffs claimed not only that they were penalized by this discriminatory race-based corporate culture – ongoing since at least April 22, 1995 – but that, despite their complaints, Coca-Cola failed to act to prevent and remedy the various acts of racial discrimination, and thus stood in violation of Section 1981 of Title VII of the 1964 Civil Rights Act. The Court found for the plaintiffs, supporting their claim that Coca-Cola's actions constituted a continuing violation of their civil right to fair employment.

In the $192.5 million settlement, Coke agreed to pay $113 million to its black employees, with the average employee receiving some $40,000. Another $43.5 million was allocated to boost the salaries of blacks so that they were comparable to those of whites, and $36 million was slotted for programs to monitor the company's employment practices. Also, Coca-Cola was held responsible for the $20 million of plaintiffs' legal fees. Even while the settlement was pending, Coca-Cola set up an Advisory Council to develop plans that would increase the company's diversity agenda with contracts to minority- and women-owned businesses amounting to roughly $800 million. Then, as a basis for the development of a variety of corporate diversity initiatives (including sending all of its American workers to diversity training), Coca-Cola indicated it would invest $1 billion for

Table 9.3. *The "Glass Walls" at Coca-Cola – senior management positions held by Caucasians vs. African-Americans*[a]

Division name	Caucasian	African-American
Corporate divisions with minimal or no representation of African-Americans in senior management positions		
Global Marketing	54	2
Information Systems	46	1
Office of the CFO	41	1
Product Integrity	42	0
Technical Operations	82	1
Corporate divisions with representation of African-Americans in senior management positions		
Corporate Affairs (PR)	16	3[b]
Human Resources	37	10

Source: Abdallah et al. v. *The Coca-Cola Company,* Filed on: April 22, 1999, *United States District Court, Northern District of Georgia, Motisola Malikha Abdallah, Gregory Allen Clark, Linda Ingram, and Kimberly Gray Orton Individually and as Class Representatives, Plaintiffs,* v. *The Coca-Cola Company, Defendant.* Civil Action No. 1-98-CV-3679 (RWS) Complaint – Class Action AMENDED COMPLAINT www.essentialaction.org/spotlight/coke/exhibitB2.html.

Percentage of African-Americans in senior management positions in *all corporate divisions:* 5.1%

Percentage of African-Americans in senior management positions in all corporate divisions *excluding Human Resources and Corporate Affairs:* 2.9%

[a] Corporate Office data as of late 1998 for all Director, Vice-President, and Assistant Vice-President positions regardless of pay grade, and all pay grade 13 and above positions regardless of job title. Data may be incomplete because race of individuals in a limited number of cases could not be identified.

[b] Two of these three individuals work in External Affairs (community relations) positions.

such training in addition to its commitment of $1.5 million in the Diversity Leadership Academy of Atlanta (DLAA), which provided a program to encourage the development and improvement of diversity-management skills of influential leaders in Atlanta, the corporate headquarters of Coca-Cola.

Yet, despite the high costs being paid by White Corporate America in responding to charges of racial discrimination in the workplace, according to the EEOC the number of these cases has increased. "During the decade of the 1990s, EEOC received a cumulative total of 47,175 such charges (6 percent of all charges filed), compared to a cumulative total of 9,757 racial harassment charges in the 1980s (1.5 percent of all charges filed)." In addition the EEOC reported that "Retaliation charges have also increased and now represent 25 percent of all charges (19,694) filed within FY 1999."[25] Neither the costs at the micro level of the firm nor the difficult-to-measure macro costs to society have put a stop to these practices.[26]

Table 9.4. *Coca-Cola Corporate Office Salary Disparities by race, 1995 and 1998*

Salary	African-American ($)	Caucasian ($)	Difference ($)
1995 Salary data for Corporate Office			
Mean	41,904	61,115	19,211
Median	34,038	55,020	20,982
75%	52,668	75,712	23,044
90%	71,431	99,545	28,114
95%	82,600	119,660	37,060
99%	114,950	187,500	72,550
1998 Salary data for Corporate Office			
Mean	45,215	72,045	26,830
Median	36,296	65,531	29,235
75%	55,903	91,207	35,304
90%	79,013	121,473	42,460
95%	97,401	144,910	47,509
99%	124,500	210,000	85,500

Source: *Abdallah* et al. v. *The Coca-Cola Company*, Filed on: April 22, 1999, *United States District Court, Northern District of Georgia, Motisola Malikha Abdallah, Gregory Allen Clark, Linda Ingram, and Kimberly Gray Orton Individually and as Class Representatives, Plaintiffs,* v. *The Coca-Cola Company, Defendant.* Civil Action No. 1-98-CV-3679 (RWS) Complaint – Class Action AMENDED COMPLAINT at www.essentialaction.org/spotlight/coke/exhibitE.html.

The first billion-dollar racial discrimination employment lawsuit was filed in January 2001 against Microsoft by seven current and former employees who claimed disparate treatment at the company based on race. They charged that they had been passed over for promotions, while positions were given to less-qualified whites.

As in the Coca-Cola case, the black employees at Microsoft claimed they were paid less than whites who worked in the same positions. Subsequently, the seven litigants moved to seek a $5 billion class-action suit to include other black Microsoft employees who had been subjected to demeaning acts of discrimination by white managers, including racial slurs. They charged that their complaints resulted in a range of hostile acts in retaliation, including dismissal from the company. Moreover, one plaintiff claimed that when he attempted to seek redress for discrimination, he was told by a high-ranking executive that "he didn't feel there was anything he [could] do."

In its defense, Microsoft claimed it had mandated "a zero-tolerance policy toward discrimination in the workplace." At the same time, the company acknowledged that "fostering diversity continues to be a challenge for the entire technology industry." A July 2000 report by a federal commission examining the technology workforce of Americans employed in science, engineering, and technology found that "African Americans make up just 3.2 percent of those in the same fields."[27] And, in this respect, according to a Microsoft spokesperson, the company "has donated more than $100 million to foster interest in technology among young women and minorities."

According to the plaintiffs' lead lawyer Willie E. Gary in 1999, "Microsoft employed 21,429 people, of whom 553, or about 2.6 percent, were African American." Gary also cited 1999 figures showing that of the firm's 5155 managers in 1999, 83 – or about 1.6 percent – were black. In the hi-tech industry more broadly, Microsoft's employment pattern of very few African-Americans at the upper-management levels differed little from those of other computer companies. In California's Silicon Valley, there were only "5 blacks, 1 Hispanic, 4 Asians and 25 women among the 379 corporate officers at 50 largest companies."[28] While the reality of the low numbers of blacks in technology can explain employment statistics at Microsoft, the racial climate that existed cannot be excluded as an important factor that limited the advancement of blacks at Microsoft. According to Gary, company management at Microsoft tolerated "a plantation-type mentality when it comes to treating African-American workers."

Ironically, there were significantly more black managers on plantations during the age of American slavery than there has been in the era of the New Economy. During slavery, 60–70 percent of the slave drivers – who were also specialists in both agronomy and the agricultural economics of cotton, sugar, and rice production – performed many managerial duties on large cotton, sugar, and rice plantations as they supervised the field labor of hundreds of slaves. Indeed, many such slave drivers were more qualified than the white overseers who "supervised" their work.[29] Of course, on the slave plantation there was little chance for mobility for the black driver as manager. But a comparable claim was made by a plaintiff in the Microsoft lawsuit – the assistant to a vice-president, who claimed that when she complained of the hostile work environment at Microsoft, a manager told her: "You will never get out of this cubicle." Another black employee claimed that a white person was recruited as a manager with the specific responsibility "to make sure that black workers were not stealing on their credit card accounts."[30]

In another instance of "plantation-type" attitudes and treatment experienced by black employees in the workplace, the EEOC negotiated a $200,000 settlement in a racial harassment and retaliation suit against the Louisiana-based Lakeside Toyota dealership.[31] The suit alleged that a former used car manager, a white person, subjected six black employees to a racially hostile work environment that included "repeated verbal harassment, racial slurs, physical threats, intimidation, and assaults with [baseball] bats."[32] While there are few examples of racial harassment in employment as flagrant as those expressed in the Toyota case, it underscores the fact that racial attitudes have changed little in some American workplaces. As EEOC Chairwoman Ida L. Castro observed: "This harassment at work sites includes egregious behavior which is reminiscent of the days of the civil rights movement."[33]

One of the most striking examples of this historical persistence of racism comes from the Texaco employment race discrimination lawsuit. In one upper-level management meeting on diversity in 1994, which was secretly taped, African-American workers at the company were referred to as "black jelly beans." Texaco maintained that racial discrimination was not tolerated at the company, but the tapes exposed the hollowness of these assertions. The revelations were especially damaging for Texaco because the meeting referred to above was held to authorize the destruction of documents subject to discovery in the lawsuit. The derisive comments on diversity in the workplace underscore the contemptuous racial attitudes held by white executives at Texaco not only toward blacks but also toward Jewish people. "This diversity thing . . ." noted one executive at the meeting. "You know how all the black jelly beans agree." . . . "That's funny. All the black jelly beans seemed to be stuck to the bottom of the bag . . ." . . . . "I'm still having trouble with Hanukkah, and I know I have Kwanza."[34]

Judicial remedies, despite successes in a few spectacular cases, seem to be limited by the structure and constraints inherent in the American legal system. A recent report has argued that in employment discrimination cases there is a "double standard" that favors the defendants. Many plaintiffs' victories are reversed on appeal.[35] Still, shifting demographics in an increasingly multicultural America perhaps will force changes in racial attitudes in employment patterns in White Corporate America. According to the Bureau of Labor Statistics, by 2008 women and people of color will represent approximately 70 percent of net new entrants into the workforce.[36] Indeed many corporations, at least on their face, are changing in their racial attitudes. And, increasingly it seems, contrary to several important court cases in higher education, such as *Hopewell* v. *Texas* (1996), which rejected race as a factor for school admission, White Corporate America is now recognizing the reality that a racially diverse workforce is the wave of the future. In the University of Michigan at Ann Arbor enrollment discrimination case, some twenty Fortune 500 corporations, including Microsoft and Texaco, filed *amicus curiae* briefs in which they claimed that

Managers and employees who graduated from institutions with diverse student bodies are better prepared to understand, learn from and collaborate with others from a variety of racial, ethnic and cultural backgrounds; demonstrate creative problem solving by integrating differing perspectives; exhibit the skills required for good teamwork; and demonstrate more effective responsiveness to the needs of all types of consumers. In their view, educating students from a wide variety of backgrounds captures America's best talents and fosters excellence.[37]

It appears that White Corporate America, with its strong bottom line considerations, is accepting that, in the twenty-first century, the nation's workforce will become increasingly diverse. Some corporations are responding to this new reality by encouraging the organization of its diverse workforce into, as the Ford Motor Company calls them, "Employer Resource Groups." In 2001, there were nine groups that reflected the new diversity of Ford's labor force, inclusive of differences in race, ethnicity, gender, and religion, including the Ford African

Ancestry Network; Ford Professional Women's Network; Ford Asian Indian Association; Middle Eastern Community at Ford; the Ford Gay, Lesbian, or Bisexual Employees; the Ford Hispanic Network Group; the Ford Chinese Association; the Ford Interfaith Network; and the Ford Parenting Network. Moreover, the percentage of black managers and officials at Ford was 10.1 percent in 2001.[38] This figure was more than double the 4.7 percent of African-Americans in private industry in 2000. Also, Ford's percentage of black managers and officials was almost twice that of Coca-Cola, where the percentage of African-Americans in senior management positions in all of Coca-Cola's corporate divisions was 5.5 percent (see Table 9.1).

Still, Coca-Cola, Texaco, and Microsoft do not stand alone in facing race-based discrimination complaints from their disgruntled black employees. In a 1998 article in *Fortune* that detailed black attitudes regarding race in White Corporate America, the responses by 750 blacks who participated in the survey to the following questions were:

1. What kind of job is corporate America doing in promoting blacks on an equitable basis?

    Excellent 1 percent; Good 18 percent; Fair 33 percent; Poor 40 percent.
2. Is workplace discrimination still common or rare?

    Common 81 percent; Rare 13 percent.
3. Are black and white employees of equal training and experience being paid equitably?

    No 76 percent; Yes 17 percent.[39]

On the other hand, White Corporate America is now confronted with reverse discrimination lawsuits by its white employees, who claim, as in the higher education lawsuits, that they are being treated unfairly in order to better position minorities. At the Ford Motor Company, a human resource manager who was passed over for promotion filed a lawsuit claiming that "he is the victim of a company-wide practice of reverse discrimination in order to achieve aggressive quotas for hiring and promoting women and minorities." Increased resentment by whites, who fear the loss of their historically privileged status, ascribed to them simply because of their race, remains an important factor that continues to exacerbate expressions of racial discrimination in the workplace in the new century.[40]

In the 1980s and 1990s, however, the race-based problems and limitations faced by blacks in White Corporate America inspired many to leave their firms. For many, employment in those companies served as a springboard for new business ventures developing the fourth wave Rise of Black Corporate America. Unable to crack the glass ceiling, many of the former black denizens of White Corporate America left to build their own enterprises. Some capitalized on the contacts and networks they had established while working in White Corporate America. In the late twentieth century, the leading African-American entrepreneurs also competed with whites in the mainstream American business community. Just as with the disparities in black salaries, however, the statistics on enterprises and their revenues are not encouraging for the black business in the twenty-first century.

BLACK BUSINESS: A SORRY PICTURE
OR A BRIGHT FUTURE?

One long-held hope for those who lament employment discrimination has been minority self-employment and business ownership. How have black-owned businesses been doing over the past decade? From 1992 to 1997, the number of African-American-owned firms increased some 25.7 percent, compared with the overall increase in American business firms of 6.8 percent. At the same time, however, black business receipts increased only 33 percent during this time, in contrast to the 40 percent increase for all American firms. Moreover, while African-American firms averaged $86,500 in receipts, the average for all American firms, excluding publicly held corporations, was $410,600. Still, nearly half (49 percent) of black firms had receipts of less than $10,000, and 23 percent had receipts of $10,000–25,000, while only 1 percent (8682) of black firms had receipts of more than $1 million.[41] Overall, then, 71 percent of African-American-owned firms had receipts of less than $25,000.

Black business performance also contrasts unfavorably with other minorities. The number of Hispanic-owned firms increased by 30.0 percent between 1992 and 1997. In 1997 there were 1.2 million Hispanic-owned firms and only 820,000 African-American-owned firms. Almost half of the black firms had receipts under $10,000, compared with 40 percent of Hispanic-owned firms and 28 percent of firms owned by Asians and Pacific Islanders. Nationally, 35 percent of all firms had receipts of less than $10,000. Consequently, despite substantial increases in the number of black businesses, their employees, and their revenues, those gains have not matched those of other minority-owned firms in the New Economy. As indicated in Table 9.5, there were 3,039,033 minority firms in the United States in 1997, with sales and receipts of $591 billion. The nation's 823,499 black firms, however, had receipts of only $71.2 billion. Yet, there were 1.2 million Hispanic firms with receipts of $186.2 billion, while receipts from the nation's 912,960 Asian and Pacific Islander firms totaled $306.9 billion. Moreover, American Indians and Alaska Natives, who numbered 2,475,956, owned 197,300 firms. This group comprised only 0.9 percent of the population but they owned 25 percent of the numbers of businesses owned by blacks and their business receipts of $34.3 billion represented almost half of that earned by African-American firms. (See Table 9.5.)

What accounts for the comparatively poor performance of African-American business? In part, the industry distribution of black business (see Fig. 9.1) as well as black consumer spending patterns account in part for the low business receipts

Table 9-5. *Minority-owned business enterprises, firms, receipts, employees, 1997*

Group	All firms		Firms with paid employees		Employees	Payroll ($1000)
	Firms (number)	Sales and receipts ($1,000)	Firms (number)	Sales and receipts ($1,000)		
Universe (All Firms)	20,821,935	18,553,243,047	5,295,152	17,907,940,321	103,359,815	2,936,492,940
Total minorities	3,039,033	591,259,123	615,222	516,979,920	4,514,699	95,528,782
Black	823,499	71,214,662	93,235	56,377,860	718,341	14,322,312
Hispanic	1,199,896	186,274,582	211,884	158,674,537	1,388,746	29,830,028
Cuban	125,273	26,492,208	30,203	23,873,193	176,428	4,162,640
Mexican, Mexican American, Chicano	472,033	73,706,753	90,755	62,270,808	695,372	13,014,996
Puerto Rican	69,658	7,461,069	10,976	5,814,069	61,509	1,496,894
Spaniard	57,160	16,922,913	12,590	15,263,807	76,338	2,045,675
Hispanic Latin American	287,314	40,997,923	42,916	34,798,421	238,612	5,862,668
Other Spanish/Hispanic/ Latino	188,458	20,693,715	24,445	16,654,239	140,487	3,247,154
American Indian and Alaska Native	197,300	34,343,907	33,277	29,226,260	298,661	6,624,235
Asian and Pacific Islander	912,960	306,932,982	289,999	278,294,345	2,203,079	46,179,519
Asian Indian	166,737	67,503,357	67,189	61,760,453	490,629	12,585,621
Chinese	252,577	106,196,794	90,582	98,233,262	691,757	12,944,824
Filipino	84,534	11,077,885	14,581	8,966,386	110,130	2,667,333

Table 9.5. (*cont.*)

| Group | All firms | | Firms with paid employees | | Employees | Payroll |
	Firms (number)	Sales and receipts ($1,000)	Firms (number)	Sales and receipts ($1,000)		($1000)
Japanese	85,538	43,741,051	23,309	41,294,865	262,223	7,106,692
Korean	135,571	45,936,497	50,076	40,745,504	333,649	5,789,472
Vietnamese	97,764	9,322,891	18,948	6,768,324	79,035	1,165,550
Other Asian	70,868	19,016,149	22,292	16,800,603	201,610	3,135,784
Hawaiian	15,544	2,250,153	2,023	1,956,793	20,698	497,950
Other Pacific Islander	3,826	1,888,205	1,000	1,768,155	13,349	286,293
Women	5,417,034	818,669,084	846,780	717,763,965	7,076,081	149,115,699

Source: The 1997 Surveys of Minority- and Women-Owned Business Enterprises Company Summary (Available for 1997 only) at U.S. Bureau of the Census www.census.gov/epcd/mwb97/group.htm.

earned by black enterprises. In many minority communities, businesses grow and expand in number by providing goods and services to members of their ethnic group. Before desegregation, this was true of black businesses as well. But in the post-Civil Rights era, with White Corporate America's competition for the black consumer dollar, it is no longer true. Specifically, black businesses no longer have a protected black consumer market, notwithstanding, for example, that in 1997 black consumer expenditures amounted to $391 billion. (See Table 9.6.) That year black businesses had receipts of $71.2 billion. As Table 9.6 indicates, a significant proportion of the black consumer dollar goes for goods and services in the following four categories: (1) household and related charges; (2) food; (3) cars and trucks; and (4) apparel products and services. In each of these sectors, black businesses have a minimal presence. In particular, whites control the financial sector that holds the mortgages of most black property owners and the rental property of places where blacks live, and consequently they take almost half of black consumer expenditure for housing. (See Table 9.6.)

In certain sectors black firms have been able to break out of these limitations, either by expanding their black consumer markets or by reaching more deeply into the general market. In 2000, according to *Black Enterprise* in its "B.E. 100s Sales By Industry" list, the leading 100 black auto dealers had sales of $8.728 billion. Total receipts of blacks in the auto industry amounted to $10.317 billion.[42] According to the National Association of Minority Automobile Dealers (NAMAD), founded in 1980, "the automotive industry generates revenue of over $1,000,000,000,000 (one trillion dollars)."[43] So while black businesses in the auto industry earned only one percent of the total revenues generated in the auto

Table 9.6. *Black American Consumer Expenditures (billions), 1996–2001*

Expenditures	Years					
	1996	1997	1998	1999	2000	2001
Household and related charges	96.5	104.8	114	117	128.1	130.7
Food	41.6	44.6	44.9	47.3	52.9	52.4
New and used cars and trucks	22	21	25.6	27.6	31.3	30.1
Apparel products services	21.2	25.2	20.5	21.2	24.7	22.3
Total (billions)	181.3	195.6	205	213.1	237	235.2
Total (billions)all expenditures	$367	$391	$441	$491	$543	$600

Source: Complied from Target Market News, Consumer Expenditure Data, "The Buying Power of Black America," from tables for the years 1996, 1997, 1998, 1999, 2000, 2001. See Target Market News at www. targetmarketnews.com/numbers/index.htm.

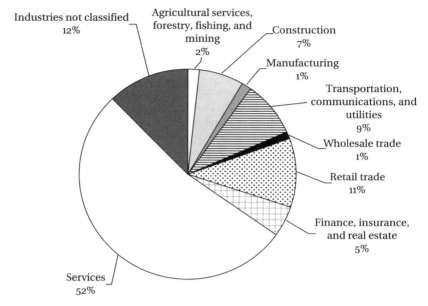

Fig. 9.1. Distribution of black-owned firms by industry division, 1997
Source: www.census.gov/csd/mwb/Blackp.htm.

industry, that percentage was significant for overall black business revenues. As shown in Table 9.6, black purchases of new and used vehicles ranked third in black consumer purchases. Overall, black expenditures for transportation in 2000 comprised 18.5 percent of total black consumer expenditures compared with 19.6 percent of white and other American consumers. (See Table 9.7.)

Higher salaries and better employment opportunities in the wake of Civil Rights increased black buying power for big ticket items like cars. In turn, black automobile dealerships have had a strong black market to serve as did other minority car dealers. According to the NAMAD: "In 1998 alone, minorities spent in excess of $60 billion dollars on new cars, used cars, and related purchases."[44] The impact of increased consumer power had reciprocal effects, increasing the number of black businesspeople acquiring new car auto franchises. In this instance, the positive role of the federal government is apparent as a factor that opened the doors to the auto franchise dealership sector for African-Americans. Especially important were federal government affirmative actions mandates in contracts and set-asides that required large corporations to give subcontracts to minorities. These also helped usher in the almost unprecedented participation of blacks in the auto parts manufacturing sector.

In the initial years of the federal government's affirmative action economic programs, their preeminent goal was to provide equal employment opportunities for blacks. At that time, assistance to black business was peripheral and indirect.[45] Title VI, "Federally Assisted Programs," of the 1964 Civil Rights Act

Table 9.7. *Transportation consumer expenditures by race, 2000*

	White and other	Black	Hispanic	Non-Hispanic
Income before taxes[a] ($)	46,260	32,657	34,891	45,669
Income after taxes[a] ($)	42,942	31,030	33,311	42,391
Transportation	19.6	18.5	20.5	19.4
Vehicle purchases (net outlay)	9.1	8.1	9.6	8.9
Cars and trucks, new	4.3	3.1	3.3	4.3
Cars and trucks, used	4.6	5.0	6.3	4.5
Other vehicles	0.1	_b	_b	0.1
Gasoline and motor oil	3.4	3.4	3.8	3.4
Other vehicle expenses	6.0	6.1	5.9	6.0
Vehicle finance charges	0.8	1.0	0.8	0.9
Maintenance and repairs	1.6	1.6	1.7	1.6
Vehicle insurance	2.0	2.3	2.1	2.0
Vehicle rental, leases, licenses, other charges	1.5	1.2	1.3	1.5
Public transportation	1.1	1.0	1.2	1.1

Source: Extrapolated and Compiled from U.S. Department of Labor, Bureau of Labor Statistics, "Table 51. Housing tenure, type of area, race of reference person, and Hispanic origin of reference person: Shares of average annual expenditures and sources of income, Consumer Expenditure Survey, 2000," at ftp://ftp.bls.gov/pub/special.requests/ce/share/2000/tenracar.txt.
[a] Components of income and taxes are derived from "complete income reporters" only.
[b] Value less than 0.05.

required that all federal agencies that provided financial assistance through grants, loans, or contracts eliminate discrimination in employment, whether of race, color, or national origin.[46] Consequently, the one specific agency in existence before the Civil Rights era that could provide monetary assistance to black businesspeople was the Small Business Administration (SBA). Established in 1953, the SBA did not become a permanent federal agency until 1958. Moreover, at the time of its founding and in the early 1960s, there was no specific attempt to reach out to black businesses. That took place in 1964, with President Lyndon Johnson's Economic Opportunity Act, which established the Office of Economic Opportunity (OEO). The OEO's specific charge was to provide loans through its Economic Opportunity Loan (EOL) Program as well as through technical assistance to inner city poverty area residents who applied to establish businesses.[47]

Unlike SBA loans to non-minority small business, EOL loans were targeted for blacks, with priority given to those with no business experience and no savings who wanted to establish small, marginal, high-risk "mom-and-pop" enterprises. The EOL program went into effect in 1965. Within a year, Congress gave full control of EOL to the SBA.[48] It would not be until the 1970s that this agency was restructured to provide support specifically to minorities with experience in business. In the interim – as America's involvement in Vietnam escalated and with black dissidence and civil disorders in American cities sharply on the rise – President Johnson took the position in his last year in office (1968) that the demands for black economic empowerment should not be limited to new employment opportunities. Perhaps also in response to Black Power demands that White Corporate America become actively involved in contributing to black business development, President Johnson established the National Alliance of Businessmen. One of the most recognized leaders of White Corporate America at that time, Henry Ford II, was appointed chairman of the NAB. Meanwhile, several major American corporations, including IBM, established factories in the urban ghetto, although by 1987, "of the 15 inner city factories built by major corporations in the mid-1960s, 9 had either been sold or closed."[49] Whether it was either national or international factors, or a combination of both, strident Black Power demands for black business expansion with the support of White Corporate America began to affect black business in very real ways by the end of the 1960s.

The federal government's Black Capitalism initiatives began with Nixon's 1969 Executive Order 11458, which established the Office of Minority Business Enterprise (subsequently renamed the Minority Business Development Agency). Also in 1971, President Nixon issued Executive Order 11625, which required that all federal agencies develop comprehensive plans and specific program goals for a national Minority Business Enterprise (MBE) contracting program. From that point on, a number of alphabet-named agencies were established to promote minority business, with the SBA specifically strengthened to provide federal support to encourage black business development. With the SBA 7(a) program, the federal government provided guarantees against defaults on bank loans made to minority businesses. Doubtless the most important provision in 1969 was the Minority Small Business/Capital Ownership Development Program, known generally as the SBA 8(a) federal government set-aside program. This legislation, drafted by black congressman Parren Mitchell, became the cornerstone of the federal government minority business policy initiatives. The SBA 8(a) set-aside program guarantees that a percentage of government contracts will go to minority businesses.[50]

Each federal agency was to establish an Office of Small and Disadvantaged Business Utilization with the mandate, found in Title IV of the 1964 Civil Rights Act, that all government agencies seek the fullest possible use of minority businesses in the agency's purchase of goods and services. In 1983, President Ronald Reagan issued Executive Order 12432, with its mandate that all federal agencies with substantial procurement or grant-making authority were required to develop a MBE development plan. As a result, minority owned businesses were positioned to secure a larger share of federal procurement contracts and subcontracts.[51] And as a result, black business finally began to capitalize on Industrial America through the automobile industry.

The federal government minority business programs became important in two ways. For the first time, blacks were able to participate in the heavy manufacturing sector of the nation's economy by establishing auto parts supply manufacturing companies. These programs also provided a basis for blacks to open new car auto dealerships and subsequently earn a substantial percentage of the top black business dollars. Until the 1970s, there were very few new black auto dealers. Also, blacks who were auto salesmen were prohibited from working on showroom floors of new car dealerships. And there were reports that some car dealers refused to sell new cars to blacks.

Civil Rights protest sensitized the auto industry to the rampant discrimination that existed in its sector of the nation's economy. At the end of the Second World War, there were about 50,000 new car dealerships. By 1977, there were 25,150.[52] The slump in the American car industry – specifically, its drastically declining profits – no doubt was an important factor that led the "Big Three" to consider opening up new car dealerships to blacks. Still, without federal government affirmative economic initiatives, one can only speculate as to whether or not White Corporate America in the auto industry would have taken steps to launch programs that would open the doors to blacks to acquire new car dealerships. Simply put, African-Americans faced very real barriers – most notably limited capital and lack of experience – in managing new dealerships. There was, however, a response from White Corporate America. Domestic car manufacturers began establishing minority dealership programs. General Motors was the first in 1971 and, in 1972, the first black to complete the program purchased a Cadillac dealership, "partially financed through General Motors, which he paid off in nine months." Ford and Chrysler subsequently developed structured programs that included placement of highly selected minorities in a training dealership. With successful completion of the program, assistance was provided in finding a dealership to purchase followed by Big Three financial support in purchasing a new car auto dealership.[53] But how successful were those programs, when one considers the rate of increase of black car dealers from 1980 to 1990? Their numbers were miniscule compared with the total number of car dealers. NAMAD's research found that from 1980 to 1990, the number of Ford's black dealerships increased from 19 to 248; Chrysler's, from 7 to 81; and GM's, from 63 to 103. But in 1990, there were "more than 10,000 GM dealerships, 5300 Ford franchises, and 5400 Chrysler outlets."[54]

The Big Three also launched Minority Supplier Development Programs (MSD) in which their First Tier suppliers were encouraged to purchase at least 5 percent of all goods and services from certified minority companies. Consequently, in the auto industry, White Corporate America's response to federal affirmative action initiatives, as well as the bottom line in seeking new profits, developed agendas that enabled black businesses in the auto industry to emerge as the strongest segment in revenues generated in Black Corporate America. Still, the downturn in the economy in the 1990s resulted in a decrease in the number of new car dealerships. In 1997, according to the National Automobile Dealers Association, there were only 22,700. This slump was also reflected in a decline in minority car dealers. At one time, NAMAD reported 584 members; but in 1997 "only about 350 of existing NAMAD dealerships are black-owned."[55]

The purchase of a car dealership runs into the millions. Even with Big Three financial support, invariably potential minority car dealers seek government support. But in doing so they must compete with other small businesses (defined by the SBA as any enterprise, regardless of race or ethnicity, with less than 500 employees). In this instance, SBA records on loan disbursements between 1990 and 2002 show that it "has made almost 2,800 loans to auto dealers, for a total of more than $860 millions. At least 425 of those loans – 15 percent, have gone to minority-owned dealers."[56] Interesting, since minorities now comprise more than 30 percent of the population, including Hispanics who indicated on the census that they are white. Racial competition has become a significant factor in determining the extent to which minorities have a "first claim" (based on membership in a historically discriminated group) to government funds and to federal, state, and local government procurement programs. In certain sectors, however, much of the expansion of black business was a result of federal government Black Capitalism policies and initiatives put in place in the 1970s.

Government set-aside programs, especially, helped blacks and other minorities by opening doors to capital and easing bonding requirements. But by the 1990s these policies were under challenge in state and federal courts. The 1989 Croson Supreme Court decision and subsequent 1995 Adarand decision, especially, made it harder for minority firms to secure contracts from state and local governments.[57] The Croson decision required that federal programs that seemingly advantaged minority owned businesses must show that the business owner had suffered past or current discrimination.[58] Consequently, the 1995 Adarand decision sought to replace race with "economic disadvantage" as the basis for awarding small business subcontracts under federal affirmative action laws. The government's use of race in identifying such disadvantaged individuals was held to violate the equal protection component of the Fifth Amendment's Due Process Clause. In 2001, the Supreme Court ruled race could be used only as a "last resort."[59]

Thus, in the Fourth Wave rise of black business, federal affirmative economic policies for minority businesses have been in retreat. This has not been the case in some instances with White Corporate America. The minority consumer market is just too big and, as the fastest growing market, with both positive and negative effects on black business. According to economist Samuel L. Myers, "Many major corporations – often faced with the enormous minority consumer power – continued to support business through set-aside programs they initiated voluntarily during the 1970s and 1980s." As Myers emphasized, "These efforts are untouched by the Croson and Adarand rulings and continue to thrive."[60] Firms in the auto industry are using the strategy of sharing profits with black businesses by expanding their purchases from black automobile suppliers in efforts to increase sales in the black consumer market.

On the other hand, in the closing decades of the twentieth century, white-owned firms in several industries launched an assault on companies in Black

Corporate America. In 1988, California-based MCA, Inc. purchased Motown Records. Founded by Berry Gordy in 1959, Motown was the first black-run company to make a major crossover in the consumer market. By the 1970s and 1980s, Motown had business receipts of more than $100 million, making it one of Black America's leading businesses, and its founder a millionaire. The Motown sound was represented by the Supremes, the Temptations, Smoky Robinson and the Miracles, Stevie Wonder, Gladys Knight and the Pips, James Brown, "Say It Loud, I'm Black and I'm Proud," and the Jackson Five (before Michael would subsequently launch a whole new industry with his spectacular music videos). And there was Marvin Gaye. Moreover, the music of these black artists revitalized the international record industry as whites – beginning with Elvis Presley and then the Beatles – rushed to imitate them, developing spin-off sounds that revolutionized white music, even Country, in the closing decades of the twentieth century.

The success of Motown, a 100 percent black founded, owned, and managed company, is significant in the Third Wave Rise of Black Corporate America for representing the first time that a black entrepreneur was able to profit substantially from the commodification of African-American culture. Its success can be attributed to Berry Gordy's management style and the corporate culture he systematically developed in growing his business. Before establishing Motown, Gordy had worked at Ford Motor Company, and in his record firm he proceeded from the Ford premise that "production could be efficiently organized and automated for the highest quality." To reach a crossover market, Motown's singers devoted careful attention to branding, packaging, and delivering its recordings in both American and international markets. The Motown Sound was so popular that its delivery expanded from radio to the first black teenage dance show on television, "Soul Train," launched locally in Chicago in 1970. The producer, Don Cornelius, also was African-American. As the show acquired a national audience, Cornelius in 1985 partnered with the Tribune Entertainment Company for syndication rights.[61]

Moreover, "Soul Train" marked the first time that a black company, Johnson Products, an ethnic hair care products manufacturer, became a sponsor of a television show. Johnson Products was one of the largest black businesses in the 1960s and 1970s. It was also the first black-owned company to be traded on the American Stock Exchange. Its success and that of other leading black hair care product manufacturing companies, including Soft Sheen and Pro-Line, however, marked the downfall of this industry, which proved to be unable to sustain the first systematic White Corporate America's assault on black business. By the 1980s, black hair care products manufacturers had combined sales approaching $1 billion. And it was also in the 1980s that the black hair care products industry was targeted for takeover by both American and multinational corporations in the health and beauty aids industry.

Indeed, a white executive from Revlon – a company that had also captured a large percentage of the black consumer market in hair care products and cosmetics – predicted the takeover back in 1986. "In the next couple of years," he observed, "the black-owned businesses will disappear. They'll all be sold to the white companies." Within only two years, white manufacturers had gained control of more than 50 percent of what was then a $1 billion plus market. By 1995, as sales in the black hair care products market approached $2 billion, the combined sales of the leading black manufacturers of these products amounted to only $203.7 million. Moreover, while only 1.5 percent of black disposable income was spent on personal care products and services, African-Americans, who represent 12.3 percent of the nation's population, made up 37 percent of the hair care product consumer market. In 1999 blacks spent $8 billion annually on these products including more than $4 billion in salons; but, by then, the three leading black hair care product manufacturers had combined sales of only $128 million.[62]

The black consumer market in the health and beauty aids industry was too profitable to be ignored. In the 1990s, within six years, the three leading black hair care product manufacturers fell, one by one. In 1993 Chicago-based Johnson Products was sold to the Netherlands-based IVAX Corporation; in 1998, Chicago-based Soft Sheen sold out to L'Oréal, the world's largest cosmetic company; and, in 1999, the Dallas-based Pro-Line company was sold to the Chicago-area industry giant Alberto Culver. Even then, there was hope that Black Corporate America would regain control of the market. In 1998 Carson Products, Inc. purchased Johnson Products from Ivax for $90 million. The Savannah, Georgia-based company, a black controlled firm that was publicly traded on both the New York and Johannesburg Stock Exchanges, was established in 1995. With its "Dark & Lovely" black hair products, Carson quickly became the nation's most successful manufacturer of black hair care products. But the company could not survive the debt incurred by its purchase of Johnson Products, and in 2000 Carson was bought out by L'Oréal USA. Carson's financial picture provided no alternative: "After trading for nearly $15 per share in 1996, Carson's stock price steadily slipped to about $3 in February as the company's long-term debt approached $133 million. L'Oréal made a $250 million offer to purchase Carson and merge the company into L'Oréal's Chicago-based Soft Sheen Products."[63]

With this transaction, L'Oréal gained control of three of the five top-selling black hair care brands, which included approximately 50 percent of the adult women's hair relaxer kits and 62 percent of the African-American hair coloring market.[64] Before the L'Oréal purchase could take place, the French-based company first had to satisfy antitrust regulations stipulated by the U.S. Department of Justice (DOJ). The DOJ, however, required only that L'Oréal divest itself of the Johnson products brand names.[65] Interestingly, L'Oréal's new Soft Sheen/Carson Ethnic division is headquartered in Chicago's ghettoized South Side black community. Both Soft Sheen and Johnson Products were located in that area before the two companies were sold. The necessity of black expertise was recognized by the white-owned companies that purchased these formerly black owned entities. Consequently, the CEOs hired to run the subsidiaries of these formerly black-founded companies are the children of the founders of Soft Sheen, Johnson Products, and the Pro-Line company.

Can the decline of the black hair care products industry be attributed solely to the assault on Black Corporate America by White Corporate America and its allied but competitive multinationals? Is it possible that, despite their success, the founder-CEOs of these companies lost the entrepreneurial drive, the innovativeness and risk-taking, and the human capital attributes that originally propelled the founding and growth of their companies? Or was their decision based on an economic reality that, with increasing white competition – not only from the leading multinationals but also from small white businesses in the industry – market share would be lost to the point where they would be unable to sustain their company's growth? With the sales of these companies, moreover, has the accumulation of wealth by black entrepreneurial families taken precedence over black nationalist economic interests, which encourage the development and expansion of black-owned businesses as a source of racial pride and emulation? Or, do the sales of large black-owned companies represent a new direction, a transition in black business growth and development that distinguishes the Fourth Wave Rise of Black Corporate America?

The sale of the Black Entertainment Television (BET) cable station to the communications giant Viacom represented a sound economic decision for Robert Johnson, who established the station in 1980. BET represented what was becoming a distinguishing feature of black business activity in the Fourth Wave Rise of Black Corporate America: many of the largest black businesses in their founding are no longer sole proprietorships. In the case of BET, Johnson held 65 percent ownership, contributing only $15,000 of his own money to establishing the station, "but was able to raise $10 million for his fledgling company by selling stakes to communications giants like Time Inc. and Taft Broadcasting."[66] Liberty Media, which put up $500,000, held 35 percent of BET. Subsequently, Johnson would give BET's president, Debra Lee, a 5 percent interest.

With the sale to Viacom for $3.1 billion, Johnson's cut of $1.63 billion represented one of the most profitable returns on an investment.[67] While continuing with the development of new enterprises, including his failed attempt to acquire an airline, Johnson now holds the position of CEO of BET, now a subsidiary of Viacom. Still, the sale of Viacom resulted in Johnson becoming America's first black billionaire. In 2000 ranking was featured on the cover of *Forbes'* annual issue of "The 400 Richest People in America", 172 with a net worth of 1.3 billion.[68] In 2001, still with $1.3 billion, Robert Johnson ranked as the 149th richest person in America. At the end of 2002 he became the first African-American majority owner in major American pro sports when the NBA granted him an expansion franchise in Charlotte, North Carolina.

The BET sale represented a loss not only to Black Corporate America in its efforts to expand and grow, but even more importantly, the loss of a telecommunications entity that in many ways epitomized and projected the voice and culture of Black America. BET's sale left only twenty-three African-American-owned television stations operating in the United States, and Granite

Broadcasting (ranked nineteenth on the B.E. 100) owned nine of those stations.[69] The BET sale to Viacom resulted in the loss of a major black-owned communications enterprise. Moreover, with the decline in black newspaper publishing, the voice of Black America increasingly has come under the control of White Corporate America.

Still, the impact of White Corporate America has had both negative and positive effects on black business. The upsurge in new forms of black business ownership and activity – pursued through joint ventures, mergers, acquisitions, strategic alliances, and equity partnerships – has provided greater access to both venture capital and development capital for the expansion of black enterprises that are surviving to compete in a global economy in the twenty-first century. The new direction of black entrepreneurship for the twenty-first century was pioneered by the business activities of Reginald Lewis (1942–93), the first black American to acquire majority interest in a multinational business with sales of more than $1 billion. Through a leveraged buy-out and with white investment capital, Lewis gained majority control of Beatrice International in 1987, and remained its CEO until his death. Within six years of his death, through divestiture and liquidation, Lewis's TLC Beatrice International Holdings no longer existed, but his surviving family was left extremely wealthy.[70]

At the end of the twentieth century, then, black Americans did not hold ownership in any enterprise with business receipts in the billions of dollars. Still, the Fourth Wave at the brink of the new century led to an increase in the number of black businesses with receipts in the hundreds of millions of dollars. Black entrepreneurs were beginning to approach billionaire status in their wealth holding. On the other hand, there have been the assaults by White Corporate America on black businesses that have contributed to the growing decline of several bedrock industries and enterprises of Black Corporate America.

A BRIGHT FUTURE?

The virtual decimation of the black America's bedrock industry – the black hair care products manufacturing sector, which had survived profitably in the first three stages in the rise of Black Corporate America – marked a transformation of black entrepreneurship in Black Corporate America to black intrapreneurship in White Corporate America. With the sale of these enterprises, former business owners are now working as employees, albeit executives, in the companies founded by their fathers. Robert Johnson, who founded BET, now reports to Mel Karmazin, President, COO, and Director of Viacom. But, perhaps, this transformation is simply business the American way. Simply put, with the BET sale Johnson's position at Viacom differs little from that of Ted Turner and other business owners who turn executives (although in the case of Turner and Johnson, both hold substantial shares in the companies where they now work).

On the other hand, in the Fourth Wave Rise of Black Corporate America, many of the most profitable companies have increased their profits and in some cases ensured their survival by pursuing forays in joint ventures, mergers, acquisitions, and strategic partnerships with White Corporate America and global multinationals. In the year 2000, three of the four largest black advertising companies merged with white companies in the industry. The New York-based UniWorld Group sold 49 percent of its company to the London-based WPP Group PLC, a leading multinational in the advertising industry, while the oldest black advertising firm, Chicago-based Burrell Communications Group LLC, merged with the France-based Publicis agency. Black advertising agencies opened the advertising world to the kind of profits that could be generated by ethnic product marketing not only to the black consumer market but also to the nation's mainstream markets. Only one top black advertising company withstood a merger, Chisholm-Mingo, which owed its survival to a federal contract for Census 2000.[71]

Black owners in the publishing industry have also had to face decisions of whether they should retain 100 percent black ownership. The privately held Essence Communications Inc., publisher of *Essence*, a magazine for black women, sold 49 percent of its company to Time, Inc. Again, the black consumer market precipitated the purchase. Don Logan, chairman and CEO of Time Inc., said that: "we expect that our relationship with Essence will facilitate the entry or expansion of other AOL Time Warner divisions into the African-American market. In addition, Time Inc.'s relationship with Essence will help us further expand our presence in the beauty and fashion advertising categories."[72] Consequently, unlike blacks in the hair care products industry, who could not survive the assault by White Corporate America, blacks in advertising and publishing acquiesced to mergers and joint ventures, while retaining a 51 percent ownership interest. When there appeared to be a take-off in the black consumer market, Black Corporate America found that it needed to share its profits with firms in White Corporate America and elsewhere.

Perhaps most representative of new black business ventures in the Fourth Wave Rise of Black Corporate America is the increasing numbers of enterprises established in hi-tech industries. World Wide Technology (WWT) was not only the leading black enterprise that capitalized on the hi-tech revolution, it was also the leading black business in 2000. The Missouri-based WWT, a distribution information technology products and services enterprise, was founded in 1990 with $812,000 in sales and seven employees. Sales increased slowly at first, but by 1998 WWT had sales of $202 million and 182 employees; by 2000, $812 million in sales and 516 employees.[73]

In several ways, WWT reflects the direction of black business in the New Economy as much as it also represents a prototype of Black Corporate America for the new century. First, in its founding, WWT was part of a joint venture between Stewart, who owed 85 percent, and James Kavanaugh (now CEO), who owned the other 15 percent. The company's growth was enhanced by the customer base developed by Stewart from his previous employment in White

Corporate America as well as from two preceding business ventures founded by him before he launched WWT. As CEO, Stewart expanded WWT strategic alliances with industry leaders, including Oracle, Lucent Technologies, Southwestern Bell, Netscape, Sun Microsystems, Dell, and IBM, supplying these Fortune 500 companies with computer hardware and software as well as telecommunications networks.

At the same time, however, the success of WWT in the high-tech and telecommunications industry reflects the continued importance of government contracts for black entrepreneurs. In both 1999 and 2000, *Washington Technology* magazine listed WWT as one of the top 100 federal prime contractors in IT. In 1999, WWT ranked 66 with contract revenues of $66.8 million and in 2000 ranked 41 with contract revenues of more than $128 million.[74] The success of WWT also reflects a continued response to changing market needs in an industry marked by rapid advances in the development of new technology. Over the years, WWT has launched several e-marketplaces in the commercial (wwt.com), government (fedbuy.com), and telecommunications (telcobuy.com) sectors.[75] In a 1999 company restructuring, WWT moved telcobuy.com from a division to a subsidiary, which now provides an on-line business-to-business marketplace for the telecommunications industry, whereby: "Its site includes more than 500,000 telecommunications infrastructure products and services representing some 3000 suppliers. Telcobuy also provides electronic procurement, technical consulting, and contract manufacturing, among other services." In the company's restructuring, telecobuy.com LLC had sales in 2001 of $604 million, with WWT sales at $320 million. The combined sales amounted to $924 million.[76]

The top-ranked African-American businessman is a Nigerian immigrant, Kase L. Lawal, the founder and CEO of Camac Holdings, an international oil exploration, refining, and trading company. In 2001 the company, with more than 1000 employees throughout the United States and Africa, had sales of $979.5 million. His holdings exemplify the expansion of black international business activities in the Fourth Wave Rise of Black Corporate America. CAMAC World Headquarters is located in Houston; CAMAC Holdings, Inc. is based in Washington, DC; CAMAC International Ltd/Allied Energy is located in the Cayman Islands; and CAMAC International (UK) Ltd. is operated out of London. The company also has offices in Lagos and Johannesburg, South Africa.[77] The company's organizational structure has been important for its success: "Spanning the globe with its projects, founder Lawal has guided Camac to success using the concept of vertical integration, combining services that might otherwise have been provided through subcontracts with other companies. The primary vehicle for CAMAC's success is a subsidiary, Allied Energy, which affords the company entrée into oil and gas producing properties both inland and outland."[78] In addition, "CAMAC's vertically integrated holdings are guiding its next major project, a $1.3 billion acquisition and relocation of process equipment from Blue Island Refinery, Illinois, USA." The refinery will be disassembled and then reassembled in South Africa.

While CAMAC is 100 percent owned by Lawal and members of his family, in the various phases of the company's development Lawal has formed strategic alliances with multinationals, including British Petroleum and Conoco: "Lawal describes CAMAC as being like Conoco but on a smaller scale." Lawal started his business in 1986 by trading in agricultural commodities and turned to oil in 1989. Some ten years later, "In 1999, CAMAC's revenues were $114.3 million. That number jumped to $571.5 million in 2000 and to $979.5 million in 2001. Lawal expects to break the $1 billion barrier in 2002 and is close already."[79] While Lawal studied Chemical Engineering at Georgia Tech, he holds a Bachelor of Science from Texas Southern University and a Masters of Business Administration in Finance and Marketing from Prairie View A&M University of Texas, both historically and predominantly black institutions of higher learning.

While education is the key to advancement for blacks, it seems that, for an African-American, an MBA from Harvard, Yale, Stanford, or Chicago does not always seem to be a requisite for one to succeed as an entrepreneur. Indeed, David L. Steward, born in Chicago and raised in Missouri, attended Central Missouri State University, where he earned a Bachelor of Science degree in Business Management in 1973.[80] The world-renowned talk show host Oprah Winfrey, the first black woman billionaire, attended Tennessee State University, a historically black college, but interrupted her education to pursue a career before earning her degree. In building her entertainment conglomerate over a period of sixteen years, Winfrey diversified with enterprises in the film, cable TV, and publishing industries, while building strategic alliances with White Corporate America.[81] Then, in 1998, Winfrey expanded her conglomerate by moving into cable-TV ownership, Oxygen Media, Inc. The cable station was co-founded in 1998 by Geraldine Laybourne (chairman and CEO and formerly with Nickelodeon and Disney), Oprah Winfrey (Harpo Entertainment), and the principals of TV production company Carsey–Werner–Mandabach.[82] In addition to Winfrey's Oxygen Media holdings, in 1999 her Harpo Entertainment Group reached a licensing agreement with Hearst Corporation to create a new magazine. In April 2000, O, The Oprah Magazine was launched. Since its initial publication, O has been one of the most successful periodicals in the country. It was reported that: "The debut issue of "O" sold out on newsstands with a distribution of 1.5 million copies, including an additional 500,000 copies printed for a second press run after the first distribution virtually sold out."[83]

The increasingly profitable commodification of African-American culture in the Entertainment Industry also is reflected in the financial success of leading black Hip Hop entrepreneurs Russell Simmons, Sean "Puff Daddy/P Diddy" Combs, and Master P (Percy Miller). Their expanding business activities, beyond the record industry, have marked one of the distinguishing aspects of the Fourth Wave Rise in Black Corporate America. Their success is significant because these young black entrepreneurs developed a whole new industry based on the African-American youth culture. And their initial success was derived from markets generated in Black America. That success was followed by the expansion into the mainstream American business community and the development of both national and international consumer markets.

The pioneer entrepreneur of the Hip Hop Industry and still the wealthiest is Russell Simmons. His entry in to the Entertainment Industry as rap producer began in 1984 as a joint venture with Rick Rubin, another record producer. They formed Def Jam Records, and subsequently CBS Records contracted to distribute their label. Def Jam's recording artists, such as L.L. Cool J and Run-DMC, reached the top of the music charts. In 1990, Simmons established Rush Communications. This firm produced the Def Jam record label, owned a management company (Rush Artist Management), a clothier (Phat Farm), and a movie production house (Def Pictures). It produced television shows – Def Comedy Jam, Russell Simmons' Oneworld Music Beat, and Russell Simmons Presents Def Poetry. It published a magazine (*Oneworld*) and ran an advertising agency, Rush Media Company, which is the largest black-owned music business in the United States.[84]

The commodification of African-American culture also is reflected in the sports industry, where black athletes with spectacular athletic abilities have become business entities in themselves. Ultimately, black athletes make money for White Corporate America. In 1997, Michael Jordan was said by *Fortune* magazine to have generated $10 billion for White Corporate America – including $5.2 billion for Nike from the Jordan Nike product line, $3.1 billion in sales of NBA-licensed sports products, sales from other products, and lucrative endorsements – all described by *Fortune* as the impact of the "Jordan effect" in generating sales.[85] At the same time, Jordan profited handsomely. Table 9.8 shows that Jordan was listed as one of *Fortune's* "America's 40 Richest Under 40" in 2001. The competitive bid for top black athletes and entertainers drove salaries higher, and in the 1990s they capitalized on their revenues to take command of their own business activities. No longer was the business side of these industries left solely to whites. In the 2002 *Fortune* listing of "America's 40 Richest Under 40," there were six blacks listed: three in the Sports Industry, Michael Jordan, Tiger Woods, and Shaquille O'Neal; and three in the Entertainment Industry, Hip Hop entrepreneurs Sean "P-Diddy" Combs, Master P, Percy Miller, and Will Smith, whose entry into the entertainment industry was as a Hip Hop artist, but who achieved even greater success in the movie industry.

The Hip Hop entrepreneurs command importance beyond their spectacular wealth accumulation. In creating a whole new industry, Russell Simmons, Sean Combs, and Percy Miller have expanded employment opportunities for young black people. So, in like manner, have an increasing number of superstar sports figures. While Earvin Magic Johnson has used his celebrity to advance his business interest, he has also provided employment opportunities for urban blacks. Johnson was ranked 33 in the *Fortune* List of the top 50 Black Executives. As CEO of the Johnson Development Corporation, according to *Fortune*, "The NBA Hall of Famer's ten-year-old, $500 million empire consists mostly of inner-city businesses: movie theaters, restaurants, shopping malls, athletic clubs."[86] Moving into movie production, Magic Johnson Enterprises released its

Table 9.8. *Fortune's "America's 40 Richest Under 40," 2001*

Rank	Name	Age	Company	Wealth
9	Michael Jordan	39	Washington Wizards	$408 million
11	Percy Miller (Master P)	33	No Limit	$293.8 million
12	Sean Combs (P Diddy)	32	Bad Boy Entertainment	$293.7 million
16	Tiger Woods	26	NA	$212 million
22	Shaquille O'Neal	30	Los Angeles Lakers	$171 million
39	Will Smith	33	NA	$113 million

Source: *Fortune's* "America's 40 richest under 40," September 16, 2002, and www. fortune.com/lists/40under40/index.html.

first feature film in 2002, *Brown Sugar*. In addition to being vice-president and co-owner of the world champion Los Angeles Lakers, Johnson's California-based company includes the Johnson Development Corp (JDC), Magic Johnson Theatres, Magic Johnson Productions, and Magic Johnson Music.

At the same time, Magic Johnson's joint ventures and strategic alliances include those with Sony Entertainment, T.G.I Fridays, and Loews Cinema in addition to his Starbucks franchises. Johnson owns 37 of Starbucks' 5,900 franchises. In a February 1998 joint venture, Starbucks and JDC formed Urban Coffee Opportunities, LLC (UCO) to enhance the development of Starbucks retail stores in ethnically diverse neighborhoods across the country. Also in 1998, Johnson partnered with Janet Jackson and Jheryl Busby, formerly of Motown, as JJB Partnership and with $2.5 million acquired a majority interest in Founders National Bank in South Central and East Los Angeles. In 2001, Johnson heading an investment group purchased Fatburger Corporation, a hamburger chain based primarily in the West.[87]

The ability of wealthy blacks to engage in this sort of business entrepreneurship has helped to shift the relationship between White Corporate America and black consumers and workers. White firms have largely seen the black community as a target for sales, rather than for investment. More recently, supermarkets, branch banks, and discount retailers have made significant investments in predominately black communities. The first Black Investment bank to go public (NASDAQ:CMAN) was also the first to respond to the increasing ethnic diversity in America by developing its trademark index, called Domestic Emerging Markets (DEM), which evaluates publicly traded companies listed on nationally recognized exchanges that are controlled by African-Americans, Asian

Americans, Latin/Hispanic Americans, Native Americans, and women. According to its founder Nathan A. Chapman, DEM companies represent a rapidly growing demographic segment of the United States population, but one that has been starved of capital. "Collectively", they [Domestic Emerging Markets (DEM) companies], "have grown faster than the major indices which benchmark foreign investments and domestic investments."[88]

Recognition of the profits that can be made in tapping minority consumer markets is also reflected in the success of joint ventures made by black businessmen with White Corporate America, such as the successes made by Magic Johnson in establishing enterprises in underserved black communities. Radio One, founded by Cathy Hughes, the first black woman entrepreneur to take her enterprise public (NASDAQ: ROIA), has followed this strategy of marketing to the Black Community. With more than sixty radio stations, she has also expanded in the communications industry through an investment in New Urban Entertainment Television (NUE-TV), an African-American-oriented cable TV company.[89] At the same time, black businesses are forging a growing number of joint ventures and strategic alliances with other minority businesses. In 1998, six minority companies in the auto supply manufacturing industry formed Global Automotive Alliance LLC.[90] In 2000 *Black Enterprise* reported that Global Alliance had sales of $260 million and was ranked ninth in its list of the top 100 black businesses. These examples, however, also indicate that the ability of black firms to survive on their own is under question. As *Black Enterprise* magazine has emphasized, the general movement toward deregulation in the 1980s and 1990s left many black-owned firms with the choice of "merge-or-be-purged."[91]

When under assault by White Corporate America and its multinational allies, the choice for Black Corporate America too often is accept defeat and sell out, as did the leading black hair care products manufacturers. Other options are to negotiate deals with White Corporate America, as did Magic Johnson; or to form partnerships and strategic alliances with other minority business, such as Global Automotive Alliance. In 1999, Michigan-based Don Coleman Advertising, Inc. (DCA) merged with True North Communications, with Coleman retaining 51 percent ownership. In doing so, he moved to expand his activities in the industry by establishing a multicultural advertising holding company, New American Strategies Group (NASG), which included a San Antonio-based Hispanic firm, Montemayor & Associates, and plans to include an Asian agency.

In many ways the American auto industry serves as one of the best examples of industries in which White Corporate America has involved itself with black business activities through joint ventures, mergers, and strategic partnerships – nationally as well as internationally. In the first venture of its kind for a black enterprise, Barden International (BI), a subsidiary of the Detroit-based Barden Companies (1981), copartnered with General Motors to secure a contract to retrofit GM cars in Namibia (Southern Africa) from left-hand to right-hand drive. In 1995 Don Barden sold his Detroit-based Barden Cablevision, which he had founded for $100 million, and soon began construction of a $15 million plant in Windhoek, the capital of Namibia, which was completed two years later. In addition to its manufacturing activities, BI established a fleet GM car and truck distributorship and a retail dealership for GM Chevrolets and Cadillacs. This venture was the result of a tripartite business arrangement that BI negotiated with GM and the Namibian government, in which the latter agreed to purchase $31 million worth of GM vehicles, while BI assumed the risk of competing against Toyota, which dominated the Namibian market. More than anything, the deal was forged because Barden had inspired the confidence of Namibian president Sam Nujoma and GM. By 2000, the Barden Companies, which now included casino gaming and real estate development, boasted sales of $136.4 million. This firm, too, exemplifies the increasing diversification in business interests by black entrepreneurs in the Fourth Wave Rise of Black Corporate America.[92]

Consequently, it appears that the more successful black-owned businesses are either reaching into the mainstream American consumer market or forming joint ventures or strategic alliances with White Corporate America. It seems ironic that in the initial stage of the Fourth Wave Rise of Black Corporate America, the bedrock industry of White Corporate America in the Industrial Age, the auto industry, had contributed significantly to the strongest segment of Black Corporate America at the dawn of the new millennium.

CONCLUSION

Yet, despite successes of the leading black entrepreneurs in business, the overall economic position of blacks vis-à-vis white American business remains relatively unchanged. Specifically, black business activity in the late twentieth century has not shown the rapid advances of other minority firms, especially in the 1990s. There always have been a few successful black businesspeople, even during the age of slavery.[93] This remains true today as well. In the "Black Fortune 100 List," published in the 2002 *Black Fortune Magazine*, BET founder Robert Johnson ranked first at $1.45 billion; Oprah Winfrey, Harpo, Inc., second, at $940 million; John Johnson, Johnson Publishing (*Ebony* and Fashion Fair), third, at $520 million; the Reginald Lewis family, inheritance from the sale of TLC Beatrice International, fourth, at $430 million; with fifth-ranked Catherine Hughes of Radio One, $420 million. In the "*Black Fortune* 100 List," published for 2003, Robert Johnson ranked first at $1.5 billion followed by Oprah Winfrey, $1 billon; John H. Johnson, $600 million; Bill Cosby, $540 million; and Bruce Llewellyn, Philadelphia Coca Cola, at $530 million.[94]

Surely, the economic status of Black America should not be measured by the success of a small handful of prominent black entrepreneurs, any more than the small handful of successful antebellum black entrepreneurs should be the measure of black business success during the age of slavery. Rather, the overall continuity of the abysmal picture of black business and the racial inequities in black wealth holding that have persisted into the twenty-first century should be the basis of measure. The bottom line is that, at the end of the twentieth century, total black business receipts amounted to only 0.4 percent of all American business receipts.

Moreover, notwithstanding increases in the numbers of blacks employed in White Corporate America, disparities in the numbers, percentages, and salaries of blacks in upper management persist, compared with whites. So while political, societal, and cultural changes in American life, brought about by the end of constitutionally sanctioned segregation, were important in opening economic doors for black Americans, racial discrimination in employment in White Corporate America has not ended. Despite Title VII of the 1964 Civil Rights Act (amended in 1991), race-based iniquities, especially in salaries and advancement, have continued to define the employment experiences of blacks in White Corporate America. Even at the end of the twentieth century, race continued to play an important part in the economic life of Black America.

What explains this disparity? In the business arena, one answer was provided over 200 years ago by a visitor to the new American states, who observed in 1788, "those Negroes who keep shops live moderately, and never augment their business beyond a certain point. The reason is obvious: the whites . . . like not to give them credit to enable them to undertake any extensive commerce nor even to give to them the means of a common education by receiving them into their counting houses."[95] That assessment has not changed much in the more than two centuries since. Today, most black businesses remain too small to access the main credit and capital lending institutions of the financial system.

As for the continued existence of race-based inequities in the workplace of White Corporate America, Alexis de Tocqueville, in his classic *Democracy in America*, observed based on his travels in this nation in the 1830s, that "In the United States the prejudice rejecting the Negroes seems to increase in proportion to their emancipation, and inequality cuts deep into mores as it is effaced from the laws." Backlash against modest black employment and business success would seem to bear out de Tocqueville. But as the observant Frenchman also noted, "Once one admits that whites and emancipated Negroes face each other like two foreign peoples on the same soil, it can easily be understood that there are only two possibilities for the future: the Negroes and the whites must either mingle completely or they must part." African-Americans are not going anywhere. Despite evidence of persistent racial prejudice, blacks and whites are mingling together, in the workplace, in educational institutions, in business partnerships, and even at the highest levels of government.

Then, too, perhaps the post-Civil Rights era in the late twentieth century represents the take-off point for an unprecedented rise in black business on a large scale. Black business activities in the 1990s produced in the twenty-first century, for the first time, two black billionaires. And for the first time, there were four blacks running Fortune 500 companies. In addition, African-Americans held powerful executive positions in White Corporate America. By 2003 it seems likely that two firms started black by entrepreneurs, one an African-American, the other an African immigrant, will achieve sales above one billion dollars. So while the twentieth century ended with anger, resentment, and rage, black Americans continued to subscribe to the American Dream of economic opportunity and equality.

In the face of the Civil Rights and Black Power protests of the 1960s, the federal government responded with affirmative action legislation to redress historic racial inequities in both the workplace and the marketplace. Yet at the close of the twentieth century and into the first decade of the twenty-first, there still are appalling examples of racial discrimination in employment, higher education, and government contracts. Meanwhile, critics of affirmative action programs have found a sympathetic Supreme Court, which has undermined the few programs that were enacted to redress the long history of racial inequality in the economy, education, and politics.[96] The biggest disappointment for black business has been in the receding role of government.

Americans tend to assume that affirmative action programs that benefit struggling black businesses and encourage more equal opportunity for blacks in employment are somehow extraordinary or blatantly unfair. But many ignore the ways in which government activities at all levels can shape the fortunes of many firms. Throughout most of American history and even today, the majority of government contracts go to white firms. Yet governments, like private capital, reflect the biases, prejudices, and interests of the powerful. As Abraham Lincoln said in 1854, before he became president: "The legitimate object of government is to do for a community of people whatever they need to have done, but cannot do at all, or cannot do so well in their separate and individual capacities." Despite the fervent anti-government rhetoric of many white businesspeople, government has assisted firms in multiple ways throughout American history. Not surprisingly, far less of this assistance has come the way of African-Americans.

Does the growth of black-owned corporations in the Fourth Wave rise of Black Corporate America signal expanded participation of people of African descent in the global economy? Or will the twenty-first century see the same sort of takeover and dominance of the most successful and profitable black firms by White Corporate America? Can black entrepreneurs participate in the mainstream of American business life through mergers and strategic alliances? Or does the sale of large black businesses that produce for the black consumer market represent a more troubling trend, one in which successful black businesses serve as incubators for competitive businesses in White Corporate America? Will there be a new black CEO added to the lists of the Fortune 500 every year? Will there be parity in salaries and advancement for blacks in employment in White Corporate America? Will black wealth holding approach that of whites, even in the twenty-first century? Historically, White Corporate America has been the arbiter of race, economics, and politics. Now, in the twenty-first century, can White Corporate America move to make the kinds of structural changes necessary to eliminate racism in the workplace, in capital markets, and at the highest levels of corporate management? In the face of increasing challenges to affirmative action policies, can the federal government partner with white-owned business to ensure blacks access to equity participation in all arenas of the nation's economic life? Capitalism thrives on profits and, increasingly, where blacks have been given the opportunity to demonstrate their profit-making capabilities, profits are taking precedence over prejudices. Ultimately, as Arthur Fletcher observed, "legislation alone is not enough to keep affirmative action alive . . . I need corporate America to do what it alleges it can do – make it work."[97]

NOTES

1. W. E. B. Du Bois, *The Souls of Black Folk* (Chicago: A.C. McClurg, 1903); with introd. by Donald R. Gibson (New York: Penguin Books, 1989). Du Bois first made this statement in London in 1900, restating it many times. See *Collier's Weekly*, 20 Oct. 1906, 30, when he said, "Many smile incredulously at such a proposition, but let us see."

2. This is hardly a new phenomenon. Early industries that promoted the nation's economic growth included Colonial American-owned slave trading vessels, slave plantation agribusinesses, along with commodity brokers and bankers that financed the production, sale, and market distribution of slave-produced commodities on international markets. For more than two centuries in the nation's agricultural-based economy, slave labor under the control of America's plantation giants fueled economic growth. These profits were shared by only a small number, and always at the bottom of this great chain of wealth accumulation were African-Americans. For the microeconomic view of White Corporate America, see Thomas K. McCraw (ed.), *Creating Modern Capitalism: How Entrepreneurs, Companies, and Countries Triumphed in Three Industrial Revolutions* (Cambridge, MA: Harvard University Press, 1997); Alfred D. Chandler, Thomas K. McCraw, and Richard S. Tedlow, *Management Past and Present: A Casebook on the History of American Business* (Cincinnati: South-Western, 1996); and Alfred D. Chandler, Jr., *The Visible Hand: The Managerial Revolution in American Business* (Cambridge, MA: Harvard University Press, 1977).

3. Juliet E. K. Walker, *The History of Black Business in America: Capitalism, Race, Entrepreneurship* (New York/London: Macmillan/Prentice Hall International, 1998), In this chapter, black business will include not only firms with 51–100 percent black ownership, but also those enterprises held by blacks as equal partners in joint ventures or strategic alliances.

4. Juliet E. K. Walker, "The Future of Black Business: Can It Get Out of the Box," in Lee A. Daniels (ed.), *State of Black America 2000 Report* (New York: National Urban League, 2000), 199–226; also Bash Ebor (ed.), *Cyber ghetto or Cypertopia?: Race, Class and Gender on the Internet* (Westport, CT: Praeger Publishers, 1998).

5. Information on "Job Patterns For Minorities And Women In Private Industry by race/ethnic group/sex," respectively, by numbers and percentages is provided in tables 1 and 2, from the Equal Employment Opportunity Report 1 (EEO-1), from data obtained from the following: public and private employers; private employers with 100 or more employees; federal contractors with fifty or more employees; and unions

and labor organizations. The data collected were compiled from "nearly 40,000 employers with more than 51 million employees." Table 1 provides information on the number employed in nine occupational categories.

6. Infra, "Blacks in White Corporate America," 340–5; also Lynn Norment, "Twelve Most Powerful Blacks in Corporate America," *Ebony* (Jan. 1998).

7. Lynn Norment, "New Faces in Executive Suites," *Ebony* (Jan. 2000), 42–8.

8. Stephanie Ernst, "African-American Maytag CEO Resigns," at DiversityInc.com, Nov. 10, 2000; and Carol Stavraka, "Avis CEO Resigns, Leaving Only Two Black CEOs Among Fortune 500," at diversityinc.com, Jan. 4, 2001.

9. Nelson Schwartz, "What's in the Cards for Amex," *Fortune* (Jan. 22, 2001), 58–70; and Tony Chappelle, "The Wealthiest African-Americans Surge into the Capital Markets," *Black MBA Magazine, Conference 2000 Issue* (Sep. 2000); also, Caroline V. Clarke, *Take a Lesson: Today's Black Achievers on How They Made It & What They Learned Along the Way* (New York: John Wiley & Sons, 2001), on Kenneth Chenault and A. Barry Rand; also see "The Top 50 African-Americans in Corporate America," *Black Enterprise* (Feb. 2000); also Richard W. Stevenson, "Moving from Big Money to Power," *New York Times* (Apr. 13, 1996), 8; Judith H. Dobrzynksi, "Way Beyond the Glass Ceiling," *New York Times* (May 11, 1995), D1; Saul Hansell, "American Express Names Apparent Successor to chief," *New York Times* (Feb. 28, 1997), B2.

10. See AOLTime Warner, Inc., 2001, "Executive Biography, Richard D. Parsons," at www.hoovers.com/officer/bio. Mr. Parsons was a key participant in driving Time Warner's growth, working closely with Chairman and CEO Gerald M. Levin and Vice Chairman Ted Turner on strategic, financial, and operational initiatives. Before joining Time Warner, Parsons was Chairman and Chief Executive Officer of Dime Bancorp, Inc., and managing partner of the New York law firm Patterson, Belknap, Webb & Tyler.

11. See "Symantec Corporation, Executive Biography: John W. Thompson, Chairman, President, and CEO," at Hoover's Online, www.hoovers.com/officers/bio notes. "Since joining Symantec in April 1999, Thompson has led the transformation of the company from a software publisher to a leader in Internet security solutions for individuals and enterprises. Symantec offers a broad range of Internet security solutions for virus protection, risk management, Internet content and email filtering, remote management and mobile code technology. Under Thompson's leadership, the company has defined a new category of Internet security software for consumers and made a number of strategic acquisitions to enhance its ability to serve the rapidly changing needs of large global enterprises for better security solutions." Also, "Symantec Names Thompson as President, CEO and Chairman," at Diversity.com/insidearticlepg.cfm.

12. Joseph P. Blake, "New Merrill Lynch President Took the Road Less Traveled," at Diversity.com/insidearticlepg.cfm; also, "O'Neal Breaks the Mould in a White Man's World," *Financial Times* (July 25, 2001); also, Robyn D. Clarke, "Running With the Bulls," *Black Enterprise* (Sep. 2000), 82–4, 86, 88, and 90; and "The Top 50 African-Americans in Corporate America," *Black Enterprise* (Feb. 2000). Also, Chappelle, "The Wealthiest African-Americans," provides a list of fourteen African-Americans, including Thompson, Raines, Ware, Parsons, and Chenault, who by Sep. 2000 held CEO or COO positions in White Corporate America's publicly traded companies.

13. Johnnie L. Roberts, "The Race To The Top," *Newsweek*, Jan. 28, 2002 44–9, on Parsons, Chenault, and O'Neal. Also, Derek T. Dingle and Alan Hughes, "A Time for Bold Leadership," *Black Enterprise* (Feb. 2002), 76–8 and 80–2 on Parsons.

14. See *Fortune*, "50 Most Powerful Black Executives in America," June 22, 2002; and at www.fortune.com/lists/blackpower/index.html. Included in the list were five blacks who held the rank of Chairman, CEO, and Publisher of the companies they founded in addition to Robert Johnson who founded BET and remains as CEO of this entity now owned by Viacom. Also, eleven of those listed are women, including two who founded their own companies, Oprah Winfrey and Cathy Hughes of Radio One.

15. Ulwyn L. J. Pierre, *The Myth of Black Corporate Mobility* (New York: Garland Publishers, 1998); also, David A. Thomas and John J. Gabarro, *Breaking Through: The Making of Minority Executives in Corporate America* (Boston: Harvard Business School Press, 1999); Sharon Collins, *Black Corporate Executives: The Making and Breaking of a Black Middle Class* (Philadelphia: Temple University Press, 1997); William R. Spivey, *Corporate America: Black and White* (New York: Carlton Press, 1993); and Sharon Collins, "Corporate America, Black Managers," in Juliet E. K. Walker (ed.), *Encyclopedia of African-American Business History* (Westport, CT: Greenwood Press, 1999); also, William A. Darity, "Underclass and Overclass: Race, Class, and Economic Inequality in the Managerial Age," in Emily P. Hoffman (ed.), *Essays on the Economics of Discrimination* (Kalamazoo, MI: W. E. Upjohn Institute for Employment Research, 1991), 67–84.

16. The data is from U.S. Bureau of the Census, 1998, "Money Income in the United States, 1997," P-60, No. 200: table B-5. For whites, 20.8 percent of all men and 6.7 percent of women earned over $50,000.

17. William D. Bradford, "Black Family Wealth in the United States," *State of Black America 2000 Report*, 116.

18. Lawrence Mishel, Jared Bernstein, and John Schmitt, *The State of Working America: 1998–9* (New York: Cornell University Press, 1999), 255–60; also, Melvin L. Oliver and Thomas Shapiro, *Black Wealth/White Wealth: A New Perspective on Racial Inequality* (New York: Routledge, 1995); William A. Darity, Jr. and Samuel L. Myers, Jr., *Persistent Disparity: Race and Economic Inequality Since 1945* (New York: Edward Elgar, 1998); also, Marcellus Andrews, *The Political Economy of Hope and Fear: Capitalism and the Black Condition in America* (New York: New York University Press, 1999).

19. See "Table 4-2 Dun Mercantile Credit Reports on Smith, Whipper and Vidal, 1853–1877," Walker, *History of Black Business in America*, 89. Whipper and Vidal were taken in by Smith as partners. In 1853, Dun notes that Whipper was worth $20,000. Vidal, Smith's son-in-law, was described by Dun in 1865 as "an educated darkey of considerable pride of char." At that time, Dun reports that Vidal was worth $30,000–50,000.

20. Walker, *History of Black Business in America*, 64–5, 157; and R. G. Dun and Company, Mississippi, 21: 81E, 82; R. G. Dun and Company Collection, Baker Library, Harvard University Business School.

21. See "Federal Laws Prohibiting Job Discrimination," Equal Employment Opportunity Commission at www.eeoc.gov/facts; also Alfred W. Blumrosen, *Black Employment and the Law* (New Brunswick, NJ: Rutgers University Press, 1971); Hugh Davis Graham, *The Civil Rights Era: Origins and Development of National Policy* (New York: Oxford University Press, 1990); Roger Clegg, "Introduction: A Brief Legislative History of the Civil Rights Act of 1991," to "The Civil Rights Act of 1991: A Symposium," *Louisiana Law Review* 54 (1994); Farrell Bloch, *Antidiscrimination Law and Minority Employment* (Chicago: University of Chicago Press, 1994).

22. Marika F. X. Litras, Ph.D., "Civil Rights Complaints in U.S. District Courts, 1990–98," Bureau of Labor Statistics, U.S. Department of Justice, Special Report, Jan. 2000, NCJ 173427 at www.ojp.usdoj.gov/bjs/pub/ascii/circusdc.txt.

23. *Abdallah* et al. v. *The Coca-Cola Company*, Filed on Apr. 22, 1999, United States District Court, Northern District of Georgia, Motisola Malikha Abdallah, Gregory Allen Clark, Linda Ingram, and Kimberly Gray Orton Individually and as Class Representatives, Plaintiffs, v. The Coca-Cola Company, Defendant. Civil Action No. 1-98-CV-3679 (RWS) Complaint – Class Action Amended Complaint at www. essentialaction.org/ spotlight/coke/index.html.

24. Gary Orfield and Susan Eaton, *Dismantling Desegregation: The Quiet Reversal of Brown* v. *Board of Education* (New York: The New Press, 1996); Orlando Patterson, *The Ordeal of Integration: Progress and Resentment in America's "Racial" Crisis* (Washington, DC: Civitas/Counterpoint, 1997); William G. Bowen, Derek Bok, and Glenda Burkhart, "A Report Card on Diversity: Lessons for Business from Higher Education," *Harvard Business Review* (Jan.–Feb., 1999), 139–49.

25. www.eeoc.gov/press/8-16-00.html.

26. Renee Blank and Sandra Slipp, *Voices of Diversity: Real People Talk about Problems and Solutions in a Workplace Where Everyone Is Not Alike* (New York: Amacom, 1994); Carol D'Amico and Richard Judy, *Workforce 2020: Work and Workers in the 21st Century* (Indianapolis, IN: Hudson Institute, 1999); Edward Hubbard, *How to Calculate Diversity Return-On-Investment* (Petaluma, CA: Global Insights Publishing, 1999).

27. Carrie Johnson, "Tech Firms Face Bias Suits as Boom Times Wane, Litigation Spreads," *Washington Post* (Feb. 23, 2001), page E1, Section: F. Also at www.geocities.com/ CapitolHill/6174/microsoft/microrac5.html.

28. Kevin Peraino, "Tomorrowland, Today," *Newsweek* Special Report Redefining Race in America (Sep. 18, 2000), 53.

29. Walker, *History of Black Business*, 54–7.

30. Paul Davidson, "Microsoft Faces Largest Racial Bias Lawsuit Ever," *USA Today* (Jan. 4, 2001), 9B.

31. The U.S. Equal Employment Opportunity Commission, News Release, " EEOC Settles Egregious Racial Harassment Lawsuit Against Louisiana Car Dealership," Aug. 16, 2000.

32. Martha Carr, "Toyota Denies Using Threat; Auto Dealer Backs Off Black Hiring Decree," *New Orleans Times-Picayune* (May 6, 2000).

33. www.eeoc.gov/press/8-16-00.html reports that: "In Fiscal Year (FY) 1999, EEOC received 6249 charges alleging racial harassment, accounting for 8 percent of all charges filed with the agency. During the decade of the 1990s, EEOC received a cumulative total of 47,175 such charges (6 percent of all charges filed), compared to a cumulative total of 9757 racial harassment charges in the 1980s (1.5 percent of all charges filed). Retaliation charges have also increased and now represent 25 percent of all charges (19,694) filed within FY 1999".

34. Bari-Ellen Roberts with Jack E. White, *Roberts v. Texaco: A True Story of Race and Corporate America* (New York: Avon Books, 1998), 1, 259, 263. Also see Kurt Eichenwald, "Texaco Executives, On Tape, Discussed Impeding a Bias Suit," *New York Times* (Nov. 4, 1996), A1; "Excerpts From Tapes in Discrimination Lawsuit," *New York Times* (Nov. 4, 1996); Thomas S. Mulligan, "Texaco Disciplines Executives in Scandal," *Los Angeles Times* (Nov. 7, 1996), D3; Kurt Eichenwald, "Investigation finds No Evidence of Slur on Texaco Tapes," *New York Times* (Nov. 11, 1996), A1; and Sharon Walsh, "Texaco Settles Bias Suit," *Washington Post* (Nov. 16, 1996), 1. See also Steven Watkins, *The Black O: Racism and Redemption in an American Corporate Empire* (Athens: University of Georgia, 1997), on a class-action suit on behalf of 120,000 black

employees at Shoney's. The lawsuit was settled at $132.5 million. The "Black O" was the blackening out on Shoney job applications to indicate an African-American applicant. The CEO was noted as saying, when he saw too many black employees, "Lighten the place up."

35. Theodore Eisenberg and Stewart J. Schwab, "Double Standard on Appeal: An Empirical Analysis of Employment Discrimination Cases in the U.S. Courts of Appeals," Prepared for Mehri, Malkin & Ross, PLLC, and Cochran, Cherry, Givens, & Smith (2001). The report compares how plaintiffs and defendants in employment discrimination cases fare on appeal, using data from the Administrative Office of the U.S. Courts, linked with data from district courts and appellate courts. The findings, based on an analysis of some 3,000 civil rights cases between 1988 and 1997, showed that: "Employment discrimination plaintiffs are far more likely than defendants to be reversed on appeal. When an employment discrimination defendant wins at trial and the case is reviewed on appeal, only 5.8 percent of those judgments are reversed. By contrast, when an employment discrimination plaintiff wins at trial and the case is reviewed on appeal, 43.61 percent of those judgments are reversed ... The 43.61 percent reversal rate of plaintiff trial victories is greater in employment discrimination cases than in any other category of cases." See www.findjustice.com/mmr/news/eisenber-schwab/schwab-report.htm, July 16, 2001. Also, Richard Epstein, *Forbidden Grounds: The Case Against Employment Discrimination Laws* (Cambridge, MA: Harvard University Press, 1992).

36. See Hubbard, *How to Calculate Diversity*.

37. *Gratz et al.* v. *Vollinger et al.* 122 F. Supp.2d 811 (E.D. Mich. Dec. 13, 2000). Also Law Offices, Jenner and Block, "Fortune 500 Corporations File Brief in Support of Diversity in Higher Education," Oct. 16, 2000 at, www.umich.edu/~urel/admissions/releases/fortune.html. For motions for leave to file amici curiae brief, see www.umich.edu/~urel/admissions/legal/gratz/amici.html. See also S122 F. Supp.2d 811 (E.D. Mich. Dec. 13, 2000). The Sixth Circuit Court of Appeals upheld that the consideration of race should continue as one of many factors in assessing applications for admission. In October 2002, the appeal was placed on the docket of the United States Supreme Court.

38. See Ford Motor Company, "More on Our Employees," at www.ford.com/en/ourCompany/corporateCitizenship/ourLearningJourney/webOnlyContent/011.htm . Information is also provided in the table, "U.S. Representation of Minority-Group Members and Women," at year-end 2001.

39. Shelly Branch, "What Blacks Think of Corporate America: An Exclusive Fortune Poll Revealed that Black Professionals are Largely Optimistic About Their Careers, Yet Still Skeptical," *Fortune* (July 8, 1998), 140(3). On Fortune's behalf, the Joint Center for Political and Economic Studies in Washington, DC, conducted a nationwide telephone poll of 750 African-American professionals and aspiring professionals between Apr. 20 and May 11, using industry-standard techniques. The margin of error was no larger than plus or minus 3.5 percentage points. Also, http://fortune.com.

40. Mark Truby, "Whistleblower Takes on Ford: Insider Offers Documents He Says Prove the Company Discriminates to Achieve Diversity," *Detroit News* (July 1, 2001) at www.detnews.com/2001/autos/0107/01/a01-242358.htm.

41. U.S. Census Bureau, "Census 2000: Overview of Race and Hispanic Origin," (Washington, DC: Government Printing Office, 2001) indicates that whites comprise 75.1 percent of the population; Hispanics, 13 percent; African-Americans,

12.3 percent; Asians, 3.6 percent; Pacific Islanders, 0.1 percent; and American Indian and Alaska Natives, 0.9 percent.

42. Alfred A. Edmond, Jr., "B.E. 100s Overview," *Black Enterprise* (June 2001), 106.

43. National Association of Minority Auto Dealers (NAMAD) at www.namad.com/index.htm.

44. www.namad.com/index.htm.

45. Walker, *History of Black Business in America*, 264–94 on "The Federal Government and Black Business: The 1960s to the 1990s."

46. See, U.S. Commission on Civil Rights, *Special Bulletin: Summary of the Civil Rights Act of 1964* (Washington, DC: Government Printing Press, 1964); also, P.L. 88–352, 88th Cong., H.R.7152, July 2, 1964: U.S. Statutes at Large, 241, for full text of the statute.

47. Gerald David Jaynes and Robin M. Williams, Jr., *A Common Destiny: Blacks and American Society* (Washington, DC: National Academy Press, 1989), 255–6 on the SBA indicates: "The impetus for the federal initiative in this area appears to have come from the National Urban League. Whitney Young, then the league's executive director, made black business opportunity a center-piece of his 'Marshall Plan for the Cities' proposal in 1963." See Whitney M. Young, Jr., "For A Federal 'War on Poverty'," in August Meier, Elliott Rudwick, and Frances L. Broderick (eds.), *Black Protest Thought in the Twentieth Century* (New York: Macmillan, 1971), 430–7, for Young's statement made before the House of Representatives, Committee on Education and Labor Ad Hoc Subcommittee on the War on Poverty Program.

48. See Arnold Schuchter, *White Power/Black Freedom: Planning for the Future of Urban America* (Boston: Beacon Press, 1968), 321–45; he notes: "the EOL program was not designed especially to help Negro businessmen make greater use of the public and private resources available to assist business." Also, Timothy Bates, "Government as Financial Intermediary for Minority Entrepreneurs," *Journal of Business* 48 (1975), 541–7; and Timothy Bates, "Small Business Viability in the Urban Ghetto," *Journal of Regional Science* 29 (1989), 625–43; also, Flournoy A. Coles, Jr., *Black Economic Development* (Chicago: Nelson Hall, 1975), 169–75 on "Federal Government Programs for Black Entrepreneurs," listed under the following Departments of Agriculture, Commerce, Defense, Health, Education and Welfare, Housing and Urban Development, Labor agencies, General Services Administration, SBA, and the Veteran's Administration.

49. "Why Few Ghetto Factories Are Making It," *Business Week*, Feb. 16, 1987, 86–7. Also, Allen, *Black Awakening*, 215–26. Also see Theodore L. Cross, *Black Capitalism: Strategy for Business in the Ghetto* (New York: Athenum, 1969), 227–54 for a survey of black businesses developed from community organizations and coalitions of White Corporate America and government agencies in coalition with black organizations; Coles, *Black Economic Development*, 177–82; and Raymond L. Hoewing and Lawrence J. Finkelstein, *Minority Entrepreneurship … A Status Report* (Washington, DC: Public Affairs Council, 1969). The Interracial Council for Business Opportunity (ICBO), founded in 1963 in New York by the Urban League and the American Jewish Congress was national, with locals in Newark, Washington, DC, St. Louis, New Orleans, and Los Angeles.

50. Shelley Green and Paul Pryde, *Black Entrepreneurship in America*, (New Brunswick, NJ: Transaction, 1990), 39–42 on the SBA; see Grayson Mitchell, "Maryland's Most Maverick Mitchell," *Black Enterprise* (July 1977), 26–33 and 54. Also, Timothy Bates, "Impacts of Preferential Procurement Policies on Minority Businesses", *Review of Black Political Economy* (Summer, 1985); 51–65 Black Entrepreneurship and

Government Programs *Journal of Contemporary Studies* (Fall 1981), 59–70; also, Theodore L. Cross, *Black Capitalism* (New York: Athenum, 1971); Timothy Bates, *Black Capitalism: A Quantitative Analysis* (New York: Praeger Publishers, 1973); George E. Berkner, *Black Capitalism and the Urban Negro* (Tempe: Arizona State University, 1979).

51. "Minority Enterprise and the Carter Administration," *Black Enterprise* (June 1977), 85, 87–9, 91, and 182–3.

52. Walker, *History of Black Business*, 146. Information on number of new car dealerships from Donna Reichle, National Automobile Dealers Association spokeswoman, at www.onwheelsinc.com/AAOWMagazine/1997_spring/feature1.asp.

53. Alcarcilus Shelton-Boodram, "Auto Dealers," *Encyclopedia of African-American Business History, 47*. According to industry reports: "The domestics started dealer development programs in the 1970s; the Asians began adding them in the 1990s. Europeans (except Volkswagen) offer no financial assistance to minorities. Though there are some Asian and Native American dealers, the rest are almost evenly split between blacks and Hispanics – except Ford, which has nearly three times as many blacks, and Mitsubishi, which has twice as many Hispanics. GM minority dealers almost have profit parity with other GM dealers, and Toyota's minority dealers (including women) are *more* profitable." See Joan Mooney, "Minority Dealerships: Will New Automakers Programs Mean More Dealer Diversity," AutoExecMag.com, June, 2001, www.aemag.com/printedition/toc2001/features/01jun/minority.html.

54. Charles Jackson, "Local Black Dealers Are Here to Survive," *Cincinnati Enquirer* (Nov. 27, 1990), section D p.1.

55. Blair Walker, "Black Dealers at the Crossroads: Association [NAMAD] Ponders Road Ahead," www.onwheelsinc.com/AAOWMagazine/1997_spring/feature1.asp.

56. Speech by SBA Administrator, Hector V. Varreto, at the National Association of Minority Automobile Dealers Annual Meeting, San Antonio, Texas, Aug. 11, 2001. www.sba.gov/news/speeches/barretoauto.html.

57. Samuel L. Myers, Jr., "Set-Asides, Minority Business," *Encyclopedia of African-American Business History, 480–2*; also, Samuel L. Myers and Tsze Chan, "Who Benefits from Minority Business Set-Asides," *Journal of Policy Analysis and Management* 15:2 (Spring 1996); and Jonathan J. Bean, *Big Government and Affirmative Action: The Scandalous History of the Small Business Administration* (Lexington: University Press of Kentucky, 2001).

58. J. Vincent Egan, "Disparity Studies," *Encyclopedia of African-American Business History*, 184–6; also, Mitchell Rice, "Justifying State and Local Government Set-aside Programs through Disparity Studies in the Post-Croson Era," *Public Administration Review* (Sep.–Oct. 1992), 482–95.

59. See (www.mbeldef.org/alert080301.htm), Amici Curia Brief in support of respondents, "Brief of the Minority Business Legal Defense and Education Fund, Inc., National Association of Minority Contractors, National Minority Supplier Development Council, Inc., and Latin American Management Association.

60. Jordan T. Pine, "Affirmative Action Backed by Bush In DOT Case on Contractors," at DiversityInc.com, Aug. 11, 2001; Myers, "Set-Asides, Minority Business," in *Encyclopedia of African-American History*, 480–2; also, 107, 185, and 514. Despite inequities, there remain challenges to set-asides; see Michael A. Carvin, "Attacking the Constitutionality of Federally Enacted Minority Set-Aside Programs," in Roger Clegg (ed.), *Racial Preferences in Government Contracting* (Washington, DC: National Legal Center for the Public Interest, 1993).

61. See Don Cornelius Productions, Inc., "The Soul Train Story," at www.soultrain. com/st/story.html.

62. Nancy Dawson, "Hair Care Products Industry," *Encyclopedia of African-American Business History*, 282–90, and related topic entries. Also, on the history of the black sector of the health and beauty aids, see Walker, *History of Black Business in America*, 302–11 and Walker, "The Future of Black Business in America," 209–10.

63. Ben Werner, "L'Oréal Finishes Carson Deal: The Massive French Cosmetics Company Receives Federal Approval to Purchase Carson Products," *Savannah Morning News*, Aug. 24, 2000, at http://www.savannahmorningnews.com/exchange/stories/082400/PULcarson.shtml.

64. "Black Hair Products Industry On Edge of Being Bought Out," *New Journal and Guide*, July 5–11, 2000, www.njournalg.com/news/2000/07/black_hair_products.html.

65. See *United States of America v. L'Oréal USA, Inc, L'Oréal S.A. and Carson, Inc.*, United States District Court for the District of Columbia, Aug. 8, 2000 at http://www.usdoj.gov/atr/cases/f6300/6324.htm. See also Soft Sheen/Carson Products at http://hoovers.com/co/capsule/1/0,2163,42061,00.html.

66. Paula Bernstein and Jill Goldsmith, "Viacom's Newest BET: Media Giant to Buy Entertainment Network for $3 Billion," *Reuters*, Nov. 1, 2001, at http://abcnews.go.com/ sections/business/DailyNews/viacom_bet_001101.html.

67. "Viacom to Acquire BET Holdings," at www.viacom.com/press; also, Stephanie Ernst, "Viacom Buys BET for $3 billion, Rise in Black Spending Cited," at Diversity Inc.com (Nov. 3, 2000); and Joyce Jones, "Betting on Black: Robert L. Johnson Sells the Largest African-American Television Network to Sumner Redstone and Viacom," *Black Enterprise* (Jan. 2001).

68. Candice Choi, "The 100 Richest African-Americans? Robert Johnson Tops the List" at, DiversityInc.com, Jan. 23, 2001. From list compiled by Securities Pro, newsletter edited by Tony Chapelle. His list does not include African-Americans in the sports and entertainment industries.

69. Sakina P. Spruell, "Could It Be a Brighter Day for the Broadcasting Industry?" *Black Enterprise* (June 2001), 45.

70. Reginald F. Lewis and Blair S. Walker, *Why Should White Guys Have All the Fun? How Reginald Lewis Created a Billion-Dollar Empire* (New York: John Wiley & Sons, 1995); Also, "TLC's Final Chapter," *Black Enterprise* (Sep. 1990).

71. Mark R. Moss, "The Battle for Urban Markets: Black Ad Agencies Surrender Partial Ownership to Compete for Their Share," *Black Enterprise* (June 2001), 187–90, 192, and 195 for list of the twenty leading black advertising companies. Also see www.targetmarketnews.com/numbers/index.htm.

72. "Target Market News," www.targetmarketnews.com/numbers/index.htm.

73. For World Wide Technology, "History Timeline," see World Wide Technology at www.wwt.com/sitemap.html.

74. "Washington Technology Magazine's 7th Annual Top 100 Federal Prime Contractors in IT," *Washington Technology*, May 22, 2000. Matthew S. Scott, "World Wide Dominance," *Black Enterprise* (June 2001), 108, and "Finding the 50 fastest-growing Technology Firms," *St. Louis Business Journal* (Sep. 21, 2001).

75. See Telcobuy.com at www.telcobuy.com and www.wwt.com.

76. See David L. Steward, Hoovers Online, www.hoovers.com.

77. Camac Holdings Inc. at www.camac.com.

78. Louri Aleta, "Kase Lawal: Making a Case in Oil & Gas. Black-owned business makes a landmark in oil & Gas," InternationalGuardian.com, July 8, 2002, at www.internationalguardian.com/070802.htm.

79. Lauren Bayne, "Black Entrepreneur Takes Top Honors Only Reluctantly," *Houston Chronicle* (Aug. 9, 2002); also, www.camac.com/news.htm.

80. See Central Missouri State University Chapter of The American Marketing Association, 1996 Distinguished Executive, David L. Steward, President of World Wide Technology, Inc., at www.cmsu.edu/market/amaexec.htm.

81. Juliet E. K. Walker, "Oprah Winfrey, The Tycoon: Contextualizing the Economics of Race, Class, Gender in Black Business in Post-Civil Rights America," in Alusine Jalloh and Toyin Falola (eds.), *Black Business and Economic Power* (Rochester: University of Rochester Press, 2002), 484–525.

82. Oxygen, Media, Inc., www.hoovers.com/co/capsule/1/0,2163,59171,00.html.

83. Seth Sutel, "Editor of Orpah Winfrey's New Magazine Resigns," *Chicago Tribune,* June 2, 2000; also, Patricia Sellers, "The Business of Being Oprah: She Talked her way to the top of her own media empire and amassed a $1 billion fortune," *Fortune* (Apr. 1, 2002), 50–4, 58, 60, 64.

84. See www.hoovers.com for Hoover's Capsule for Company information, sales, growth percentages, and number of employees for both Russell Simmons and Sean Combs; also, Alan Hughes, "Phat Profits," *Black Enterprise* (June 2002), 148–50, 153, and 156. The extent to which Hip Hop has impacted on American culture is reflected in Russell Simmons' participation in the 2002 Milton S. Eisenhower Symposium at Johns Hopkins University, along with such distinguished speaker as the grandson of Mahatma Gandhi. The theme of the symposium was "Changing Times: Who Are We? An Introspective Look at American Identity in the 21st Century." The title of Simmons' lecture was: "The Beat Goes On: The Influence of the Hip Hop Revolution on American Identity."

85. Roy Johnson, "The Jordan Effect: The World's Greatest Basketball Player is Also One of Its Great Brands. What is His Impact On the Economy?" *Fortune* (June, 1998); also, Jeffrey E. Walker, "Sports, Athlete Enterprises and Entrepreneurs," *Encyclopedia of African-American Business History*, 530–40.

86. See *Fortune*, "50 Most Powerful Black Executives in America," June 22, 2002, and at www.fortune.com/lists/blackpower/index.html.

87. Fatburger Corporation at www.hoovers.com/co/capsule/3/ 0,2163,58303,00.html.

88. See Chapman Capital Management www.chapmancompany.com/ccm.html.

89. Radio One, founded by Cathy Hughes, the first black woman entrepreneur to take her enterprise public (NASDAQ: ROIA). See Keith Alexander, "Quiet Storm: Cathy Hughes Rolls Across America's Airways Building Her Radio Empire," *Emerge* (Sep. 1999), 44–9; Lynn Norment, "Ms Radio, Most Powerful Woman in the Industry," *Ebony* (May 2000), 100–8; also, "Radio One," at Hoover's Online, http://hoovers.com/co/co/ capsule. According to Hoovers, in 2001, Radio One had sales of $243.8 million, a 56.6 percent sales growth, and 2001 net income of $55.2 million.

90. Stacey R. Green and Rosville Embry, "People on the Move," *AAOW Magazine* (Fall 1999) at www.onwheelsinc.com/AAOWMagazine/1999_fall/pg18.asp.

91. Alfred A. Edmond, Fr., "B.E. 100s Overview," *Black Enterprise* (June 2001), 106.

92. In the B.E.100s for the year 2000, the Barden Companies ranked 25th, with sales of $136.450 million. Also see Dingle, *Black Enterprise Titans*, 213–32.

93. Walker, *History of Black Business in America*, 83–149.

94. *Black Fortune Magazine* at www.blackfortunemag.com/partiallist.htm.

95. J. B. Brissot de Warville, *New Travels in the United States of America, 1788* (Cambridge, MA: Belknap Press of Harvard University, 1964), 1, 239; Also, Walker, *History of Black Business*, 48.

96. What challenges do these recent court decisions present for black economic interests in the coming decades? Higher education is more important than ever for access to good jobs and for would-be entrepreneurs who want to take advantage of rapid technological change. Court rulings that make it more difficult for black students to gain admittance to top schools will be especially damaging to future black economic interests.

97. Arthur A. Fletcher, "Business and Race: Only Halfway There," *Fortune* (Mar. 6, 2000), F-77–F-78.

10

Wall Street Women's Herstories

Melissa Fisher

In 1975 long-standing restrictions on stock brokerage commission rates ended, ushering in an era of financial deregulation. In the wake of these changes, Muriel Siebert, the first woman to buy a seat on the New York Stock Exchange (NYSE), helped to pioneer the concept of the discount brokerage house. Seeking to distinguish herself and her new company, Siebert took out a full-page advertisement in the *Wall Street Journal*, an ad that showed her cutting a hundred dollar-bill in half. According to Siebert:

When we first shot it, he [Jack the adman] didn't like the expression. He said: "Mickey, you have to look like Ginnie Sweetest. You are cutting their commissions." So, I said, "Okay. Girl Scouts of America all the way."[1]

Thus, at the moment in which fictitious capital (electric money) threatened to displace paper money, Siebert literally and metaphorically cut commodity money in half, as her scissors cleaved the portrait of Benjamin Franklin that adorns every $100 bill. At the dawn of an era in which it seemed possible to conjure up enormous sums of wealth by engaging in risky market practices, she destroyed the icon most closely associated with the American Protestant work ethic linking hard work to success.

Twenty years later, on a cold March Manhattan night in 1996, one hundred and fifty well-groomed professional–managerial class women gathered in the ballroom of the Philip Morris building to meet Muriel Siebert and other celebrity women.[2] They and I, in the midst of my fieldwork on Wall Street women, were there to attend an event entitled: "Celebrating Women's History: Defining Moments in the Lives of Five Leaders." Organized for the fortieth anniversary of the Financial Women's Association (FWA), the affair had an invitation that opened with the following questions:

At what point in your career did you first know you were successful? When did you realize that you had power and influence? What, so far, has been your greatest moment? Has it all been worth it? You've probably been asked these kinds of questions from time to time. If you're curious about how other women would answer, then join us for a panel discussion featuring five, prominent, accomplished, history-shaping women. Each will candidly recount "herstory": The pitfalls and pinnacles, roadblocks and opportunities, choices made, challenges undertaken, resulting risks and rewards.

The evening began with women filing past metal detectors into the ballroom. They received name tags with gold, red, or "no" stars. Gail Miner, FWA President and Controller at McGraw-Hill, greeted the audience. She stated that FWA members averaged forty-four years of age; earned an average income of $160,000; and possessed average household net worth of $1 million or more. Miner recounted the founding story of the FWA. Eight female security analysts working on Wall Street in 1956 formed their own organization. She then introduced the panelists and presented Muriel Siebert. Siebert, Miner said, attributed her meteoric success on Wall Street to the following formula: "*Work, Risk, Luck, and Pluck*".

For the rest of the evening Siebert and the panelists told "herstories" about their corporate triumphs and failures. I was especially struck by Siebert's recipe for success in finance as "work, risk, luck, and pluck." I was intrigued because she was referring to a similar constellation of attributes and meanings I was picking up in interviews with women in my Wall Street fieldwork about gender, power, capital, and business practices.[3]

WALL STREET WOMEN: CULTURE, POWER, GENDER, AND AGENCY IN HIGH-FINANCE

I highlight these two stories – Siebert's advertisement and the FWA dinner – because I am interested in locating women's accounts of corporate life in relation to historical factors, including and encompassing the contest over women's legitimate place on Wall Street and the transformation of gendered relations amid the upheaval in institutional structures produced by global capitalism. Specifically, this chapter follows the lives, problems, and successes of the first cohort of executive women on Wall Street during the latter part of the twentieth century. It is about their entry into the white male dominant professional–managerial class world of high finance; it is also about the ways they reproduce, unravel, and sometimes transform that hegemonic order, through everyday practice and struggle. This chapter, at another level, is about the changing relationships between gender and class in contemporary financial America. And, at the broadest level, this is an essay about the possibilities of integrating developments in two (relatively) separate bodies of work – feminist practice theory in anthropology and neo-institutional theory in sociology – in order to think about culture, late capitalism, gender, and agency.[4]

Sociological and economic research on corporations utilize a range of loosely interrelated theories that come under the rubrics of neo-institutional and neo-evolutionary theory.[5] Much of the work in these areas focuses on institutional reproduction. However, scholars are concerned with developing frames to understand change and dynamic processes of interaction in firms, industries, and markets. Much of the neo-institutional literature has yet to incorporate ethnographic methods that treat the cultural dimensions of shifts in gendered relations over time and space. Moreover, scholars tend to use relatively static concepts of structures, and conceive of structures in purely relational (sociological) terms as opposed to, or in conjunction with, cultural ones.[6] While these analysts engage in valuable research on organizational structures, they are less successful in capturing the historical dynamics and continually shifting cultural categories that provide some kind of underlying logic to them. Moreover, they rarely, if ever, take the view of structures as competing, interactive, dynamic, shifting, conflicting systems of power and meaning, of gender and class. And, in large part as a result, they rarely, if ever, focus on practice in terms of the multiple forms of agency in which corporate actors engage as they confront, reproduce, and sometimes transform the various structures that, in part, constrain them.

In attending to feminist theories of scholarship and practice theory, anthropologist Sherry Ortner's (1996) "serious game" model works out of similar theoretical concerns circulating within neo-institutional research, but handles them somewhat differently, especially in relation to questions concerning culture, power, agency, and gender:

> The idea of the "game" is meant to capture simultaneously the following dimensions: that social life is culturally organized and constructed, in terms of defining categories of actors, rules, and goals of the games, and so forth; that social life is precisely social, consisting of webs of relationship and interaction between multiply shifting interrelated subject positions, none of which can be extracted as autonomous "agents"; and yet at the same time, there is "agency," that is actors play with skill, intention, wit, knowledge, intelligence. The idea that the game is "serious" is meant to add into the equation the idea that power and inequality pervade the games of life in multiple ways, and that, while there may be playfulness and pleasures in the process, the stakes of these games are often very high. It follows in turn that the games of life must be played with intensity and sometimes deadly earnestness.[7]

By focusing on games, specifically on the creativity with which Wall Street women play serious games, this chapter attends to the cultural and social constraints women face in the financial world and the multiple forms and degrees of agency in which they artfully engage. To make sense of the games that Wall Street women play, it draws attention to their career narratives as a means to unpack the ways women draw on dominant American free-market discourse, and the slippages, disruptions, and ruptures they make in its reproduction.[8]

THE GENDERED DISCOURSES OF FINANCE

One of the major "serious games" played on Wall Street entails risk-taking and risk-avoidance.[9] Notably, women's narratives about their careers draw on gendered

discourses of risk. These discourses operate in relation to the ethos of hegemonic American regimes of finance. On the one hand, the rhetoric of women
in research and brokerage tends to draw on natural attributes of American femininity, such as conservative risk-averse behavior. In this way, femininity can be
inserted within traditionally masculine areas. In particular, women in these
fields invoke and reframe the figure of the "consumer" as feminine in order to
lay claims to their own ability to forecast, sell, and buy stocks. To play the game
of risk, they seem to use gender assumptions about their roles as mothers
making family purchases in order to sell themselves as professional subjects of
economic expertise in the market. In this way, women construct themselves as
authoritative financial subjects.

Women positioned in investment banking, on the other hand, provide a
different articulation of playing games of risk. Their narratives draw on supposedly masculine characteristics of cool calculated rationality, adventure, and risk-
taking. Investment bankers are directly responsible for capital accumulation, in
contrast to women in research and brokerage. Risk-taking is important here. Yet,
because risk-taking women invert all that is traditionally proper about gender,
Wall Street treats these women as "anti-mothers" of the professional–managerial
class. Female bankers become demonic mothers who do not care about their
employees or, in some cases, their real-life children.

In addition to constructing discourses of risk, women elaborate upon serious
gender games in finance that are based on American notions of individualism
and the associated rhetoric concerning the efficacy of deregulation in freeing
the financial market and citizens in general from the power of the state. Here,
they link their mobility histories and success stories to supposedly gender-
neutral economic images and entrepreneurial practices of hard work, production, and performance.[10]

This chapter is divided into three sections. The first focuses on changes in the
world economy and financial institutions during the past seventy years. This
section provides the historical setting and contemporary stage necessary to
situate women's narratives about serious gender games in high finance. The
second centers on women's discourse about games of risk. The final section
examines their talk about Wall Street games that require hard work and
production.[11]

THE POST-SECOND WORLD WAR ERA
ON WALL STREET

Between the Great Stock Market Crash of 1929 and the Second World War, Wall
Street emerged as a state-regulated, closed, domestic financial space. Crash,
depression, and war had significant effects on the regulation and structure of
investment banking. During this period the industry shrank and faced serious
public distrust. Bankers, nicknamed "banksters," were considered manipulative

at best and corrupt at worst. Financial market stabilization was finally achieved by a series of governmental acts under New Deal reforms, notably the Glass–Steagall Act in 1933 and the Securities and Exchange Act in 1934.[12]

Glass–Steagall separated commercial banking (deposit and lending) and investment banking (mediation between sellers and buyers of various assets). Unbeknown to the majority of Americans, banks during the twenties had gambled with and lost their depositors' money in bad investment deals. To avert future massive losses, Glass–Steagall forced banks, such as J. P. Morgan, to choose one of two institutional paths. In the Morgan case, the firm decided to maintain its commercial practice and private banking clients. Several partners, however, remained in investment banking and built Morgan Stanley.

The "Chinese Wall" separating the two financial-vendor groups' businesses created a cartel-like structure. Wall Street investment firms were protected from competition by commercial banks. Governmental measures also restricted high risk practices that might produce another crash. The Securities and Exchange Act of 1934, which set up the Securities and Exchange Commission (SEC), was designed to insure that the American public was provided with adequate information regarding securities and trading practices in order to make wise investment decisions.

New Deal reforms helped the domestic situation, but the Second World War had a devastating effect on international financial practices. It destroyed confidence in bond issuers and credit institutions.[13] Out of this situation emerged strategies intended to ensure the growth and stability of national capitalist economies and agendas. The postwar years witnessed the organization of a new international regulated space composed of nation states managed by a set of international institutions. Under the Bretton Woods system, constructed in 1944, governments of leading economies practiced collective financial management based on a set of agreed upon rules, including fixed exchange rates and national controls over employment, savings, and interest rates.[14]

During World War II banks were caught in an impoverished war environment for underwriting and trading. In contrast with the large institutional structures and volume of business conducted by commercial banks, Wall Street firms experienced a relative dearth of activity.[15] A handful of firms, Morgan Stanley, First Boston, Dillon, Read, and Kuhn Loeb, emerged in the reorganized industry as the strongest and most prestigious investment banks.[16] The Street hired only small numbers of new personnel, and those who were hired reflected the visible religious–ethnic characteristics of different investment banks that went back to their nineteenth-century origins. Morgan Stanley's roster of clients was composed of blue-chip corporations. The firm's partners matched their client's WASP, Ivy-League, "white-shoe" pedigree.[17] First Boston, a spin-off of Chase Bank, also boasted a blue-chip clientele.[18] These financial institutions did not compete for their clients. A "gentleman's agreement" existed in which firms did not raid each other's client list. Bankers engaged in ongoing professional and social relationships with industrial capitalists and affluent individuals. The "three martini lunch" symbolized masculine styles of long-term "relationship banking" practices.

Partnerships, in both WASP and Jewish firms, were the predominant organizational form, though these partnerships often were closer to the model of the "family firm" of nineteenth century business.[19] The banks were deeply hierarchical. At the upper tiers male partners – "fatherly executives" – exercised total control of decision-making. A small supporting cast of predominantly male clerical workers operated in the lower tiers. Entry and advancement into the higher echelons depended on family, religious, and school connections. Fathers prepared their sons (and nephews and sons-in-law) to take over their positions as partners of their firms.

In spite of religious/ethnic differences between banks, the men occupying the power structure worked predominantly in an elite homosocial world. Although the white upper-class male dominant order was never completely dominant or static, gendered boundaries remained fairly rigid until bankers and office workers were forced to join the armed forces during Second World War. In the men's absence, Wall Street firms recruited women with experience in education, hospital administration, and welfare work to replace males in the financial services industry.[20]

The go–go years in finance

During the Eisenhower bull market (1954–69), the power structure and elite family cultures of Wall Street slowly began to unravel. These shifts – in class, ethnicity, and, as we shall see, generation – were reflected in changes in relationships between financial firms and their corporate clients. Such alterations were manifest in new corporate forms and subjects that transformed the established male leadership of the Street. The period of the extended postwar economic expansion witnessed the emergence of new firms, managerial practices, executive entry routes, and ways of training men. The dearth of men during the Depression and War contributed to a generational gap between the partners of firms (who were mostly in their sixties) and the majority of men working their way up the corporate ladder. While some sons went into their fathers' firms, firms that were not family owned now recruited others.

A combination of old and new timers transformed American business and financial practices. Two tycoons – Thomas Mellon Evans and Charles Merrill – plus the entry of Eastern European Jews, shook up the relatively staid world of postwar Wall Street. Evans, along with a handful of others, pioneered the first corporate raids of the period. Nicknamed the "white shark," he built the first conglomerates by merging disparate industries such as canned goods, textiles, and clothing into single massive corporations.[21] He reshaped the ways these companies conducted business with their workers, executives, and shareholders. Long before the advent of "investor capitalism" the 1980s and 1990s, Evans insisted that firms operate for the benefit of their stockowners. He wielded a ruthless corporate machismo that focused on downsizing companies to achieve the maximum profits.[22]

Wall Street embraced the new conglomerate "glamour stocks" in electronics, plastics, and other Cold War inspired technologies.[23] Merging enabled companies to capitalize on their current stock value.[24] In the midst of speculative stock fever, self-made men arose out of yet another group entering Wall Street – the "New Crowd" of Eastern Jewish descent. This group made its way in the burgeoning areas of money management, trading, and brokerage.[25] They contributed further to introducing a brash machismo into the air of finance.[26] Journalist John Brooks suggested that they exhibited "a style more inclined to dash and daring as opposed to respectability, less concerned about preservation of values and appearances and more sympathetic toward speculation and outright gambling."[27]

A second figure, Charles Merrill, transformed Wall Street practice in a different way. He built a brokerage firm designed to draw the middle class investor back into the market from which he/she had been absent since the 1920s.[28] He transformed brokerage by advertising aggressively and making the selling of stocks to individuals into a salesman's art. He modernized the brokerage business by creating a new kind of organizational form on Wall Street – a large retail house with complex administrative and operations structures, expanded research departments, hundreds of branch offices, thousands of enterprising salesmen, and a new training program for brokers.[29] By the late 1950s, more than 1300 men had graduated from the program.[30] Merrill also hired women to write for the firm's business news publication, *Investor's Reader*. Marguerite Beer Platt became the *Reader's* senior editor during the 1960s.[31]

The new retail firms began to disrupt the classed and ethnic hierarchy in finance. In the public imagination, established firms such as Morgan Stanley were replaced by Merrill Lynch and other so-called wire houses (firms that did most of their business by telephone).[32] Several brokerages developed advertising campaigns, including "services" such as free courses in investments, targeted specifically at women.[33] The meaning and position of stockbrokers were elevated to heights previously unknown on Wall Street. Outcasts generations earlier, stockbrokers crept into the highest status group of the professional–managerial class including doctors, executives, and judges.[34]

In the so-called "go–go" and "boom–boom" years on Wall Street, the new male hero – the stockbroker – made sense in the increasingly fast-paced landscape of 1960s American finance. The appearance of these men partially dislodged the hegemony of an earlier gentlemanly banker masculinity. Forms of masculinity emerged that elevated qualities excluded from the earlier ideal. Aptly nicknamed "gunslingers," brokers embodied a youthful "Marlboro Man" salesman masculinity. Their success, like those of the "new crowd" of Jews, supposedly was less dependent on their family and class connections than on the "performance" – the new buzz word in finance – of themselves and their stocks.[35] The revolution in the stock market brought the cultural revolution of the 1960s to Wall Street. Journalist Martin Mayer documented what he called the brand-new "performance oriented world" of late 1960s Wall Street. His opening chapter was entitled: "Performance: New Money Calls Forth New Market." The second part was called: "Performers: And New Markets Call Forth New Men."[36] The American public loved the new heroes. Department stores sold adult games called "transaction," "Broker," and "The Stock Market."[37]

BROKERS, RESEARCH ANALYSTS, AND CRACKS IN SERIOUS GENDER GAMES ON WALL STREET

Mayer also noted the presence of one Asian-American, one African-American, and one woman – Muriel Siebert. Siebert's first job, notably, was in research. To make sense of Siebert's and other women's entry into research requires paying further attention to male brokers and research analysts, and to the power relations between these men. To be a successful man on Wall Street has always depended upon men's ability to make deals and money. Classed and gendered definitions embedded in the kinds of skills, forms of training, and types of occupations have, however, shifted over time. During the 1950s and 1960s, building a career in the brokerage business entailed becoming admired for one's technical and intuitive ability to quickly pick and sell hot stocks.[38] The rules of the brokerage game included acquiring, maintaining, and growing an established client base of investors. Selling stocks required that brokers spend time outside of the firm traveling, visiting, and calling upon clients. A large, highly active client base allowed brokers to make huge sums of money, to become celebrities on the Street, and, at times, to move up into senior positions. Brokers sometimes made it appear as if they were making all this money, and achieving power and fame on their own. However, one of the major strategies they used in the stock picking game was to rely on the work and written reports about industries produced by analysts, mainly men, working in the undervalued area of research.

In contrast to brokers, analysts were less well paid and less visible on the Street, and in American culture in general. Brokers were picked for their charm, "frat boy" outgoing personalities, "risk-taking" nature, and ability to make friends and sell to the public.[39] Analysts were regarded, for the most part, as introverted, quiet, detail oriented college men who spent the bulk of their time hidden from the public eye – squirreled away in cubbyholes writing their reports.[40]

Brokers were part of the front-line of finance. Analysts remained at home in the back office. Male analysts, thus, were lower ranking, and, arguably, symbolically feminized men. "Domesticated men" or not, they were structurally disadvantaged players in the games of finance. They held less prestigious jobs and lived in less exclusive areas than their broker counterparts. However, the hidden and feminized nature of the work helped crack open the door to women's entry into research. Eight female security analysts, for example, launched the Young Women's Investment Association in 1956. A decade later, there were still only about sixty professional women on Wall Street, but the majority of them worked in research.[41] The only other women on Wall Street occupied "non-professional" clerical and secretarial positions.

DROWNING IN EXCESS PAPER AND PERSONS: THE "CAGE" VS. MANAGEMENT ON WALL STREET

Known informally as "the cage," the backroom of firms in the 1960s was mixed in terms of gender and race.[42] The cage was Wall Street's equivalent to the factory shop floor. It operated, I argue, as a Foucauldian heteropia "capable of juxtaposing in a single real place several spaces, several sites that are themselves incompatible" but "function in relation to all the space that remains."[43] A dilapidated place, furnished with often broken typewriters, its purpose was "to move physically money and stock certificates in conformity with transactions in the front office."[44] To accomplish these tasks, the cage was subdivided into a bewildering vast array of departments and menial clerical jobs.

Coordination within and between the backroom and the enormous volume of trading in the front office was chaotic.[45] Indeed, by 1968 as the bullish stock market set new volumes nearly every day, the backroom was unable to keep up with the mass of paper produced by such intense activity. Some stock certificates never were issued. Others were lost or, according to one Wall Streeter, turned up "stuffed behind pipes in ladies' rooms, at the bottom of trash baskets, in the backs of filing cabinets with old letters."[46] Articles in the *Wall Street Journal* exposed stories of slippery bookkeeping, and fantastical valuations for common stocks.[47]

Traditional forms of management, composed along partnership lines, were not prepared to successfully govern the evolution of firms into giant investment and brokerage houses. The majority of partners were not schooled in modern business disciplines such as cost accounting, financial controls, corporate planning, or the use of new information technologies.[48] Unable to deal with the vast changes in institutions and the burgeoning need for more permanent capital, 1960s Wall Street slowly began a shift from the partnership to the corporation as the predominant organizational form. Transformations in power relations followed as the shift of market knowledge and earnings moved away from partners and toward traders and mid-level managers.[49]

In spite of organizational change, the New Deal securities acts, based on self-regulation, were still largely intact. The NYSE, like its member firms, was initially slow to respond to the challenges facing investment banks. It was not until 1968, when the nation was in the midst of the Vietnam War and other major events, that the paper crisis on Wall Street reached a critical mass. By the end of the year, the postwar bull market was but a memory. By 1969 several brokerage firms fell into bankruptcy.[50] The *Wall Street Journal* ran an article warning investors that "A spectre haunts Wall Street . . . The spectre is the possibility that troubles in handling high stock trading volume could cause the collapse of some major brokerage houses in a financial chain reaction."[51] The NYSE was also in danger of collapsing.[52] Calls for monetary and banking reform were in the wind.

THE REFORMATION AND GENDERED REORGANIZATION OF FINANCE: THE 1970s TO 2001

By the early 1970s, the NYSE was losing business to other exchanges because of its high charges for executing orders. Commission rates were high and fixed.[53] During this period, New York City's position as a major center for financial intermediation was weakened.[54] Several office buildings on Wall Street were half-empty.[55] Speeches were made proposing exchange reforms, including switching to negotiated commission rates. The restructuring of the NYSE, called by some "the club," did not go uncontested by the established financial community. Struggles over business practices and the implementation of technological devices, such as the composite ticker tape, were highly visible.[56]

A sense of financial crisis was not contained exclusively within the geographical borders of Wall Street. The decade of the 1970s was the crucial period when some of the calls for national as well as international deregulation, in the making since the 1960s, took hold. By the early 1970s, conditions supporting the 1945 Bretton Woods agreement – the international set of institutions and rules for global trade – were falling apart.[57] The United States led the trend toward deregulation when President Nixon suspended convertibility of the dollar into gold. The fracturing of the link between currencies and gold, the basis of the international monetary system, led to the disintegration of the fixed exchange system in 1973.[58] On May 1, 1975 – "May Day" – the SEC finally abolished the rules fixing the commissions charged by stockbrokers to allow institutions to compete more intensely with each other.[59] The effects of eradicating fixed rates were dramatic and far-reaching. Commission rates soon dropped to between 40 and 50 percent of their earlier fixed-rate levels. The new business environment placed considerable strain on firms, especially the research boutiques that traditionally provided analysis freely to banks in return for commissions on their business. Some were liquidated while larger institutions acquired others.[60]

During the 1970s, however, research, the area occupied by women, became increasingly important to business operations in the organizations that survived.[61] In a competitive atmosphere, firm research capacities grew as banks diversified into national and international business areas. The arts of financial forecasting were also on the rise.[62] Firms came to depend on the expertise of analysts, both women and men. Many current high-ranking Wall Street women started their careers in research during this era. Initially, they provided a source of cheap labor in the bear market. As one senior woman, Patricia Riley, a woman I discuss in some detail later, recalls:[63]

My first job was at a firm where the director of research used to brag that he was the only one hiring women because he could get the talent cheaper. And I at least appreciated that he was honest. He used to hire one female college graduate every year. He paid you less than the secretaries got paid, but you were so glad for the professional opportunity. And, he did provide really good training – which was of course what you wanted.

Although a few women in the early 1970s entered finance with business degrees, most combined working by day with business courses by night at Columbia University or New York University. Training programs on Wall Street did not open up to women until the mid-1970s. Women acquired analytical skills on the job. As Patricia described her first job as a research associate securities analyst trainee:

I worked with a senior analyst. I got stuck working with the utilities analyst, a consumer product man. It was the pre-computer age. Before they even had calculators you were using adding machines. You had to do all these spread sheets by hand. It was really boring. But what you did was learn the relationship among numbers, value, and what made for good stock.

Research and, to a limited degree, sales became more feminized in the new era of competition. Both research and sales were associated with new, seductive forms of labor, and also with traditional maternal images of nurture and care. A few women working in research recognized the shift toward feminized sales-games. Maydelle Brooks, another contemporary high-ranking Wall Street woman, began her career in research. She recalls her decision to move into sales:

I was working in one of the premiere institutional research firms. They said to me: "Do you want to be a salesman or do you want to remain a research analyst?" I looked around the firm and noticed that there was one other woman – an analyst. So, I said I'll be a salesman. In those days there were three or four women in institutional sales. The client base – most of them institutional investors – had never seen a woman salesperson. I thought it was a great advantage because I think women tend to be much more client, service, and relationship driven, and that was very much a relationship and client driven business. I found it was terrific because being a salesman was being a bit of an actress – being able to play differently to different clients, being able to sense the client's needs and moods.

The accelerated pace of competition also produced openings for Wall Street women in brokerage. After May Day, new organizational forms, including discount brokerage firms, entered the mix. Muriel Siebert discovered the art of trading on female images, in this case her own, to draw in clients. In her 1976 *Wall Street Journal* ad for her new discount firm, Siebert metonymically displaced the SEC cutting fixed rates with her own image snipping a $100 bill in half.

MODERN-DAY WALL STREET

Beginning in the 1980s, Wall Street witnessed even greater changes.[64] There was a huge expansion of employment in the financial services industry in the United States, as well as in Britain and Japan.[65] The globalization of markets, the introduction of new risk-management technologies to deal with increasing volatility and uncertainty, and securitization (the conversion of non-marketable assets into marketable ones) all radically reshaped the institutional landscape of Wall Street.[66] In response to these changes, firms dramatically expanded their research, trading, and banking departments and capabilities.[67] For example, when the financial economist Henry Kaufman began his career in 1962 at Salomon Brothers, he joined a new six-person research department. By the time he left the firm, in 1988, he was managing a research staff of more than 450 employees.[68] The growth and internationalization of the industry forced institutions to enlarge their managerial structures and emphasize leadership and partnership.[69] Indeed, as markets and firms went global, a new global power structure in finance emerged. High-status and well-paid jobs in the higher echelons of management became increasingly concentrated in global cities such as New York, London, and Tokyo.[70]

The contemporary period is witnessing the emergence and solidification of a new category of professionals – a transnational elite that includes financial managers, advisers, and consultants.[71] These elites are highly mobile, and embrace lifestyles and values far different from their predecessors. They are more focused on consumption, with their ubiquitous luxury automobiles and nifty electronics goods. This new class is still, however, composed for the most part of men, particularly at the higher professional echelons.

During the past three decades women have worked their way into the top tiers of Wall Street, but at the highest level they are still a distinct minority. Only 5.9–13.6 percent are managing directors.[72] Although EEOC data reveals that 29.6 percent of managers are women, many of these women still occupy lower level positions. By title they are listed as senior officers, but most are in staff positions in personnel or administration, rather than in line jobs that directly affect profits. Many women today still occupy research positions.[73] Even here, despite some success stories, surprisingly few have reached the top of the research department. Barely a handful of women have gone on to become executive research heads at major firms, the first being Margo Alexander at Paine Webber in the early 1980s.[74]

During the past decade Wall Street has continued to hire more female researchers and some more brokers. This decision is, in part, a response to the increasing numbers of women in the workforce making money and coming of retirement age. Over 40 percent of American households with assets of $600,000 or more are headed by women.[75] Thus, in recent years Salomon Smith Barney has tripled the number of women in its broker trainee programs.[76] In addition, an entire Internet industry has sprouted up devoted to the growing numbers of female investors. Here, too, Muriel Siebert is paving the way for the gendered Internet revolution. In October of 2000, Siebert bought two Internet operations – Women's Financial Network and Herdollar.com – devoted to offering financial education, advice, and services to women.[77]

In the emerging new economy atmosphere of increased competition for clients, traditional masculine games of long-term "relationship banking" have all but disappeared. They are being replaced by faster, more transaction-oriented games of deal making.[78] Indeed, in the wake of what political scientist Susan Strange calls "casino capitalism," a "predatory market machismo" is displacing more gentlemanly and paternal forms of doing business.[79] As feminist scholar Cynthia Enloe observes, "risk taking" is now at the core of masculinized conceptions of banking. "Just as travel to exotic regions was once imagined to be a risk and therefore a particular masculine form of adventure," she writes, "so risk taking is thought by many financiers to be integral to competitive international business."[80]

Although men still hold the highest positions on Wall Street, women, nevertheless, have been the unexpected beneficiaries of the fallout from the increasing pace of globalization, deregulation, technological innovation, and speculative practice.[81] To be sure, the rise of feminism, the presence of the EEOC, and a number of publicized antidiscrimination suits on Wall Street have and are continuing to play a major role in women's emergence.[82] My point here, however, is that given women's initial structural position in research, and given changes such as deregulation and increased competition in finance, women have gained a new position on Wall Street.

THE GENDERED DISCOURSE OF RISK IN FINANCIAL CAPITALISM

In the course of my Wall Street fieldwork, I began to consider whether Muriel Seibert's success formula – "work, risk, luck and pluck" – cited at the Financial Women's Association's "herstories" evening could be understood in terms of transformations in serious gender games in financial capitalism, especially regarding the new value put on risk. Indeed, Seibert's prescription seemed to bridge a divide between older, more traditional games linking hard work and pluck to material reward, and newer ones connecting the deployment of risk-taking practices and luck to producing wealth in the new casino economy without perceptible production.[83]

Women's talk about themselves and their careers seemed to share part of its cultural logic with the logic of games in financial capitalism. Could what we think of and naturalize as economic truth be a particularly powerful way in which the values of the free neoliberal market are being internalized, making a contribution not only to new forms of work but also to configurations of American professional managerial class femininity and masculinity?[84] What kinds of discourses do women draw on to further elaborate gender difference? What do their narratives about global financial markets tell us about contemporary structures of feeling operating within the American professional–managerial class in late modernity? And what do they tell us about how corporate actors – in this case, those caught up in the reordering of capitalism – understand shifts in everyday business games on Wall Street?

Patricia Riley

To begin to address these questions, consider then the following exchange between Patricia Riley and myself. Patricia was the first woman I spent time with on the first day of my fieldwork. Our meeting took place within her office in one of the major transnational financial firms headquartered in midtown Manhattan. Her office is on the smallish side. Her desk is filled with reams of papers and a large computer. Behind her desk a large window looks onto the city skyline filled with other corporate headquarters and midtown hotels. Patricia is forty-seven years old, divorced, and lives with a male partner, a doctor, and her three children from her former marriage. She is taken to donning dark green suits that match her softly dyed, neatly cropped reddish hair. She is a vivacious and articulate person. Indeed, it is not hard to see why Patricia is repeatedly invited to be on television programs to talk to the public about developments in the market.

Patricia has remained in research her entire career. She found her first job in Wall Street by answering an ad in the *New York Times* for a securities analyst trainee in the early 1970s. Climbing the executive ranks, she is now an investment strategist specializing in helping to create her current firm's overall policy for dealing with individual clients, who, according to Patricia, "range from very wealthy people who are investing large amounts of money down to people – yuppies – who are just trying to build for the future." During our interview, Patricia and I spoke about many things, including her views on women's businesses practices on Wall Street. Below is a piece from our first talk:

Fisher: Do you think that women face particular challenges in terms of bringing business in than men do?

PR: There is an advantage and a disadvantage. The disadvantage is they don't have a lot of women friends and contemporaries making a lot of money. Just because of the way things are. On the other hand, some of the most successful brokers are women. You can see why. Women tend to be *sympathetic.* They are not afraid to *spend time with the client.* They really *listen* to what the client wants. They tend to be very *service oriented.* You can build an incredible amount of business by just *caring about* your client. Women tend to be much more *conservative,* more *long term investment oriented* than "lets buy the hot technology stock." So, when I look at successful women brokers here, I see a consistent pattern. They are very *conservative.* They *don't take too many risks.* They have good, *long term relationships* (emphasis mine).

Fisher: Why do you think there are differences?

PR: You know it is funny. Oppenheimer commissioned a study of women investors to see if there is a difference. In fact, there are. One of them it that long term, conservative orientation, risk averse thinking helps you in the market. I think that women, just the way things have been, tend to balance a lot more. I think that women have always had so many *responsibilities* that it almost in an easy sense translates to stocks. I mean as corny as it sounds, let's say that you decide to buy a new blazer. You can walk down the street to Saks. You know that you are going to pay full price. You know that you are going to get good quality. You know if you go to Loehmanns. You know what you are getting at Filene's Basement. I mean you are constantly making decisions of price and value.

I think that when women look at stocks they have a lot more respect for the concept of risk. This serves them well. Men are classics. I constantly get this – they are at a cocktail party, and they get a hot tip. If you suggest electronics they want to buy it. But women will sit there say "like my family's IRA account" or whatever. The women want something conservative, something long term, something that they can hold on to for a couple of years. Meanwhile the men always want something that is going to double the next week. I don't know whether it is good or bad. But, in terms of the outcome, I think that women's attitudes are better for investing.

How can one begin to approach Patricia's narrative?[85] In the first place, we can insist that her account of gender difference must be understood within the context of a global market and its relation to the fetishization of risk-management underlying new economic games. However, we can further attempt to situate her articulation of the gendering of risk as simultaneously involving American debates of the *longue durée* about gender. Indeed, purportedly feminine attributes of serving and caring historically have provided a rationale for women successfully occupying a range of traditionally female positions such as nursing, teaching, and even in selling insurance in the earlier part of the twentieth century[86] Hence, women's performances of femininity – of risk aversion – can be interpreted as one way they creatively insert themselves in male dominated financial games. They subtly transfer the womanly qualities which they demonstrate in the act of advising and selling to the stocks they endorse. Their performance suggests that similar traits will be attributed to their client's portfolio and future market success.[87]

Indeed, women imaginatively draw on the historical identification of femininity, of womankind, with consumption (shopping).[88] They do this in order to distinguish themselves as especially well equipped to engage in games of exchange within the market. The story Patricia Riley tells equating buying blazers and buying stocks provides one way in which, as Arjun Appaduarai argues, "consumption has now become a serious form of work" in which "the heart of this work is the social discipline of the imagination, the discipline of learning to link fantasy and nostalgia to the desire for new bundles of commodities."[89]

The first approach, however, only provides partial insight into Patricia's narrative. It gives us a deeper sense of the ways women's career stories (and games) must be understood in terms of the ways global capitalism only exists insofar as it is indigenized and culturally understood within each locality.[90] It does not, however, fully situate how their narratives operate within the particular segment of American society – the professional–managerial class – engaged in contemporary market activity. It seems to me that producers and marketers of stock advice, such as Patricia Riley, construct research products (embodied in reports and in their performances of selling) that draw upon, rework, and incorporate structures of feeling operating within their clientele, primarily the professional–managerial and upper classes.

Studies on the professional–managerial class reveal that one of the major structures of anxiety involves the ways in which this class cannot pass on its status to its children.[91] This anxiety appears to be in some ways operating across the class board, in spite of vast differences in recourses to effectively "cushion" those who might "fall from grace."[92]

To be sure there are important differences regarding structures of feeling that operate on professionals and managers and those operating on the very wealthy. However, one of the reasons why women like Patricia Riley are successful in research is that they perform acceptable forms of womanhood – namely, they act as mothers who care about the future and reproduction of their client families in an age of enormous economic and cultural uncertainty.

HISTORIES OF GENDERED DISCOURSES OF RISK ON WALL STREET

Images of corporate domesticity, motherhood, and female success in the financial services industries are not entirely new. Indeed, as I suggested earlier, women resurrect and revise American gendered discourses to insert themselves into contemporary Wall Street. They reconfigure an earlier gender-business ideology that imagines relationships between executives and clients, and between managers and employees, as those between mother and the family as nation. Female narratives about risk-aversion, particularly those elaborated upon by women positioned in research, such as Patricia Riley, draw on an earlier corporate domestic discourse which views educated middle-class businesswomen as "motherly" saviors of the nation. In Patricia's narrative, we can see the ways Wall Street women reiterate and elaborate a set of gender norms derived from an earlier turn of the twentieth century financial management ideology identified by historian Angel Kwolek-Folland as "corporate domesticity".

According to Kwolek-Folland, male life insurance executives adopted a gender ideology of "social motherhood" to incorporate and provide a means for educated clerical women to symbolically and literally help advertise and sell life insurance products to the public. Building on images and discourses associated with the late nineteenth century social motherhood movement, executives tapped into the argument that "women's place should expand into the realms of politics and public welfare because the unique qualities of womanhood would bring sympathy, nurturance, and enlightened responsibility to the public arena." Just as "educated women became the mothers or guardians of the whole society," insurance companies imaginatively portrayed the corporation as a benevolent mother, watched over by "fatherly" executives, all of whom were collectively responsible for insuring the safety and future of the nation through placing and selling a monetary value on each and every individual's life.[93]

Patricia Riley's articulation of Wall Street women's unique gendered qualities also can be understood as a further legitimation of what Dean has identified as the privatization and commodification of risk protection in place of protections traditionally provided by the welfare state.[94] In the context of neo-conservative economic policies, Patricia Riley's narrative reveals much about the ideology of the professional class. Behind her elaboration of caring corporate motherhood lurks a class ideology designed to maximize the power of what Michael Lind refers to as the "new American oligarchy, the white overclass".[95] Images of social corporate motherhood, nevertheless, continue to refer to women's "natural" orientation to the home and emotions. Even at a time when women like Patricia are participating in an economy of radical individualism, high risk, and instability for many workers, Patricia's narrative, thus, reveals a key means by which Wall Street subsumes females into the workforce without explicitly rejecting the old connections between femininity, motherhood, and work.

MONSTER MOTHERS ON WALL STREET

But what happens to women who exceed the norm and are identified as risk-takers? To address this question we must now turn to a different narrative of risk. The following "herstory" exists alongside Patricia's risk-averse account. This narrative about risk-games is articulated by a high-level executive woman named Maydelle Brooks.

Maydelle is a good friend and member of Patricia's female cohort. Like Patricia, she self-identifies as coming from a "middle class" background. She is a single 49-year-old mother of one. Maydelle is taken to wearing traditional navy blue suits and tasteful gold jewelry. Unlike Patricia, she works in investment banking and is directly involved in making deals to produce capital accumulation for the firm and its clients. Though Maydelle also started out as a research analyst, she made some highly unusual career moves for a woman, advancing further and further into all-male territory. In the 1970s, she moved into sales; in the 1980s she switched, from sales into investment banking. She spent the 1980s and 1990s working her way up the corporate ladder of a financial services firm.

In a number of striking ways, Maydelle's career history and experience differ from Patricia's and other research women. Unlike Patricia, who spends relatively little time supervising others, Maydelle is responsible for managing a group of approximately 100 employees.

In Maydelle's narrative, she moves nervously back and forth between two contrasting articulations of her publicly and privately imagined self. She notes that she is perceived professionally as a "demonic" mother, both in relation to her employees and her real-life children. Violent gendered images often accompany her self-description as a "risk-taker" in the firm. Yet she simultaneously reiterates her subjectively understood private reality as a caring mother and, relatedly, as a self-described, non-risk oriented person in her "normal life." Indeed, throughout our interview, she expressed a deep desire to convince everyone in the firm, as well as me, that she was a "good mother." Engaged in a career in which she was the exception to the norm, Maydelle articulated acute anxiety over the ways Wall Street attempts to code her identity as a masculine risk-taker. In our interview, she proudly presented herself as a "risk-taker" in a variety of professional guises. In descriptions of her publicly performed self, she typically occupies the more masculinized subject position of measured "risk-taker." She seamlessly attaches to herself dominant American values of choice, calculation, responsibility, and agency. For example, when I ask her to tell me more about her unusual career move from sales to investment banking, she assures me that

I have always figured that sometimes you have to take a half step back to take three leaps ahead. But, my risks are real calculated. People do view me as a risk taker. But, I usually know that 51 percent of the time it is going to work out.

The quotation above indicates the ways in which Maydelle's meteoric career depended, in part, on her ability to project a "masculine" risk-taking performance that produces recognition from her employees and peers. Yet, the firm's reception of her risk-taking qualities also reveals some of the ways in which speculative games, celebrated in "predatory market machismo," can be reinterpreted in women as the dangerous and negative forces of sexual excess, especially in women occupying top leadership positions.[96] Consider Maydelle's discussion regarding the "hard times" in her career:

There were times, especially after I made the transition into investment banking, that because I wasn't from Harvard I was assumed not to be as bright, good, or successful. All the intangible and perception stuff is hard to deal with. Over the years I got a reputation in this firm as being very tough and very aggressive – and, therefore the assumption is that I will always be a ball buster. Even in the last few years, the people that know me well assume that I kept this place in order – got the business turned around – because I must have been shooting people.

Maydelle's description, suffused with images of violence and sexuality, provides an important glimpse into the masculinization of powerful Wall Street women. Her reputation as a "ball buster" reveals corporate fears of emasculinazation that also accompany the rise of women into the ultra-moneyed executive ranks. There is, however, an important interrelated class, ethnic, and status subtext lurking throughout her narrative that should not be lost. In the quotation above, Maydelle alludes to cultural obstacles she faced in the early 1980s in making a set of unusual career moves for a woman into banking. In particular, she mentions the difficulties she faced switching out of what was typically perceived as the rough and tumble, white (Irish or Eastern European Jewish, depending on the firm) "working class" and "middle class" male world of trading and sales, into the traditionally prestigious closed universe of investment banking occupied by blue blood Harvard men.

For Maydelle, dispositions perceived as firmly rooted in her outsider, less polished, aggressive, salesman, middle class habitus appear to follow her throughout her career trajectory. This perception works both to her disadvantage and advantage. On the one hand, Wall Street brands her with the "iron maiden" image that sociologist Rosabeth Moss Kanter has identified as the stereotype imposed on tough and strong businesswomen.[97] On the other hand, Maydelle fortuitously enters into banking at the moment when, under deregulation, "predatory market machismo" begins to partially usurp earlier forms of Wasp and "old crowd" Jewish paternal and gentlemanly deal-making games.

Just as the notion of benevolent social corporate motherhood is not completely novel, so too the masculinization and demonization of powerful women is not a total creation of 1990s Wall Street. What is novel, however, is the way in which these images register with the celebration of risk-taking and risk-management techniques. Wall Street women, whether they are biological mothers or not, are straddling competing gendered discourses of risk. Depending on their career–family trajectories, some women negotiate these discourses more comfortably than others, as the contrasting narrative cases of Patricia and Maydelle reveal.

Throughout our talk, Maydelle moved back and forth between taking a more masculinized professional position of risk-celebration and a feminized private position of risk-aversion that more closely matches Patricia's motherly narrative. Consider, for example, how Maydelle answers my question regarding why she thinks "some women manage to break through career barriers, while others do not":

I think that some people, men or women, still wait to be given an opportunity basically. And, sometimes you have to take a risk and basically go out and do it. You are either going to succeed or you are going to be told, "No, No. Stay back." But, if you don't try, nothing ever happens. Now some will tell you that these are some of the fundamental qualities of good leadership, but they first have to come within you before you can try and instill it others. I don't know because I am not a risk-oriented person. I don't like to ski. There are certain things that in my normal life I would never have seen, because I consider myself a risk-taking person.

As the fragment above begins to reveal, one of the structures of anxiety running throughout Maydelle's narratives is her discomfort over a split between what she identifies as "the inner plays in the mind between the personal and the professional." Maydelle articulates a divide between public risk-taking and private risk-avoiding.

A perverse cultural logic calculates her presumed brutal, late capitalist risk-taking on Wall Street to construct her as a kind of poster woman for the corporate "anti-mother." This notion, in the end, produces the most unease in Maydelle. During our interview, and throughout our subsequent meetings, she repeatedly told me about the ways in which people in the firm imagine her as an "ogre who beats her husband and kids." (Based on my discussions with other executives she is probably not entirely wrong about the ways in which they build fantasies and fears that link her aggressive speculative practices to her motherly behavior. Although managers relatively rarely spoke about her private life, they most often drew on evocative testosterone-like qualities – her "swagger" and "bigness" – to conjure up an image of her body and corporate style for me.)

Given Maydelle's comments, we can begin to make sense of the kind of masculinized stigma and polluted motherly status that is stamped on very high-level women. The potency attributed to Maydelle derives in part from the dual tension between her assuming different levels of cross-cutting gender (masculine and feminine) and class (working-class and professional) identities. Indeed, a brief look at the great lengths Maydelle takes to convince Wall Street that she is a good mother gives us some insight into how women who exceed gendered class norms cope with abjection. After nearly two decades of working in the same firm, she for the first time invites her entire department to her country house for a day. She held the event for two reasons: "team building" and to show everyone that "I'm pretty down to earth. I don't beat my kids. I don't push them around."

In the end, the image Maydelle tries very hard to portray is close to the picture articulated by her counterpart, Patricia, of the caring mother. Patricia, however, assures us that professional working women will still take care of, and reproduce, the nation's children, or at least the children of the upper class. By contrast, Maydelle's account enacts deep neo-conservative concerns about the current and future state of the American family. The masculine tropes she draws on reveal structures of what I suspect are class-wide anxieties about "who will do the caring" in this era of a small but growing presence of financially and culturally independent women.[98]

THE "GENDER-NEUTRAL" DISCOURSE OF CORPORATE NEOLIBERALISM

While Wall Street women's career stories about risk construct gender difference, their narratives also elaborate discourses of neoliberal individualism and the associated rhetoric concerning the efficacy of deregulation in freeing the market and citizens from the power of the state. Here they link their experiences of mobility games to supposedly gender-neutral economic images and entrepreneurial practices of work, production, and performance. In particular, they invoke the American dream of success – that any individual woman or man who works hard enough will be rewarded. They insert this more traditional ideology of success directly into their accounts of the marketplace. Consider a further exchange with Maydelle Brooks:

Fisher: Do you think there are glass ceilings?

MB: Yeah. But glass ceilings are made to be broken. I think that too many people sit and wait for the ceiling to break. You've got to figure out how to break it.

In this business it is easier to do that because it is a business where performance and production are non-gender specific and non-race specific. I know that that is very different from working in corporate America.

Fisher: How is performance evaluated?

MB: If you are a producer, performance is evaluated in terms of securities bought and sold, transactions done. If you are a banker it is in terms of deals brought in, executed, and business developed. That is production. That has tangible numbers and measurable results. It's how many calls have you made this year, whereas being the brand manager at P and G is very different.

Fisher: So, you think there is a real difference between corporate and financial America?

MB: Absolutely. Corporations and banks are more of a bureaucracy. I mean on Wall Street you are talking about loose organizations and affiliations and individual entrepreneurs with real measurable result, results that can transcend race and gender.

Maydelle's account of "gender neutrality" and "race neutrality" can be understood within the context of the free market, and the heightened emphasis on competitive individualism and entrepreneurial values. Her assertions fit within a long history of American belief in the work ethic. Individuals, regardless of gender, race, or ethnicity, are able to control their occupational, and hence class, destiny.[99] Her account of millennial Wall Street, however, unmoors this success ideology from its traditional berth in the workplace and the national economy. In an era of corporate neoliberalism, she locates the entrepreneurial American self *directly* in the global marketplace of "loose organizations and affiliations."

Women's career stories need to be understood in terms of the dialectical interplay between the "local" and the "global." Yet, this alone does not fully situate their accounts in relation to structures of feeling connected to changing gender relations among members of the professional–managerial class in the United States. Maydelle's discussion offers significant insight into the ways Wall Street female elites articulate an ideology of gender neutrality in the American public sphere. However, feminist theorists have argued that seemingly neutralizing discourse is still gendered and racialized.[100]

To this observation I would add class. As Sherry Ortner argues, and as I have tried to show throughout this chapter, Americans lacking a strong overt class discourse tend to displace "class frictions into the discourses and practices of gender and sexual relations."[101] Consider the following observation Maydelle makes in her further discussions about "productivity":

MB: This business breeds insecurity, especially among women. But that is what makes people more productive. That is what makes people more competitive. And like most women, even not in this business, but most successful women, I look at the bag ladies and say "there but for the grace of God go I." You can call it immigrant mentality, but I never was born with a sense of entitlement.

Maydelle's comment about her relation to bag ladies and immigrants is striking emanating from a woman standing at the very top of the corporate ladder, making millions of dollars. Nonetheless, she, like a great number of women I spoke to, imagine their fears within female figures and "others" positioned near and or at the very opposite bottom end of the class scale. Their observations suggest that in era of economic and corporate restructuring, anxiety about massive capital loss, and spiraling downward mobility, register even among elites.

CONCLUSION

In this chapter I have argued that, in general, the two career narratives about women's success on Wall Street draw on and refashion two contradictory and competing American discourses. On the one hand, narratives such as that of Maydelle Brooks represent a traditional "old economy" emphasis on serious games based on individual achievement and success. On the other hand, her and Patricia Riley's articulations about risk also reveal the ways women's insertion into masculine games draw on and produce debates and performances that elaborate gender difference and inequality, both between men and women and, I have argued, among women. Maydelle's parting words to me, perhaps, sum it up best:

I like to able to think things through and be rational and come up with the right answer. In the equity business you sometimes have to go with the tape, go with the flow. I recognized that in myself that, at some point, that was going to top me out because I would always fight the tape. You know the market is a consensus of psychology at any point and time, and you have got to go with the flow. I mean there are reasons why I think in different markets women have different skills. The real issue is risk. I mean, in our business, the risk is like immediate. You are right or wrong. You see it right there. And you've sort of got to be able to pick and go on to the next trade or transaction.

In an increasingly accelerated volatile market, Wall Street women's (and men's) prospects in playing serious games in finance are indeed measured by their risk-avoiding and risk-taking "abilities." Siebert's formula of "work, risk, luck and pluck" draws additional attention to the ways in which Wall Street women ideologically straddle the divide between newer and more traditional ideologies of success.

NEW ECONOMY POSTSCRIPT

During the past few years, a new typology of professional woman has emerged in the world of "new economy" Wall Street. Mary Meeker of Morgan Stanley has been nicknamed by *Barrons* as the "queen of the net." Meeker is part of a new breed of analyst, a breed that blurs the traditional lines between giving advice and making deals. Her ability to move between two supposedly conflicting positions is a product of the ways in which the so-called 'Chinese wall' once separating research from investment banking is eroding in the new economy.[102]

While it may be too early to tell, Meeker may be in the process of fashioning a new game of negotiating risk-taking and risk-avoiding financial practices. Lauded by the Street and the financial press for anticipating the rapid growth of the Internet, Meeker saw her star fade with the lackluster performance of dot.coms. In a recent *Fortune Magazine* article, Meeker reportedly concedes that, even as she foresaw the possible downturn, Morgan Stanley "had to take risks . . . We couldn't not be in that game."[103]

Now blamed for taking such risks, Meeker appears on the May 14, 2001, cover of *Fortune Magazine* with the words "can we ever trust Wall Street again" scribbled across her face in bold type. Once more, it would seem, a risk-taking woman has been taken to task for daring to exceed the gendered norms of the Street.

NOTES

1. *Institutional Investor* (June 1987), 90.
2. It will be useful here to introduce the definition of the professional-middle class. Also described as the new middle class and the professional–managerial class, this class is, according to John and Barbara Ehrenreich, located between labor and capital. Barbara Ehrenreich and John Ehrenreich, "The Professional-Managerial Class," *Radical America*. Pt. 1. Mar.–Apr.; pt. 2, May–June (1977). It comprises a wide range of professionals, including the wealthy and influential managers in American business and finance. Some top-ranking executives are also variously referred to as members of America's ruling corporate elite or white overclass. For a further discussion see Barbara Ehrenreich *Fear of Falling: The Inner Life of the Middle Class* (NY, 1989).
3. I conducted fieldwork on Wall Street during the mid-to-late 1990s.
4. Paul J. Dimaggio and Walter W. Powell, "Introduction," in Powell and Dimaggio (eds.), *The New Institutionalism in Organizational Analysis* (Chicago, 1991); Sherry B. Ortner, "Making Gender: Toward a Feminist, Minority, Postcolonial, Subaltern, etc. Theory of Practice," in *Making Gender: The Politics and Erotics of Culture* (Boston, 1996).
5. Richard Nelson, "Recent Evolutionary Theorizing About Economic Change," *Journal of Economic Literature* 33:1 (1995), 48–91.
6. Business studies, until recently, have tended to conceptualize firms as Goffmanian-like "total institutions". Relatedly, they often turn to a more classical Geertzian anthropological concept of culture (as a shared system or field of meanings) and apply it in order to focus on corporate culture. As a result the culture concept in the majority of this work tends to be relatively simple. Culture is generally viewed as an all-encompassing causal force permeating all aspects of corporate life that persists over time and is shared by all. The result is that business research relatively rarely situates corporations and executive life within the larger social and cultural structure and hegemony of contemporary American life and the global economy within which they operate. For a critique of the uses of culture in business studies, see Susan Wright, "Culture in Anthropology and Organizational Studies," in Susan Wright (ed.), *Anthropology of Organizations* (NY, 1994).
7. Ortner "Making Gender," 12–13.

8. There is a small but important and growing interdisciplinary literature that specifically analyzes the discourses of managers, including their talk about corporate culture as a window onto shifts in the social and cultural construction of business life. See Eric Guthey, Chapter 11, this volume; George Marcus (ed.), *Corporate Futures: The Diffusion of the Culturally Sensitive Corporate Form* (Chicago, 1998); Chris Newfield, "Corporate Culture Wars," in George Marcus (ed.), *Corporate Futures*. This body of work takes the point of view, as do I, that we can learn a great deal by examining "how social actors, in this case caught up in the reordering of managerial capitalism, are rethinking their habits of thoughts in the face of inadequately understood conditions of deep transformation that challenge past modes for neglecting, taking for granted, or at least comfortably operating with a conception of the broader social order functions." Marcus, *Corporate Future*, 7. By focusing ethnographic attention to the metaphors and tropes Wall Street women draw on to elaborate their career experiences, this chapter builds on and contributes to this new body of scholarly work.

9. For provocative discussions of risk in finance see Ann Capling and Michael Crozier, "Insuring Risk: Systems of Global Finance," in *Thesis 11: Capitalism After Labour?* Number 53 (May, 1998).

10. For an interesting analysis of the changing notions of risk and work in new capitalism see Richard Sennett, *The Corrosion of Character: The Personal Consequences of Work in the New Capitalism* (NY, 2000).

11. This is not meant to be a complete history of twentieth century American finance. For recent work see Brian Axel (ed.), *From the Margins: Historical Anthropology and its Futures* (Durham, NC, 2002); Charles Geisst, *Wall Street: A History* (NY, 1997); Doug Henwood, *Wall Street: How it Works and For Whom* (NY, 1997); David Rogers, *The Future of American Banking: Managing for Change* (NY, 1993). On Wall Street and American culture, a good place to begin is Steven Fraser, "Toward a Cultural History of Wall Street," *Raritan* 22 (Winter, 2003), 1–16. For a popular account on Wall Street women, see Ann Fisher, *Wall Street Women* (NY, 1990). For recent ethnographic works on finance, see Ellen Hertz, *The Trading Crowd: An Ethnography of the Shanghai Stock Market* (NY, 1998); Linda McDowell, *Capital Culture: Gender at Work in the City* (Malden, MA, 1997). For a financial history of the 1970s, see Susan Strange, *Casino Capitalism* (NY, 1986). Additional information on Wall Street women's stories can be found in Melissa Fisher, "Wall Street Women: Gender, Culture and History in Global Finance," Ph.D. dissertation, Columbia University Department of Anthropology, 2003.

12. Saumel L. Hayes and Philip Hubbard, *Investment Banking: A Tale of Three Cities* (Boston, 1990), 98–102.

13. Hayes and Hubbard, *Investment Banking*, 25.

14. Stuart Corbridge and Nigel Thrift, "Money, Power and Space: Introduction and Overview," in Ron Martin and Nigel Thrift (eds.), *Money, Power, and Space* (Cambridge, MA, 1994) Susan Strange, "From Bretton Woods to the Casino Economy," in *Money, Power, and Space*.

15. Hayes and Hubbard, *Investment Banking*, 103–4.

16. Hayes and Hubbard, *Investment Banking*, 105.

17. Paul Hoffman, *The Dealmakers: Inside the World of Investment Banking* (NY, 1984), 36.

18. Hoffman, *The Dealmakers*, 49.

19. Angel Kwolek-Folland, *Engendering Business: Men and Women in the Corporate Office, 1870–1930* (Baltimore Press, 1994), 129.

20. Angel Kwolek-Folland, *Incorporating Women: A History of Women and Business in the United States* (NY, 1998), 149.

21. Diana Henriques, *The White Sharks of Wall Street: Thomas Evans and the Original Corporate Raiders* (NY, 2000), 16–17.
22. Henriques, *White Sharks*, 4–7.
23. Charles R. Geisst, *Wall Street: A History* (NY, 1997), 284.
24. John Brooks, *The Go-Go Years* (NY, 1973), 156.
25. Judith R. Erlich and Barry J. Rehfeld, *The New Crowd: The Changing of the Jewish Guard on Wall Street* (NY, 1989), 34.
26. Ehrlich and Rehfeld, *The New Crowd*, 13.
27. Brooks, *The Go-Go Years*, 118.
28. Edwin Perkins, *Wall Street to Main Street: Charles Merrill and Middle-Class Investors* (NY, 1999).
29. Chris Welles, *The Last Days of the Club* (NY, 1975), 146.
30. Martin Mayer, *Wall Street: Men and Money* (NY, 1959), 113.
31. *FWA Newsletter* (1996).
32. Welles, *Last Days*, 146–7.
33. Robert Sobel, *The Last Bull Market: Wall Street in the 1960s* (NY, 1980), 13.
34. Geisst, *Wall Street*, 281.
35. Martin Mayer, *The New Breed on Wall Street* (NY, 1969).
36. Mayer, *The New Breed*.
37. Sobel, *Lost Bull Market*, 215.
38. Robert Sobel, *Inside Wall Street: Continuity and Change in the Financial District* (NY, 1977), 107.
39. Sobel, *Inside Wall Street*, 116–39.
40. Mayers, *Wall Street*.
41. Brooks, *The Go-Go Years*, 108.
42. Brooks, *The Go-Go Years*, 191–5.
43. Foucault cited in Edward W. Soja, "Postmodern Geographies: Taking Los Angeles Apart," in *NowHere: Space, Time and Modernity*, Roger Friedland and Deirdre Boden (eds.) (Berkeley, 1994), 154.
44. Brooks, *The Go-Go Years*, 192.
45. Alec Benn, *The Unseen Wall Street of 1969–1975* (Westpoint, CT, 2000), 17.
46. Brooks, *The Go-Go Years*, 191.
47. Sobel, *Inside Wall Street*, 253.
48. Welles, *Lost Days*, 146.
49. Henry Kaufman, *On Money and Markets: A Wall Street Memoir* (NY, 2000), 85.
50. Benn, *Unseen Wall Street*, 250.
51. *Wall Street Journal*, Jan. 31, 1969, p. 1, cited in *Unseen Wall Street*, 28.
52. Benn, *Unseen Wall Street*, 83.
53. Benn, *Unseen Wall Street*, 125.
54. Geoffrey Ingham, "States and Markets in the Production of World Money: Sterling and the Dollar," in Martin and Thrift (eds.), *Money, Power, and Space*, 45.
55. Sobel, *Inside Wall Street*, 17.
56. Welles, *Lost Days*, 303–4.
57. Sassen, *The Global City*; Geisst, *Wall Street*, 299–327; Susan Strange, *Casino Capitalism*, 3.
58. Andrew Leyshon and Nigel Thrift, *Money/Space: Geographies of Monetary Transformation* (NY, 1997), 77.
59. Susan Strange, "From Bretton Woods to the Casino Economy," in Martin and Thrift (eds.), *Money, Power, and Space*, 58.
60. Hayes and Hubbard, *Investment Banking*, 109.

61. Fisher, *Wall Street Women*, 14–15.

62. Kaufman, *On Money and Markets*, 148.

63. Patricia Riley is not her real name.

64. For an excellent analysis of contemporary Wall Street see Doug Henwood, *Wall Street: How It Works and for Whom* (Verso, 1997).

65. Sassen, *The Global City*.

66. Kaufman, *On Money and Markets*.

67. Geisst, *Wall Street*.

68. Kaufman, *On Money and Markets*, 149.

69. Robert Eccles and Dwight B. Crane, *Doing Deals: Investment Banks at Work* (Harvard Business School, Cambridge, MA, 1988).

70. Sassen, *The Global City*.

71. Sassen, *The Global City*.

72. Abelson, Reed Abelsom, "A Network of Their Own: From an Exclusive Address, A Group of Women Only," *New York Times*, Oct. 27, 1999, Business Section, C1.

73. Susan Harrigan, "A Whiteman's World: Diversity in Management/Female execs Endure Wall Street Bumps," *Newsday*, Nassau and Suffolk Edition, Apr. 14, 2000.

74. McGroldrick and Gregory Miller, "Wall Street Women: You've come a short way, baby" *Institutional Investor*, June 1985.

75. Ann Marsh, "Wall Street Chases Women," *Forbes Global*, Sept. 21, 1998.

76. Marsh, "Wall Street Chases Women."

77. Toddi Gutner, "A Street Legend Sets up Shop on the Net," *Business Week*, Nov. 13, 2000.

78. Eccles and Crane, *Doing Deals*.

79. For the study of paternal managerialism in the early years of financial services see Kwolek-Folland, *Engendering Business*. For a discussion of the movement from paternalist managerialism to "predatory market machismo" under neoliberalism, see Eric Guthey, "Ted Turner's Corporate Cross-Dressing and the Shifting Images of American Business Leadership," *Enterprise and Society 2 (Mar.* 2001), 11–142. For in-depth discussions of "casino capitalism" see David Harvey, *The Condition of Postmodernity: An Enquiry into the Origins of Cultural Change* (Basic Blackwell, 1989); Susan Strange, *Casino Capitalism* (Oxford: Basil Blackwell Ltd., 1986).

80. Cynthia Enloe, *Making Feminist Sense Of International Politics: Bananas, Beaches, and Bases* (University of California Press, 1988), 158–9.

81. Fisher, *Wall Street Women*.

82. Kwolek-Folland, *Incorporating Women*, 174–83.

83. For pathbreaking work on the "rise in occult economies: in the deployment, real or imagined, of magical means for material ends" under neoliberalism see Jean and John L. Comaroff, "Millennial Capitalism: First Thoughts on a Second Coming," in Jean and John L. Comaroff (eds.), *Millennial Capitalism and the Culture of Neoliberalism*, Public Culture, Volume 12, No. 2 (Duke University Press, 2000), 291–343.

84. For an interesting analysis of the ways contemporary scientific principles produce new gendered images of the body reflecting features of flexible accumulation in late capitalism, see Emily Martin. "The End of the Body?" in Lancaster and Di Leonardo (eds.), *The Gender Sexuality Reader: Culture, History, Political Economy* (Routledge, 1997).

85. My analysis of Patricia Riley's narrative is inspired, in part, by Paul Silverstein's superb analysis on the role of a Nike advertisement in late twentieth Century France. Paul Silverstein, "Sporting Faith: Islam, Soccer and the French Nation State" *Social Text* 65 (2000) 25–53.

86. Kwolek-Folland, *Engendering Business*.

87. For an analysis of the importance of having the "right body" and self-presentation to insure occupational success and class mobility, see Pierre Bourdieu (translated by Richard Nice), "The Habitus and the Space of Life-Styles," in *Distinction: A Social Critique of the Judgment of Taste* (Harvard Press, 1984). For a very important essay suggesting ways of linking work on the economy of global cities to theoretical work on the body, see S. Sassen, "Analytic Borderlands: Race, Gender, and Representation in the New City," in A. King (ed.), *Re-Presenting the City: Ethnicity, Capital and Culture in the 21st-Century Metropolis* (NYU Press, 1996). For a discussion of some of the recent literature that addresses the range of ways in which new service occupations "demand an embodied and visual performance," see Linda McDowell, "Thinking through Work, Gender, Power, and Space," in *Capital Culture: Gender at Work in the City* (Oxford: Blackwell, 1997).

88. For a discussion on the gendering of consumption see Victoria de Grazia, "Introduction," in Victoria de Grazia with Ellen Furlough (eds.), *The Sex of Things: Gender and Consumption in Historical Perspective* (University of California Press, 1996).

89. Arjun Appadurai, *Modernity at Large: Cultural Dimensions of Globalization* (University of Minnesota Press, 1996), 82–3.

90. Sahlins, Marshall, "Cosmologies of Capitalism: the Trans-Pacific Sector of the 'World System'," *Proceedings of the British Academy* 74, (1988) 1–51.

91. For a path breaking analysis of the multiple structures of anxiety concerning mobility and success within the American middle class, see Sherry B. Ortner, "Generation X: Anthropology in a Media-Saturated World," in George. E. Marcus (ed.), *Critical Anthropology Now: Unexpected Contexts, Shifting Constituencies, Changing Agendas* (SAR Press, 1999). See also Ehrenreich, *Fear of Falling*.

92. Katherine Newman *Falling From Grace: The Experience of Downward Mobility in the American Middle Class* (Free Press, 1988), 14.

93. Kwolek-Folland, *Engendering Business*, 17, 136.

94. Dean 1997 cited in Deborah Lupton, *Risk* (Routledge, 1999), 99.

95. Michael Lind, *The Next American Nation: The New Nationalism and the Fourth American Revolution* (Simon & Schuster, 1995), 181.

96. Stories of bad things happening to powerful women are widespread in cultural narratives. For a discussion of the unmaking of female agency in cultural accounts, see Sherry Ortner, *Making Gender: The Politics and Erotics of Culture* (Boston, 1996). For an account of the ways women are made to feel out of place on the trading floors and dealing rooms in the London financial market, see Linda McDowell, *Capital Culture*, 137–80.

97. Rosabeth Moss Kanter, *Men and Women of the Corporation* (Basic Books, 1977), 236.

98. Elizabeth Traube, "Who Will Do the Caring?" in *Dreaming Identities: Class, Gender, and Generation in 1980's Hollywood Movies* (Westview Press, 1992).

99. Robert N. Bellah, Richard Madsen, William M. Sullivan, Ann Swidler, and Steven M. Tipton, *Habits of the Heart: Individualism and Commitment in American Life* (Harper and Row, 1985).

100. Susan Chase, *Ambiguous Empowerment: The Work Narratives of Women School Superintendents* (University of Massachusetts Press, 1995), 19.

101. Sherry Ortner, "Reading America: Preliminary Notes on Class and Culture," in Richard Fox (ed.), *Recapturing Anthropology: Working in the Present* (School of American Research Press, 1991), 171.

102. Richard Elkin, *Fortune Magazine*, 2001, 71.

103. Richard Elkin, *Fortune Magazine*, 2001, 80.

11

New Economy Romanticism, Narratives of Corporate Personhood, and the Antimanagerial Impulse

Eric Guthey

. . . a certain type of person who has recently made it big in Silicon Valley could have made it big at no other time in history. He made it big because he was uniquely suited to this particular historical moment. He was built to work on the frontier of economic life when the frontier was once again up for grabs. He was designed for rapid social and technological change. He was the starter of new things . . . .

. . . As it turned out, the main character of this story had a structure to his life. He might not care to acknowledge it, but it was there all the same. It was the structure of an old-fashioned adventure story. His mere presence on a scene inspired the question that propels every adventure story forward. What will happen next? I had no idea. And neither, really, did he.[1]

Just one year after its publication, Michael Lewis's *The New New Thing [A Silicon Valley Story]* belonged to an already extinct and short-lived literary–historical movement, one that in retrospect deserves the name New Economy Romanticism. At once glib, iconoclastic, and portentous, most of the popularized writing about Silicon Valley and the Internet revolution in the latter half of the 1990s took on the same inflated, go–go qualities as the high-tech stock market bubble that inspired its many hyperbolic pronouncements and excesses.[2] This kind of writing syncretized elements from a variety of contradictory cultural sources – among them free market libertarianism, the sixties youth counterculture, the guru school of managerial advice, computer hacker culture, millennial futurism, business leader hagiography, and the California wing of the human potential movement. Out of this mix came a style that mirrored,

Select portions of this chapter were adapted from Eric Guthey, "Ted Turner's Corporate Cross-Dressing and the Shifting Images of American Business Leadership," *Enterprise and Society: The International Journal of Business History* 2/1 (Mar. 2001), 111–42.

oddly enough, several of the central characteristics of the Romantic movement in English literature that had flourished nearly two centuries earlier.

The literary Romantics were preoccupied with the idea of revolution, and rejected the strictures of Neoclassicism and the linear rationalism of the Enlightenment. In place of the stifling aesthetic discipline of the traditional guilds, poets such as Wordsworth, Shelley, and Blake elevated the spontaneous outpouring of emotions, the passionate freedom of the imagination, and the importance of unconscious intuition in the creative process. In a like manner New Economy Romantics celebrated a generation of impassioned revolutionaries who tilted against the suffocating hierarchies and droning procedural straightjackets of American big business. According to guru consultant Gary Hamel these "radicals, activists, and guerilla fighters who fashion bullets made of ideas" were building not only a new economy, but also a "new industrial order where imagination counts for more than capital and rule-busting insights are more important than mere knowledge."[3] In just this spirit the hero of Lewis's *The New New Thing*, Netscape founder Jim Clark, had become "deeply irritated by the rules of American capitalism," and had "lifted one big middle finger in the direction of the enormous gray corporation." In fact, Lewis maintains, in the inspired moment that Clark launched the Internet browser Netscape, "a lot of the old rules of capitalism were suspended."[4]

The New Economy Romantics also emulated the radical individualism of their literary forebears. In both movements, hot-blooded protagonists take on prophetic stature, changing the course of history with their insatiable passions. Thus, Michael Lewis describes his protagonist as the "character at the center of one of history's great economic booms," the representative creative genius behind "the greatest legal creation of wealth in the history of the planet." He is a "disruptive force" and a "catalyst for change and regeneration," because he is always grasping for something new. For Lewis, Clark's individuality derives from this restless searching, and this echoes another central element of literary Romanticism. Citing William Blake's declaration that "Less than All cannot satisfy man," M. H. Abrams explains that, for the Romantics, man's original sin had become his most heroic quality: "he refuses to submit to his limitations and, though finite, persists in setting infinite, hence inaccessible goals."[5] In a like manner, Lewis' Clark always needs something else, something more – another billion dollars, a boat bigger than Larry Ellison's, a new way to outsmart Microsoft. The inaccessibility of his goal becomes paramount in Lewis's description of Clark's Holy Grail, the new new thing. "It's easier to say what the new new thing is not than to say what it is," Lewis explains. "It's the idea that is a tiny push away from general acceptance and, when it gets that push, will change the world." But even after that push, Lewis observes, Clark keeps groping in the dark. "No matter how well Jim Clark did for himself, it was always two in the morning in his heart, and he was lying awake."[6]

Those who would dismiss New Economy Romanticism as just so much business press carnival hype will have to stand in line: the movement's own enthusiasts have been earnestly disavowing it themselves ever since tech stocks started falling precipitously in mid-2000. Besides, there are some good reasons to pay closer attention to this kind of writing. In what follows I argue that New Economy Romanticism and its erstwhile companion genre – the more venerable and longer-lived tradition of business biography – function to rework and popularize themes from a body of literature that many fewer people actually read, but that academics concerned with the corporation take more seriously – corporate legal theory and corporate governance literature. The cultural framing of corporate activity in the business "folklore" of the commercial media translates some very serious debates over corporate leadership, legitimacy, and control into vernacular language and imagery for public consumption. From this perspective, Lewis's portrait of Jim Clark as the consummate billionaire capitalist anti-hero rehearses in dramatic form a significant ideological transformation in the rhetorical and legal construction of the American corporation that has occurred over the last twenty-five years – the shift from managerialism to anti-managerialism.

Throughout much of the twentieth century, the managerialist picture of the American firm served to legitimize corporate prerogative by elevating the corporation's status as an autonomous entity, an artificial or even a natural person before the law. Starting in the 1970s, a number of economists and legal scholars sought to wield the raw energies of the market to erode the principles undergirding managerialism. They rejected the separation of ownership from control and the notion that management should serve in any way as a trustee of the public good. The new economic (but not yet "New Economy") theory of the firm dismissed the doctrine of corporate personhood as a "mere" fiction, and characterized corporate activity as nothing more than an aggregation of individual market transactions, or a nexus of contracts. "As a corporate genre, the contractarian approach is as distinctive to the United States as Faulkner and Hemingway," remark Gerald Davis and Michael Useem. "The emphasis on voluntarism and individual liberty, and the suspicion of viewing the corporation as a social entity with obligations to constituencies other than shareholders, are recurrent themes in American law and economics."[7] The genre's real-world protagonists were the corporate raiders and takeover artists of the 1980s, who in the name of shareholder maximization toppled managerial hierarchies, broke them up into their aggregate parts, and sold them off in chains of transactions that rendered the boundaries between individual firms and the market itself increasingly fluid. The debate between managerialist entity and anti-managerialist views of the corporation hinges to a great extent on the question of whether the corporation should be considered a quasi-public institution or a piece of private property.[8] Within academic circles, corporate legal theory has served as the most widely recognized forum for this debate.

But popularized business writing of the sort that appears in glossy magazines and management self-help manuals also functions as an important mechanism for fixing the line between public and private with respect to the corporation, and here too this issue gets all wrapped up in notions of personhood. In particular, media profiles and pop biographies of celebrity business figures – corporate persons, if you will – fold individual personalities together with corporate structures and render "private" lives public in ways that mirror the persistent debate over the nature of the American firm. In a curious inversion of corporate legal doctrine, then, such supposedly well-known corporate persons as Ted Turner, Bill Gates, and Jim Clark are themselves fictions. From a narrative perspective, their life histories function less to reveal how certain deserving flesh-and-blood entrepreneurs actually made it big, and more to structure and legitimize competing ideological visions of the corporation. Turner, Gates, and Clark occupy distinct but contiguous points on the spectrum from managerialism to antimanagerialism. A closer look at the rhetorical and narrative construction of these fictional persons can help sort out the shifting politics of corporate personhood, and can illuminate the cultural backdrops to contemporary debates over the relationship between corporate agents, shareholders, stakeholders, and society at large. As I will argue, one important backdrop for understanding both New Economy Romanticism and the antimanagerial impulse is the very familiar narrative of American exceptionalism, which also celebrates the notion that radically atomistic individuals can achieve a clean break from the shackles of the past and from oppressive institutions in order to create a New World.

This approach also calls into question the strong, personality-based causal and empirical claims exerted by business biography, and highlights its status as ideologically charged literature, as well as the need to interpret it as such. This approach also reformulates the focal question of corporate legal theory: is the corporation a fictional person? In the traditional version of this question, various understandings of the nature of the corporation function as dependent variables to be measured up against individual identity and personality. These latter concepts figure as fixed coordinates on the cultural map, near-universal givens that we can take for granted without much question or debate. But there are at least two good reasons to suspend this tacit assumption of the self-evidence of personhood. First, the kind of super-personhood bestowed upon those individuals who embody corporate identity is very much a fiction. Jim Clark simply is not the revolutionary historical prime mover Michael Lewis makes him out to be – not because someone else is, but because history does not work according to this kind of hero-centered causal logic. Second, there is a strong argument to be made that personhood itself is a cultural construct that can change over time. Critical attention to the fictional nature of corporate persons like Clark, Turner, and Gates can help illuminate the constructed nature of personhood in this more general sense.[9]

On the basis of this latter argument one could ask: If we bestow personhood on corporations, and the meaning of personhood has changed over time, does this mean that our understanding of corporate identity has changed as well? In her chapter in this volume, Naomi Lamoreaux presents a convincing version of this argument by conducting a careful investigation of the ways that personhood has been applied to both corporations and partnerships throughout the twentieth century and up to the present.[10] But in keeping with most of the work on corporate personhood, Lamoreaux does not question the empirical and explanatory validity of personhood per se. Rather, she queries the meaning of personhood *as applied to associations*, and how that has changed over time. I want to supplement Lamoreaux's argument by pointing out that there is no reason to assume that the causality runs only in one direction. That is, there is no reason to assume only that our understanding of corporate identity has changed as a result of changes in what it means to think of corporations as persons. In fact, the opposite appears equally likely – that shifts in the nature of some of the most powerful institutions in our society have caused shifts in the way that persons relate to those institutions, and consequently shifts in the cultural meaning of personhood itself.

It is not necessary to strike some fashionably postmodern critical pose in order to question the self-evidence of personhood and to reconceptualize corporate figureheads as fictional characters. The solidly modern Yale law professor and New Deal antitrust czar Thurman Arnold made just such an argument in very forceful terms as early as 1937 in his book, *The Folklore of Capitalism*. Taking a cue from Arnold, I argue here for an expanded notion of what counts as corporate governance literature, one that includes this notion of "folklore." Arnold was not just talking about Horatio Alger novels. "By the folklore of capitalism," he explained, "I mean those ideas about social organization which are not regarded as folklore but accepted as fundamental principles of law and economics."[11] By calling some of these principles into question, we can revive the progressive aspects of Arnold's arguments about why corporate governance matters. In the narrowest sense, corporate governance addresses the problem of how to get managers to serve as effective and obedient agents for owner/shareholders, or principals. But even the most mathematically circumscribed, game theoretical perspective on managerial shirking and the free-rider problem raises issues of power, control, agency, structure, and representation.

Once we scratch the surface of these political dynamics, it quickly becomes apparent that corporate governance constitutes a much more vital discourse about how to deal with the challenges the corporation poses for the American liberal imagination, how to reconcile the ideals concerning individual freedoms and democratic representation with the fact of massive, collective concentrations of wealth and power. In the broadest sense, then, corporate governance literature, including the kind of popularized writing about corporate activity that I discuss here, constitutes a complex cultural discourse about what it means to be a person in a corporate society.[12] In his analysis of the political subtext of computer hacker culture, Thomas Streeter argues that "net libertarianism" rests on a limiting, romantic understanding of what it means to be a person that renders it incapable of developing any meaningful critique of the neoliberal direction of communications policy debates or the commercialization of the Internet.[13] I argue here that antimanagerialism has developed a similarly romantic and exceptionalist understanding of corporate personhood, and that for this reason its critique of corporate power functions ultimately to legitimize corporate activity on new terms for a new historical moment.

THE INSTITUTION OF (CORPORATE) PERSONHOOD
AND *THE FOLKLORE OF CAPITALISM* REVISITED

In the preface to the 1962 reprint of *The Folklore of Capitalism*, Thurman Arnold remarked that he originally had written the book "to describe the frustrating effects, in times of revolutionary change, of ideals and symbols inherited from a different past." He explained that enormous changes had occurred since 1937, and that several of his arguments, including his chapter on "The Personification of the Corporation," had become obsolete. "We no longer feel that government control of industry is something that will end in the destruction of individual liberty," said Arnold, noting that the high levels of government regulatory interference into business possible in 1962 would have been unthinkable in 1937. From a vantage point at the turn of the twenty-first century, Arnold's observations can induce a certain historical vertigo, because regulatory interference has fallen back out of favor, and many of the statements Arnold disavowed in 1962 once again seem to describe, in very apt terms, the current climate of deregulatory zeal, corporate concentration, and free market triumphalism. On the other hand, the Thurman Arnold of 1937 assailed corporate prerogative with a vigor and confidence that many would now consider unthinkable as well, and the brazen sarcasm of his critique highlights a crucial difference between American attitudes toward the large corporation at the beginning and the end of the twentieth century. In the former period, unbridled corporate power did not enjoy anywhere near the levels of uncontested legitimacy it does today.[14]

Indeed, the rise of the large managerialist corporation in the early part of the twentieth century sparked considerable debate and dissent, because such unprecedented levels of market concentration and privilege challenged an American liberal imagination predicated on the Jeffersonian ideal of a democracy of small property holders. "The quandaries created for liberal thought by the rise of the giant business corporation were many, but most of them can be seen as versions of one central dilemma," explains sociologist Thomas Streeter. "If the legitimacy of a market society rests on its control by individuals, how can one justify a capitalism dominated by the giant impersonal collectivities we call corporations?"[15] Streeter and others have highlighted how *corporate* liberalism developed as a means of resolving this quandary by reconciling traditional liberal ideals regarding individual liberty with corporate capitalist imperatives. From this perspective, Arnold's *Folklore* delivered a bracing critique of corporate personhood as a central tool in the corporate liberal arsenal – a tool that justified powerful capitalist collectivities in individualist terms.[16]

"One of the essential and central notions which give our industrial feudalism logical symmetry is the personification of great industrial enterprise," Arnold observed. "The ideal that a great corporation is endowed with the rights and prerogatives of a free individual is as essential to the acceptance of corporate rule in temporal affairs as was the ideal of the divine right of kings in an earlier day." Corporate personhood had subverted the meaning of the constitution, Arnold charged, and had thrown the American liberal polity completely out of balance. "Every phrase of the Constitution designed to protect the submerged individual has become an instrument for the protection of large organizations," he complained. "The arguments often appeared nonsensical, but it should be remembered that for the purpose of binding organizations together nothing makes as much sense as nonsense, and hence nonsense always wins."[17]

In corporate legal terms, the device that had performed this sleight of hand was the separation of ownership from control. According to this arrangement, managers would serve as neutral trustees situated halfway between shareholders and society at large, responsible for weighing the interests of both, but invested with an authority all their own. Management expertise would ensure that shareholders received an optimal return on their investment, while managers' autonomy and social responsibility would guarantee that the staggering levels of economic power inherent in the corporate form would not threaten the rights of individual citizens. At the same time professionalization and public service obligations would guard against renegade managers who would seek "prestige, power, or the gratification of professional zeal" instead of shareholder value, as Adolf Berle and Gardiner Means feared they would in their 1932 book, *The Modern Corporation and Private Property*. "Indeed, it seems almost essential if the corporate system is to survive," they concluded, "that the 'control' of the great corporations should develop into a purely neutral technocracy, balancing a variety of claims by various groups in the community and assigning to each a portion of the income stream on the basis of public policy rather than private cupidity."[18] This notion of an autonomous and accountable managerial hierarchy buttressed the legal conception of corporate personhood and provided the foundation for the corporate liberal doctrine of managerialism.

But, as Arnold insisted, we cannot understand an institution like managerialism merely by reference to legal devices and organizational principles. These do not make sense on their own terms, he emphasized, because "their content and their logic are the least important things about them." (21) Their meaning only takes shape in connection with a series of "mental pictures," an institutional "mythology" and a pantheon of "imaginary personalities" that give form and logic to the institutional structure and bring the words to life. "Back of every creed is a hierarchy of heroes or divinities whose imaginary personalities give meaning to those words," said Arnold. "Without an emotional understanding of this hierarchy we cannot even guess the meaning the words will finally take." While such mythologies function primarily to organize and legitimize social institutions, Arnold argued, "the power of any currently accepted mythology lies in the fact that its heroes are thought to have a real existence."[19]

Organizational sociologists use different terms and generally avoid the kind of polemic in which Arnold reveled, but some of them have described corporate personhood in much the same way. Gerald Davis, Kristina Diekmann, and Catherine Tinsley help explain how the entity concept in corporate legal theory built upon a tradition of naturalizing social institutions through the analogy of the "organization as body." They draw on the work of anthropologist Mary Douglas to explain that an institution is a social convention that becomes legitimized, often by means of such a "naturalizing analogy," which they define as "a parallel cognitive structure that sustains the institution by demonstrating its fit with the natural order." These analogies, they add, "provide a source of stability for conventions by 'scripting' behavior, and they are a potent rhetorical resource for ordering social arrangements." The body analogy also "implies a way of thinking about what an organization is – a bounded social structure composed of members – as well as a set of desiderata (e.g. growth and survival) that can guide action and provide a basis for the adoption of organizational practices and forms."[20]

Barbara Czarniawska emphasizes the narrative aspects of the "organization as body" analogy in her book, *Narrating the Organization: Dramas of Institutional Identity*. She also highlights the constructed nature of the anthropomorphic image of the organization as a "super-person," that is, "as a single powerful decision maker, personified in a leader or leadership group, or expressed in the notion of the organization as collective." The problem with this simplifying metaphor, she explains, is that organizations are not people at all. They are "nets of collective action undertaken in an effort to shape the world and human lives." But rather than dismiss the metaphor of the "organization as super-person" altogether, Czarniawska points to its continued rhetorical power as a narrative of institutional identity. That power derives, she explains, from the fact that individuality also is a modern social institution with a history, and that individual identities are narratives that produce, reproduce, and maintain the self in conversation with others as well as with the social institution of individuality itself.[21]

Czarniawska helps explain the connection between corporate personhood and the responsibilities attached thereto under managerialism, because she emphasizes that responsibility, or accountability, provides the basis for the institution of individuality itself. From her narrative perspective, individual identity hinges on "an ability to account for one's actions in terms that will be accepted by the audience." By the same token, Czarniawska explains, organizations get anthropomorphized in order to produce accountability of the sort attached to the managerialist corporate person. In this formula, accountability performs the crucial function of linking individuality to the other two predominant institutions in the modern liberal narrative: the market and the state. "The invention of a 'legal person,' which makes organizations accountable both as citizens and as consumers and producers, constitutes a necessary link between the three," Czarniawska says, "and is then reflected in everyday language."[22]

In the process of highlighting the narrative logic of corporate personhood, Czarniawska joins Harrison White in delivering a critique of the socially constructed nature of personhood itself. In *Identity and Control*, White calls the social sciences to task for assuming the priority of bounded identity or "entityness," both at the individual and at the organizational level. "Effective theory of social relations is hindered by assuming that social action comes only from individual biological creatures – humans – as a consequence of their nature and consciousness as persons," says White. "This mirage of the person as atom breeds an obverse mirage of a society as an entity." He argues instead for an approach in which "persons should be derived from, rather than presupposed in, basic principles of social action." From White's perspective, actors do not necessarily precede action, and need not be persons at all. Individual identity arises from a social field of contention in which contingencies and uncertainties are met with attempts to construct and project continuity and control. "Identity here does not mean the common-sense notion of self, nor does it mean presupposing consciousness and integration or presupposing personality," says White. Instead, identity amounts to any source of action upon which observers project meaning, including an employer, a crowd, a corporation, or one's own self. One potent means of projecting this coherent sense of identity is through stories, and on this basis White also emphasizes the centrality of narrative to the process of identity construction.[23]

It is difficult to imagine a lucid historical narrative that would not presuppose the existence of persons as actors at some level. But even if we do not pursue the most radical implications of White and Czarniawska's arguments about personhood in general, they help explain the fictional nature and narrative function of the "imaginary personalities" that legitimize the institution of corporate personhood. Contrary to what Thurman Arnold says, it makes sense to talk about corporations as fictional persons because we can productively understand personhood itself as a fiction – a narrative project the goal of which is to convey a sense of coherent identity and to exert control over the social world. But, as Arnold would agree, it is crucial to this project that business divinities like Ted Turner, Bill Gates, and Jim Clark are thought to have a real existence, even though the recurrent public celebration of their existence serves mainly ideological rather than descriptive purposes in the context of a narrative that functions to reinforce and legitimize the institution of corporate personhood.

TED TURNER: CAPTAIN OUTRAGEOUS IN THE BOARDROOM

In a revealing profile titled "The Lost Tycoon" that appeared in an April 2001 issue of *The New Yorker* magazine, media writer Ken Auletta describes Ted Turner's deep sense of loss over his recently failed marriage to Jane Fonda and his ousting from power over what used to be his own company. The sixty-two-year-old Turner had spent his entire adult life developing the regional outdoor advertising operation he had inherited from his father into a significant provider of news, sports, children's programming, and movies to the cable and broadcasting industries. The Turner Broadcasting System had merged with Time Warner in 1996, and when America Online bought the latter in 2000,

Turner had become the largest individual shareholder in the largest media conglomerate in the world. As Auletta explains, Turner had expected to take a major hand in steering AOL Time Warner, but within four months Time Warner chief Gerald Levin essentially fired Turner, abrogating Turner's five-year contract to manage the Turner Broadcasting divisions, handing the control of Turner's former company over to AOL's chief operating officer Robert Pittman, and relegating Turner to one of two vice-chairmanships and the additional, titular position of "Senior Advisor." According to Auletta, Turner learned most of these details from a perfunctory press release faxed to his ranch in New Mexico. "Ted went white," recalls fellow media mogul John Malone, Turner's guest when the fax arrived. "He was very upset. He thought it was extremely bad behavior for them to do it that way."[24]

Auletta complements this insider information about AOL management politics with intimate details about Turner's marital problems and divorce. Turner complains to Auletta that Fonda had decided to become a born-again Christian without discussing it with him. Fonda counters that she chose to keep her decision from her husband of eight years because he was an overbearing former debate champion, and would have talked her out of it. Friends and associates talk politely around rumors that Turner could not control his attraction to other women throughout their marriage, and Fonda places much of the blame on Turner's deep insecurity. "He needs someone to be there one hundred percent of the time," Fonda tells Auletta. "He thinks that's love. It is not love. It's babysitting."[25] She points out that Turner has often compared himself and been compared to Rhett Butler (the Clark Gable moustache long ago became a staple of Turner's iconography), but that he actually relates much more closely with the more vulnerable and insecure Scarlett O'Hara.

The Auletta profile offers up a wealth of personal and professional detail, but it does not really help us know and understand better the person called Ted Turner. Rather, the new revelations serve to rework the central theme of what I have elsewhere called the Turner media legend. That legend has evolved over the years in countless such profiles, in six or seven remarkably similar pop/commercial biographies and "insider accounts," and in a ghost-written autobiography that Turner decided not to publish. All these sources insist that Turner's unique and outlandish personality provides the key to understanding his career. By contrast, I have argued that Turner's personality does not sufficiently explain the many changes in the media industries attributed to him, nor does it even account fully for his own business success. With respect to each of Turner's celebrated achievements, a whole network of intersecting causal factors also come into play, including economic, regulatory, and social developments in broadcasting, cable, and satellite technology; other people's ideas, decisions, connections, and skills; and even more slippery cultural shifts beyond any individual's control. This does not mean that the Turner legend is merely false, however, or that his personality does not matter at all. The Turner legend folds his personality together with these broader causal forces in such a way that it becomes nearly impossible to distinguish between them. Turner's private life and personality matter because of the ways they have come to intersect with and stand for a particular narrative understanding of the proper relationship between individual agency, market activity, and corporate power.[26]

From this perspective, the Turner legend is fictional in the deeper sense that its primary effect is thematic rather than descriptive. Its central theme always has been the power of an individual entrepreneur to buck the establishment, to break free of the entanglements of collective government, bureaucratic, and corporate encroachment, and to bring about a global communications revolution along the way. Throughout his career, Turner has railed against the regulatory protection and stifling managerial power of the large managerialist corporation. He has compared the broadcast network presidents and such powerful competitors as Rupert Murdoch to Hitler, and fashioned his own business ventures as moral crusades on behalf of his ever-expanding market share. In this manner Turner has served as a leading figure in the construction of antimanagerialism.

The Turner legend has invoked time and again the corporate threat to liberal individual agency, while at the same time helping to redefine the corporate liberal solution to the problem. Turner's symbolic effect has been to supplant managerialism's gray-templed bureaucratic rationality with youthful and aggressive entrepreneurship, its technical expertise with an "aw-shucks" enthusiasm for satellite gadgetry, and its paternalistic trusteeship with a populist, near-missionary zeal for expanded consumer choice. In this regard, he has embodied the market exuberance that we associate with the new economic theory of the firm, and this is why he has never legitimized corporate media management in the top-down, paternalist mode of a Henry Ford or a William Paley. "What makes me root for Turner is not his self-proclaimed virtue but his wild vitality, his unruliness," declared a 1985 *New York Times* op-ed piece celebrating Turner's quixotic takeover bid for the CBS television network. "No force short of Turner could shock [CBS] out of its tedious complacency."[27] Still, in spite of the challenge Turner poses to traditional conceptions of managerial identity, he does not dispense with the managerialist conception of the corporation as a person altogether. Rather than separate ownership from control, or do away with both, Turner's effect has been to recombine both ownership and control in his own person. In this manner he has come to represent a new, tangible, antibureaucratic, and antimanagerial brand of corporate personhood.

Again, this narrative project pivots on the synergies between Turner's professional and personal life. For example, when Turner Broadcasting folded into Time Warner in 1996, the icon of antimanagerial rebellion appeared to sell out to the very large gray corporation he had fought against for years. In the media and even in Turner's own public statements, his conjugal union with Jane Fonda came to serve as the naturalizing analogy that helped police the contradictions created by this corporate union. "How could somebody who's been his own boss go and work for somebody else after 35 years?" he asked during a speech in the midst of the merger negotiations. "Well, when I married Jane Fonda, I mean, I was taking a real risk there, too . . . If I can do that I can probably live with the executives of Time Warner. At least they let me go home at night, and I get a few hours a day when I'm free and I can do whatever I want."[28] Because Turner himself had made clear that Time Warner threatened to emasculate and feminize him – as many Turner fans feared Fonda also would – the reassertion of his legendary masculinity became a condition for the legitimacy of both mergers.[29] Glossy magazines such as *Newsweek* and *Vanity Fair* published reassuring references to Turner's virile behavior with his star-power wife, and the *Wall Street Journal* celebrated the fact that America's favorite cowboy capitalist was giving the largest media conglomerate in the world "a one-man dose of culture shock."[30] With the help of such imagery and language, Turner enacted the introduction of competitive and disruptive market energies, individual entrepreneurial agency, and even male sexual potency into the large managerialist organization itself.[31]

The Auletta profile at first seems to rub against the grain of this narrative, because it presents Turner as a near tragic figure who has failed in both business and personal terms, and whose persona can no longer manage to contain both ownership and control. Turner's grand visions have been supplanted by profit–growth targets and cost-cutting directives, while his trophy wife, the symbol of his continued vitality and virility, has left him for Jesus. But rather than contradict the Turner legend, the near-eulogistic tone of Auletta's lament over these misfortunes highlights the fact that Turner's heroic and hyper-masculine postures always have been largely compensatory, masking a deeply rooted fear that the forces of corporate encroachment would win out over the power of individual agency in the end. During his heydays, Turner helped stave off that threat by providing living proof that real men could still stand for real companies, and by serving as the most visible figurehead for the shift from managerialism to antimanagerialism. The tension between these two poles still governs the ideological debate over the American corporation, but the task of personifying that shift has passed to other hands.

BILL GATES: MANAGERIALISM REDUX

In *One Market Under God: Extreme Capitalism, Market Populism, and the End of Economic Democracy,* Thomas Frank singles out Bill Gates as the contemporary exemplar of what he calls "market populism." As Frank explains, the 1990s bore witness to the rise of a new American consensus, which held that markets constitute a popular system, and a much more democratic form of organizing and directing modern life, than democratically elected governments. "Markets expressed the popular will more articulately and more meaningfully than did mere elections," Frank says. "Markets conferred democratic legitimacy; markets were a friend of the little guy; markets brought down the pompous and the snooty; markets gave us what we wanted; markets looked out for our interests."[32] According to Frank, popular attitudes toward the richest man in the world illustrated how thoroughly market populism had seized the American imagination. Far from a plundering robber baron or symbol of blatant economic inequalities, Gates had become "*our* billionaire, *our* Rockefeller." Microsoft's power could not really pose a threat to liberal ideals, because it's leader was nothing more than a friendly nerd. "He dressed in humble chinos and sweaters, not stiff suits. He built corporate 'campuses,' not skyscrapers," observes Frank. "We spoke of him as though We the People had built him, had knowingly piled up our treasure at his feet, and we thrilled to the news of his philanthropy, of his faintly creepy Seattle chateau as we would to the deeds of our own relatives."

Frank's observations highlight the similarities between Gates and Turner, and make clear the Microsoft founder's ideological debt to Turner's own brand of market populism. Like Turner, Gates has been credited with many innovations for which he really had at best tangential responsibility.[33] This has not stopped him from becoming the most visible figurehead for the computer industry, a centerpiece of the new discourse about information technologies and how they will change the world. The kind of blue sky sloganeering about cable television and satellites Turner popularized helped pave the way for the now familiar talk about the "revolutionary" potential of personal computers and the consumer benefits of the Internet. Gates, by virtue of his youth and his computer geek veneer, was for many years a free rider on this same pseudo-countercultural mystique. Hi-tech utopian rhetoric permeates his speeches and writing, even though his business plans have pursued market domination rather than anti-establishment or even vaguely communitarian postures.[34] Both Gates and Turner celebrate unlimited choice and consumer sovereignty in a way that presumes to negate the need for positive state intervention or managerial trusteeship. As historian Jackson Lears has pointed out, Gates's brand of "friction free capitalism" has little to do with managerialist notions of social responsibility. "It is merely a fantasy of commercial harmony through applied technology."[35] One might speculate that if Turner's assault on paternalist managerialism had not made it safe for corporate leaders to shed their responsibilities toward the public interest in the name of empowering consumers, Gates could not have thrived as long as he did without even pretending to recognize that social obligations might attach to his own wealth.

But the Microsoft antitrust trial, and the way Gates' public persona has attempted to adjust to that challenge, bring to the fore the crucial differences between these two corporate fictions. Turner has never been the target of anything like the sheer venom directed at Bill Gates over Microsoft's iron fisted lock on the computer operating systems market. Throughout the trial, the federal government and a cadre of smaller software interests sought to portray Gates as a raging monopolist and greedy robber baron. But they only added to a tide of anti-Gates sentiment that had been swelling for years. A brief search on the Internet can unearth an endless stream of sites devoted exclusively to the project of hating Bill Gates. There's a site called "Microsoft – The Evil Empire," another called "Bill Gates is Satan," and a game called "Billy Killer," which allows players to shoot at Gates the way they would at ducks in an arcade. There are number of sites called "Punch Bill Gates," at which visitors can do just that, and another site called "www.microsuck.com," which features links to, among other Microsoft and Gates hate sites, the "Microsoft Boycott Campaign Superlist of Anti-Microsoft Sites."[36] When this assault on Gates's character spilled over from the Internet to the courtroom, pro-Microsoft forces launched a philanthropic and media counteroffensive designed to portray the richest man in the world as nothing more than the benevolent whiz kid next door who just happened to make it big, and who wanted to share his good fortune with everyone else. Frank correctly interprets this latter Gates narrative as the ultimate expression of market populism, but he may not give enough weight to the anti-Gates counter-narrative, or to the possibility that it reflects a deeply felt discomfort with the very notion of corporate power as embodied by Gates.

Unlike Turner, Gates has not been able to fuse his public relations project and his private life in a seamless fashion. He never had been one to reveal intimate details about his private life. Suddenly he seemed to wax emotional about his young daughter whenever he got the chance, as if to make clear that he was just a caring father and warm family man. "She's a little redhead with brown eyes, the happiest person I've ever met," said Gates at the outset of a *Newsweek* cover story titled "Behind the Gates Myth" that went on to compare him to the children's television character Mr. Rogers. "Everything she does is just so fascinating."[37] At one particularly ham-handed point during the antitrust trial, Gates actually went so far as to sing "Twinkle, Twinkle Little Star" to a misty-eyed Barbara Walters on prime time network television – just as he does for his daughter every night before bed, he said.[38] In spite of such touching displays, the media deployment of Gates' personal and family life often has been perceived as just that: an orchestrated and awkward attempt to salvage an image that had become a major liability for the Microsoft Corporation. This perception was not helped when, in the spring of 1998, the *Los Angeles Times* exposed Microsoft's secret efforts to fund and orchestrate a "grassroots" campaign in support of the company and its operating system.[39] Nor did Gates' sudden interest in philanthropy after the antitrust indictment convince everyone that his motives were genuine.[40]

The nagging insinuation that Gates's philanthropy merely serves his business goals has given his largesse the whiff of still more top-down, corporate meddling. His attempts to hold up his daughter as a means to soften his image raise overtones of managerialist paternalism as well. He may have inherited certain stock antimanagerialist rhetorical tropes, including the gospel of consumer sovereignty and the vision of abundance through the graces of new technological innovations. But while Turner used these devices to attack the Big Three networks as monopolies, Gates has mobilized them to defend his company against similar charges. Gates's image has never incorporated the macho and rebellious aspects of Turner's antimanagerialism, even when he has acted as a monopolistic aggressor. In a 1999 made-for-television movie called "The Pirates of Silicon Valley," (coincidentally produced by Turner Network Television), Gates's character appeared first as a sweaty computer geek turned entrepreneur and later as a lurking and diminutive control freak prone to shrill fits of anger.[41] The role of the rakish corporate rebel was reserved for Gates's rival, Apple founder Steve Jobs.

In the end, Gates is a corporate fiction, not because the market populist image of him as the disheveled nerd next door is just plain false, or because he is really a nefarious and scheming monopolist out to rule the world. He is a fictional character because he can function as either of these, depending on the narrative context. The elaborately staged representational struggle over Gates's image has little to do with the "real Bill Gates" and everything to do with the long-running American debate over corporate authority, individual agency, and antitrust. The distance between the two fictional persons named Bill Gates points to the depth of American ambivalence over these issues. From this perspective, the debate over whether Gates is a good person or not obscures the crux of the antitrust issue, which has less to do with the actual personality, or moral character, or parenting skills of any one individual, and more to do with the manner in which narrative representations of individuals and technologies crystallize shifting and conflicting hopes and fears about the democratic and anti-democratic aspects of corporate organization and control.

JIM CLARK: ANTIMANAGERIALISM AD ABSURDUM

According to its book jacket, "*The New New Thing* describes a vast paradigm shift in American culture: away from conventional business models and definitions of success, and toward a new way of thinking about the world and our control over it." But there is something more than vaguely familiar about the many such paradigm shifts that have emanated from the business world in recent years. For all the bluster about being so radically different and subversive of the norms and certainties of that boring old economy, the "new" economy came wrapped in tropes and clichés that had been around for a long time. Michael Lewis reproduces this contradiction when he compares Jim Clark's life to an "old fashioned adventure story" on the grounds that Clark himself does not know what will happen next. Lewis inadvertently signals here that he will serve up a generic, adventure story version of unpredictability, and asks his readers to at least pretend that they do not know how such stories always proceed, so as not to dampen the thrill of the ride.

"This book is about a search that occurs on the frontiers of economic life," Lewis declares at the outset. He adds that this search lies "near the core of the American experience," which he associates with innovation, material prosperity, certain kinds of energy and freedom, and transience. Because of these central aspects of the national character, he maintains, the United States occupies a special place in the world, and Silicon Valley occupies a similar place in the United States. "It is one of those places . . . that are unimaginable anywhere but in the United States," Lewis says. "It is distinctively us." He drives home his point about American distinctiveness by peppering his book with disparaging comparisons to various lackluster Europeans. The Dutch have "pallid Dutch skin and lank Dutch hair," and the group of young Dutch businessmen Clark meets with to promote his latest "new new thing" understand nothing about the Internet. "What could it mean to a dozen Dutchmen who were still getting their minds around the idea of electric power?" Lewis asks. In fact, he declares, Europeans as a whole are "famously clueless about new things, not to mention new new things." This is because they are mired in tradition and rules, and completely averse to risk, much like the "paunchy Swiss banker in his humid gray suit" with whom Clark meets to open an account. The "Swiss recipe for handling money" is in Clark's mind "a recipe only for mediocrity and stability." The niggling questionnaire the banker asks Clark to fill out contains "all the attitudes designed to keep people locked in one place." Just asking such a revolutionary financial genius to fill out such a form amounts to "a social gaffe, on the order of inviting the fastest gun in the West to court at Versailles," says Lewis. Clark has no patience with the rigid traditions and confining small-mindedness of the Old World, he explains, because "He was creating a new one."[42]

In this manner Lewis gives his adventure story the shape of the very familiar romance of American exceptionalism. For all of its sound and fury about rejecting rules and traditions for something ineffable and unprecedented, *The New New Thing* adheres religiously to the strict confines of that time-worn generic formula. Exceptionalist ideology maintains that the New World is not only different, but also morally superior to the Old World, because it provides an opportunity to wipe the slate of history clean and to break free from the shackles of an oppressive past. "The clean slate suggests most powerfully a freedom of choice – the freedom to be the designer of one's own life unaided or unimpeded by others," explains historian Joyce Appleby. "It also denies the force of history, for it is past actions that clutter up the metaphorical slate."[43] This is why Clark refuses to discuss his own past ("I don't give a shit about the past," he grumbles) and why Lewis insists that "As a practical matter, Clark had no past, only a future."[44] Clark becomes for Lewis the new Adam, a stock figure of American exceptionalist mythology that historian Garry Wills characterizes as "untrammeled, unspoiled, free to roam, breathing a larger air than the cramped men behind desks, the pygmy clerks and technicians."[45] Lewis's portrait of Clark alters the traditional exceptionalist formula in only one significant respect, replacing its emphasis on nature and landscape with computer technology. The Internet becomes Clark's frontier, a new, technological source of unlimited freedom and abundance that will wipe the slate clean. The Europeans Clark encounters cannot understand the Internet any more than they can understand the romance of the American West.

In a series of chapters interspersed throughout the book, Clark literally reenacts the mythic journey to the New World, navigating his fully wired and computerized yacht, "Hyperion" – at the time the world's largest single mast sailing vessel– from its shipyards in the Netherlands across the Atlantic to the United States. But Clark is not really concerned with leaving the Netherlands behind, nor is he rebelling against some real or imagined European past. The Old World functions in this narrative primarily as a metaphor for the true source of mediocrity and uniformity that vexes Clark. Even more than Europe, the large gray corporation is top-heavy, bureaucratic, and deserving of all the derision Clark can muster. Lewis fashions Clark as the pure embodiment of the antimanagerialist impulse, a "Disorganization Man" who is constantly "throwing sand in capitalists' eyes."[46] Clark's every encounter with "the American professional management class" convinces him that there is "a whole layer of people in American business who called themselves managers who were in fact designed to screw up his plans."[47] So poorly does he fit into the large managerialist organization that when he leaves Netscape, he resolves to design "all future large organizations without a place for himself inside."[48] Clark despises large organizations, but not because of the threat they pose to the liberal democratic polity. He is chiefly annoyed by their encroachment on his own individual agency and personal wealth. "Just for one moment, I would kind of like to have the most," Clark responds wistfully when asked whether he'd like to have more money than his rival, Bill Gates.[49] If only he could devise his own tollbooth, if only he could become a monopoly like Microsoft, then he could achieve that goal, and he would never have to put up with the "Serious American Executive" again.

In his last chapter Lewis pictures Clark wandering "along the top of the cliff overlooking the U.S. economy, deciding which rock, if kicked, would wipe out the largest section of the slope below." Clark settles on launching a new, Web-based service called "myCFO," which he hopes will solve the many hassles associated with becoming a billionaire by allowing him to oversee his far-flung investments on a single web site. Clark would offer this service to others, and his customer base would consist of "the wealthy masses," that 0.6 percent or so of the American population who also own $10 million in assets or more. Once they had collected all of their financial clout under one roof, the wealthy masses could use their power anarchically, cutting themselves a long list of special deals, minimizing taxes and overhead, and maximizing wealth. "If myCFO did not seize control of the levers of capitalism, it could at least remove the lever from the capitalists' hands," says Lewis. "Once the number of dollars became sufficiently huge, they could sit on top of the financial world like an operating system sat on top of a personal computer."[50] Lewis here displays how deeply reactionary and self-contradictory the antimanagerialist impulse can become. The central theme of this brand of antimanagerialism turns out to be the natural and legitimate right of certain individuals to amass obscene amounts of wealth, as long as they strike the properly anti-corporate poses. But what could be less revolutionary than the idea of a cabal of the wealthiest people in the wealthiest country in the world forcing their will down the throats of everyone else?

We can explain how Lewis, through Clark, manages simultaneously to despise "the capitalists" and to elevate capitalism's basest impulses to the level of a revolutionary crusade only by reference to the deep connections between antimanagerialism, American exceptionalism, and New Economy Romanticism. In his analysis of the romantic roots of computer hacker and net culture, Thomas Streeter emphasizes that what he calls "net libertarianism" does not merely employ radical postures as a rhetorical ruse. In many instances, it does appear sincerely to prioritize an "expressive, exploring, transfiguring idea of the individual" over the "calculating, pleasure-maximizing utilitarian individual characteristic of conservative economic theory." Streeter argues that "there are positive lessons to be learned from this romantic individualism, both in its compelling, popular character and in the key role it has played in technological and social innovation." We can take the antimanagerialist critique of the corporation just as seriously for expressing real concerns about the deleterious effects of corporate organization on individual agency. But as Streeter also points out, net culture rests on the foundation of "a pathological and illusory vision of isolation and escape from history and social context." Antimanagerialism suffers from a similarly limiting version of romantic individualism, one that reduces complex issues of corporate governance to a struggle between heroes and villains, and that renders any kind of meaningful critique or vision of change impossible. As *The New New Thing* illustrates well, antimanagerialism's affinities with American exceptionalism instead lead it to a fantasized flight from history and from corporate entanglement, as well as to a deep confusion over some very basic conceptual matters, such as what actually constitutes a capitalist.[51]

But it is not just the particular manner in which Lewis's Clark embodies the new economy that makes him such a perfect example of the shortcomings of antimanagerialism. It's also the very fact that he does so. In one of the more reasoned attempts to describe what might actually be different about the current economic moment, Gerald Davis and Doug McAdam catalog the increasingly diffuse and intangible forms of corporate organization that have developed over the last several decades. They highlight as a major aspect of this shift the decline of the mass production paradigm, along with the Fordist organizational forms and social structures related to it. Even the largest firms have begun evolving from stable organizations into fluid networks, Davis and McAdam observe. The rise of this global and flexible corporate universe calls into question traditional notions of managerial prerogative and monopoly capital, as well as those social theories of capitalist society that hinge on such notions. "Organization theory traditionally treats corporations as meaningfully bounded, actorly entities analogous to organisms," the authors point out, drawing from the work of Harrison White mentioned earlier. "This was a reasonable imagery for some purposes in analyzing the organization of the postwar American economy, but the metaphors of 'sovereignty' and birth and death no longer make sense of the corporate sector."[52]

In Davis and McAdam's view, managerialist modes of organization are on the wane, and the new forms rising to replace them do not resemble bodies or persons very much. But as *The New New Thing* clearly illustrates, New Economy Romanticism continues to attribute even these changes to the work of heroic antimanagerial figures out to transform the corporate world in their own image. In this chapter I have suggested two possible explanations for this contradiction. From one perspective, if such familiar tropes and clichés still suffice to describe the new economy, then it can not be that radically new after all. The strong connections between New Economy Romanticism and American exceptionalism reinforce this point. These kinds of observations serve the useful purpose of tempering the excessive amount of hype wrapped around the notion of a new economy, but they do no justice to the changes Davis and McAdam describe, nor to the ways in which corporate persons have changed as a result.

A closer look at the differences in the narrative construction of corporate personhood from Turner to Gates to Clark points toward an intensification of the antimanagerial impulse, and toward an ever more romantic and atomistic understanding of what it means to be a person in a corporate society. Ted Turner's brand of antimanagerialism argued that corporations could best fulfill their public interest obligations not by the regulatory imposition of managerial trusteeship, but rather by the expansion of consumer choice, in his case made possible by cable and broadcast deregulation. But notions of corporate responsibility and the public interest do not even appear on Jim Clark's radar screen. He strikes anti-corporate postures without even recognizing the corporate threat to meaningful participation in the democratic polity. For Clark, the corporation is simply a drag, because it prevents him from enjoying the abundance of material goods and entrepreneurial opportunities made possible by the Internet. In this manner New Economy Romanticism completes the task of erasing citizenship and elevating consumption as the vital core of what it means to be a person in a corporate society. As a social type, Clark exhibits all the characteristics of the ultimate consumer: a restless addiction to accumulation for its own sake; a short attention span for each latest acquisition; a preference for immediate self-gratification over commitment to sustainable institutions; and a narcissistic obsession with keeping ahead of the Joneses – or Bill Gateses, or Larry Ellisons.

In this chapter I have used Thurman Arnold's critique of corporate personhood to trace the development of this emphasis on abundance and consumer sovereignty in antimanagerialist rhetoric, but, ironically, Arnold turns out to be a significant figure in this development himself. Historian Alan Brinkley has argued convincingly that Arnold's approach to antitrust enforcement helps explain why, in the late 1930s, antimonopoly sentiments in American society virtually vanished just as they seemed ready to take center stage. "Eclectic as it had been, the antimonopoly impulse had usually included a belief that the public interest would be best served by ensuring that the institutions of the economy remained accountable and responsive to popular needs and desires," Brinkley observes. "It had rested on essentially democratic aspirations."[53] But Arnold ran the antitrust division of the Justice Department according to the principle that the only standard by which to judge the presence of monopoly was price to the consumer. "Any organization, regardless of its size, that did not harm the consumer had nothing to fear," Brinkley points out. By elevating the sovereignty of the consumer over that of the citizen, Arnold reflected a halting but decisive shift in American liberal thought. "They were beginning to develop a prescription for the state that rested less on reining in corporate power and more on promoting economic growth and expanding mass purchasing power, less on regulating production and more on stimulating consumption." Arnold was no romantic individualist. As Brinkley puts it, his was "an ideal tied to a vision, not of restoring power to individuals and communities, but of expert management of the economy through centralized state bureaucracies."[54] But his adherence to the burgeoning belief that consumption was the fundamental core of personhood in a corporate society took the bite out of his otherwise incisive critique of corporate power and personhood. It also helps us understand the traditional liberal roots of New Economy Romanticism and Antimanagerial Exceptionalism, as well as the reasons why in the final analysis they don't provide anything like a constructive critique of the problems created by the concentration of corporate power in a democratic society.

NOTES

1. Michael Lewis, *The New New Thing [A Silicon Valley Story]* (New York: Norton, 2000), 14, 16.
2. Other notable works in this genre include Kevin Kelly's *New Rules for the New Economy: 10 Radical Strategies for a Connected World* (New York: Viking Press, 1998); George Gilder's *Microcosm* (New York: Simon and Schuster, 1989), and *Life After Television* (New York: WW Norton and Co., 1994); and Gary Hamel's *Leading the Revolution* (Cambridge, MA: Harvard Business School Press, 2000), but the list goes on and on, and the countless unread New Economy books struggle for attention with just as many glossy magazines like *Wired, Fast Company*, and *Business 2.0*.
3. http://www.leadingtherevolution.com. See also Hamel, 2000.
4. Lewis, 85.
5. M. H. Abrams, "The Romantic Period," in Abrams (ed.), *The Norton Anthology of English Literature, Fourth Edition*, vol. 2 (New York: WW Norton, 1979), 12.
6. Lewis, 261.
7. Gerald F. Davis and Michael Useem, "Top Management, Company Directors, and Corporate Control," in Andrew Pettigrew, Howard Thomas, and Richard Whittington (eds.), *Handbook of Strategy and Management* (London: Sage, 2002).
8. See, for example, Alan Wolfe, "The Modern Corporation: Private Agent or Public Actor," *Washington and Lee Law Review* 50 (Fall 1993), 1673–96.
9. In *The Emerson Effect: Individualism and Submission in America* (Chicago: University of Chicago Press, 1996), Christopher Newfield argues that the late nineteenth century gave rise to a new kind of "corporate individualism" that would accommodate American ideals about freedom and agency to an economic sphere in which those ideals would meet with increasing challenges and limitations.
10. Naomi Lamoreaux, "Partnerships, Corporations, and the Problem of Legal Personhood in American History," Unpublished draft of Oct. 17, 2000.
11. Thurman Arnold, *The Folklore of Capitalism* (New Haven: Yale University Press, 1937), 14.
12. For a complementary argument that expands the boundaries of corporate legal theory even to include an episode of *Star Trek: The Next Generation*, see Jeffrey

Nesteruk, "A New Narrative for Corporate Law," *Legal Studies Forum* 23/3 (1999), 281–91. (Nesteruk analyzes the episode entitled "The Measure of a Man," in which the android Lieutenant Commander Data goes to court to avoid being taken apart for scientific study.)

13. Thomas Streeter, "'That Deep Romantic Chasm': Libertarianism, Neoliberalism, and the Computer Culture," in Andrew Calabrese and Jean-Claude Burgelman (eds.), *Communication, Citizenship, and Social Policy: Re-Thinking the Limits of the Welfare State* (Oxford: Rowman & Littlefield, 1999), 49–64.

14. See Alan Brinkley, "The Antimonopoly Ideal and the Liberal State: The Case of Thurman Arnold," *Journal of American History* (Sep. 1993), 557–79; and Richard Hofstadter, "What Happened to the Antitrust Movement? Notes on the Evolution of an American Creed," in *The Paranoid Style in American Politics and Other Essays* (New York, 1965), 188–237.

15. Thomas Streeter, *Selling the Air: A Critique of the Policy of Commercial Broadcasting in the United States* (Chicago: University of Chicago Press, 1996), 51.

16. See, for example, R. Jeffrey Lustig, *Corporate Liberalism: The Origins of Modern American Political Theory, 1890–1920* (Berkeley: University of California Press, 1982); and Martin Sklar, *The Corporate Reconstruction of American Capitalism: The Market, The Law, and Politics* (Cambridge: Cambridge University Press, 1988).

17. Arnold, 185.

18. Adolf A. Berle and Gardiner C. Means, *The Modern Corporation and Private Property* [revised edition, 1967] (New York: Harcourt, Brace, and World, 1932), 312.

19. Arnold, 21, 22.

20. Gerald F. Davis, Kristina A. Diekmann, and Catherine H. Tinsley, "The Decline and Fall of the Conglomerate Firm in the 1980s: The Deinstitutionalization of an Organizational Form," *American Sociological Review* 59 (Aug. 1994), 551, 565. See also Mary Douglas, *How Institutions Think* (Syracuse, NY: Syracuse University Press, 1986), ch. 4.

21. Barbara Czarniawska, *Narrating the Organization: Dramas of Institutional Identity* (Chicago: University of Chicago Press, 1997), 1, 41, 46.

22. Czarniawska, 46.

23. Harrison White, *Identity and Control* (Princeton: Princeton University Press, 1992), 13.

24. Ken Auletta, "The Lost Tycoon," *The New Yorker* (Apr. 23 and 30, 2001), 138.

25. Auletta, 156.

26. See Eric Guthey, "Ted Turner's Media Legend and The Transformation of Corporate Liberalism," *Business and Economic History* 26/1 (Fall 1997) 184–99; and Eric Guthey, *Ted Turner: Media Legend/Market Realities* (book mss. under revision).

27. James Traub, "Turner Might Save CBS From Itself," *New York Times* (May 1, 1985), A27.

28. Jenney Conant, "Married . . . With Buffalo," *Vanity Fair* (Apr. 1997), 213.

29. In a speech before the National Press Club in 1989, Turner complained about the way Time Warner used its majority voting bloc on its board to stifle his creative energies by comparing himself to Egyptian teenage girls subjected to genital mutilation. Ted Turner, "National Press Club Luncheon," *Federal News Service* (Sept. 27, 1994).

30. Johnnie L. Roberts, "Main Men: the Time Warner–Turner Deal Will Create the World's Biggest Media Company," *Newsweek* (July 29, 1996) 42; Conant, "Married . . . With Buffalo," *Vanity Fair* (Apr. 1997), 213; Eben Shapiro, "Ted's Way: Brash as Ever, Turner Is Giving Time Warner Dose of Culture Shock," *Wall Street Journal* (Mar. 24, 1997), A1.

31. Guthey, "Ted Turner's Corporate Cross-Dressing and the Shifting Images of American Business Leadership," 139.

32. Thomas Frank, *One Market Under God: Extreme Capitalism, Market Populism, and the End of Economic Democracy* (New York: Doubleday, 2000), xiv.

33. For a good account of how many of Gates' "breakthroughs" he had nothing to do with, see Jennifer Edstrom and Martin Eller, *Barbarians Led by Bill Gates: Microsoft from the Inside* (New York: Henry Holt and Company, 1998).

34. See Streeter, "That Deep Romantic Chasm." See also Bill Gates, *The Road Ahead* (New York: Penguin, 1995); and *Business at the Speed of Thought: Using a Digital Nervous System* (New York: Warner Books, 1999).

35. Jackson Lears, "Unsweet Smell of Success: How Bill Gates Makes J. P. Morgan Look Good," *New Republic* (Oct. 18, 1999).

36. For an extensive description of the Gates hate culture, see Gary Rivlin, *The Plot to Get Bill Gates* (New York: Random House, 1999), especially ch. 12, "Bill Gates is Satan."

37. Steven Levy, "Bill Just Wants to Have Fun: Behind the Gates Myth," *Newsweek* (Aug. 30, 1999), 41ff.

38. "20/20," ABC Television Network, Jan. 30, 1998.

39. Greg Miller and Leslie Helm, "Microsoft Plans Stealth Media Publicity Blitz," *Los Angeles Times* (Oct. 4, 1998), A1.

40. Jackson Lears, "Unsweet Smell of Success: How Bill Gates Makes J. P. Morgan Look Good," *New Republic* (Oct. 18, 1999). See also "Room at the Bottom," *Economist* (Jan. 3 1998); "Philanthropy: Giving Your All," *Economist* (May 29, 1999); James V. Grimaldi, "Where, and When, Gates Gives," *Washington Post* (Apr. 17, 2000), A10.

41. *The Pirates of Silicon Valley* (Martyn Burke, director, 1999).

42. Lewis, 14, 22, 165, 176, 181, 182.

43. Joyce Appleby, "Recovering America's Historic Diversity: Beyond Exceptionalism," *Journal of American History* 79/2 (Sep. 1992), 427.

44. Lewis, 43.

45. Gary L. Harmon, "Review of Garry Wills, *John Wayne's America: The Politics of Celebrity*," H-PCAACA, H-Net Reviews, June, 1999. URL: http://www.h-net.msu.edu/reviews/showrev.cgi?path=28722929651235.

46. Lewis, 101.

47. Lewis, 63.

48. Lewis, 98.

49. Lewis, 260.

50. Lewis, 252, 255.

51. I do not mean to deny that any form of individual autonomy could provide a basis for the constructive critique of corporate activity. For two convincing attempts at articulating such a position, see Mats Alvesson and Hugh Willmott, *Making Sense of Management* (London: Sage, 1992) ch. 1; and Christopher Newfield, "Corporate Culture Wars," in George Marcus (ed.), *Corporate Futures: The Diffusion of the Culturally Sensitive Corporate Form* (Chicago: University of Chicago Press, 1998), 23–62.

52. Gerald F. Davis and Douglas McAdam, "Corporations, Classes, and Social Movements After Managerialism," in Barry Staw and Robert I. Sutton (eds.), *Research in Organizational Behavior* (Oxford: Elsevier Science, 2000), 22, 195–238.

53. Brinkley, 570.

54. Brinkley, 579.

Afterword: Toward New Renderings

Kenneth Lipartito and David B. Sicilia

The preponderance of scholarly research about the American corporation adds up to a more or less coherent master narrative: Corporations took root in British North America as a monopoly privilege bestowed by the Crown. In the nineteenth century, the corporation was transformed from an instrument of exclusion into a mechanism for exploiting opportunity. Antebellum joint stock companies served as a rational and convenient way of mobilizing capital and limiting owner liability. Giant managerial corporations emerged in the Gilded Age to dominate many core industries by exploiting economies of scale and integrating mass production with mass distribution. As more and more economic power was concentrated into fewer and fewer giant firms in core industries, the corporation increasingly came under attack from social reformers, small and medium size firms, workers, and others of a republican stripe. But – according to the standard narrative – because the economic benefits and economic power of the modern corporation far outweighed its social and political disadvantages, it persisted as the preeminent economic institution throughout the twentieth century. Now, early in the twenty-first century, corporate finance is suffering a crisis of confidence, but American-style corporate capitalism is an international juggernaut.

This view accommodates the corporation's defenders, who see it as the triumph of professionalism, rationality, and efficiency, as well as its critics, who lament its power, its ubiquity, its exploitation of labor and natural resources, and so on. Across the ideological spectrum, there is widespread agreement that corporate managers try to maximize profit and insulate the corporation as much as possible from the buffeting forces of social change, politics, regulation, ideology, and social values. The prevailing view holds that corporations prefer to define their agendas in economic terms and to control their own destinies, within these terms, as much as possible.

The chapters in this book challenge the master narrative about the emergence, growth, and proliferation of the American corporation on several fronts. Three seem most salient to us, and point the way toward new investigations of the central institutions of capitalism.

RECONFIGURING PERIODIZATION

The era from the Civil War to the First World War has long been the defining moment in the historiography of the American corporation. It was then – according to scholars and textbook writers alike – that the barons of iron and steel, petroleum, automobiles, electrical machinery, and other heavy industries figured out how to build giant firms and dominate entire industries. Much of how we think about what happened both *before* and *after* the Age of Giant Enterprise is defined by the dramatic transformations of that period – as preamble to the triumph of corporate capitalism, and as variations on a theme after the fact. In this way, business history largely has been an exercise in the backward and forward projection of the *fin de siècle* paradigm.

The chapters in the first section of this volume, however, suggest that the periodization of American corporate history needs to be rethought, with each era considered in its own right. In the antebellum period, the corporation was one of several viable ways of organizing economic activity, and grew in prominence through a complicated process of negotiation that had as much or more to do with legal tradition and ideology as it did with capital markets and economic coordination. More than that, the antebellum corporation did not spring up like an insidious capitalist weed in an otherwise pristine republican garden, but rather emulated forms of social organization and social control commonly practiced by utopias and commonwealth communities. As the U.S. corporation evolved in a more autarkic direction, it did so through a contested process and, when viewed from a comparative perspective, in a distinctly American fashion. As a regulatory state was fashioned to rein in the corporation's burgeoning economic salience, the growing demarcation between public and private interest was reified through the rejection of a pragmatic approach to state oversight in favor of one construed more strictly in terms of markets and capital.

In these and other ways, the antebellum period was one of competing models and visions for how to organize economic life, with both the alternatives and the outcomes flowing from legal traditions, values, and familiar forms of social organization as much as from problems associated with capital markets and transactions costs. Even as the large industrial corporation gained sway after the Civil War, it mobilized resources along well-worn paths that effectively excluded Jews, African-Americans, and other traditionally marginalized groups from participating as owners, managers, workers, and customers. What became the dominant form of economic organization, therefore, rested largely on forms of exclusion that were not based on meritocracy, efficiency, and profit maximization. At the same time, as the giant, integrated corporation moved further toward ostensible isolation from its cultural and political environment, its relationship with state actors became more adversarial.

In the long run, the strategy of isolation proved to be ineffective. The corporation's claim to focus narrowly on the twin ambitions of maximizing efficiency and profit became especially problematic in the second half of the twentieth century. In technologically rich domains, U.S. corporations found that partnerships with the state were both desirable and inescapable. The turn-of-the-century adversarial model for dealing with the antitrust issue became increasingly irrelevant in an age of global competition. And social movements and other forms of collective action posed new challenges to the large corporation's social role and legitimacy, particularly when it came to race, ethnicity, the environment, and public health. The narrow economic construction of the corporation's mission gave way to a multiple stakeholder approach that elevated the interests of consumers, regulators, and politics to the highest strategic level of the firm. At the same time, the turn-of-the-century heritage proved to be intractable when it came to excluding or limiting participation based on race, ethnicity, and gender.

This book, therefore, identifies multiple stages in the evolution of the American corporation that extend from the early nineteenth century to the present. The model that dominated in the late nineteenth and early twentieth century neither flowed inevitably from the rational operation of the market before the Civil War, nor endured into the post-Second World War period. It was a time-bound phenomenon, a moment when both the American corporation and American culture stood closest together in the mistaken belief that business and society were and should be separated by the corporation's "pure" economic functionality.

PERMEABLE BOUNDARIES

Our second theme concerns the boundary between the corporation and the rest of society. In the dominant meta-narrative of American corporate history, this boundary is seen as strong and impermeable. Such boundaries exist, of course. Without them the corporation would lose its identity. But we argue that corporations interact with their environment across a permeable membrane constructed (and periodically reconstructed) from law, ideology, and cultural history. In some cases, the corporation's stake in society can be seen in the ways that economic structures are embedded in social context. Race and gender remain important to management and strategy; law and politics are key influences on corporate capabilities. In other cases, corporations are best seen as actors caught up in the very process of defining or constituting the social order. Debates over and definitions of the corporation actually help to construct the environment, by defining key issues, such as citizenship, power, rationality, and efficiency.

In either case, history indicates that when the corporation attempts to cordon itself off from its environment too firmly, challenges soon follow. Corporate–social boundaries began to harden in the mid-nineteenth century. The antebellum corporation had been a close cousin to the partnership, governed by a one-person, one-vote democratic structure and both inspired by and emulating commonwealth forms of social organization. The postbellum corporation was governed by professional managers and owners who exercised plutocratic control, and who organized workers into rigid bureaucratic hierarchies. The antebellum corporation was viewed as an instrument for pursuing economic opportunity and social improvement; the postbellum corporation as an obstacle to opportunity and a threat to the public good.

In the twentieth century, two world wars and the Cold War helped infuse the corporation with a renewed sense of social purpose. The Great Depression undermined the imperious corporate isolationism of the 1920s. After the Second World War, a series of new challenges to corporate legitimacy further impeded corporate unilateralism, and over time the corporation responded by engaging its challengers in new ways, both real and rhetorical.

PRESENTATION AND REPRESENTATION

From the start, the corporation has depended on social and legal sanction. States expected corporations to provide benefits that outweighed the costs of their special privileges. But the economic realities of the bargain were never, to use modern parlance, wholly "transparent." As the power of industrial corporations grew in the late nineteenth century, so did the intensity of debates about their legitimacy. Their defenders took up the challenge by offering a rationalistic model of economic efficiency that resonated with the temper of the times and overwhelmed alternative notions proposed by Brandeis and others. This cultural project was carried out only in semi-deliberate ways; contrary to the claims of Marxists and Gramscians, society constructed the giant industrial firm as much as the reverse.

The motives and methods of corporate self-definition changed dramatically in the twentieth century. On the public relations front, chapters in this volume extend into the postwar period Roland Marchand's work on the interwar decades and the Second World War.[1] Having largely rehabilitated the corporation's image by the late 1940s, its managers soon encountered a host of new challenges to its reputation, and responded in ways that reached well beyond the earlier techniques. By the 1980s, it was difficult – and, according to many insiders, irrelevant – to discern the difference between business practice and rhetoric. So lauded was the corporation in the 1990s that many declared the permanent end of unemployment and the business cycle. The dot.com crash and financial scandals that quickly reversed those gains underscore the fragility and constructed nature of the corporation's image. Unlike previous periods, however, the business of "stakeholder management" now infuses corporate strategic thinking.

[1] Roland Marchand, *Creating the Corporate Soul: The Rise of Public Relations and Corporate Imagery in American Big Business* (Berkeley: University of California Press, 1998).

As globalization marches forward, the corporation rivals race, ethnicity, class, gender, and nationality as a site of individual identity construction. Whereas the rhetoric defines the corporation as a level-field meritocracy, in reality such identities often clash, as they do – rather, *because* they do – in the larger society. The same is true of political economy: the boundaries between state and the private economic sphere have expanded and contracted throughout the twentieth century, depending on the success of each in defining those boundaries. Here, again, the turn-of-the-century model fails to illuminate the postwar period. In John D. Rockefeller's day, captains of industry could afford to be far less concerned with workers, regulators, conservationists, and other "stakeholders."

Born of many possibilities before the Civil War, reified as the paragon of efficiency by the turn of the century, forced by crisis to soften its boundaries, ever-engaged with the state, and now a contested terrain of individual and social identity, the American corporation has been anything but the static, rational, transactions-based ideal type depicted in neoclassical economic theory and in the prevailing interpretative frameworks of business history. With new methodologies and with an openness to multiple vantage points, students of the corporation face exciting possibilities for rendering the corporation's many lives.

INDEX